PRIMITIVE ART

ERWIN O. CHRISTENSEN

PRIMITIVE ART

BONANZA BOOKS · NEW YORK

This edition published by Bonanza Books, a division of Crown Publishers, Inc., by arrangement with The Viking Press, Inc.

LIBRARY OF CONGRESS CATALOG CARD NO. 55-11109

Manufactured in the United States of America

CONTENTS

INTRODUCTION 7

I AFRICA 11

Historical relations. Political divisions. The religious and social basis of Negro sculpture. Materials and techniques. The place of the artist in society. General characteristics. Figures and masks. Regional and tribal styles: West Africa; The West Guinea coast; The Central Guinea coast; The East Guinea coast; The Benin style; The Ife style; Ibo, Ibibio and Ekoi styles; Cameroons; Central Africa. Contemporary art.

II ALASKA AND THE PACIFIC NORTHWEST COAST 56

Alaska and the Eskimo: Beliefs; Eskimo art. Northwest Pacific coast Indian art: Country and tribes; The psychological background; General characteristics; Totem poles and house posts; Masks; Figures; Drawing and painting; Blankets; Utensils. Recent and contemporary art.

III THE UNITED STATES: FORESTS, PLAINS AND DESERTS 113

Physical environment and religious beliefs. The historical background. General characteristics. The Eastern woodlands; sculpture and pottery: Masks. The Great Plains: Plains Indian painting; Quillwork and beadwork. The arts and crafts of the Southwest: Petroglyphs; Mural painting; Navaho sand painting; Prehistoric pottery; Contemporary pottery; Pueblo and Plains Indian sculpture; Basketry; Weaving; Masks and Kachinas; Silver. Contemporary Indian painting.

IV MEXICO AND THE ANDEAN REGION 161

Countries and peoples. The historical background. Religious beliefs. Magic versus art. General characteristics. Regional styles. Tarascan clay figurines. Maya art: Old Empire sculpture; Work in stucco; New Empire sculpture; Painting; Drawing; Pottery; Wood carving; Jades. The Olmec style. The Zapotec style. The Mixtecs. The Totonac and Huasteca styles. Toltec art. Aztec art. Central American styles outside the Maya area: Jade, stone sculpture, ceramics. Work in gold in Central and South America. Peruvian art: Scope; Andean stone sculpture; Peruvian ceramics; Textiles; Wood carvings.

V THE SOUTH SEAS AND AUSTRALIA 273

The islands; settlements and races. Regions. Beliefs and customs. Crafts, materials, tools. Style groups. Melanesia: Ornamental styles; Figure styles. Micronesia. Polynesia: The Hawaiian Islands; Easter Island and the Marquesas; The Maori of New Zealand. Australia.

VI EUROPE AND AFRICA: CAVE PAINTINGS, CARVINGS AND ROCK ENGRAVINGS 299

Prehistory. Caves and rock shelters. Styles and periods. Aurignacian art. Magdalenian art. Sanctuary and studio. Magic. Origins of art. Scandinavian Paleolithic sites. Figure sculpture and minor arts. The East Spanish style. North African rock pictures. South African Bushman paintings. Rock paintings of Southern Rhodesia. Scandinavian Bronze Age rock engravings.

ACKNOWLEDGMENTS 365

SELECTED BIBLIOGRAPHY 367

INDEX 377

INTRODUCTION

Primitive art is produced by people who have not developed any form of writing. The word "primitive" applied to art commonly means Negro African sculpture, aboriginal American art, the arts of the South Seas, and other tribal arts in different parts of the world. There is no one primitive style, but many styles ranging from simple patterns to portrait sculpture that would rank as masterpieces anywhere. Primitive does not mean crude and is used in the sense of undeveloped only in certain specific instances.

The history of art is not a straight-line progression advancing from early imperfections to late fulfillments. There are, instead, cycles of development, with early, mature, and late stages. Of the more developed styles, some flourished a few centuries ago, others thousands of years ago, and still others fairly recently.

Primitive art uses materials provided by nature, derived from plants and animals or taken from the earth, such as clay and various kinds of stones and metals. Often these materials are used in the natural state, but sometimes they are refined by man.

On the level of simple ornamentation in such techniques as braiding, basketry, weaving, pottery or pictographs there is a good deal of similarity. Simple patterns have been developed independently in various parts of the world, or in some instances have been diffused from common centers.

Geometric design and pictorial representation occur in primitive as in all art. Basic principles of design, such as sequence, rhythm and balance, and simple modes of representation, such as straight line and line with flat tone, are common to many styles. Symbolism—by which a part suggests the whole—is as widely used in primitive art as in our own.

Primitive craftsmanship at its best is superior. In the making of tools and utensils, early man applied his mind to the solution of practical problems. Coordinating hand and eye, he made tools out of the hardest stones, thinned out clay into vessels without loss of strength, and made threads into textiles of the closest weave. The posture of an ancestral figure may be purely frontal with arms closely attached to the torso in the simplest possible manner, but the carving is often excellent and the surface carefully finished. Even in difficult processes such as casting of bronzes, as in Benin, the work is as well executed as in the best European practice.

What may appear to us as the limitations of primitive art are not necessarily due to any lack of skill or of industry, nor are they due to a lack of devotion or of a sense of beauty. They can be considered the by-products of man's slowly evolving intellectual powers. With little knowledge and few facts to reason with, primitive man's endeavor to explain the universe was largely swayed by his emotions. What beliefs he developed served to assuage his fears and thereby to contribute to his sense of security. Frequently the personified forces of nature were induced to serve his needs. In primitive cultures ritual was as important as belief, and art occupied a prominent place in ritual. Often, therefore, it is not art that is limited, but the underlying belief for which it serves as a vehicle. Although primitive art is admired today and is readily adapted by modern artists, we have no comparable admiration for magic, known to us as superstition, that once impelled the primitive artist.

We see the effects of belief in the relative development of the major arts of painting, sculpture and architecture in primitive cultures. Architecture seems eminently practical to us, and we might assume that necessity would have led to its early development. Sculpture and painting we might regard as luxury products which would arrive late in history. On the contrary, architecture was the last to develop, and its major structural problems were not solved until the Roman period, while painting began in the Ice Age, and sculpture, at least as carving, was widely distributed in early art. As we see it today, monumental architecture aims to create ground plans to serve many human needs and to enclose space to unite under one roof a large number of people. Simple plans, and the post and lintel system, served all pre-Roman cultures, including Sumer, Egypt, India and Greece, as well as ancient Mexico. Pyramids and ziggurats, though impressive and ornate, were essentially glorified hills with a stone facing and a small chamber for the statue of the god; in Egypt pyramids were tombs. Everywhere such structures served the purposes of religious ceremonials held in the open; they were of no practical use.

Painting in primitive art was limited to representation in one plane; it did not advance to representation of space. Depth, through perspective, and a full visual effect were not attempted, though Aztec manuscript illustration was veering in that direction at the time of the Spanish Conquest.

Primitive sculpture in Maya reliefs attained some freedom of movement and even showed initial stages promising further development. Aztec sculpture hardly aspired to that stage where the figure is infused with life, revealing an activity stirring from within. Basically, primitive man can be said to have been limited by his superstitions in reacting creatively to many aspects of his environment. That, more than any other factor, accounts for the particular directions of his art. Since he was impelled to act along comparatively narrow paths, his lack of inner freedom precluded that broader creativity open to the individual today.

We have forceful proof, however, that intellectual limitation did not prevent the creation of significant art. All art of the past has worked within its own style; it has always developed competence, often distinction, whatever its limitation and restrictions. There is a presumption that the power of tradition in primitive art operated as a handicap to originality and the development of individuality. But historic art in nonprimitive periods has also stressed tradition. It will be noted that an insistence on a maximum of originality and a strong emphasis on the individuality of the artist are more characteristic of our own time than of any previous period. We cannot properly divide art into primitive and civilized; the difference is one of philosophy and not of art, which is essentially an integrated whole. The modern artist consciously seeks aesthetic values; primitive art used them primarily to give intelligible form to religious concepts.

Through his arts and crafts man left us an important link, giving continuity and direction to his culture. Art did not depend upon language to be understood, and writing played no part in its development. A language in its own right, art is often the only clue we have to the life of early man.

In deciding what styles to include under primitive, we have followed precedent by including the highly cultivated art of Mexico and Peru. By definition of primitive, as preliterate, this is permissible. Solely on an artistic basis, ancient Middle American art is on a level with the arts of the literate cultures of ancient Egypt, Sumer and India. To group the arts of these urbanized cultures with the arts of the Eskimo, the Plains Indians and the Australians may seem incongruous. But this incongruity is more apparent than real. What here stands out in sharp contrast are often not the arts of these widely separated regions, but the material cultures of which the arts are a part. The limitations of these more primitive peoples have to do rather with the available material resources, and less with the merits of individual works of art. When we focus on artistic quality of styles rather than on their elaboration and variety, differences become less significant. With that in our mind, Eskimo walrus engravings and Mimbres pottery bowls hold their place; it would be unprofitable to compare them with Maya stelae and Paracas textiles.

But there is one inevitable result of bringing together the arts of highly favored and less favored regions: the variety of Middle American art assures these styles a major portion of text and illustrations. With this pre-eminence of Mexican and Andean art, the arts of the Americas necessarily assume a commanding place in any survey of primitive art.

Within each of the six art regions, the subject matter is dealt with in a four-fold approach: (1) a general orientation, (2) some matters of anthropology, (3) the psychological background, and (4) an emphasis on art or design. These aspects are taken up in each chapter in about that order.

The illustrations in this book constitute virtually a treasury of primitive art, selected from the great collections of the world, except where caves and rocks have been painted, or carved boulders and stelae are still resting in tropical jungles.

AFRICA
Algiers
Oran
ATLAS MOUNTAINS
Sahara Atlas
Susfana V.
Tarhit
TUNISIA
ALGERIA
Ahaggar Mountains
Tripolitania
Fezzan
LIBYA
Libyan
EGYPT
Dakhla Oasis
Kharga Oasis
Nile R.
Desert
Uwenat Hills
Khargur Thal
SAHARA DESERT
French Sudan
FRENCH WEST AFRICA
Senegal R.
Niger R.
French Guinea
Ivory Coast
GOLD COAST
Togo
Dahomey
Nok
NIGERIA
Benue R.
Ife
Benin
Abomey
Cross R.
SIERRA LEONE
Sherbro Island
LIBERIA
Lake Chad
FRENCH EQUATORIAL AFRICA
Cameroon
Ogowe R.
Gabun
CABINDA
ANGLO-EGYPTIAN SUDAN
ETHIOPIA
Congo R.
BELGIAN CONGO
Kasai R.
Kwango R.
Buli
Lake Victoria
Lake Tanganyika
TANGANYIKA
Lake Nyasa
ANGOLA
Zambezi R.
Mtoko
S. RHODESIA
Fort Victoria
SOUTHWEST AFRICA
Madagascar
UNION OF SOUTH AFRICA
Orange Free State
Orange R.
1. Baga
2. Bambara
3. Dogon
4. Mendi
5. Dan
6. Bobo
7. Guro
8. Baulé
9. Senufo
10. Ashanti
11. Yoruba
12. Beni
13. Ibo
14. Ibibio
15. Ekoi
16. Bekom
17. Bangwa
18. Bamum
19. Fang (or Pangwe)
20. Ogowe River Style
21. Bakota
22. Bateke
23. Bayaka
24. Bapende
25. Mangbetu
26. Warega
27. Bakuba (or Bushongo)
28. Bena Lulua
29. Basonge
30. Warua
31. Baluba
32. Badjokwe (or Batshioko)
33. Barotse
34. Makonde
35. Hereros
36. Bushmen
37. Hottentots
JAB

I

AFRICA

ART HAS ALWAYS REFLECTED THE PHYSICAL ENVIRONMENT OF THE COUNTRY WHERE IT DEVELOPED and matured. This is particularly true of the art of people who live close to nature, and are at the mercy of their environment. Africa is no exception to this rule; the land and its climate had a profound influence on African art. In contrast to Europe with its heavily indented coast that makes for subdivisions and brings many sections into close contact with the sea, Africa forms a more solid mass. Nothing in its coastline encouraged seafaring excursions. Africa has received waves of other races from Asia and from Europe, but has itself remained passive, turning its back to the ocean, in self-sufficient isolation. The continent was slow to reveal itself to outsiders. Little is known of its past and only Egypt, in contact with Asia, has played a part in history. African self-containment is reflected in its art, which is virtually, though not exclusively, Negro sculpture. Considering the large area which produced sculpture, its style shows a remarkably unified character.

Of the indigenous races of Africa, Caucasian Hamites and Semites inhabit the northern part of the continent, north of an imaginary line drawn from the Senegal River in the northwest to Ethiopia in the east. The true Negro, dark-skinned and with woolly hair, is restricted roughly to the Guinea coast and its hinterland from the Senegal River to the mouth of the Cross River in the south at British Cameroons. Negroes mixed with Hamitic strains, the Bantu-speaking tribes, occupy the Congo River region. These two races are responsible for African Negro sculpture. Non-Negro people, the Bushmen, Hottentots and pygmies, are also outside the sculpture area.

Within the grand simplicity of this solid continent, climate has produced an equally simple division of desert, parkland (savannah) and forest. Only the least developed tribes sought the rain forests as a refuge. Less dense forests and more open parklands furnished the best conditions for agriculture, and it is in these regions that African art flourished.

Generally speaking, primitive arts are either an expression of a nomadic hunting culture or of a sedentary agricultural economy. Of these two basic economies in Negro Africa, only a primitive agriculture based on the use of the hoe was an indigenous growth. It has been suggested that nomadic Hamitic cattle raisers entered the country in two places; in the northeast and in the southeast where no heavy forests blocked the way. It is not known how or when these early invasions took place, but they were well before the Christian era.

The invasions from the northeast eventually spread to the west coast, from the mouth of the Senegal River to Nigeria. At some unknown dates the Ghana Empire and the Melle Empire were founded in the western Sudan, where large cities with clay-built houses existed as late as the nineteenth century. On the Atlantic coast were the kingdoms of Ashanti, Dahomey and Benin, all of which have left a heritage in art.

In the southeast, in the region of the Zambezi River, large and small groups are presumed to have come from Arabia, India and Indonesia. The stone architecture of southern Rhodesia has been related to these invasions. Important states once existed along the path of this penetration, like the Monomotapa Empire, which is believed to have flourished between A.D. 1000 and 1500, and a Sudan Empire on the upper Kasai and Zambezi rivers. Other modern reflections of these non-Negro Hamitic invasions are found in the cattle-raising Hottentots and in the Herero tribes of the southwest. Though history has produced little to fill in the great void of Africa's past, there probably was a general southward movement that left cities and empires, of which ruins still remain.

In the seventh century after Christ the Moslems conquered North Africa. The Mohammedan occupation, lasting into modern times, laid a barrier between the Mediterranean world and the rest of Africa. Thus, Negro Africa was cut off from the north not only by the Sahara but also by people who were hostile to sculpture and would hardly transmit sculptural influences.

Some contacts from Europe reached Negro Africa by way of the Atlantic Ocean. We know from European history that Africa north of the Sahara was more definitely related to the Mediterranean than was the rest of the continent. Berbers, Phoenicians, Romans, Germanic Vandals, Byzantine Christians and Moslems at one time or another inhabited the coastal regions. West European contacts involving Portuguese, Dutch and Germans brought firearms to Africa, founded commercial settlements and introduced Christianity. Further contacts were made through the Arab slave trade.

In the sixteenth century the ancient Congo Empire temporarily adopted Christianity and named its capital, the modern Cabinda or Angola, São Salvador. The realm remained Christian until 1717 when relations with Portugal and European Christian culture were broken off. When the missionaries returned in 1870, the country and art were divorced from Christianity.

Such relations with Europe and Asia have had some influence on Negro art; just how much is a matter of conjecture. West European trade settlements on the west coast did leave imprints on African art, as in Benin and the Congo, without permanently affecting its development. That Phoenicians, Carthaginians and Romans may even earlier have contributed something is also possible. To what extent the mingling of cultures has exerted influences on the art is unknown, but as tribes moved from one region to another, there was a very considerable cultural exchange among the natives.

Africa developed, on the one hand, court art styles, and on the other hand, informal or folk styles which did not serve courts or the nobility. Native capacities developed variety, richness and complexity, and always gave foreign influences an unmistakable African character.

Works of art, that have been recovered through excavation, are not readily placed within a proper historical setting because our knowledge of African history is still too sketchy. Any dating of works of art is likely to be unreliable and is not often attempted. Exceptions are the Bakuba statues of kings, based on a known genealogy and the Benin bronzes, for which a tentative classification has been suggested. Moisture and termites affect wood sculpture by destroying the more ancient examples. Much of African wood carving is of fairly recent date, at best of the nineteenth century, while individual pieces may be nearly contemporary. Even where works of stone, terra cotta, bronze, and ivory exist from earlier centuries, they often represent late stages of a development of which the beginnings are unknown.

POLITICAL DIVISIONS

At the present time the largest part of West Africa is French colonial territory, which touches the Atlantic in French Guinea, the Ivory Coast, Dahomey, and French-mandated Togo. Where the African coast turns abruptly south lies the French-mandated Cameroons which adjoins the Congo. Out of French West Africa several smaller segments are cut: Portuguese Guinea, the British Sierra Leone and Sherbro Island, Liberia, the British Gold Coast and British Nigeria. French Equatorial Africa is largely north of the equator, and the Belgian Congo lies on both sides of the equator.

As the political divisions cut into the country rather arbitrarily, a simpler division into four major sections is more serviceable. On that basis, the sculpture area may be divided from west to east into West Africa, with the western Sudan; the province of Cameroons; and Central and East Africa.

THE RELIGIOUS AND SOCIAL BASIS OF NEGRO SCULPTURE

This art is a means of relating the individual to the universe. It gives him some feeling of security and acts as a safeguard against the forces of nature. Art was not the first step in his struggle against insecurity. Man's feelings, his fears, came first; they prompted his beliefs, and his beliefs found expression in art. Nor were his fears confined only to natural forces; his fear of fellow men, animals and the spirits of the dead prompted the creation of various sculptural forms with which he sought different kinds of protection.

The sedentary cultivator of the soil and the nomadic hunter developed magic and ritual, but the hunter was less troubled by the spirits of the dead, which he left behind. His major concern was the appeasement of the spirit of the animal he had killed. But the agriculturist lived with the spirits of his ancestors he wished to appease and to whom he also turned for comfort.

Veneration of ancestors and fear of demons have produced much of the motivation for primitive sculpture. In some cases ancestral figures, fetishes and masks were more important than statues of gods. Some tribes, like the Dogons and the Yoruba had a more developed hierarchy of gods, which were the special concern of a small group of priests. In the case of the Dogons, a group of high priests had their own ritual, which found expression in art.

Ancestral figures are sometimes the homes of the spirits of ancestors. After death the soul may be separated from the body and may wander about the village. This is often considered undesirable, and the purpose of the ancestral figure is to tie the soul to a fixed place. "The spiritual principle of the ancestor freed from the body by death would enter this new receptacle and cease wandering abroad to the hurt of mankind. . . . The sculptor's art . . . had to offer the ancestor a pleasant sanctuary which he would enjoy inhabiting." (Himmelheber, 1935) Those who have passed on are not really dead, for their spirits are still about. They may not be entirely satisfied with their fate and may even harbor feelings of revenge toward the living, hence it is necessary to appease these spirits and make their existence as pleasant as possible.

The sanctuary did not have to be a realistic likeness of the person; a soul would recognize his figure and come to rest in it, remaining there until it went to the hereafter. The figure was talked to as if it were alive.

Next in importance to ancestral figures are "fetish" figures. A fetish figure is carved and a magical substance added to give the figure a soul or power. The figure can be petitioned to act as an intermediary to specific spirits from whom the petitioner expects to receive what he has requested. Fetish figures were employed to cure ailments, to relieve a person from worries and difficulties. Their possibilities for doing good were unlimited, though fertility fetishes existed for that one purpose only.

One interesting type of fetish figure is the so-called "nail fetish," particularly popular in the lower Congo. These are large, roughly hewn wooden figures, undifferentiated as to sex. One hand was on the hip, the other raised holding a dagger. To call the attention of the fetish to a particular request and to remind it to do its duty by the petitioner, a nail was driven into the fetish.

Certain fetishes of the Mendi tribe (Sierra Leone) served as oracles to answer questions regarding the curing of ailments. They were kept in a separate hut, in the house of the Yassi, a female society devoted to the curing of the sick. These fetishes received their power through anointment. After anointment they were placed next to the medicine, to absorb its diagnostic capacities. Then the second in command of the Yassi society sank into a "dream sleep." When she awoke the figure was once more rubbed with oil. Then the leader of the society would take the figure, present it twice before the Yassi fetish, and turning the figure toward herself and holding it by the hips would swing it. From this motion of affirmation the answer to the question would be deduced. This ritual of the Mendi may illustrate how art served in the curing of illness, without implying that it was used in the same way elsewhere in Africa.

Most African tribes have men's societies, which are often secret. Although they are also concerned with legal procedures, health and military service, one of their chief functions is to introduce boys, at the age of puberty, to the responsibilities of adulthood. This is accomplished by following a prescribed initiation ritual, for which masks are often used. These ceremonials form an important element in tribal life and contribute to the preservation of traditions. There are also in many tribes comparable societies for women. One of the best known is the Bundu society of Sierra Leone in Liberia.

MATERIALS AND TECHNIQUES

African Negro art is mostly wood carving; it is rarely painted. All kinds of woods are used, hard as well as soft. Freshly cut wood was often used, as this is more readily carved. The fact that wood is also known to have been set aside before use may point to an older tradition of aging the wood to eliminate the sap.

Materials like pieces of textiles, beads and shells, human and animal teeth, animal claws, feathers, plant materials, metal, mirrors and string are sometimes added. These materials might contribute additional power through magic, occasionally they may have been added for decorative purposes. Sheets of brass and copper are found on the well known Bakota figures.

The Basonge of the Congo also occasionally covered large fetish figures with narrow strips of copper. Animal skins are used by the Ekoi to cover ceremonial masks, perhaps as substitutes for human skins; and shells and beads were used to cover wooden stools and masks, adding to the decorative effect through color.

Though wood is the common material, there are notable achievements in metals and in ivory, and to a lesser extent in terra cotta and stone. Stone sculpture usually refers back to earlier periods, although recent human figure and animal carvings in soft steatite have been discovered in Sierra Leone. Ivory was occasionally used for masks and other objects. In Benin whole tusks surmounted bronze heads which were placed on the altar of the royal palace. Ivory statuettes occurred in central and eastern Congo, especially in mother and child representations.

The use of clay for many purposes is found in the Sudan and clay was used in Togoland for ancestral figures and animals, and in Nigeria for the Ife terra cottas; ceramic faces were made by the Mangbetu in northeastern Congo, and the "Bali clay pipes" were made in the Cameroons. Very fine terra cotta heads of the so-called Nok culture of Nigeria (Fig. 1), known through excavations, have been attributed on an archaeological basis, to a date before the Christian era.

Cast bronze vessels were made by the Ashanti, as containers. These so-called "kuduos" have lids showing groups of animals in combat. Gold was an important commodity in the Ashanti kingdom of the eighteenth century, and gold gave the whole coast its name. This precious metal was cast for small masks and other objects for personal wear.

Africa, with her great wealth of minerals, has known the use of iron since a very early period, and her knowledge of the forging of tools is unique among primitive peoples. Neither the Americas nor Oceania enjoyed this advantage before contact with the white man.

Several different tools were used in wood carving: the adz for rough shaping and a bent instrument to hollow out. Difficult parts were cut with a small knife shaped like a kitchen knife. The African carver used one hand and his knees to hold the block of wood. This gave him less freedom of movement than European carvers, who, with the block held in a vise, could work with both hands free.

We are told of one case where the carver would visualize the figure he planned, and would then choose a block to suit his conception. Instead of blocking in the whole mask or figure first, some carvers finished the head completely before progressing to the rest of the figure. Only the roughest outlines were marked on the block, although eventually all parts from head to feet were carved with equal care. Some carvers explained that they made "corrections" as the work progressed.

The use of color was restricted to a few pigments provided by nature. Red and blue were used from local dye plants, white from white earth. For black various procedures were employed, including the use of mud; yellow and green were unknown. Gilding was also used by the Atutu, carvers also being gilders.

METHODS, MOTIVATIONS AND TALENTS

What is here reported is based largely on recent information from two studies brought by Hans Himmelheber and Justine M. Cordwell from restricted areas of the Ivory Coast (1935) and Nigeria (1950), which have long been subjected to European contacts. It may not reflect earlier practices, or perhaps only imperfectly. But as many African wood carvings are also fairly recent, this information may be valid for its own time and place. The carver was usually trained to work using some existing statue or mask as a model. In Africa, copying of a given form and style was the prevailing teaching method and the artist remained anonymous. Although some names of modern African carvers are known, self-expression in our sense of the word, which places the emphasis on the individual, was not involved. Yet African wood carving was by no means static, but included changes of style. It has been suggested that, in the case of the Baluba, art may possibly be related to a dynamic Baluba philosophy, above the level of animism (William Fagg), as set forth by Temples. As philosophy deals with general ideas, a philosophic system may be expected to help us to understand the general character of Negro art, if not its stylistic variations. The picture we get from observations reported from the Ivory Coast by Himmelheber throws no light on any relation of art with philosophy for that region.

There art or craft was looked upon as something that could be taught; it was not based upon magic nor was it believed to be a matter of unusual talent. But a few individuals must have revealed a creative drive beyond the needs of the craft. Individual variations within the tribal manner occur even in conservative Africa, and such variations must be in part due to the exceptional artist. The importance of the tribal style has often been stressed, and properly so, but less has been said about variations introduced by the artist.

Talent was widely distributed, but it also varied with the tribes. Some tribes, even within the sculpture area, hardly carved at all. A single Atutu village, Afotobo, on the Ivory Coast, once had about one hundred carvers, including virtually the whole male population, and still had thirty in 1933. Such specialization in wood carving also occurs elsewhere, as in the Belgian Congo.

In some tribes a craft was a family occupation, the son taking it over from the father. In other tribes, a craft was open to anyone who demonstrated a talent and who chose to become apprentice to a master. In the case of wood carving, two or three years of apprenticeship would usually produce a capable carver.

An investigation of the arts of the Yoruba and the Beni of Nigeria, carried on by Mrs. Justine M. Cordwell in 1949 and 1950, brought to light a wealth of firsthand information. As another corrective study opposed to a purely theoretical approach to African art, this investigation presented valuable contributions, calling attention to the differences between the traditional style of the older generation and the more contemporary one of younger artists.

No evidence was found, as far as the carvers were aware of, that would justify the importance placed by some writers on distortions and on a three-dimensional aspect of sculptural form. The Cordwell findings differed from Himmelheber's in details and their emphasis on the cultural background. If we make allowances for differences of culture between Africa, and Europe and America, the basic artistic creativity, and probably motivations, seemed to have much in common. In spite of differences of religions and customs, as here presented, there is hardly a single basic factor relating to African art that does not have its parallel in our own culture. Even the fact that African carvers, along with those in other pre-literate cultures, do not use preliminary sketches is a matter of method; artists everywhere depend more or less on working conceptually from their imaginations.

Mrs. Cordwell talked to and observed twenty-one Yoruba carvers and apprentices, who varied from persons of title to commoners. Some were farmers, builders, tailors, and native doctors on the side. In spite of rigid traditions, "individual aesthetic play in creative activity" was found to have its place, motivated by "pleasure in producing artistic forms," as well as by prestige which comes "with social recognition for excellence in carving." Among Yoruba carvers, due to changing economic conditions, the trend today seemed to be to carve for customers rather than for the sake of the creative activity itself. The existence of talent was recognized, not as a "mysterious force that enters into a person," but as an inherited ability which in turn needed practice and development in order to enable one to become a successful carver. Wishes of the customers were complied with as they would recognize what might please the god (orisha) in cases where a statue was to be carved for a religious society. Original creative activity was found to exist among a few with superior talent. Such persons on occasion carved as a result of direct inspiration received from observation of persons or animals, but used remembered experiences. Three types of work could be differentiated: (1) typical, (2) specialized, according to an agreement with a customer, and (3) freely creative, growing out of an aesthetic emotional experience. Yoruba carvers were found to be versatile in mastering a large repertoire of forms, more so than so-called "primitive" artists are sometimes thought to be capable of. The creative process was found to be non-verbal, in Africa as in Europe and America. The Cordwell study admits other than purely aesthetic factors, as we admit such factors in our culture. A carved statue is important, not only for its artistic form, but as an aesthetic container for the power of a spirit. Architecture and costume are included in art, which is not limited to masks and figures. Costume is important for the part it plays in reinforcing or elevating position in society, as is the case with us. Of twenty-six carvers all but three left the choice of color to the customer.

Where colors were said to be naturalistic, the colors used did not necessarily imitate those of nature, and judgment on colors did not necessarily agree with our color preferences. Color in wood carving, in the opinion of the carvers, counted for less than form and texture. The method of carving proceeded swiftly, the carver constantly turning the block and examining it from different angles. Distortions in Yoruba carving served meaningful rather than purely aesthetic purposes, even though information on such meanings was difficult to determine. Formal analysis alone proved to be insufficient to explain motivation.

Stylization was found to be less rigid than it may appear to us; the artist would take liberties within the framework of the style, and the Yoruba carver had no words to differentiate naturalistic and stylized. The same Yoruba carvers were at times found to be equally competent in stylized and naturalistic carving. Yoruba carving differed in one respect from other West African carving; the shape of the block exercised less influence on the final form. The "tree trunk" theory seemed to apply less, at least in the Yoruba style. It is not as confining or influencing a factor as is commonly supposed. Mrs. Cordwell, after having seen carvers at work, came away with the idea that the "tree trunk" idea can be applied only "to a few areas where it is consistent with all forms the carver makes."

In Africa the woodworkers often continued to till the soil. But a tendency toward labor division between men and women is typical in early cultures and a trend to specialize in the crafts is also noticeable in Africa. Men carved while women were restricted to other handicrafts. The fact that carving was linked to religion, in which the role of women was limited, may account for this.

In the Sudan, the smith devoted all his time to his craft. At times he occupied a place in the secret society second only to the chief. Here the smith was also wood carver.

Where a feudal organization of society existed, as in some regions of the Zambezi River, the Congo and the Atlantic coast, some craftsmen became attached to the courts of rulers. Even kings, as with the Bakota, or members of the nobility, on occasion became craftsmen. Among the Bakuba of the Belgian Congo the wood carvers occupied the first place among the representatives of the crafts on the king's council, which exercised a restraining influence on the king's absolute power. In the Sudan the wood carvers have retained a guild-like organization. No artist achieved such fame that his name lived on through the centuries, but during his lifetime the artist held a position of respect, often achieving a considerable reputation.

The wood carver had a public on which he could depend; masks and figures were always in demand. Where there was a king and a court, the demand also included more elaborate works to reflect the importance of those who could afford luxuries not available to the common man.

Where a man of means would carve his own figures, as has been reported from Dahomey, because he felt the urge to do so, he carried on this activity secretly. He would do this in order not to be placed in a position of obligation to accept orders from others. To do so would be expected of him, once his skill as a carver would become known, but this would also be felt as a humiliation to his family, as well as his ancestors, and lower his prestige in the village (Herskovits).

GENERAL CHARACTERISTICS

Within the whole field of Negro African sculpture there are certain characteristics that apply more or less to all regions, thus cutting across the tribal styles which vary between the relatively abstract sculpture of the Fang and Bakota, in central Africa, for instance, and the more naturalistic sculpture, such as that of the Yoruba and Ekoi tribes in Nigeria. Briefly, these characteristics are (1) a disregard for the natural proportions of the figure, (2) an emphasis on the head in some styles, (3) frontality of posture, (4) a disinclination to explore movement to any marked extent, (5) a preference for monochrome, though polychromy occurs in some regions.

There are exceptional examples that show a different spirit and do not fit into the general style. To this group belong the before-mentioned terra cotta heads from Nok, which are definitely early, and the much-discussed heads from Ife, both in Nigeria. Perhaps, in time, others will be found.

FIGURES AND MASKS

There are two main classifications of Negro wood-carving: figures and masks. In addition, some architectural carving is to be found, and there are various objects of utility ranging from carved stools and chairs to a variety of smaller articles including spoons, spools, reels, pulleys, boxes and the like.

African wood carving is usually portable, varying from statuettes to small figures about half life-size. The African householder could keep his ancestors close at hand and take them along when he moved. Each figure is carved out of a limb or a section of a tree trunk. As is often the case in art, the material sets limits to form; figures carved out of logs the world over have a basic repose. Figures in Africa are, with occasional exceptions, carved in one piece, so that projections, like arms, come out of the log; they are not made of separate pieces doweled in.

The single figure is shown in standing, sitting or kneeling poses, and is usually free standing, except in architectural wood carving as in the Cameroons. Groups are not entirely absent, but they are subordinated to an external structure like a doorpost or lintel. There are a few groups like mother and child, two or more figures supporting a stool or holding a bowl.

The preservation of the skull is considered of importance in Africa, as in Oceania, for one reason or another. Figures of ancestors go back, according to one theory, to a cult of the skull and an early custom of erecting a pole over the grave. It has been argued by some scholars that the skull may have been placed on the pole. Eventually a carved head is said to have replaced the skull, and the wood carved ancestral figure came into existence. Some Fang figures suggest a survival of the skull or spirit pole; the skin-covered Ekoi masks (Color Plate 1) and the Bakota figures may also relate to an earlier skull cult. All pole-like forms in wood sculpture lend some plausibility to this theory, especially in the doorposts of Cameroon chiefs, carved with superimposed heads. The beginnings of African Negro sculpture are hypothetical, and no one theory has been generally accepted.

To speak of African masks as distortions is misleading, for that term implies that a concept of the human countenance is the objective, the mask a mere variation of a real face. Actually a Negro mask starts with a block of wood, and a fairly close resemblance to a human face often results. But it also happens that the interpretation may be very free. A nose may be elongated or form a vertical ridge, eyes may be small circles or huge window-like apertures, they may be egg-shaped and bulging or they may protrude like cylinders. A mouth may be tiny with lips all but suppressed, or large, curved and full-lipped with teeth showing. Design may be abstract or realistic. In some masks animal forms are used as freely as human features. The origin of mask design may have been determined by magic and myth, but esthetic considerations have also contributed refining influences.

Masks have been distinguished by their origin, as having evolved from skulls, mummies and animals. Some masks are painted white to suggest the spirits they represent, like the Ibo masks of Nigeria. Masks were worn by dancers in religious and social performances. Originally the dancer wore a long grass gown frame which covered the figure entirely, minimizing the head.

The methods of cutting into the wood blocks also determined styles. Thus, in certain masks the telescope eyes, nose ridge and mouth form the outside of the block, from which the carver cut back to form the cheeks. A semi-egg-shaped block could bring mouth and nose to touch the surfaces of the curved outlines, from which the carver chiseled out the wood to make the main features stand out. This technique in two planes explains the block-like character of many African masks.

In some few cases, masks worn by dancers in a pantomime were fastened to long garments that completely concealed the figure. The dancers in their masks represented the ancestors, who went through a ritual to arouse feelings of awe. Figures are usually brown or black, masks may show color where they are overlaid with closely spaced strings of red, blue and white beads.

REGIONAL AND TRIBAL STYLES

WEST AFRICA

The number of African Negro tribal styles is large. A comprehensive list might include one hundred or more styles that have been identified and are known by the tribal name. The examples of Negro African sculpture here dealt with are mostly from museums and private collections. They represent tribal styles as they functioned before they were subjected to modern European influence.

West Africa may be divided into a northern part of open grasslands, the savannah, and a southern part of tropical forests. The northern part, the Sudan, is well suited to agriculture and includes a varied fauna, especially many varieties of antelope.

Five tribal styles best represent Sudanese wood carvings: the Dogon, Mossi, Bobo, Bambara and Senufo; the location of these and other tribes is indicated on the map included in this chapter. The Sudan is characterized by a geometric style, which includes rigid frontality, a tendency to elongated forms in the human figure and a limited use of color. Of the many types of figures and masks, a few characteristic examples have been selected.

The Dogon tribe lives in the mountainous plateau within the great bend of the Niger River. Protected by the wild character of the country, they have preserved their own culture and art, though surrounded by Moslems. Dogon ancestor figures show long, cylindrical torsos surmounted by sharply defined heads contrasting with thin arms and legs. Rectangular forms in uncompromising verticals stand out against others which project horizontally. In some cases scarification patterns cover certain of the broad surfaces, hairdress, beards and frontal postures are analogous to those of ancient Egypt. A simple and structurally sound technique, cutting mainly with and across the grain of the wood, using diagonals sparingly and avoiding entirely long curves, results in a monumental style. A magnificent funeral group of a seated male and a female figure in the Barnes Collection, Merion, Pa., and a single female figure, illustrate this style (Fig. 2).

A variation of this style occurs in grave statuettes, of which only about ten specimens are known. The essential characteristics are repeated in a sturdier, but also simpler, less involved manner. The figure is an elaborated pole made in three parallel sections for torso, arms and legs. The breast appears to be attached to the shoulders. On the hands, six grooves for fingers form an ornamental pattern. A primitive structural origin developed directly into geometric abstraction, apparently by-passing realism.

The most spectacular of all Sudan styles is the Bambara. This large tribe adjoins the Dogon to the southwest. Their style is equally abstract. A type of wooden headdress, used in fertility dances, shows antelopes, often two animals combined, in a great variety of designs. These headpieces are a characteristic expression of Bambara art and rank among the finest of all African wood carving.

If we examine one of these antelope headpieces (Fig. 3) we are impressed by the rhythm in its play of line, the relation of the open spaces left between solid forms, the silhouette, the elegance in the curved neck and the sensitive merging of flat planes and sharp ridges into rounded forms. The flatness of the original plank is preserved in the effective side view. The use of repeating rectangles and triangles gives the design a sturdy coherence. This search for repeating shape is characteristic of effective design, and is here strikingly demonstrated. What gives a final touch of refinement is the differentiation of textures through the use of shallow surface ornamentation in the form of chip carving, shallow relief, and incised lines. Borders are judiciously placed and nowhere does decoration interfere with structure.

This headpiece is worn in dances at the sowing and harvest seasons, to propitiate evil spirits. The steps of the performers in the dance ritual would imitate the mating dance of antelopes. Anyone familiar with the antelope will recognize in the mask the grace so characteristic of this animal. But the artist has freely adapted the form to the purposes of decoration. Here the antelope's long, slender legs and cloven hoofs are made into sturdy supports, attached to a base that could be fitted to a cap, the wood being lighter than it appears. The carver has retained the bridge of the animal's nose and the camouflage spots of the young one standing on its mother's back. The artistic quality, so pronounced in this headpiece, is not unusual in African wood carving. Every village using this type had its own designs so that the antelope motif appears constantly varied.

The cylindrical torso of a Bambara human figure (Fig. 4) is reminiscent of the cylindrical neck of the carved antelope (Fig. 3). Gouged-out borders with rings are at the base of the human torso as well as the antelope neck. Both animal and human forms show the same types of ornamental borders; even the heads have something in common in the triangular shape and the prominent nose ridge. Heads suspended on slender, pole-like necks are in the tribal tradition, as are the cone-shaped breasts and the paddle-like hands with notched ends for fingers, similar to the block feet with grooved toes.

The Senufo have produced a variety of art forms such as musical instruments, masks, statues—some holding a dish to serve as an offertory table—fertility statuettes, ointment boxes, weavers' pulleys. The bird is a common motif on masks and dancing staffs. The Senufo style relates the abstract Sudanese manner to that of less severe and softer coastal styles.

A Senufo mask (Fig. 5) over one foot high fuses the stylization of the Sudan with the curves of the Baulé style. The semi-oval projections on either side of the face and the short legs coming out of the chin are typical, but their meaning is unknown. Probably more than purely aesthetic considerations explain the style. The wing-like projection might relate to a bird and indicate a soul or spirit significance and the closed eyes of the smaller head on top could point to death. A Senufo male figure (Fig. 6) about three feet high, said to be from Lorogho village, now in the Verité Collection in Paris, has the short legs and forward thrust of the Senufo style. A comparison of the Senufo mask (Fig. 5) with the head of the statue reveals the tribal style. In contrast to the mask, this Senufo figure is imbued with an extraordinary elegance and vitality. A sense for dramatic contrasts, a feeling for linear consistency and beauty of surface texture makes this figure a great work of sculpture.

THE WEST GUINEA COAST

The style of the small Baga tribe of French Guinea is abstract and is related to the simplified, geometric Sudanese manner. The most pronounced feature of the Baga style (Fig. 7) is the head which projects horizontally far to the front, suspended from a post-like neck. Figures, half figures and large male and female masks, made to rest on the shoulders of the wearer and look like busts, have the same type of heads. The profile is a succession of incisive curves of great vitality. Carved ornamental borders, in the manner of bridles or straps, are laid across the head, which is beautifully related to the curved surface of the two pendent breasts. A sense of superhuman power is obtained through shapes that are precise in carving and only faintly human in appearance. The forward extension of the head might be based on the reminiscence of a man carrying a mask in front of his face. The female mask is said to represent a tribal ancestor and maternity symbol of the Baga. "The female ones are called 'nimba' and are said to be containers for maternity and fertility spirits or powers." (Wingert)

The chief tribe of Sierra Leone, the Mendi tribe, is known for masks and figures associated with the Bundu and Yassi, female secret societies. Soft forms with high coiffures and bulging foreheads overbalance the compressed features. A figure (Yassi) in the Mendi style, about a foot and a half high (Fig. 8), was used by the priestesses in a divination rite. From the unadorned bowl the figure rises in a graceful curve. Arms and shoulders exist as part of a gently swelling form that reaches a climax in the rounded forehead and elaborate headdress. Hands are important as a part of posture and as an accent of pleasing texture, distributing the interest. Refinement is here developed to a high degree. As the carved figure was believed to be capable of conveying the decision of spirits, stylistic changes were probably discouraged for fear of offending them. So the carver adhered to the old styles that had proved effective. Any changes would be motivated by a desire to make a traditional type more attractive. Neck rings according to African custom denote wealth, and the elaborate headdress, carefully carved and embellished with decorations, would do honor to the spirit who made his home in the statue. No other parts are equal to the headdress in precision; it is the most realistic part of the figure.

These sloping shoulders and this receptive, self-effacing posture seem to parallel the painted and sculptured saintly virgins of the Christian Middle Ages. The high forehead and narrow eyes recall a Sienese or Byzantine manner, though there is no close resemblance as the details are African. This figure comes from Sherbro Island, off Sierra Leone.

Stone sculpture in the form of small steatite figures (Fig. 9) has been found throughout Sierra Leone. This crouching figure with low forehead, large frog eyes, hook nose, thick lips, differs from the modern Mendi wood carving, but belongs stylistically to Sierra Leone. "It seems unlikely, in spite of local traditions, that these stone carvings are ancient." (Wingert)

Several west Guinea coast tribes, including the Mendi, had the Poro, a man's secret society, in common. Three styles of masks are known. One shows simplified human features; another, heavily indented sculpturesque forms with a movable lower jaw, telescope eyes and a semi-coneshaped nose; and a third, under a foot high, combines a human face with an animal (Fig. 10). Both human and bird types are emphatic in their curved surfaces. Though unlike in expression, they are related in style. Their vitality is perhaps the most noteworthy characteristic. Each mask has a fresh vigor due to the technique of direct cutting of the block. Some Poro masks are rough, lumpy and massive in appearance. The Mano, Geh, and Gio tribes of Liberia are represented in these Poro society masks.

An abstract sculpturesque mask from the Liberian border (Fig. 11) is related to the Bambara style. It is of one piece but looks as if it had been constructed of separate shapes of rounded surfaces bounded by flat planes. Brows, cheeks, jaws and nose project. Tufts of fiber for whiskers fill the recesses and contrast with smooth surfaces and elliptical edges. White streaks emphasize projection, and curved horns round out the mask on a lid-like top. In its use of geometric shapes and its logic of design this mask has a certain affinity with modernism. With its gaping mouth it conjures up some strange beast, its shagginess increasing the fearful effect, but horns and jaw indicate a ram, probably not meant to inspire fear.

The Dan tribe includes several groups in eastern Liberia and the western Ivory Coast. Their art is one of masks; statues are unknown; but there are also ladles and brass castings. The masks range in style from abstract to realistic types; some are close to portraits. Of the Dan tribe of the Ivory Coast, masks are known in various degrees of stylization, emphasizing form rather than surface. An emphasis on pyramidal shapes clearly suggests how the style evolved out of the technique. There are few curves and rounded surfaces. The effect depends on angles and plane surfaces chopped out with the adz and cut down with the knife, producing masks that look cubistic.

THE CENTRAL GUINEA COAST

The large Baulé tribe adjoining the Dan on the west Ivory Coast has produced some of the finest and best known Negro sculpture. Restrained elegance is combined with technical perfection in stylized masks and figures. Pure aestheticism finds its fullest expression in the Baulé style.

Calm and passive, these ancestral figures (Fig. 12) appear like reassuring phantoms from another world. The heads are given a major interest. A measure of idealization combines with a mingling of heavy African eyelids with long straight noses and small, button-like mouths. Nothing is known of the historical development, but forms so finished and so perfect in detail seem like end products of a long development.

When we compare female with male figures, the unity of the style is apparent. Oval heads on cylindrical necks show mask-like faces. Torsos rest on dwarfed legs and have purely ornamental arms. There are individual variations, even in the proportions. Care is taken to enrich the surface with detail, and headdress and features are developed into patterns primarily for artistic ends. The heads are overlaid with the tribal scarification marks in relief. Wood carving is here accomplished with patience and much labor. The main surface had to be cut back to bring out details. Hard wood, closely grained, is made smooth and polished, its effect depending on wood finish rather than on color. The pieces are allover black, gray or red.

A seated female ancestor figure (Fig. 13) shows in side view the tribal characteristics, but these are somewhat varied in proportion and details. We recognize the Baulé style and yet every part of the figure combines to make for a personal expression. This figure is distinctive in its fullness and breadth. Hairdress, scarification marks, breasts, thighs and calves express a love of full-blown form. Other Baulé figures emphasize slenderness of form and a precision of ornamental detail which is almost metallic.

The general characteristics of the Ivory Coast style appear on a female figure in the Smithsonian Institution not definitely attributed to a particular tribe. Baulé type eyes are here combined with a nose with spreading nostrils more characteristic of Benin and Cameroons figures, whereas the mouth suggests one of the many variations common to the Congo. One feels in such a figure that the carver lingered over every part of the figure, head, torso and legs, to give each its full measure of attention, as if to improve and idealize. Hairdress, scarification marks and breasts are realistic, everything else is stylized, but the total impression is one of consistency and unity.

Baulé masks are highly sophisticated. In a stylized mask from the Buffalo Museum of Science the mouth all but disappears. Eyebrows and wedge nose form one line into which the eyes are fitted, semi-almond-shaped, open only in a fine slit. The sawtooth fringe of the lower half of the face fits into the stylization, while the hair forms a flat net of curves and linear patterns. In its extreme elegance the Baulé style stands out in contrast to a more robust naturalism in other styles. Von Luschan has suggested that the elaborate collars of the Benin ivory heads may be due to a reminiscence of European lace collars. The zigzag contours around the necks of these Baulé masks might reflect a similar source.

The general pattern and the individual details are the same in Baulé masks, but there are subtle differences. All express repose and some show a more rounded (Fig. 14) or more elongated (Fig. 15) facial contour, more nearly horizontal eyes, full lips and bulging curves to describe the hairline. Each of these masks is a perfect solution of its kind; straight lines and curves, flatness and relief, smooth and textured surfaces are combined with a calculated finesse. Baulé carving also exists in the form of weaving pulleys, drums, divination bowls, gong mallets, spoons and bowls.

The Guro tribe occupies the region to the west of the Baulé. Their style is close to the Baulé style, varying only in details. It seeks the utmost in seemingly self-conscious artistry. A Guro mask (Fig. 16) with horns and bird is one of Africa's most sympathetic carvings. With what exhilaration the bird surmounts its human support! Below, the features timidly break through the surface; above, the supernatural takes command in a bulbous forehead, two powerful horns and the triumphant bird raised high above its base. The spirit that moves the dancer is in control, subordinating the human actor to its will. Rarely has feeling found such an exalted expression. In such masks of cultivated elegance and refined dignity (Fig. 15), the Guro and Baulé artists, the Botticellis of wood carving, represent a high point of excellence within the whole field of primitive art.

The Ashanti, an important Gold Coast tribe, lived under a king in a feudal type of organization. As a kingdom it flourished from the end of the seventeenth century. Royal courts have always used the arts as a source of articles of luxury made to enhance their position and contribute to their prestige. For that reason the Ashanti developed decorative forms rather than important sculpture. The Ashanti kings had a monopoly on gold and its use in manufacture. There was also much cast brass in the form of ceremonial vessels, and smaller casts for the purpose of weighing gold dust. The Ashanti tribe became notorious for warfare and human sacrifice. Raids on neighboring tribes secured captives which were sold as slaves. When the country became a British protectorate in 1895, the kingdom came to an end.

Ashanti figure sculpture is rare, but is not entirely lacking. An Ashanti seated figure of mother and child (Fig. 17) has an easy relaxation which differentiates the Ashanti from the more precisely defined Baulé type (Fig. 13). The carving of objects of utility, plates, spoons, calabashes and combs, was highly developed. Of carved figures, fertility fetishes were most common. A woman who wanted children carried the fetish, wrapped in a neckerchief, upon her back. It is said a round head indicated that a boy was wanted, a square head, a girl. The same symbolism, round heads for males, square for female, prevails in Navaho sand painting.

Gold weights, cast in bronze, brass and copper in miniature size by the "cire perdue" process, included birds, fish, insects, plant forms, articles of everyday use, as well as weapons and firearms, which betray the contact of the Ashanti with Europe. Geometric designs are believed to be the oldest type. Though each piece is individual, because it required a form of its own which was destroyed in the process of casting, the same types were recast many times. Their appeal is in naturalism and in the representation of action. Proverbs and religious subjects were often represented. It has been said that if the proper weight did not result in the casting, a limb might be broken off, or a piece of metal added, to bring the piece to the proper weight, without regard for the appearance of the finished cast. Every Ashanti in comfortable circumstances formerly had a collection of from forty to sixty gold weights, and the well-to-do had several hundred. As a folk art the Ashanti gold weights are in a class of their own and should not be judged by the standards of sculpture (Fig. 18).

Larger objects of cast gold, from three to four inches in width and breadth, are of fine craftsmanship. A gold crescent-shaped pendant showing two eyes and a nose (Fig. 19) is carefully made and well designed. The smaller brass objects are soft and fluid in form, pictorial in design, and loose and sketchy in execution; but the gold pendants show greater reserve and are of superior craftsmanship. This is also true of ceremonial bronze urns or vessels. The hinged lid often shows an animal or two animals in combat.

Dahomey, like Ashanti and Benin, was once a kingdom with a court art centered at the capital of Abomey. The arts of brass casting, clay modeling, cloth appliquéing and the carving of calabashes were the prerogative of king and nobles. Brass casting was reserved for a family guild serving court and nobility, but wood carving was in the hands of the people. It varied in quality depending on whether it was of professional origin or the work of laymen. Silver, brass and iron were also used in sheets to cover wooden statues. Figures were made in gold, silver and brass, which was as highly valued in ancient Dahomey as gold. Animals cast in brass included symbolic representations of lions, buffalo, elephants. No religious significance was attached to the human figure; it was used as a motif in brass casting in a purely secular way. The craft came to Dahomey from Europe, and according to tradition the more recent kings had amassed wealth in the form of cloth, gold, silver, and brass figures (Herskovits). The style is one of elongated figures in lively action (Fig. 20) showing man in combat with animals. Each piece was separate, but the figures and animals were set up in groups. Somewhat larger than Ashanti gold weights, the Dahomey brasses are thin and sleek, quite different from the lumpy Ashanti style. Their surfaces are finely chased, suggesting a relationship to Benin bronzes.

The making of appliquéd cloth for various purposes, including hammocks, wall hangings, umbrellas, is the monopoly of one family guild in Abomey. But the cloth itself is sold to all who can buy it. The backgrounds are gold or black, human figures are red or black and the pattern is in red, blue, green or white. Brass and cloth appliquéing have their own traditions. The general trend of Dahomey art is naturalistic, but the character of the material also played its part in affecting style and technique.

As late as 1930, Melville J. Herskovits found wood carvers at work on commissions for native patrons. The few wood carvings that have come out of Dahomey may vary considerably in style. Dahomey figures, like those of the Herskovits collection, are massive and pole-like, with a minimum of articulation below the round head, and oval eyes that recall the Yoruba style. The arms are thin, except for lumpy hands, and cling to the body. The original tree trunk is retained as a base.

Masks on a carved wooden door (Fig. 21) show a marked resemblance to Senufo masks in the shape of the head, with its lateral extensions, and in the features. As a matter of fact the attribution is uncertain and the official museum attribution is, "Senufo, French Sudan or Ivory Coast." Some carved figures may be called folk art, but this developed pattern in its elegance and technical excellence is clearly the work of a professional carver.

THE EAST GUINEA COAST

The southwestern part of Nigeria, between Dahomey and the Niger River, occupies a unique place in African sculpture. Three important styles are located here; the style of the Yoruba, the art of the Beni, once holders of the powerful kingdom of Benin; and the style of some extraordinary bronze and terra-cotta heads, excavated at Ife.

The Yoruba tribe, one of the largest in Africa, numbering about five million, is divided into several sub-tribes. Their art is strikingly unified and is characterized by color and a largeness of scale. Besides masks and divination bowls, the Yoruba carved statues of their gods, to serve as dwelling places for their spirits. This art is massive, vigorous and naturalistic, expressive of a taut energy, with large open eyes, curved noses, and thick lips (Fig. 22). It uses various postures; standing, sitting, kneeling and squatting poses, groups (Fig. 23), and motifs taken from life. The Yoruba are related to the Beni and Ife styles culturally and artistically.

Characteristic Yoruba features (Color Plates 2 and 3) include egg-shaped eyes, cylindrical necks and oval faces. The Yoruba dancer's staff (Color Plate 2) used in the Shango cult is here combined with the double ax. Shango, the god of thunder, in another famous piece of Yoruba sculpture, in the Newark Museum, takes on the outward form of an armed horseman who carries a divination bowl on his head. Such bowls were carved in what amounts to a high relief out of the plank-like section left after the bowl had been outlined. Had there been no bowl, horse and rider would have shown considerable breadth, as happens in a well-known example of a Yoruba mask with a superimposed horse and rider.

A large number of seated figures that look like Yoruba wood carving, but are carved in soft talc stone, were found in 1934 in the Nigerian village of Esie. There were enough to fill a small museum built to house them. All exhibit the same vigorous style with robust head and large eyes. The mass-produced manner made according to a tradition seems to dominate, yet individual styles are also represented.

Traditional Yoruba style characteristics are retained in a wooden door from Ikerre (Nigeria), now in the British Museum, carved around 1900 by an artist by the name of Olowere. In a lively manner, less stylized than Benin art, each frame relates an incident. Figures walk in procession, an attendant stands behind a king seated on a folding chair, soldiers with sword in hand return from a decapitation scene, prisoners are led to their death; in the lower frame two servants carry a figure wearing a European hat in an African-style sedan chair. Though the mannerisms of the style are emphasized, characteristics like differences of age, as expressed in the heads, are also brought out.

The Beni, with their city of Benin, are the best known of the former West African kingdoms, and have a history based on oral tradition that goes back seven or eight centuries. Their kings (Obas) claim descent from the legendary progenitor of the Onis of Ife. Benin bronzes contributed much to the recognition of African art in the eyes of the west.

THE BENIN STYLE

In February, 1897, the ancient kingdom of Benin came to an end, after a British expeditionary force had taken over the city. The story of human ritual sacrifice, as reported by H. Ling Roth, is part of ancient Benin's ancestor worship, but is not represented in art. A vast cache of well over two thousand art objects of bronze, ivory, iron, coral, glass and a few wood carvings and textiles was taken to Lagos, Nigeria. Some twenty-four hundred items were listed under sixty-four subdivisions. What was not retained by the British Museum eventually became available to other museums and private collectors.

As examples of bronze casting the Benin pieces are technically equal to the best of European work. Felix von Luschan claimed that "Benvenuto Cellini could not have cast them any better." Benin bronzes composed of copper and zinc, rather than copper and tin, were cast to an even thickness to assure uniform cooling of the liquid bronze and thereby avoid cracks. As is often the case, the castings when removed from the mold had to be worked over with tools for the final finish. A single small plate, according to expert testimony, may have taken weeks and months to polish.

The Benin style (Fig. 24) is close to Yoruba wood carving; there is a resemblance between the large heads and egg-like protruding eyes. Compare this example with the Benin bronzes in reliefs, and in the over life-size bronze heads of the kings (Obas). (Color Plate 4) This head represents an ancestor and served the king as his own personal fetish. The ceremonial dress has coral bead neck bands; the headdress has strap-like side supports for the carved elephant tusks. The Yoruba style of wood carving here appears refined to soft, swelling forms as if gently inflated. The bulging eyes project less, are large and close to the front of the skull. In the bronzes the features are more or less stylized, making for a cultivated but still ornamental realism. A feeling similar to the Yoruba wood carving is here expressed in a softer technique, that of the craftsman in bronze who models in wax.

For eyes accustomed to realism, Benin bronzes are easy to appreciate. Naturalism and stylization are attractively blended in the head of a young woman (Fig. 25). Lines stand out as such in subtle contrast to the modeling of the cheeks, like the lower eyelids, a line separating the nostrils from the end of the nose, and a linear ridge along the lower lip. Strings of coral beads are treated with great reticence, in the net-like cap, to form pendants in front of the ears and to encircle the neck. European court costume of the more extravagant periods was more confusingly barbaric than this dignified style that subordinated headdress to the person.

A bronze cock (Fig. 26), about life-size, and with an allover pattern, is a triumph of craftsmanship. The surface is overlaid with painstakingly executed details. We feel here a burst of energy that delights in an expression of splendor.

The same is true of ivory leopards (Fig. 27), made in pairs and inlaid with copper studs. Each leopard is about a foot and a half high and about two and a half feet long, including the tail.

Most ambitious of Benin bronzes are the high reliefs once used architecturally in the royal residence. According to a report by Dr. Olfert Dapper, a seventeenth century Hollander, the wooden piers of the royal palace had been covered from top to bottom with bronze reliefs. Culturally, aesthetically and art-historically, these plaques are of the greatest interest. A particularly magnificent specimen is one with seven figures (Fig. 28). On first sight it seems confusing in the abundance of detail; but in the original it gives a more unified impression owing perhaps to the color of the patina. The king is in the center with a high officer on either side, each with a shield. Four smaller attendants are in between. One holds two bells upside down, while his companion to the right blows a horn. Under him the third has a ceremonial sword and the fourth a fan. The chieftain is nude except for a tooled leather loin cloth, but he wears an eight-ringed coral necklace, a coral sash, a coral net helmet, coral and chain puttees and holds a ceremonial sword in his right and an ornamental spear in his left hand. The spear bearer on the chieftain's left has just handed the weapons to his master, who presents them in ceremonial fashion.

Such emphasis on arms, armor and bodily adornments to denote rank, clearly bespeaks a highly stratified society based on the hereditary power of kings. This is official court art, intended to enhance the ruler by a display of pomp. We have in these panels a reproduction, in miniature, of the miscellany that went into a Benin state ceremony. The same Dapper, to whom we owe the report of the use of the bronze reliefs, left a water color of a royal Benin procession. This shows leopards led by chains and followed by men ringing bells for the calling of the spirits.

It is significant that a realistic style is highly developed within a basically African orientation. Arms and weapons are thrust into space, entirely separating them from the background, and legs and feet are minimized. The artist appreciates contrasting textures, as in nude portions against incised patterns, flat areas against high relief, as well as the necessity of subordinating minor attendants to give dominance to the king. Numerous reliefs with four or more figures are known; von Luschan gives thirty-four. They show that the Benin artist experimented with compositions, all based on symmetry. Benin art, compared to other African styles, more nearly parallels the aims of official court art everywhere.

Among the hundreds of bronze reliefs there are a number representing Europeans. The features, as shown in eyes, nostrils and mouth, are in the African style, but the nose becomes elongated and the man has a beard. They are not superior to the others, but have a special interest in that the costumes indicate their approximate periods, such as pleated skirts similar to those on late fifteenth century German woodcuts. The African artist tried his best to represent accurately strange dress and weapons. As he knew them only by sight, he made mistakes, like showing buttons but no buttonholes. Bronze casting was known to the Beni before the Portugese arrived in 1472. The extent to which the Portugese contributed to Benin metal work, if at all, is not clear. The style of Benin bronze casting is admittedly African and its chronology has been tentatively charted (Struck), and also questioned and amended (William Fagg).

Benin ivory carving offers us examples of superior craftsmanship, such as armlets in two pieces, one inside the other, which would rattle as they rubbed each other.

A much-admired example (Fig. 29) is a small ivory mask, about six inches high, one of five known specimens. The elongated head shows a coral neck below a chin necklace and a coral net cap fringed with a row of small European heads. Eyes and forehead are inlaid in metal. The typical Benin eyes and nose are refined and softened toward realism; in proportions the stylization has gone toward length rather than breadth of head. The immaculate, sensitive treatment of the surface, smooth and evenly rounded, is like a "classicizing" tendency in the African mode.

A Benin ivory container (Ill. 1), attributed to the fifteenth century, is an interesting example of the fusion of European motifs with African styles. The central Crucifixion, with the two doves of the Holy Ghost above the Virgin Mary (on the left) and St. John with his chalice (on the right), shows the Christian symbols and bearded heads common to the European tradition. The flanking figures (beginning on the left), are: St. Andrew with his "Andrew" type of cross, St. Peter with key, St. Paul

Ill. 1. Ivory container with the Crucifixion, St. John, Virgin Mary, and four saints. Benin style (Nigeria). *Collection, Melville J. Herskovits, Evanston, Illinois.*

with sword and St. John with chalice. The ornamental border with zigzags and curved linear elements are African, though similar details are found in other styles. The beards are distinctly separate from the serrated collar beneath each beard, if the zigzags may be interpreted in that way. In the case of the Virgin the same motif could mean the starched edge of a nun's hood. Shapes unfamiliar to the Beni, like the heads of the doves, are barely recognizable. The owner of this container, Melville J. Herskovits, has pointed out in this connection the hold that style has upon the artist, style being likened to a mold into which a foreign content is poured.

An ivory standing cup in the British Museum is one of a number of Benin ivories that show European influence. In costume and weapons, as in the pleated skirt and the long sword, and details such as the long bearded heads of the figures wearing crosses on chains around their necks, an influence, perhaps from German late fifteenth century woodcuts (Hans Burgkmair, the Elder), is apparent. There is relatively little in the style that could be called African. Such ivories were apparently carved for Europeans directly in imitation of European designs. Except in technical matters, they owe little to Africa and had no influence on the native style.

THE IFE STYLE

Between 1910 and 1912 Leo Frobenius startled the world with the discovery at Ife of an extraordinary bronze head, which in its style seemed to contradict the then prevalent conceptions of African sculpture. In 1938 eleven bronzes came to light at Ife, published by Bascom in 1939, and in 1949 Bernard Fagg excavated terra-cotta heads at Abiri, ten miles from Ife. The bronze (brass) head known as Olokun (Fig. 30) was a portrait of the Oni, the divine king, founder of the present Yoruba dynasty. Comparable in style is the British Museum copper head supposedly of Obalufon II (Fig. 31), an early Yoruba king, the third Oni of Ife of the tenth century. Their refined naturalism and their technical perfection gave rise to various speculations as to origin and dating. It had been variously suggested that the artists who made them came from Nubia, the Mediterranean (Etruria) or from Asia (Persia), and until recently a Greek contribution appeared to be plausible. The question may well have been answered, at least as far as origin is concerned.

It now appears, according to Justine M. Cordwell, that the terra-cotta and bronze heads, as well as bronze figures, belong to funeral figures which are indigenous to a wide area from Lake Chad to Dakar, and to the area south to the coast of West Africa. Small heads of terra-cotta and stone, in different styles and degrees of excellence, have been found in archaeological sites in this area. According to Mauny, these Benin and Ife bronzes are part of this pattern.

After extensive research (1945-50), Mrs. Cordwell has suggested that these heads are African, linked to the naturalistic art of the so-called second funeral. The second funeral, the *ako*, was a part of the ancestral cult. Some time, from three months to three years, after death and burial, the body of the deceased chief or king or head of a family was disinterred and reburied in a ceremonial funeral. This was done to please the ancestor, as any honor bestowed on him increased his prestige in the spirit world. A puppet was made to represent the deceased. The head was lifelike; the body only served as a rack on which real clothes were draped. The long, funnel-like neck was used to attach the head to the puppet; only the head was important. Holes in the top of the head were used to attach a crown.

We are hardly in a position to judge the degree of resemblance to the person represented. Apparently the purpose of the artist was to create a resemblance to the deceased that would serve in this important public ceremony.

IBO, IBIBIO AND EKOI STYLES

The Ibo tribe of eastern Nigeria, with its numerous sub-tribes, is known particularly for its masks used at funerary rites (Fig. 32). The masks are patterned after the skull, with closed eyes, high foreheads, fallen cheeks and exposed teeth. They are painted white to suggest a spirit of the dead. Through these masks, the ancestors were believed to speak on the occasions of mortuary ceremonies. That the artists worked with reverence is evident in the careful execution. These masks infuse death with dignity as an expression of regard for ancestors, and the effect is both startling and beautiful.

The Ibibio tribe, on the left bank of the Niger and south of the Ibo, is linked to the Ibo through secret societies. Masks are more important than statues. The style is characterized by bold, simple forms, without detail or surface enrichment (Fig. 33). Within a general pattern secret society masks vary considerably, and some Ibibio masks have movable jaws.

The Ekoi with their sub-tribes are a large group in eastern Nigeria next to the English-mandated Cameroons. Their particular specialty is wooden masks, which represent ancestors and are used by the secret societies at burials. The double-headed Janus mask is black on one side, representing the male, and white on the other side, representing the female. Another type of mask has two horns, which are surmounted by figures of animals or human beings. A third type, a variation of the Janus double mask (Color Plate 1) or single mask, was covered with human skin, the skin of slaves or slain enemies being used. The skin of monkeys or of antelopes has since replaced the use of human skin. For hair, wool or human hair was used, teeth and eyes were of metal or wood. The skin color, darkened by age, shows up as an orange brown and is decorated with black. They show extreme realism, as if carved after the human skull. These skin-covered masks are stylistically the opposites of the severe Bambara and the sophisticated Baulé masks. The Ekoi masks were usually worn on top of the head; those worn in front of the face are considered rare.

CAMEROONS

The province of Cameroons, to the east and south of Nigeria, is inhabited by small tribes related in culture and language. The sculpture of these tribes is remarkably unified in style. Crafts handed down from father to son use wood, brass, beaded fiber (Fig. 34) and argillite. Among the sculpture-producing tribes are the Bamum, Bangwa, Bafum and Bali. Various types of masks are produced as well as numerous objects of utility, including stools, beds, carved doorposts and lintels, house posts and free-standing posts with superimposed figures (Fig. 35). The art tends toward a robust and realistic manner, and animal motifs, like antelopes, lizards, monkeys and snakes, are common.

Cameroon figures excel in movement and are lively in facial expression (Fig. 36). A rough vigor is apparent but does not exclude care and precise workmanship, as in the deftly cut features and the rendering of teeth. We note similar tribal characteristics in a Cameroon mask. The mouth is open and the expression is definitely jovial, unlike the usual calm features of most African art. The shape of ears and eyes follows a definite style. Strength expressed through the directness of the technique, with the tool marks showing, is characteristic of both figures and masks.

An oxhead mask, about a foot and a half high, attributed to the Bamum tribe, represents a stylized approach. A red clay Bali pipe bowl, in spite of the difference in material, clearly shows the typical eyes, ears and mouth, though individually varied. Both these items are in the Carl Kjersmeier collection in Copenhagen.

CENTRAL AFRICA

French Equatorial Africa

French Equatorial Africa and the Belgian Congo are the two main political divisions of Central Africa. The French section is to the west and north of the Congo River and joins the Cameroons on the west side. Three tribes live in the southern part or near the coastal region. From north to south they are: the Fang, also known as Pangwe or Pahouin, the Bakota, and Ogowe River tribes. In contrast to the Cameroons area, these three tribes are restricted each to one kind of sculpture.

An Ogowe River tribe female mask about a foot high suggests Asiatic influence. The mask is white with black hair and scarification marks and red lips. These masks represent the spirits of ancestors. The high lobes of the hairdress, arched eyebrows, sharply edged projecting lips, combine with a smooth surface and an elegant oval contour in an effective manner. The eyes are often closed, and each mask has an individuality of its own.

Fang figures are believed to be among the oldest of surviving African wood carving. The Fang, a warlike tribe, entered the country from the northeast as conquerors. In Fang style (Fig. 37), the basic pole structure is overlaid by arms and interrupted by projecting thighs. The cutting of the statue out of the tree trunk is clearly visible. A long torso, a cylindrical neck and short legs are typical. Bulging and tapering forms cling to the body, in this example even fuse with the body, and abruptly emerge at the hips, before the thighs descend into massive calves and block feet. The figures functioned as guardian spirits over the skulls of ancestors, which were kept in cylindrical boxes.

The extreme simplification of the Fang figures also appears in the mask shown in Fig. 38. Boldness of cutting, simplicity of shape and purity of line combine to suggest delicacy. Tiny slits for eyes emphasize the place where the curves converge. Thus, accents and contours contrast with the larger blank spaces of forehead and cheeks, making one aware of the extraordinary sensitivity of African Negro art.

A Gabun mask (Fig. 39) from the region of the Congo border shows somewhat similar stylistic characteristics: an oval-shaped head and a concave facial area. The effect depends on a smooth facial surface and a curved outline contrasting with a straight lined nose raised, like the eyes, above the curved surface of the face. We feel here an economy of form in which each element is varied to produce the greatest effect. A simple border introduces a suggestion of surface decoration in a mask that otherwise depends on form alone.

Bakota carved wood funerary figures are less than two feet high and are covered with thin sheets of copper (Fig. 40). The oval-shaped head, slightly convex, connects to what has been called a neck, which is attached to legs with knees flexed. Extensions project out on either side of the head. Metal is used in sheets and strips and the features are embossed in simple shapes making the most of the beauty of the material. The style shows the greatest reserve in the treatment of the metal and the subdivision of the surfaces. Though the pattern is standardized, individual figures are different in almost every detail.

There has been some speculation upon the origin of this unusual type. The usual explanation is that the figures are guardians of ancestors, since they were placed in the baskets containing ancestral skulls.

An influence from the mask shape has been suggested, and they have been related to styles of hairdress said to have been customary in neighboring tribes. Some figures are double, Janus-like, with a face on either side. Most of them are concave, said to be female; a few, believed to be older, are convex, and said to be male. Andersson, who has most recently studied the problem of their origin, suggests that the figures were originally gods of the dead, rather than mere guardians of ancestral spirits or spirits of ancestors. In this connection it might be pointed out that the wings suggest the headdress of the Egyptian god, Osiris, the god of the future life, to whom the dead were said to have gone. The legs suggest faintly the *ankh,* the Egyptian symbol of enduring life, except that the original loop has become angular, leg-like. It is impossible to say whether such resemblances are valid, indicating an historical connection, or whether they are purely accidental.

The Belgian Congo

The other part of Central Africa consists of the Belgian Congo south of the Congo River, and a section of Angola. The more productive area for sculpture is in the south. From west to east this area can be divided into several tribal regions. In the Western Congo region are the Bateke, Bayaka and

(continued on page 49)

Fig. 1 (top left). Head, terra cotta, H. 8¾ in., from the region of Nok, Nigeria, period 500 B.C.–1 B.C. *Nigerian Government.*

Fig. 2 (left). Female figure, Dogon style, Sudan. *University Museum, Philadelphia.*

Fig. 3 (above, right). Antelope headpiece, Bambara style, Sudan. *Frobenius Institute, Frankfurt am Main, Germany.*

Fig. 4 (right). Figure, Bambara style, Sudan. *University Museum, Philadelphia.*

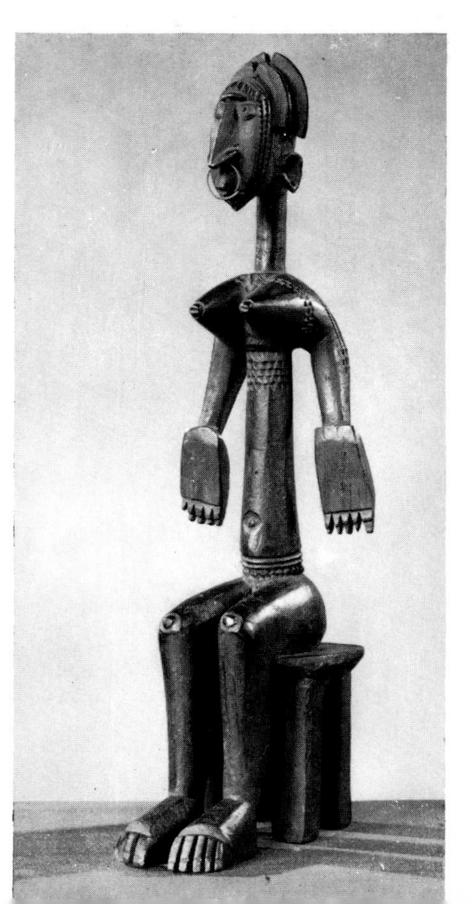

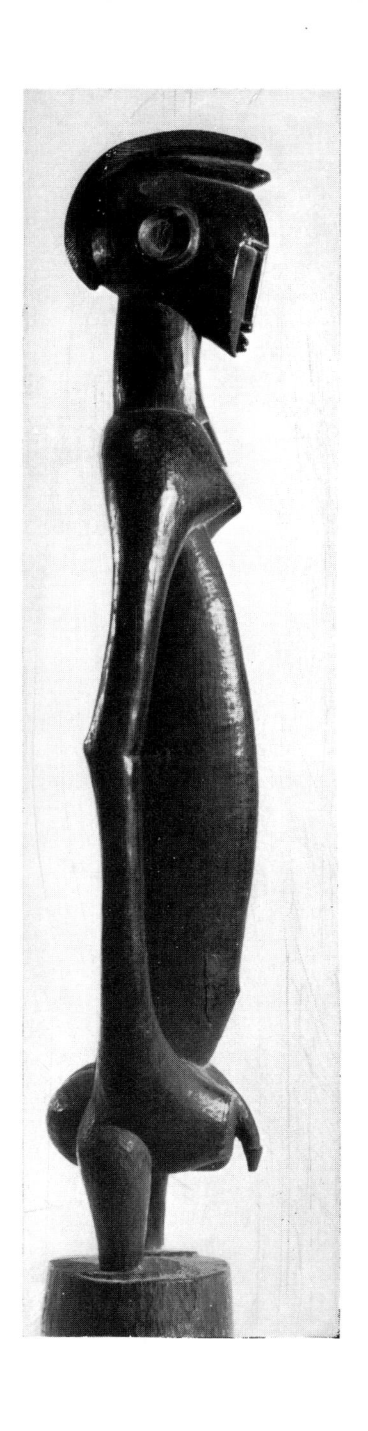

Fig. 5 (left). Mask, Senufo style Ivory Coast. *Verité Collection, Paris. Photo: Eliot Elisofon.*

Fig. 6 (above). Male figure, Senufo style, Ivory Coast. *Verité Collection, Paris. Photo: Eliot Elisofon.*

Opposite page:

Fig. 7. Female half figure, Baga style, Sudan. *British Museum. Photo: Eliot Elisofon.*

Fig. 8 (right). Female half figure, Mendi, Sierra Leone. *University Museum, Philadelphia.*

Fig. 9. Soapstone (steatite) figure, Sierra Leone. *Klejman Gallery, New York. Photo: Eliot Elisofon.*

Opposite page:

Fig. 10. Poro bird mask, West Guinea Coast (Liberia). *British Museum. Photo: Eliot Elisofon.*

Fig. 11 (above). Mask, Ivory Coast, Liberian border. *Smithsonian Institution.*

Fig. 12 (left). Male figure, Baulé style, Ivory Coast. *University Museum, Philadelphia.*

Fig. 13 (lower center). Female figure, Baulé style, Ivory Coast. *Collection, Vincent Price, Beverly Hills, California.*

Fig. 14 (above). Mask, Baulé style, Ivory Coast. *Collection, Mr. and Mrs. Ralph C. Altman, Los Angeles.*

Fig. 15 (extreme left). Mask, Baulé style, Ivory Coast. *Baltimore Museum of Art.*

Fig. 16 (left). Mask, Guro style, Ivory Coast. *University Museum, Philadelphia.*

Fig. 17 (below). Seated figure, mother and child, Ashanti style, Gold Coast. *Collection, Mr. and Mrs. Ralph Altman, Los Angeles.*

Fig. 18 (lower left). Ashanti bronze weights for weighing gold, Gold Coast. *British Museum.*

Fig. 19. Gold mask, Ashanti style, Gold Coast. *Pierre Matisse Gallery, New York.*

Fig. 20 (left). Cast brass figure, Dahomey style, French West Africa. *Collection, Melville J. Herskovits, Evanston, Illinois.*

Opposite page:

Fig. 21 (top). Wooden door, Dahomey style, French West Africa. *University Museum, Philadelphia.*

Fig. 22 (bottom). Mask, Yoruba style, Nigeria. *Denver Art Museum.*

Fig. 23 (extreme right). Mask, Yoruba style, Nigeria. *University Museum, Philadelphia.*

Fig. 24 (extreme left). Bronze pendant in form of a head, with catfish collar, Benin style, Nigeria. *Museum of International Folk Art, Santa Fe, New Mexico.*

Fig. 25 (left). Bronze head of a young woman, Benin style, Nigeria. *British Museum.*

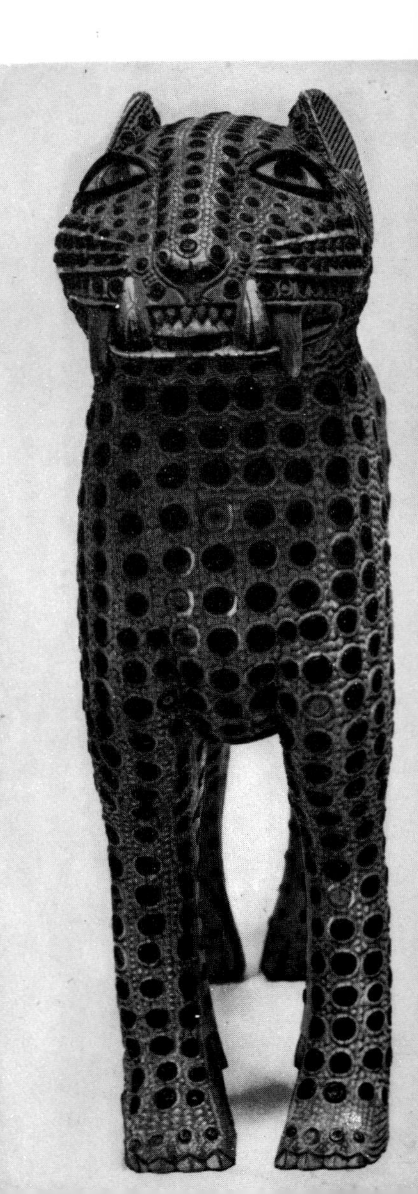

Fig. 26 (left). Bronze cock, Benin style, Nigeria. *University Museum, Philadelphia.*

Fig. 27 (right). Ivory leopard with copper studs, Benin style, Nigeria. *British Museum.*

Fig. 28 (above). Bronze relief, Benin style, Nigeria. *University Museum, Philadelphia.*

Fig. 29 (above, right). Ivory mask, Benin style, Nigeria. *British Museum.*

Fig. 30 (right). Bronze (brass) head, Olokun. Portrait of the king (oni), Ife style, Nigeria. *British Museum.*

Fig. 31 (extreme right). Copper head (mask), Obalufon II, Yoruba king, Ife style, Nigeria. *British Museum.*

Fig. 32 (left). Mask, Ibo style, Nigeria. *American Museum of Natural History.*

Fig. 33 (lower left). Mask, Ibibio style, Nigeria. *Baltimore Museum of Art.*

Fig. 34 (above). Beaded fiber mask trimmed with red cloth, Bamum style, Cameroon. *Denver Art Museum.*

Fig. 35 (right). Carved doorpost, Cameroon style. *Museum für Völkerkunde, Basel, Switzerland.*

Fig. 36 (below). Figure, Cameroon style. *Chicago Natural History Museum.*

Fig. 37 (right). Figure, Fang style, Gabun. *Denver Art Museum.*

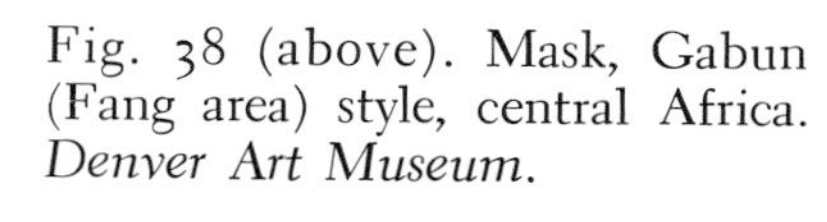

Fig. 38 (above). Mask, Gabun (Fang area) style, central Africa. *Denver Art Museum.*

Fig. 39 (left). Mask, Itumba region, border of Gabun and Congo. *Museum of Modern Art.*

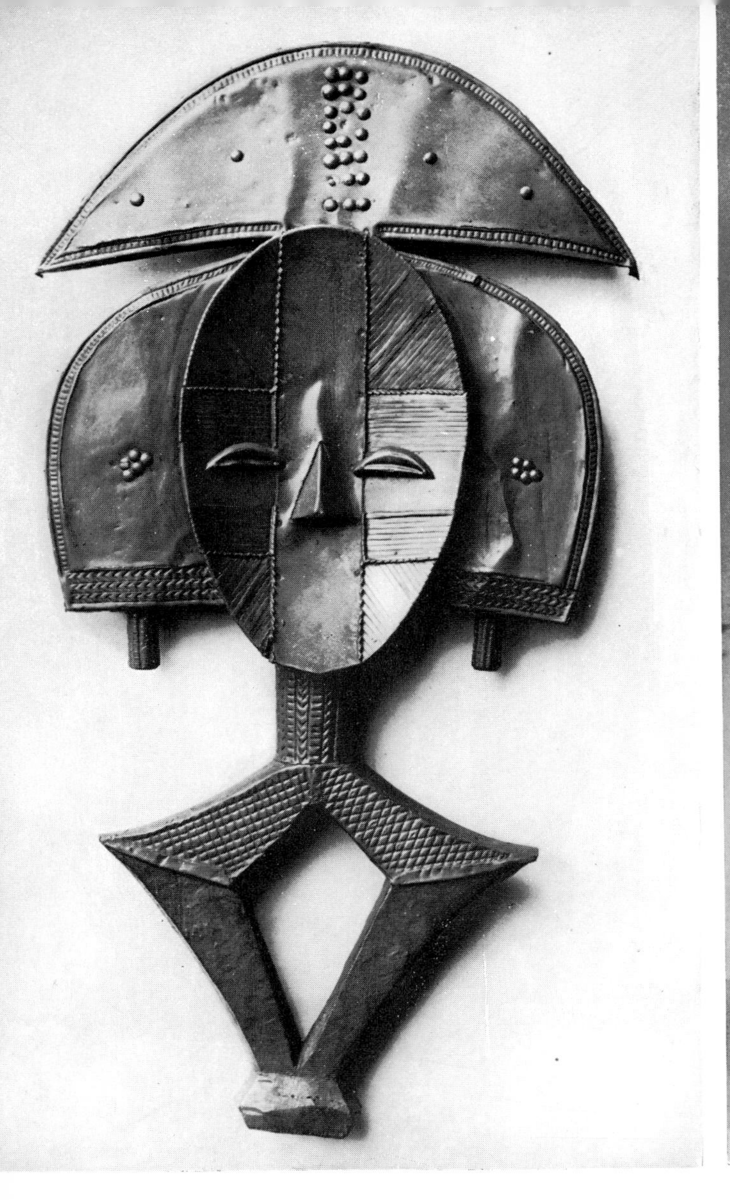

Fig. 40 (above). Mask, wood and copper, Bakota style, Gabun. *Smithsonian Institution.* Fig. 41 (above, center). Figure, mother and child, Bayombe style, Lower Congo. *Royal Museum of Belgian Congo, Tervuren.* Fig. 42 (extreme right). Figure, Bakuba (Bushongo) style, Kata Mbula, 109th king of Bakuba (1800-1812). *Royal Museum of Belgian Congo.* Fig. 43 (right). Mask, Bakuba (Bushongo) style, Central Congo. *Baltimore Museum.*

Opposite page:

Fig. 44 (left). Mask, Bakuba (Bushongo) style. H. 13 in. *Courtesy, Ladislas Segy, New York.* Fig. 45 (top right). Figure, Baluba style, Eastern Congo. *British Museum.* Fig. 46 (lower right). Figure, Basonge style, Central Congo. *Cincinnati Art Museum.*

Fig. 47 (left). Mask, Basonge style, Central Congo. H. 13½ in. *University Museum, Philadelphia.*

Fig. 48 (above). Chief's stool, detail, Baluba style, Eastern Congo. *Royal Museum of Belgian Congo, Tervuren.*

Bapende tribes. On the coast at the mouth of the Congo River are the Lower Congo tribes. The Bakuba, also called Bushongo, and related tribes are in Central Congo, and the Baluba tribes live in the east and south. Within the Baluba region on the north are the Warua and Warega, and considerably farther north the Mangbetu, and in the Southern Congo are the Badjokwe; though the actual number of tribes is much larger, these tribal names designate the important centers.

Frans Olbrechts has analyzed the Congo styles in figures as to posture, proportion and details. Postures may be sitting, standing or kneeling, with variations of the sitting poses. Proportions may be slender, as in the Bena Lulua, or muscular, as in the Baluba.

Shoulders, back and abdomen are given special emphasis in the treatment of the torso. Arms may cling to the body, be separated or freely detached. The hair arrangement differs. It may be kept together, helmet-like, separated into horizontal crests or divided into a number of lobes. Scarification patterns also differ, but the greatest variation occurs in individual features; eyes, ears, nose and mouth. The eyes are basically oval or more fully rounded, but occur in a dozen different variations. They may dip down to a point, and may be open or be closed to a narrow slit. Ears are treated in a more summary fashion, varying from a rough approximation of the natural contour to a mere knob-like protuberance. The mouth may be horizontal, may show lips with the center dipping down or pulled up or it may suggest a figure eight in a horizontal position. Noses may be peg-shaped, wedge-shaped, or more nearly rectangular.

The Lower Congo tribes are settled to the south of the Congo River between Matadi and Leopoldville. These tribes constituted the most important section of the ancient Congo kingdom. They are united by history, culture, and by dialects of a common language. Their sculpture came temporarily under European influence after 1482, when Portuguese merchants and missionaries entered the country.

This contact is believed to have contributed to the formation of the Lower Congo style, which is characterized by an opulent naturalism. Racial characteristics are brought out, like flat noses, thick lips and projecting cheek bones. Gestures are realistic. A fetish may brandish a knife; in groups, arms may be intertwined; and figures may turn their heads which show painted eyes.

The Lower Congo styles are characterized by commemorative ancestral figures and by fetish figures, including the nail fetishes. One type of ancestral figure represents a mother and child in seated position (Fig. 41). The motif of the child forms a satisfying counter-attraction to the realistic head and the shoulders elaborated with scarification marks. There is a sense of balance in the composition which gives repose and dignity to the group. Such groups were commemorative of individual persons. They were not worshipped and had no religious meaning, but were kept by descendants and, in recent times, placed over tombs. They probably owe something to the Christian influence of the missionaries.

In another instance, a smaller figure is seated in front of a larger one. This type shows a considerable amount of action. The mouth is open, the head thrust forward, the arms are freely extended, well separated from the body, producing an open type of composition contrasting sharply with the usual closed, massive, block-like figure.

The Bateke, Bayaka and Bapende tribes live in the area of the Kwango and Kasai rivers. A certain angularity of form is a common element in these styles, the Bateke forming a style province of its own.

Here masks are less important than figures. The Bateke figure style is one of abbreviated simplicity.

The oval-shaped head ends in a small, helmet-like top. Examples show scarification marks covering both cheeks with closely shaped parallel lines. A triangular, peg-like nose combined with a prominent quadrangular beard, a segmental mouth and oval eyes all together, form a single geometrical pattern. This same sharply delineated schematic design in smooth surfaces without details is carried into torso and legs. Arms are hardly differentiated from the straight-lined torso. Such statuettes, under ten inches high, are widely distributed throughout Central Africa. According to Maes, they were used by the Bateke as fertility fetishes and child guardians.

In the Kwango River region the Bayaka style is important. The war-like Bayaka ancestors are said to have invaded the Congo kingdom in the sixteenth century. The heads show characteristic knob-like projecting ears and large noses, sometimes turned up at the ends. The figures vary from small to life-size and some figures and masks have smaller figures or animals, such as buffalo, antelope, dog, anteater or bird, on top. A Bayaka initiation mask (Color Plate 5) is one of a type that was carried by the handle in front of the face. This shows the typical long nose with the curved end.

Wooden masks were used in the initiation ceremonies of the Bapende tribe, and smaller masks of wood or ivory, bone or cast brass, copper or lead were worn around the neck by adults as talismans against sickness. The masks are realistic, death-like in appearance, with lowered eyelids, hollow cheeks and prominent cheekbones. Eyebrows forming a single V-shaped motif carved in relief, drooping eyelids, triangular noses and broad mouths, compressed or open with teeth showing, are combined with variations.

Bakuba (or Bushongo) is a name applied to a Central Congo political confederacy of tribes formerly under the rule of a king.

The king's absolute power was limited by a council of men and women. No war could be declared without the consent of the women, the representatives of mothers and wives. In 1885 the kingdom was still flourishing, but by 1908 it had disintegrated. But even then there were living old men who could recite the names of one hundred and twenty-one kings who had ruled over the Bakuba from about 490 A.D. Eighteen carved wood king statues are known, thirteen have been identified. The oldest statue of the series, now in the British Museum, is of Shamba Bolongongo, the ninety-third king, who ruled from 1600-1620. He is credited with having introduced the custom of having statues carved in honor of the king. As the Bakuba remained without contact with Europe longer than most tribes, much of the material culture of the Bakuba has been preserved.

The kings are seated with crossed legs in strictly frontal postures, as in the example of King Kata Mbula, the 109th king of the Bakuba (1800-1812). (Fig. 42). They are calm and aloof in expression, as considered appropriate to their eminent position. The head is given special emphasis and is large in proportion to the torso. The shaven skull shows the hairline and the features are treated in considerable detail—following the tribal manner and yet with a degree of individualization. The crown is shaped like a mortarboard.

In one hand, usually the left, the king holds a knife with its knob facing forward, and on the front of the base an object is carved symbolizing some important deed associated with the ruler. King Bope Pelenge, who was a famous smith, is given an anvil; another king has a small human figure, believed to represent the slave girl he married. One has a game board, another a drum. These king statues are carved out of hardwood and are highly polished. They are about one and a half to two feet high.

The utilitarian arts were fully developed by the Bakuba and constitute a style that existed side by side with the court style. Some Bakuba carved cups assume the shape of heads or even complete human figures; some are double or even quadruple cups. These cups, carefully carved of hardwood and polished, are designed for palm wine drinking, poison ordeals and sorcerer's white earth (Wingert). The features represent the tribal characteristics and show hairdress patterns. Other objects carved by the Bakuba are hands, chests and boxes decorated with figure and animal motifs in relief.

Bakuba masks (Fig. 43) are extraordinarily rich in the way form is combined with polychromy, in addition to beads, shells, raffia and cloth. The top of the head, eyebrows, the ridge of the nose and the mouth are overlaid with shells and beads, and forehead and cheeks are painted with a pattern of diamonds and lines made into broad ornamental bands. In a Bakuba initiation mask (Fig. 44) the features are developed into a stylized form of great dignity. The long, narrow slits of the eyes, in dramatic contrast, are set within a larger well-defined area reminiscent of the bony skull structure. The nose is cone-shaped, the mouth a projecting oval. This initiation mask (Fig. 44) is as reserved as the one in Fig. 43 is extravagant, but still uses painted decoration with a measure of restraint in keeping with the basic severity of the design.

Among the most effective of all African masks are the so-called Kifwebe dance masks (Fig. 47). Eyes, nose and mouth are expressed in simplified form, conforming to the simplicity of the total shape. The ample surfaces are overlaid with a pattern of closely spaced, incised parallel curves that converge from two sides toward the center. Form and line unite with extreme severity in a superb design, restrained and still highly dramatic. Such masks were originally used at chiefs' burials, were later (1905) used at dances for the reception of dignitaries and at present are used by the lion society.

One of the large tribes is the Baluba. Originally nomads, the Baluba have been credited by some reports with founding kingdoms in the early sixteenth century and adapting themselves to agriculture and ancestor worship. Ancestral figures (Fig. 45) are usually larger than fetishes, a foot and a half to three feet in height. They are carefully carved and finely polished. Ancestral figures are conceived as individuals, even as portraits. Statues of women predominate (Fig. 46). A pattern of scarification marks covers the abdomen. Hands are placed on the breasts, the expression is calm and pensive. Statues of men usually show no scarification.

Another type of Baluba mask shows a well-shaped human head with ram's horns. The face is treated as a single undisturbed broad surface, placid and idealized, suggestive of an Egyptian-Nubian character. The horns are not an integral part of the skull but are attached, cap-like, from the rear. According to one hypothesis, the horn trophy of the Sudan, presumably the antelope headpiece, traveled south to the Congo, there fusing with masks (Karutz). But the ram's horns also suggest Ammon as much as hunting trophies.

The three most characteristic types of Baluba wood carving are: chiefs' stools and head rests, or pillows, supported by one or two figures (Color Plate 6 and Fig. 48); figures supporting a bowl overhead, and two figures holding a bowl out in front (Fig. 49).

The ancestral figures supporting chiefs' stools constitute some of the most expressive wood carving of the whole Congo. As this society was a matriarchy, the figures are female. Aesthetically and technically they are among the supreme examples of Negro sculpture.

Baluba caryatid figures may show angular proportions with cylindrical torsos and dwarfed legs folded back and carved in a flat style closely adhering to the base. But the most noteworthy Baluba caryatid figures are represented by a small group of a unified style in the Tervuren, the British and the Darmstadt museums. Two were found in the Baluba village of Buli, and Frans Olbrechts has referred to this group as the long-faced style of Buli. The style is well illustrated in Figs. 48 and 49.

In the ancestral chief's stool (Fig. 48), we sense in the slight forward bend of the head the resignation of old age. The highly individualized face with half-closed eyes might originally have been based upon a portrait, probably of a revered person.

The way in which the features are contrasted in a bold, slashing manner imbues the head with significance. Where the structure requires solidity, the hands are freely enlarged to supply the necessary bulk. With great skill the artist has elaborated his shapes to include a variety of directions, verticals and diagonals playing against each other. Though anatomically impossible, the combination of volumes, shapes and planes is entirely convincing, suggesting bones and muscles imbued with a sense of nervous energy.

The kneeling figure with bowl (Fig. 49) illustrates the third Baluba type. A long head with bony structure reveals the same tribal characteristics in eyebrows, eyes, nose and mouth as indicated in the figure beneath the chief's stool. Here are the same unstructural hands, curiously contrasted with the sharply defined head. Such bowls, set before a house where a child was expected, invited alms for the spirit of maternity.

A ceremonial Baluba bowl (Fig. 50) shows two seated figures looking at two lizards on the lid. In this compact design the figures are carved from the same block as the bowl, but are detached. A base is distinguished from the bowl proper, and rim and lid have incised borders and centers in relief. The figures hold the bowl between them, and the bowl conforms in structure to the idea of base, bowl and lid. The Baluba also carved chiefs' staffs and musical instruments. The influence of their wood carving spread to other tribes.

The Bena Lulua, of Baluba origin, developed a style of their own. In the figures the torsos, arms and legs are thin, the joints thick and articulated and the heads prominent. Scarification patterns in curved lines are more pronounced than in other African styles.

A Bena Lulua female figure holding a child (Fig. 51) is essentially an ornamental bust on a stand with a base. The carver continued the short pole-like staff above the shoulders into an elongated neck. Head, neck, shoulders and arms are overlaid with a crisply carved pattern, marks of scarification. The emphasis is on the head of the mother; the child is a mere emblem. To carve human flesh to resemble floral decorations is so outside our experience that we need to disassociate ourselves from its reality. We can appreciate and admire the Bena Lulua style as ornamental form if we banish all thought of scarification as a custom, lest it become an impediment to artistic enjoyment.

A mask worn by comic dancers of the Bena Biombo tribe is monumental in its cone-like eyes and its peg-shaped nose enhanced by contrasting color (Color Plate 7).

The Warega inhabit a region in which elephants were plentiful. Ivory masks made by this tribe are of great simplicity, and superior to ivory statuettes. Some ivory masks are symbols of high office. Two styles exist, one of round, the other of angular forms. Where tattoo marks occur, they form rows of circles and dots across the features, as in a head on a neck, about nine inches in height (Fig. 52).

The Badjokwe (Batshioko) tribe is one of the nomadic hunting and warlike tribes of the Southern

Congo and Angola. In 1887 they conquered the Lunda empire. They were active in sculpture and have produced some of the most powerful figures, the older statues exceeding more recent ones in an expression of vitality. A Badjokwe figure is a study in contrasts (Fig. 53). Bent knees contrast with a perpendicular torso which is continued above the head into a handle and opposed by feet, hands and head projected out horizontally. A small head, carved with open mouth, contrasts with a knob-like backward extension, as if conceived as part of a handle. Delicate features, intensely alive, are opposed to massive weight in the lower portion. The carving is as much an object to be placed about as it is a figure; use in ceremony may help to explain its freely conceived proportions. Such a distribution of weight may have been useful to make the figure stand firmly.

Badjokwe masks represent men and women, but are worn by both, and go back to an ancient ritual. Characteristically about seven and one-half inches high in the wood part, the carving is expressive of bold defiance. Their bark cloth initiation masks are of a fantastic design which exaggerates the tribal style in a grotesque manner.

There are also combs used by men, carved with small figures attached, tobacco pouches carved with figures, soup ladles, musical instruments, divination baskets, clubs and lances. Figure-carved stools and chairs represent scenes from life in superimposed rows on top of the rungs.

The sculpture of the north is uniform in style and shows few types, chiefly standing figures in frontal postures. An important style is represented by the Mangbetu tribe in the extreme northeast.

The Mangbetu entered the country as conquerors from the north at some unknown early period. They founded a dynasty of kings that attained its greatest power during the mid-nineteenth century. Early influence, possibly from Egypt or from neighboring tribes, has been noted in Mangbetu culture, such as artificially elongated skulls and a high hairdress. Wooden statues are said to be either dolls or decorative rather than ancestral figures; there are no masks. Objects of utility are also carved with figures or heads. A few old ivory statuettes are known, but modern ivory carvings are inferior. Ceramic jugs with human heads, effigy jars, are of superior artistic quality (Fig. 54).

In styles to the east and south of Central Africa human figures are rare and only a few masks were carved. Exceptions are the full length standing female figures of the Makonde tribe of southwestern Tanganyika. Naturalistic proportions and the use of lip-plugs are characteristic for this style. The slightly carved masks show simple, painted decoration.

The styles of East Africa are characterized by painted and some carved decoration applied to weapons and utensils. The Barotse tribe, of Northern Rhodesia, along the Zambezi River, carved bowls with animals on the lid. Neck-rests of a geometric type are common with other tribes. Though individual examples of design are distinguished, this eastern province as a whole lacks the wealth and variety of carving of other African tribes.

Religious beliefs have motivated art throughout the primitive world. The desire of the individual to relate himself on a friendly basis to his ancestors, and the unseen but powerful forces of nature, became important for art. Ancestor veneration and animistic beliefs were at the base of Negro African sculpture. Animism, by virtue of a belief in spirits, as well as the existence of secret societies, also contributed to the production of sculpture. Where an organization of society on a feudal basis existed, court art made for a differentiation of styles, allowing the more primitive examples to exist side by side with court art. Purely secular aims promoted artistically embellished utensils. Wood was the common material, but metals such as iron, gold, brass and bronze, as well as ivory, clay and other materials were also used.

A variety of tribal styles can be demonstrated but not related to the past in any organized fashion. Without a knowledge of African history and with only an incomplete supply of works of art available from the past, African sculpture is known largely on the basis of its more recent development. Even this incomplete record makes it clear that artistically and technically, in variety and quantity, African sculpture has made noteworthy contributions to art as a whole. Among the many styles a kind of aesthetic perfectionism, based on the work of the individual artist, brings Negro African sculpture close to contemporary taste.

CONTEMPORARY ART

Collectors and museums interested in African sculpture pay most attention to the tribal arts, which were virtually uninfluenced by Europe. But another type of wood carving, representing the white man, in the form of small statuettes and drawings appeared during the nineteenth century. These works reflect the Negro's reaction to soldiers in uniform carrying rifles, and sailors, missionaries or travelers in European costume. Utensils of a foreign cast, including dolls, bicycles and all kinds of ships, are also common. The style is realistic to a degree, and varies in skill and competence with the artists. From the point of view of indigenous African art, this new art is a regression, if not a degeneration.

In our own day the native African has become a modern artist, particularly during the last few decades on the Gold Coast, in Nigeria, in the Belgian Congo, and no doubt in other regions. These artists work in European techniques and sign their work. Illustration, landscape and portrait painting are practiced as easel-painting. Art societies have been established in the cities, art is taught in the schools, and children are taken to the newly established museums to become familiar with their artistic heritage. The crafts, encouraged by the several European governments, also continue and include ebony and ivory carving, pottery, leather and other techniques. The Moroccan style of leather-work originated in Nigeria. Utensils made for domestic use are distributed by Hausa merchants.

Artists from Nigeria have studied in London and returned to Nigeria to teach art in the schools. Out of this experience two Nigerian artists have developed. Ben Enwonwu, a sculptor, has distinguished himself in wood carving and terra cotta. After a period of training at the Slade School in London, Enwonwu has developed a style that is modern, based on a Negro tradition. His work has been shown in London, New York and Washington. Felix Ibudor works in the Benin tradition and is known in England and America. On behalf of the government he has been commissioned with work in a college chapel in Nigeria.

"Carving was revived in Benin City by Oba Eweke II, ruler of Benin, after the death of his father in 1914. The palace was rebuilt; clay bas reliefs and carvings were used, bronze and brass casting revived, and ebony wood was added to the old materials of iroko and ivory. An arts and crafts school was established in 1929, open to young men who had not belonged either to the traditional families of carvers or to the class of swordbearer in the palace, who had been taught to carve by Oba Eweke II up to that time. The old traditional carvers were left to depend on orders from local shrines of both deities and ancestors of nobles, and less on those coming from the royal palace, which were now commissioned in the oba's own school and the new arts and crafts workshop. The rejected carvings of apprentices and students in the school were bought up by itinerant Hausa and sold along the West Coast to foreign sailors and travelers passing through the ports and to civil servants, both European and African.

"The subjects favored in the arts and crafts school are traditional ones chosen by the oba himself, who is a carver in his own right. These are expressed in a style which combines the tradition of the old bronze bas-reliefs, now largely in European museums, with a contemporary Western naturalism. A slightly different style of carving has developed in recent years in the city of Lagos, springing from the migration of former swordbearers of the oba to the Yoruba area port town, though in the workshops only Beni youths are taken as apprentices. The original Benin style has there been modified to fit the demands of tourists, soldiers, and the Hausa traders who also carry this style up and down the coast." (Justine M. Cordwell)

Gold Coast artists have also been trained in London. They are active in painting, wood carving and making pottery. Most artists are employed as teachers in the schools. Kofti Antubam is a Gold Coast artist, who studied art at Goldsmith's College, of the University of London. He has had exhibitions of his drawings and paintings in several European countries and in the Gold Coast itself. Antubam is now Senior Art Master at Achimota. In 1954, an exhibition of works of thirty-nine Gold Coast artists was held in Accra under the auspices of the West African Cultural Society.

The first introduction of machine-made utensils adversely affected native crafts, a regrettable, though inevitable result of industrially made products brought into competition with the handicrafts. The Commission for the Protection of Native Arts and Crafts, created in 1935, has "helped toward that renaissance which is discernible in all expressions of art in Belgian Africa" (Belgian Government Information Center, 1954). In a school at Muschenge, Bakuba art is said to be flourishing again, and pupils of the painting studio founded by Pierre Romain-Desfosses, at Elizabethville, have become known for decorative panels.

In the Belgian Congo the Church, as well as the Ministry of Colonies, has encouraged local artists; and exhibitions of Congo art have been held in Belgium. Religious art, statues of the Madonna and Child, of saints and objects of religious art, chalices and crucifixes, form part of the contemporary art of the Belgian Congo. Even where efforts to encourage the native arts have produced works above the tourist ware level, they have not always met with the approval of critics. This may be in part due to the fact that modern African art is subject to the same controversy that all contemporary art is subject to, and does not reflect upon the competence of the artists, who have high professional standards. Separated from ancient tribal customs, this work may be too recent to represent an integrated style.

Nigeria and the Gold Coast look forward to an early independence, but, properly speaking, the linking of these tribal styles to contemporary western art is outside our field. The story of what becomes of primitive styles in a world that grows smaller has a human significance. We should not assume that such contacts of cultures necessarily spell death to the native arts. Given encouragement and opportunities, art lives on, though styles change. This is what is happening in Africa today.

II

ALASKA AND THE PACIFIC NORTHWEST COAST

AT SOME PREHISTORIC PERIOD, GROUPS OF ASIAN HUNTERS BEGAN TO ARRIVE ON ALASKA'S WEST COAST by way of narrow Bering Strait. Far to the south, early navigators of the Pacific may also have reached the American mainland, perhaps repeatedly. Settlements of the New World began, dispersed groups gradually occupying the entire continent, north and south. By the time Columbus arrived, a variety of cultures had developed throughout the Western Hemisphere, including the advanced, urbanized civilizations of Middle America and the Andean highlands of South America. The level of achievement of these civilizations was in many ways equal to that of Old World cultures. The Maya excelled in a knowledge of astronomy, and the ancient Peruvians in ceramics and textiles. Until the coming of the white man, the aboriginal inhabitants of this continent did not know how to smelt iron, but they had hematite and softer metals and bronze alloys were used. They were generally unfamiliar with the wheel, which they knew only as a toy, and had few domesticated animals. The more advanced cultures, with notable results in the arts, were developed independently, but not, according to some scholars, to the total exclusion of all relations with peoples across the Pacific.

The tribes that drifted into North America probably arrived with very little, mainly a knowledge of the use of stone implements, handled and missile weapons, and with a multitude of inherent capacities. The magnificent arts of wood carving in the north, and of stone sculpture and various crafts in the regions of Middle and South America, were developed substantially in isolation. Differences in material cultures developed as between the settled agricultural people of the south and the Indians and Eskimo of the north, who lived by hunting and fishing and only incidentally depended on agriculture. Eskimo and Indians are Mongoloid, as are the peoples in Asia and Indonesia, with brown racial characteristics rather than black or white.

It may seem surprising that the Eskimo remained in such an unfriendly environment when they might have moved south where living conditions were less severe. There are two theories that attempt

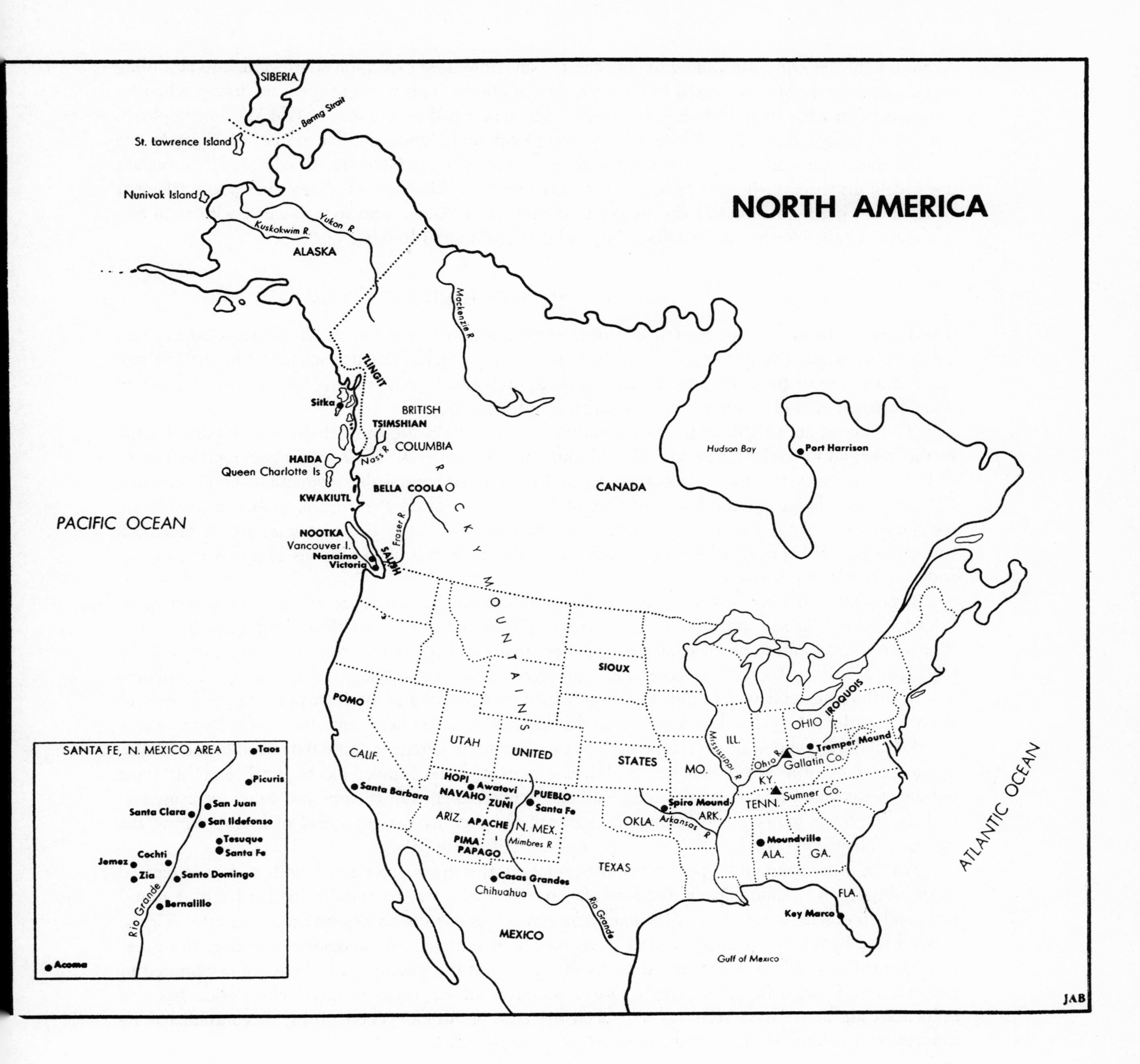
NORTH AMERICA
SIBERIA
Bering Strait
St. Lawrence Island
Nunivak Island
Yukon R.
Kuskokwim R.
ALASKA
Mackenzie R.
TLINGIT
Sitka
BRITISH
TSIMSHIAN
COLUMBIA
Nass R.
HAIDA
Queen Charlotte Is
BELLA COOLA
KWAKIUTL
Hudson Bay
Port Harrison
CANADA
PACIFIC OCEAN
NOOTKA
Vancouver I.
Nanaimo
Victoria
SALISH
Fraser R.
ROCKY MOUNTAINS
SIOUX
IROQUOIS
POMO
OHIO
ILL.
Mississippi R.
Tremper Mound
SANTA FE, N. MEXICO AREA
Taos
Picuris
San Juan
Santa Clara
San Ildefonso
Tesuque
Santa Fe
Cochti
Jemez
Zia
Santo Domingo
Bernalillo
Rio Grande
Acoma
CALIF.
UTAH
UNITED
STATES
MO.
Ohio R.
Gallatin Co.
KY.
HOPI
Awatovi
NAVAHO
ZUÑI
PUEBLO
Santa Fe
Santa Barbara
Spiro Mound
ARK.
TENN.
Sumner Co.
ARIZ.
APACHE
N. MEX.
OKLA.
Arkansas R.
PIMA
PAPAGO
Mimbres R
Moundville
ALA.
GA.
TEXAS
Casas Grandes
Chihuahua
Rio Grande
FLA.
Key Marco
MEXICO
Gulf of Mexico
ATLANTIC OCEAN
JAB

to answer this question. According to one, the Indians prevented expansion southward, and according to the other the Eskimo remained in the north out of choice. This may not seem so strange when we remember that settlements elsewhere in North America occurred on the base of Old World complexes. The Finns sought the northern lake country; the Dutch and Danes, the flat southern farmlands; the Mesabi mines received European-trained mining groups; whereas Germans, Swedes and Norwegians are widely dispersed in both rural and urban communities. What is more likely than the settlement of the bleak northern shores of the American continent by Asians who were familiar with such surroundings, or the Northwest Coast by groups who knew fish and forests?

ALASKA AND THE ESKIMO

The Eskimo live in the vast stretch of frozen coastal region across the Arctic between Siberia and eastern Greenland. The northern limit of tree growth only touches the area inhabited by the Eskimo, but driftwood from the rivers and the sea has always furnished wood, mainly for weapons, boats and sled construction, and in some regions enough also for carving.

The immediate neighbors to the Eskimo of western Alaska are the Athapascan-speaking Ingalik of the lower and middle Yukon and Kuskokwim River settlements. Their masks and representations of human and animal forms closely approach in style and technique the productions of neighboring Eskimo groups living on the lower reaches of those rivers. Since the Ingalik masks invariably are inferior to those of the Eskimo craftsmen, it may be assumed that in this particular area Eskimo culture provided a richer spiritual basis and technical ability than that of the Indian, and that the Ingalik Indian was a heavy borrower.

Archaeological work in the arctic area in south Alaska, St. Lawrence Island and Bering Strait (Okvik, Old Bering Sea and Ipiutak styles) and in regions farther east has thrown light on the prehistoric past. Excavations so far have uncovered an essentially unified culture back to the beginnings of the Christian era. Even the earliest bone and ivory carvings are advanced in style, showing curvilinear motifs that recall modern Melanesian designs. The part of Eskimo art here presented is largely of the nineteenth century. It is this more recent development that has been collected widely by museums.

Of all the Eskimo in the world, perhaps one-half, or some sixteen or more thousand, live in Alaska. Eskimo of the entire arctic were accomplished carvers of bone comparable to the Paleolithic bone carvers of Europe. Fur and animal skin, feathers, braided fiber, walrus ivory and wood were used in their crafts. Since hunting and fishing are seasonal, the men have a good deal of leisure during the intervals. They look upon hunting as a sport and enjoy it thoroughly.

On the other hand, in support of his interpretation, this investigator also found (as communicated to the author) an Eskimo grave in the Kuskokwim region with two faces on a wooden board, a round male and an oblong female face. "To make a long face," is a common expression to indicate chagrin; a round face by contrast is interpreted as an expression of content. Psychologically speaking, this interpretation makes good sense; it is based on facial expressions the meanings of which are not limited to one country. Though tradition plays a part in primitive art, on occasion direct observation has also influenced art, as we have seen has also been the case in Africa. Where theory is contradicted by experience, a common-sense explanation may be perfectly valid.

The Eskimo of southwestern Alaska, along the Kuskokwim River and Nunivak Island, carved and painted objects to be given away at the time of the winter festivals. At these celebrations, held for the sake of religion, amusement and sociability, the gifts were exchanged between men and women of neighboring villages. Several weeks each year were devoted to walrus ivory carvings of small objects of jewelry, labrets, earrings and nose ornaments, harpoon knobs and points, fishhooks, knives, pipestems, as well as wooden masks and wooden dishes.

Compared to the major occupations, art played a minor role in the life of the Eskimo. Hunters and kayak builders enjoyed greater prestige, and until recently carvers gained no great fame. But the individual artist took pride in his work. Artists were in no way different from other persons; they hunted, fished and set traps, as all others did. Artists did not imitate each other, speak ill of each other's work, and were not aware of themselves as a group. Carving of masks was placed on a level with kayak making and ahead of bowl carving. Kayaks are the one-man, skin-covered canoes of the Eskimo. Masks, when carved for others, were paid for, but neither ivory engravings nor masks were made as objects to be sold. Those who stood out as artists, as noted by Himmelheber (1936), were the more intelligent individuals, but they did not stand out as personalities different from others. The Eskimo artist worked steadily and finished a project the day he started it, and worked on one piece at a time. He did not work from nature or from models, but depended on his knowledge and familiarity with the animals he represented, though imaginative animals, believed to have existed in olden times, were also represented.

BELIEFS

Animism and sympathetic magic underlie the use of dance masks. The spirits of animals were said to participate through the masks in the celebrations. At a specifically announced time during the festival, while the dances were going on, a dance dedicated to a particular species of animal was put on in order to encourage these animals to appear in large numbers during the next hunting season. The hope and expectation was that a dance, in which an animal was mimicked, would encourage the animal to make itself available for the hunter at the proper time. By making masks resemble animals in one way or another, the soul of the animal was believed to be present at the feast. All this would not make sense either from the point of view of the Eskimo, who invited seals to become his victims, or from the point of view of the seals to heed such an invitation. To appreciate what is here involved we must remember that primitive people the world over, including the Eskimo, believe animals have souls. To compensate the animals for being killed, the Eskimo held the belief that the animals they killed would be restored to life. To bring this about the Eskimo held the important "bladder festival." The souls of the animals killed were believed to take refuge in the bladder. For that reason each hunter preserved the bladders of animals killed by him. Inflated, they would be suspended in the Men's Houses until the souls would be restored to the water at the end of the rituals. "The bladders are taken to a hole in the ice, and, after being opened, are thrust into the water under the ice so that the shade may return to its proper element. The shade is supposed to swim far out to sea and there to enter the body of an unborn animal of its kind, thus becoming reincarnated and rendering game more plentiful than it would be otherwise." (Nelson) In that way, by restoring them to life, the hunter has demonstrated to the animals that he has dealt fairly with them. "The animals will not be afraid when they meet him (the hunter) again in their new form and will permit him to approach and kill them again without trouble."

The purpose of mask dances was to influence the small human-like being which lived in the mask. This living being (soul) was immortal, and had the ability to bring on the multiplication of its own species. Again, according to Nelson, "The object of these faces (masks) is to propitiate and to do honor to the animals or beings represented by them, and thus to bring about plenty of game . . ." This ritual took place at the "inviting-in" feast. The "shades" of the animals were invited to the feast "to enjoy the songs and dances, with the food and drink offerings, given in their honor."

At the "inviting-in" feast the animal souls were invited to participate; at the bladder festival the souls of the killed animals were restored to life. Against such a background it becomes clear why masks were not made solely for their artistic quality. Attraction and appeasement of the animals through entertainments, at which masks were used, were the basic objectives of masks, rather than the artistry of the masks themselves. Even so, this does not mean art was neglected or artists not appreciated.

ESKIMO ART

In the engraving of walrus ivory the Eskimo developed a kind of pictorial writing which is unequaled in its economy of means (Ill. 2). Much is expressed by a shorthand, graphic style that gives action and describes life accurately but not realistically. Eskimo graphic art was at its best in the country west of the Mackenzie River and south of the Bering Strait, which includes most of the coastal fringes of Alaska. Fire-drill bows and tobacco pipes were decorated with geometric patterns and illustrated from everyday life. Usually two sides of a quadrangular pipe show ornamental designs, while the remaining sides are reserved for the illustrations. In the contrast of the ornamental and the pictorial, this art reveals excellent taste (Figs. 55 and 56). The engravings are delicate as well as fresh, spontaneous and timeless in their appeal. The ornament consists of linear borders and concentric circles; with single-stroke linear elements in silhouette. As the long sides of the pipestems are less than one inch wide, the decoration becomes an art of miniature drawing. The incised lines are filled in with red ocher or made black with soot.

Walter James Hoffman (1899) has illustrated and described these engravings in a comprehensive manner and in considerable detail. To read Hoffman's text and to study his illustrations becomes an event for any reader fortunate enough to come upon this magnificent record. The following interpretations follow those of Hoffmann. Each strip here reproduced describes in a detailed manner the various things that can happen to an Eskimo in and outside the house on a busy day (Ill. 2). In strip 5 we see a village near the water. The owner of the house suspends fish from a pole (Nos. 1-3); festoons of food are hung up for drying (Nos. 4-7); a granary with stairs is shown (Nos. 8-10); boats are placed on racks for the skins to dry (No. 11); a summer habitation (No. 12) has an open door; someone is stirring food in a kettle (No. 13); there is smoke and a kettle over the fire (No. 14); a man acts excitedly (No. 15), because harpooned walruses are being dragged ashore (Nos. 16-22); and an old man is walking with a stick (No. 25). By the same device old age is indicated on Egyptian hieroglyphics. In this lively fashion the ivory engravings give us a record of the daily life of the Eskimo. For completeness these

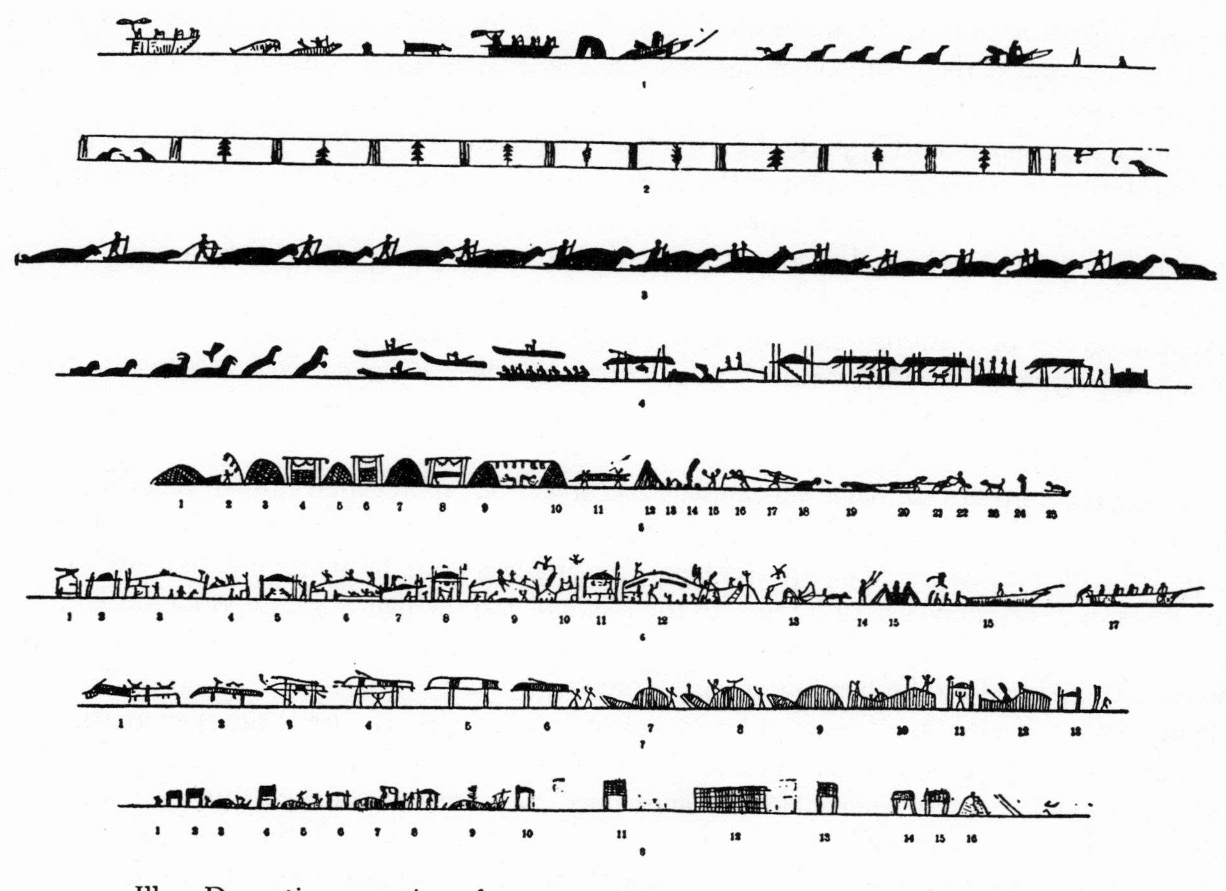

Ill. 2. Domestic occupations, from engravings on walrus ivory, Alaska. *After W. J. Hoffmann. Smithsonian Institution.*

engravings rival, in a miniature, abbreviated style, the larger tomb paintings of ancient Egypt, and for animation they are on a level with the hunting scenes of the African Bushmen.

These engraved objects were collected during the nineteenth century; how far back they go we do not know. It has been suggested that this type of Eskimo carving and engraving may be of the period of 1700-1850. The graphic arts of the Eskimo seem to have developed after contact with Russian missionaries in the seventeenth century. The reason for this dating is believed to be the fact that the missionaries had nothing to say about engravings, although they reported a great deal about many other things (Sydow).

The motifs of Eskimo art, outside of these engravings, were animals that constituted his food supply: seal, walrus, fish, whale and reindeer; but others, like otter, fox, wolf and bear, also occur. The human figure was used in masks, grave figures, and dolls. Eskimo art was realistic in details, but imaginative in the way details were combined. But meaning according to the dictates of religion determined what was to be combined, rather than a conscious intent to make a work of art. The results, as in certain masks, may seem surrealistic to us, but the impetus on the part of the artist may be assumed to have been religious. The verbal explanations on the part of the artists seem to support this point of view. On the other hand, the works themselves give ample testimony that artistic considerations guided the artist and perhaps subconsciously played a larger part than is usually admitted.

Tambourines covered with skin and also wooden bowls were painted with figures and animals representing extraordinary and important events that happened to ancestors. Such stories were handed down from father to son and constituted the subject matter for painting. The stories had to do with events of the hunt, which were often fantastic and brought in a supernatural element. The square skylights used in the Men's Houses, made of strips of seal intestine sewed together, were also painted, and presented as gifts at the festivals.

Another group of paintings and engravings dealt with ownership marks carved or engraved on weapons and painted on wooden bowls. The subjects were likewise taken from events that happened to an ancestor. Compared to the drum paintings, ownership marks on bowls represented events in a concentrated, simplified fashion.

Painting for purposes of magic was applied to the kayak. Abbreviated human faces were painted on the underside to keep the kayak from tipping over. Mineral colors mixed with blood and urine were applied with brushes made of squirrel hair. Painting was done by men only, drawing by women. In both cases the story alone was of interest to the Eskimo, and the paintings, important as communications, were accompanied with verbal explanations. The stories painted on the drums are also dramatized in dances accompanied by the beating of such drums.

Paintings for wooden trays represent a composite animal (Ill. 3) part reindeer, part white whale, and a strange mythical crocodile-like animal (Ill. 4). This latter animal was also painted on the sides of boats (umiaks). Local traditions relate this animal to "the climate in ancient times . . . when . . . the climate was very much warmer" (Nelson, p. 444). However this may be, the drawings have an easy fluid line that is most attractive. In another example we find four sea lions and a duck, supposedly caught in a net intended for seals, painted separately with no intent to suggest action. That part was taken care of by the verbal explanation. The painter devoted his energies to setting forth the objects, mentioned in the story, in a style impeccable for brushwork and quality of line. In yet another painting a huge whale is placed beside a seal net. According to the story here, the whale caught in the net had to be salvaged by using six inflated sealskin floats.

In the painting of drums many grades of artistic quality were found. The artist among the Eskimo was the person who could draw a line well. Competence in draughtsmanship was appreciated, and those lacking in skill would engage someone else with more skill to decorate their wooden bowls.

Though carving was a fairly general occupation among men, mask carving was a specialty thought to be more difficult than drum painting. Painting required no preliminary drudgery such as hewing out the block before the more interesting knifework began, as was the case in wood carving. Since results appeared at once, the Eskimo artist took readily to painting.

Eskimo masks have a style of their own; though compared to Northwest Pacific Coast masks, the range is narrow and its means to achieve effects limited. Within its field, the Eskimo mask is still varied in design and ingenious in many ways. Its style was perhaps in part a result of a lack of a plentiful supply of wood. To develop a fully rounded style that could freely exploit the thickness of solid blocks and make the most of long slabs that could be split to any thickness, there had to be wood in quantity. Though there was often no actual scarcity of wood, the thinness and sparseness of the wood-carved

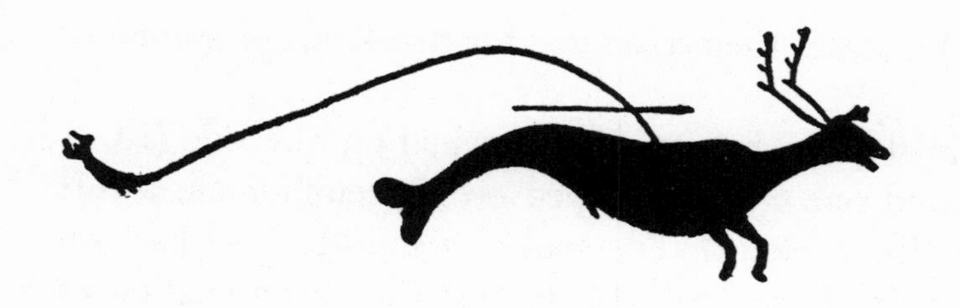

Ill. 3 (left) and Ill. 4 (right). Eskimo paintings of a composite animal in a wooden tray. *After Nelson. Smithsonian Institution.*

Eskimo masks was due perhaps to the absence of huge forests with an abundance of timber. The Eskimo carver did his best with the driftwood he had. He enlarged masks by extended rims, and added emblems and feathers. Wooden masks were highly developed in the southern region, among the Eskimo of the Kuskokwim River. Three types of masks were made: (1) masks based on animals and plants serving hunting magic, (2) masks used by actors in humorous plays, (3) masks made for the assistants of a shaman, commonly called a medicine man. He received his power from supernatural beings, and served as an intermediary between the world and the world of spirits.

Masks with human faces were given an animal-like character to symbolize the animal soul. Masks of this type appeared to be based on the concept that an animal's soul must have a human aspect. But not all masks have this human aspect. Some represent only the animal part, others consist of fantastic combinations of animal and human details (Fig. 57) in which the several parts are freely put together with no intention of creating any realistic resemblance to living creatures.

In masks used at festivals to produce laughter, members of tribes not held in high repute were known to have been caricatured on such occasions by a fantastic mask. Even known individuals who had a particular facial characteristic, like a crooked nose, were taken off by a mask designed to exaggerate the nose.

Masks to represent the assistants of a shaman were based on specific events. A shaman who wished to impress a neighboring village with his power would have a carver make a mask that referred to some extraordinary event he experienced while he sent his soul on a migration to the spirit world. Shaman masks have a number of wood-carved attributes attached to wooden rims that project out from the edge of the mask. These two concentric rings have been said to symbolize the real world, in the inner ring, and the world above us, in the outer ring. The masks themselves are for two kinds of spirits, of friendly helpers and of evil demons.

A mask of a black bear from the lower Yukon shows a human face attached on one side (Ill. 5, No. 2). Another mask, white with a red spot around one crescent-shaped eye, is semihuman, a tuft of reindeer hair protrudes from its circular mouth (Ill. 5, No. 4). The soul of a short-ear owl has two unequally shaped eyes and two mouths on either side of the beak (Ill. 5, No. 1). A combination of an animal with its soul is shown in a wooden mask, about a foot high (Fig. 58). A seal is combined with one-half of a human face to represent the dual character of the seal with its human-like soul. Attached feathers and carved pieces were economical ways of elaborating the mask; whether or not any symbolism is involved is not known. Another mask (Fig. 59), elaborated by attachments, was probably used in a humorous skit. An undistorted human face is represented in a mask from the region south of the Yukon mouth (Ill. 5, No. 3). A deerskin is pegged in around the edge of the mask, and globular labrets are attached at the corners of the mouth. These masks are small, under nine inches in height. Of two larger masks, twenty-two and thirty inches high (Ill. 6), one (b) is a double mask showing two animals with a small human face at the top; it is from the lower Yukon and bears some resemblance to Tlingit masks from southern Alaska. Characteristically, Eskimo masks are painted white or blue and are accented in red.

There is a thinness and leanness about Eskimo art. In drawing, painting and carving, effects were obtained with a moderate expenditure of effort. A dearth of materials set limits to the achievement of that fullness and complexity which is so characteristic of the Northwest Coast style to the south, but ingenuity on the part of the artist compensated for what the region lacked in material resources. The Eskimo were gifted artists, and their style was by no means an impoverished one, as is well demonstrated in the engraved pipestems and fire drills. Here limitations determined style, but did not interfere with its development.

Ill. 5 (No. 1, No. 2, No. 3, and No. 4). Masks, wood trimmed with fur and feathers. Eskimo, Alaska, from the lower Yukon. *Smithsonian Institution.*

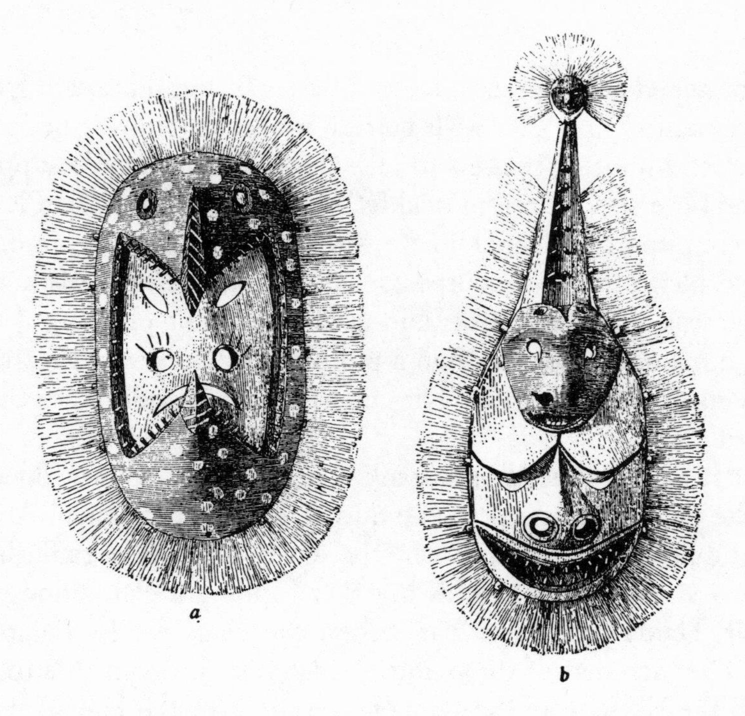

Ill. 6, *a* and *b*. Masks, trimmed with fur. Eskimo, Alaska, from the lower Yukon. *Smithsonian Institution.*

NORTHWEST PACIFIC COAST INDIAN ART

COUNTRY AND TRIBES

The Northwest Pacific Coast Indians inhabit a rugged country, a narrow coastal strip between the sea and the mountains from Yakutat Bay in Alaska to the Columbia River in Oregon. Their villages were built along the inlets and on the islands. The tribes from north to south were the Tlingit, Tsimshian, Haida, Kwakiutl, Bella Coola and Nootka. South of them, within the state of Washington, were Salishan tribes, and also Chimakuan, Wakashan and Chinookan. This Salishan group is here touched upon only incidentally. We are well informed as to their carving through a study by Paul Wingert, written both from the stylistic and the ethnological points of view.

Various aspects of the art and culture of the Northwest Coast have been studied, particularly by Franz Boas, C. Marius Barbeau and others. William H. Holmes pointed out in one of his early papers that an aboriginal art area extending from San Francisco Bay to northern Alaska emphasized wood carving of the human figure, particularly facial features. Though perhaps a matter of opinion, this has been considered to have reached its greatest development among the Haida of the Queen Charlotte Islands, B. C., tapering off in quality and quantity both to the north and to the south.

Communication by water was available to all tribes, but the mountains to the east formed a barrier which kept the coastal Indians separated from those of the interior. Intercommunication between the coastal tribes and seclusion from contacts beyond the mountains contributed to a homogeneous culture and a fairly unified style in art. The people of this area were divided into a number of groups, but here as elsewhere a difference of language did not interfere with cultural exchanges.

The problem of securing a living was not difficult for the Northwest Pacific Coast Indians. The sea abounded with porpoise, seal and many kinds of fish, the rivers provided quantities of salmon. The land also provided game, especially bear, deer, elk and mountain goat, as well as wild fowl. In addition they supplemented their diet with berries, roots and bulbs. Enough food could be secured during the best fishing and hunting seasons to give the Indian an ample supply, which was stored for the winter months and for elaborate ceremonial feasts. As a result, they had leisure for cultural activities, of which the arts were important. The climate with its heavy rainfall produced an abundance of forests which made wood plentiful for all purposes, houses, canoes, utensils and carving. The cedar tree provided bark, which was beaten into fiber and used for making clothing.

The fauna of the country had a profound influence on the art. Certain animals were represented in the carving and textile crafts. They constituted, in addition to the human figure, practically the only motifs used.

Great stress was placed upon rank. The tribal society was divided into chiefs, freemen and slaves. Most of the people belonged to the middle group of freemen. Above them were the chiefs, fewer in number, and below the freemen were the slaves. In order of rank there were the chiefs of tribe, of clan, and of houses, several households together forming a clan among the northern tribes. In the case of the Tlingit, Haida and Tsimshian tribes, the clans were separated into two or four groups, called phratries. The members of the phratries related their origin to a totem animal. Generally speaking, the Raven and the Eagle were the symbols of totems of the Haida; the Eagle, Wolf, Raven and Bear, of the Tsimshian, the Wolf and the Raven of the Tlingit. There were modifications of this division. The Raven side of the Haida had the killer whale as its principal crest, and on the Eagle side the beaver was as important a crest as the eagle. Among Tlingit, Haida and Tsimshian there were sub-groups, each with its own crest animals (Boas).

The combination of an ample food supply that gave leisure, a social system that included slaves (captured in war or brought from other tribes), as well as rich and powerful chiefs and an abundance of raw materials laid a foundation favorable to art. An intense rivalry between chiefs for prestige further stimulated the arts which were used to enhance the personality of one chief in competition with another. Much of this accumulation of surplus food, utensils and works of art was ostentatiously given away at the special festive occasions of the potlatches. These elaborate feasts were given primarily to enhance the social position of the host, but they were also held to celebrate different occasions such as dedications, or as commemoration of a dead relative. Reasons varied from tribe to tribe. On other occasions feasts were held at which valuable objects were destroyed or burned, again with the object of elevating the owner's social status.

Myths are at the core of the art of the Northwest Coast, and ancient tales and legends were handed down from generation to generation. Ceremonials consisted of re-enactments of myths, and members of secret societies, elaborately dressed and masked, impersonated supernatural beings, the spirits of fish and various mammals and birds, which in many aspects resembled human beings.

THE PSYCHOLOGICAL BACKGROUND

It is interesting to explore the motivations that may have fostered basic beliefs that developed folklore and gave content and direction to what was carved and painted. Admittedly, explanations involve conjecture, but they are not wholly speculative.

To understand what is back of this tribal art, it is necessary to take into account once more that man, living at a primitive level and depending directly on nature for his livelihood as hunter or tiller of the soil, feels a very close relationship to nature. He is part of an outdoor environment and must cope with it as best he can. He is impressed by the wind, by storms, thunder and lightning, by wild animals, and fears those uncontrollable forces to which he is exposed. Self-preservation urges him on to come to terms with a hostile world. If he cannot eliminate what he fears as threats to his well-being, he tries other means to maintain a sense of security. What man cannot overcome through his own strength he may attempt to appease and befriend.

The creation of statues of ancestors, as in Negro Africa, the use of animals as family crests, as on the Pacific Northwest Coast, and the representation of gods in stone, as in ancient Mexico, seem to be linked in one way or another with man's basic need for security. In psychological terms, this is accomplished in Mexico through identification, and in Africa, and particularly on the Pacific Northwest Coast, where a sense of guilt is involved, through appeasement. We must now touch, rather briefly, upon one aspect of totemism which found such striking expression in Northwest Coast art.

In Northwest Coast culture, totemism meant that man was related in a close and particular way to certain animals or to mythological beings. Man and animal had so much in common that they were considered to be on much the same level. In myths, man and animal united in marriage and their offspring provided proof of their equality. It is usually said in explanation that man desired to have certain superior abilities which he lacked, but which the animal had. Even if the Northwest Coast Indians are recorded as having made these statements as to their beliefs, they may not be completely revealing. The sober fact is that man, without the strength and agility of the animals, did very well with what ability he possessed. He hunted and killed the animals, and not the other way around.

Animals played an unusually important part in Northwest Coast art, in a large measure furnishing the artist with his motifs. Animals were not selected as motifs at random; only certain ones could be used, according to identification with a particular clan or narrative. Totems had a significance comparable to that of ancestors in Africa. Their importance and expression in art calls for a more convincing explanation than a desire to equal the animal in his superior abilities in a world where man completely dominated the animals.

To appreciate the significance of the psychological situation, we must keep in mind that these Indians lived largely by hunting and fishing. This meant that, in the light of what has already been said about the close relation of man to animal, they were virtually killing their own relatives. As a result, the sense of guilt must have been considerable. To compensate for this a correspondingly large measure of devotion to the totem was required to maintain emotional equilibrium. The individual had to kill some animals in order to live, but he made up for this by being on particularly intimate terms with other animals who, he considered, were his friends.

We may look upon the fact that totem animals are not eaten as one form of appeasing a sense of guilt. It must be kept in mind that this explanation relates back to origins of customs, the understanding of which may not be completely settled by reference to statements made by nineteenth century Indians. The perhaps incomplete ethnological evidence obscures the true situation. Certain animals used for crests, totem animals, like bears, wolves, ravens, eagles, frogs, killer whales, and "fish with heads at each end or monsters . . ." were not eaten for various reasons. Wolves were not eaten because they ate corpses, and ravens because they ate unclean things. Grizzly bears were not eaten because they kill people, nor killer whales for they were people, and so on. A long list is given (Franz Boas, *Tsimshian Mythology*, pp. 501-502) of crest animals which were not eaten for varying reasons other than the one we suspect was significant—that these animals were regarded, subconsciously, as symbols of atonement for other animals which were killed as a matter of necessity.

Franz Boas (*Tsimshian Mythology*, p. 501) quotes Mayne and Duncan, who say, "The Indian will never kill the animal which he has adopted for his crest, or which belongs to him by birthright." Frazer, quoting this passage, points out that no other writer refers to it, as if it had been overlooked by others. Boas was never able to get evidence from the Indians on this point. The reason for this may be that the Indians did not know what had kept their ancestors from eating certain animals. As far as they were concerned, they were following tribal customs by repeating the customary explanation. They were part of their heritage and not subjected to further scrutiny. The sense of guilt could have operated at the time the customs were established and perhaps even then on a subconscious level. That hunting cultures involve a sense of guilt is suggested by the beliefs consciously held by the Eskimo in regard to the restoration to life of animals killed. With fewer species to choose from, the Eskimo solved the guilt problem by life restoration rituals rather than by means of totemic animals honored by crests. The Northwest Coast Indians did not have to invent conscience relieving myths that restored killed animals to life. They appeased guilt by choosing other animals as favored substitutes for those killed.

Other customs may be traced to the need to allay fear in addition to the appeasement of conscience. As animals had souls and were equal to man in importance, killing them created a responsibility that called for appeasement by means of a special ritual. The Nootka Indians at Koryak propped up a slain bear in an upright position before the chief and placed food before the bear, who was invited by words and gestures to eat. At such ceremonies, the bearskin was taken off, and one of the women put on the skin and danced in it, offering meat to the bear and entreating it not to be angry. This act of dancing in the bear's skin is presumably a symbolic identification, not unusual in dances. The purpose of this performance was perhaps to allay fear that the bear's soul might seek help from other bears to take revenge. This is the same belief in appeasement of the souls of dead animals that we have reason to believe functioned in prehistoric cave painting of Europe and about which we shall have more to say in the last chapter under "Magic." This same motive of a ceremony of animal appeasement is still a subject in native Indian painting of the Southwest.

Another explanation in connection with wood carvings might serve to account for the use of sharks, sea lions or swordfish carved on wooden clubs. Sharks, sea lions and swordfish were feared by the Indians, but by the action of sympathetic magic their carved images assisted man in his work. Possibly, too, the intent may have been to relieve themselves of blame by deceiving the salmon, making it believe that one of its natural enemies was attacking and killing it.

GENERAL CHARACTERISTICS

We shall not attempt here to differentiate rigorously between tribal styles, all of which have contributed to the formation of a relatively unified Northwest Coast design. For our purposes it will suffice to deal with Northwest Coast design as if it were one style with variations which may be due to tribal or to individual differences or to both. A linear, ornamental, surface-covering trend is much in evidence. A basic shape was inherent in the tree trunk in poles, in the contours of the animal in masks, or in the function of the object in utensils. Both abstraction and realism were used, but often the two principles fused. Realism bordering on portraiture also occurred as well as a free development of form to suggest the supernatural. Standing postures were the rule for larger, individual figures, and other postures were used decoratively. An expression of action in the freely posed figure was the exception, and symmetry was universally preferred.

A repetition of forms is generally apparent, and in some details, such as eyes, a preference for rounded rather than angular shapes. Color was used on wood carving, except smaller utensils, as well as in decorative painting. The type of design based on animal motifs is believed by Boas to have had its home in British Columbia and southern Alaska, whereas the tribes of Vancouver Island made more use of geometrical ornamentation. It has been suggested that the geometric style may represent an early indigenous style, and the lush ornamental manner that we usually think of as the Northwest Pacific Coast style may be linked to a later immigration. The origins of the style are unknown, but it is reasonable to assume that this style has had a long history on the North American continent. Wood was the preferred material. Bone, horn, argillite and copper and, for weaving textiles, plant and animal fibers, were used.

Northwest Coast art has developed, in connection with animal design, a number of symbols which are widely applied in various materials and different techniques. Boas, who first published his findings in 1897, has been justly credited with having solved the meaning of these symbols. The animal symbolism, he discovered, has three basic aspects. First, an animal was identified by a single detail attached to a generalized representation. Animals and mythological characters had to be identified, but it was not necessary to represent them realistically. Human and animal heads are hardly differentiated, and one does not realize immediately what animal the artist had in mind until one notes that each animal is characterized by specific details always repeated in the same way. Large incisors indicate the beaver (Ill. 7), a large curved beak indicates the hawk (Ill. 8) if the beak is turned back, but the eagle (Ill. 9) if the beak is turned down. Large heads and large mouths are the symbols for the killer whale (Ill. 10); the shark has a depressed mouth (Ill. 11) and sharp teeth. The bear shows paws, sometimes holding a stick (Fig. 80). Other symbols were used for various animals so that identification was specific. As soon as these tell-tale details have become familiar, the animals can be named.

Second, joints in the bony structure of the anatomy are given a surface indication by ovals or circles called "eyes." They are distinguished from real eyes by not showing the triangular corner made by the joining of the lines of the lids.

Third, individual parts of the animal are drawn separately and arranged close together in a compact design with no background showing in symmetrical front view (Ill. 12) or in profile view (Ill. 13). The parts often do not combine into recognizable animals (Ill. 14). The original idea may have been to have the animal design enclose the object or, in the case of a blanket worn by a chief, fold around the body.

Northwest Coast art includes totem poles, house posts, mortuary poles, masks, figures, drawings and paintings, textiles and utensils. In addition, the late nineteenth century period has produced carvings in slate, called argillite (Haida), and stone sculpture and petroglyphs have come to us from the prehistoric period. Whether or not these stone carvings and petroglyphs are in any way related to the Indians who produced the Northwest Coast art of more recent times, is unknown.

TOTEM POLES AND HOUSE POSTS

Some Northwest Coast totem poles are memorial columns, bearing the carved totem animals of the family. Other poles illustrate myths as well as clan affiliations. The totem animals are heraldic devices comparable to European coats of arms. Totem poles are the most impressive work in wood of aboriginal North America, comparing favorably with Aztec and Maya work in stone. They are the world's largest wood carvings and in monumental grandeur surpass anything produced by wood carvers anywhere.

In many cases, the ranking nephew of the deceased would commission a carver to design and supervise the carving. The carver selected his team of assistants, decided on the cedar to be used for the pole and assigned to each subordinate the section he was to work on. According to one report, it took most of the male inhabitants of a village a year or so to carve a totem pole (Adam). How much effort was spent on totem poles is evident from the fact that every house in the village Kitkatla of the Tsimshian tribe, had a totem pole from thirty to fifty feet high. Exceptional poles in Haida villages and on the Nass river in British Columbia stood as high as eighty and ninety feet above ground, and were correspondingly thick. The poles are in scale with the large houses in front of which they stood; these sometimes accommodated several hundred persons.

In the nineteenth century, when totem poles became the vogue, Indians of wealth acquired an extra supply of totems by various means; in warfare, by purchase, exchange, through marriage and in other ways. The more totems a man had, the greater his prestige. To accommodate all these totems, the poles tended to increase in height. Sometimes frogs were added when additional crests were wanted. Frogs were common, and no one officially laid claim to them. In common with European heraldry, crest design has symmetry, angularity and severity, but on a plane with sculpture rather than simple ornament.

The earlier poles were hewn with stone axes and clearly show the tool marks, which are often more neatly smoothed down on poles made with iron tools. These iron tools are believed to have reached the Indians through white traders in the eighteenth century or else iron was secured from other sources as from wrecked ships washed up on the beaches. According to Boas, the Indians adopted iron slowly and clung to native jade blades. In spite of this persistence of stone blades, the highest development of the totem pole occurred from 1840 to 1880 and later, as a result of the increased prosperity of the Indian chiefs owing to the fur trade, which began in the late eighteenth century. Reports of early explorers from the last quarter of the eighteenth century mention only mortuary poles and house posts. Whether this was due to the fact that the early ships did not go where the totem poles were, or whether they did not develop until later, is not entirely clear. By the time Captain Cook came to Nootka in 1778, iron tools were already in use, but they probably did not include the saw. The setting of the pole was a major engineering problem, accomplished by digging a sloping trench connecting with the hole, down which the pole could be maneuvered into position with the aid of wedges and ropes. Often a potlatch would celebrate the dedication.

Totem poles, especially in near view, look compact in their repetition of motifs, one on top of

Left, top to bottom: Ill. 7. Painted legging, beaver on man's head. Haida. Ill. 8. Headdress, hawk. Tsimshian. Ill. 9. Slate model of totem pole, eagle surmounting shark. Haida. *Center column:* Ill. 10. Carving, monster with bear's head, paws; and body of killer whale. Tlingit. Ill. 11. Slate dish, shark design. Haida. Ill. 12. Slate box, sea monster. Haida. Ill. 13. Slate carving, sea monster Wasku. Haida. *Above:* Ill. 14. Totem pole, sea monster. Haida. *All after Boas. American Museum of Natural History.*

another. One section, representing one animal crest, is apt to stop abruptly without transition to the one above. The pole is overlaid with a complex linear design that affords the eye little rest. There is much vigor in the variety of motifs but the effect is also bewildering, owing to an equal emphasis on every lineal foot all the way up to the top of the pole. Where in addition the pole is painted with contrasting colors, completely covering the wood surface, the clamor for attention is most insistent. Poles more nearly in the original unrestored state show a rich gray color caused by the weathering of the wood and the bleaching of the pigments. In the early period the Indians painted only eyes and ears and other details, using mainly black, red, blue-green and occasionally white. Color was for emphasis only. To paint poles all over in bright color is a modern innovation. Some poles, even from a moderate distance, show greater unity and do not look as if cut into sections (Fig. 60).

If we examine one section of the carving by itself (Fig. 61), we can admire how sensitively an eye is carved, the way it is shaped and projected from the recessed area and how this depression joins the main level by means of a soft roll. If we let our eye move up, as we face the pole, we note how bold details are set against large smooth surfaces. We become aware of light areas contrasted against dark depressions, and we note with what elegance curves are repeated in deep, narrow, ribbon-like bands. Eyes and foreheads made by patterns repeat the same shapes. In terms of design, if we ignore total composition, individual passages are most attractive. A largeness of scale, a feeling of breadth and power in a single head are entirely admirable (Fig. 62).

The limitations of the post and the necessity of using the whole animal encouraged the use of a few standardized animal postures, and a certain rigidity of pattern inevitably resulted. Animal heads fold around part of the pole; bent or folded legs and drooping paws are brought out in relief against the tree trunk which is cut back from the surface. Smaller poles (Fig. 62) avoid the extreme complexity of the taller showing many crests. Each animal head is characterized so that it is recognizable. The projecting snout of the beaver (Fig. 60 bottom, left pole) differs from the beak of the raven (Fig. 60 middle, left pole). Bodies are carved so that the legs assume a few typical postures. It could hardly be otherwise and still make a satisfactory design. Something had to be repeated in the complexity of the pattern; as the heads had to be different, the bodies were wisely carved to bring rest into an already crowded composition.

So far, research on totem poles has emphasized the symbolism, which includes the stories that are linked to each animal represented in the carving. Folklore rather than folk art has been the usual object of study, and much less has been written about the carving as such. The names of a few carvers are known, but often they have not been linked to particular styles. A comparison of the heads in two poles (Figs. 61 and 62) will show that the cutting is different, bold, with strong relief in one pole (Fig. 62) and delicate, flat and linear in another (Fig. 61).

As many as six hundred poles were estimated to have been standing at the end of the last century, and in 1938 about two hundred poles were salvaged by the U.S. Forest Service program.

Other carved and decorated poles used by the Northwest Indians were mortuary poles and house posts. The mortuary poles were used as supports for wooden boxes containing ashes of the dead. House posts, an integral part of the structure of the buildings, supported the roof and part of the interior and were carved with family crests in relief (Fig. 63) or in the round.

A Tlingit house post (Fig. 63) carved in a flat relief and incised represents the style in one of its most attractive aspects. The distribution of the motifs in strict symmetry, contrasting small carved heads in the center with larger incised heads on the border, is impeccable in its refinement. The carved heads stand out against the flat surface of the wood, where fine tooling creates texture. For excellence this carved panel, ten feet high, would be difficult to match in any style. The post has a companion in the same style. From the top down, the center crests represent: woodworm, human face, frog, the bear man, dogfish; on the right side, whale (?), dragonfly; on the left side, eagle and sea lion.

MASKS

Second in interest only to the several kinds of poles are the carved and painted wooden masks used in a great variety of forms at the potlatches and winter festivals, when members of secret societies impersonated mythological beings. Masks were either the usual kind fitting close to the face (Fig. 64) or they included birds' beaks several feet long (Fig. 65), or the body of a killer whale six feet long with movable tails and flippers. The mask used in the Cannibal dance, representing a bird, may have a beak twelve feet long, supported by two men of the Cannibal society.

The work of the secular carver was done in the open for anyone to see, but the sacred work of the exclusively religious carver was done in seclusion. To observe it was punishable by death. Among the Tsimshian tribes, some carvers specialized in religious objects. Carvers of the Tsimshian and Kwakiutl tribes, and others too, produced ingenious mechanical devices, double masks (Fig. 66), sometimes equipped with strings. In certain dances, the outer mask would open up to reveal the human manifestation of the spirit. Some of these masks were made to roll the eyes back. In a composite mask the sun is represented above a man and a doubleheaded snake, all connected with strings to make the attachments move (Color Plate 8).

Masks are stylized in form and color and may reflect the style found in the totem poles (Fig. 67). Color and form may also be used to distort the human countenance, to emphasize the supernatural characters of the actors. Eyes are shaped as on totem poles, and black stripes cut across the forehead. Color emphasizes mouths, eyes and noses (Fig. 64), and a varied relief in the carving provides depression for shadows.

A trend toward the grotesque and dramatic is characteristic of the religious masks of the Kwakiutl. They were worn indoors and at night by the light of the great log fires that were kept up in the community house during the winter festivals. To suggest the power of the supernatural beings represented, Kwakiutl masks were heavy in features, at times distorted, and exaggerated in the eyes. The combination of flat color and deep shadow must have been highly effective.

Northwest Coast design was sufficiently flexible to include the weird as well as the realistic and the decorative. In a mask ten inches high representing Tsonoqua, an uncanny, fear-inspiring character is emphasized (Fig. 68). This mask of an ogre with high cheek bones, small eyes and a large mouth with a labret, represents the spirit of a wild woman who lives in the woods and kills and eats children, an Indian parallel to our own witch of the fairy tales. The sinister, threatening expression suggests that this type owes something to a realistic trend in Northwest Coast art.

The wolf's head mask (Fig. 69) was worn on top of the head. This mask, with a cedar bark tail and teeth made of Dentalia, was used in the wolf dance where the performer dressed in blankets would imitate the motions of the animal. The mask itself combines carving in broad surfaces with painted details. "Its style is not known to have changed in the last century." (Boas)

Mask and headdress carving did not vary a great deal among the tribes as far as the carving technique was concerned (Fig. 70). Wood, cedar or alder, was the usual material, occasionally whale bone among the Nootka, or beaten copper among the Tlingit. Small adzes served for the preliminary shaping of the block; straight and curved knives and a primitive drill were used for the actual carving of the detail and dogfish skin for the final smoothing of the surface. Powdered pigments mixed with chewed salmon eggs and applied with brushes of bristles and vegetable fibers left a flat, slightly glossy surface after drying. It was a kind of tempera painting applied directly to the wood. This supplied a solid and durable coating that contributed to the effectiveness of the mask. Yellow, brown, and red ocher, black and white and, more rarely, blue-greens were used.

The fusion of man and animal in masks has resulted in combinations suggestive of the fantastic extravagances of Oceanic art, though part of the American development. In an eagle mask, in the Portland (Oregon) Art Museum, the mouth is human, the eyes only partially so, but the nose is an eagle's beak. Bird and man preserve their identity, and yet the combination looks like a new creation. Shredded bark cloth and a four-pronged feathered crown on top of the head further emphasize the novelty of the invention. Fitted with strings, such a contraption could be made to twirl around.

The mask shown in Fig. 71 comes close to being a portrait. Without the stylization of the totem pole crest, it still reflects the Northwest Coast style. Tsimshian masks were used in broad daylight, and this fact gave them a character somewhat different from the Kwakiutl style. The most characteristic Tsimshian masks are related to the dramatic presentations staged in connection with the potlatch feasts to portray supernatural events, or they were used for comic skits, or take-offs on rival chiefs and foreigners. Several tribes also had a headdress ornament worn by the chiefs (Fig. 72). They were attached to headbands, decorated with sea lion whiskers, feathers and skins, which would drop down to the shoulders. Fur, hair and cedar fibers were also attached to masks, and abalone shells were used to represent teeth.

Some of these masks may seem weird, but they have an artistic appeal and are never shocking. Not as much can be said for some of the incredibly repulsive rituals in which they functioned in connection with the secret society. However, taking a mask out of its place in a particular dance to which it once belonged does not diminish its artistic significance.

FIGURES

In the carving of the figure, the Northwest Coast Indian arrived at a style entirely different from African figure sculpture, as in the carving of a Tlingit chief (Fig. 73). The intent is realistic, and the effect at times recalls the totem pole manner. At their best, Northwest Coast statuettes have a natural ease, a certain unaffected grace, different from the involved forms of Africa. Such a statuette may suggest movement when carved with a forward slant, as in the Haida statuette illustrated in Fig. 74. This is under two feet in height. Far from being awkward, these statuettes are sophisticated. The treatment of the eyes, brows and face is in the typical ornamental tradition. Haida carved figures are enhanced through the use of color: a red-orange body with green and blue details.

In a carved ceremonial figure of the Kwakiutl, only the head is developed beyond the merest contours of the figure (Fig. 75). This is a speaker, a real person who is making an address, as is indicated in the parted lips. The painted decorations and the carved details are in the familiar style pattern but carved in a rough and sketchy manner. A Vancouver Island and Fraser River type of mask with telescope eyes (Fig. 76) is definitely sculpturesque.

The style of the Salishan tribes at the southern extremity of the coastal region of British Columbia seems to derive from different sources. In its simplest terms, this carving is the notched post refined and elaborated into an art form of distinction. It is represented in shaman figures, loom posts, house posts, spirit canoe figures and grave post figures. These southern examples are distinct and perhaps only incidentally related to the northern style.

A close-up of the head of a Quinault Indian (Salish) shaman's figure (Fig. 77) shows clearly what really fascinated the carver who was working within a tradition. It was his problem to reduce a post into a few finely related shapes in which surfaces and contours retain a primary attraction. The major task fell to carving, color was used for contrast and accents were added. Eyes, using shells, were placed beside the nose, the mouth between nose and the end of the chin. The effect of the finished head is a direct result of tools, materials and a simple technique. From forehead to chin the face is expressed by a series of subtly curved surfaces in which tool marks and wood grain add to the effect.

DRAWING AND PAINTING

Painting was practiced in its own right for the decoration of the gable ends of houses. The smooth, tooled surfaces of the wide planks were decorated with huge totem animals, sometimes in groups and relating to well-known myths. In large scale and in bold stylized designs, these magnificent motifs stretched across the whole front. Painted house fronts, rather than wood carving, are mentioned by early explorers. Painted panels like the one shown in Fig. 78 were used on the inside of the houses. They show the same love of largeness found in the giant poles. The same motifs are used, but in asymmetrical compositions.

Where and how the Northwest Coast style of drawing and painting originated is unknown. The ornamental linear style may have developed originally out of a type of drawing still in evidence in rock drawings, as at Nanaimo, Vancouver Island (Adam). A long period of development must be assumed to lie between the early, truly primitive beginnings and the late phase of the style of the late eighteenth and nineteenth centuries. The stylized manner was already flourishing when Northwest Coast art came to the attention of the white man. Figure drawings of an early type may have led to the later ornamental style. Certain line elements used on primitive figure drawings for the joints have been explained as possible sources for the ornamental styles. Later this convention may have developed into the so-called "eyes" used in house painting, on leather dance aprons, on Chilkat blankets and elsewhere.

Northwest Coast design has a strong family resemblance. Postures of animals repeat; so do shapes like limbs, paws and claws, as well as eyes, noses and mouths. Shapes are standardized like words in a vocabulary.

Essentially the same style of painting is used in a painted ceremonial shirt (Color Plate 9) showing a remarkable elegance in its sweeping curves and precise details, as well as boldness and simplicity. We admire a sureness of touch and an easy control of shapes. Each part takes its place in a complex design. A mighty head cuts across verticals, rising from a horizontal base; a rectangular contour restrains the details, and compact massiveness is the result. The head is broad to emphasize the rectangular outline of the whole design, thereby adding to a feeling of power.

The painted bear is essentially a design filled in with color. It could have been applied to wood and carved, giving wood carving a linear, ornamental character. Nevertheless, the artist made certain that the animal, the bear, would be recognized.

Another bear painted on a drum panel, now in the Portland Art Museum, Oregon, shows the same style used on the painted shirt in Color Plate 9. There, too, the brushwork, with its fluent strokes and precise details, is used to express a conventionalized anatomy. The drum had a name, "Bear coming out of his hole," which was also the name of its owner.

BLANKETS

Besides poles, dance masks and rattles, Northwest Pacific Coast art revealed its finest work in woven blankets. Such blankets were made on a primitive loom consisting of two upright posts connected by a horizontal top bar. Mountain goat wool, stained black, yellow and blue-green, was used for the woof threads, and cedar bark threads for the warp. The weaving was tapestry-fashion, the weft threads being continued only as far as each color was needed in the pattern. Men furnished the design on wooden pattern boards, and women did the weaving.

The finest products from these looms were ceremonial blankets made by the Chilkat (Fig. 79), who belong to the Tlingit tribe. They were worn only by chiefs over the shoulder at festivals, and were placed over the chiefs' funeral chests.

The attraction of the Chilkat blankets is in the harmonious relations, partly of the colors, blue-green, yellow, and white on a black ground, and partly of the shapes. The total effect is one of compactness, with a horizontal feeling dominating.

The rounded rectangles enclosing a linear shape, ending in points on either side, are spoken of as the "eyes." Where these shaped corners are missing, the ovals or "eyes" are the ball and socket joints of an animal in cross section. The inner oval stands for the ball, the outer for the socket. Both motifs, characteristic details in painting and carving, are transferred to weaving unchanged. Curves remain curves, contrary to the rectilinear character of the loom. To an uninitiated eye the blanket designs do not suggest any recognizable animal. The blanket is often divided into a wide central and two narrow side panels. The artist aimed to get as much of the animal as possible into the central panel, and the side panels were merely filled in; nevertheless, the side panels were believed to represent the reverse, unseen, portions of the animal. With all sides of the animal indicated, if not realistically represented, the blanket was like an animal skin that could envelope the wearer.

Even as late as 1907 the idea of the blanket standing for a magic cloak had not entirely died out among the Indians. From the ethnological point of view Chilkat blankets are objects of rank and prestige that were standardized long ago. That is as far as we can go without bringing in conjecture. But from the point of view of their development, which can no longer be traced, there was probably a time when magic and symbolism entered. It may be even less plausible to assume they were never more than symbols of rank without a magical connection. Chilkat blankets, in a psychological sense, might have been substitutes for animal skins suggesting, no doubt, identification on the part of the wearer with his totem animal. A Chilkat blanket design suggests a compromise between the demands of magic and the requirements of art. Northwest Coast art had a vocabulary of art forms which it put to use to serve the interests of magic by using symbolism rather than realism. The animal was symbolically indicated on the central panel; the artist combined parts of the animal and left out other parts. A large head, various sections of the body, joints, limbs, paws, and tails are pushed together more or less as these parts join on the live animal; actually the resemblance is difficult to follow through.

The painted dance aprons of leather are related to woven blankets in the type of stylized patterns. Northwest Coast design was a well-developed style, its details could be cut out of cloth, in wood, painted or woven. In Haida dance shirts appliquéd with a design of a bear in red flannel, motifs appear practically unchanged. Even proportions do not vary much, and the basic character and the shapes that express each animal remain the same.

UTENSILS

Tradition and ritual determined what was to be carved. Rattles used in the winter ceremonies, and by chiefs to welcome guests to the potlatches, were made in various styles. The paw of an animal like a bear may be carved with a human face (Fig. 80), or a rattle may include man or animal (Fig. 81). It seemed natural to the Indian carver to combine human and animal form in the same work to express the dual character of man and animal. Thus, spirits could have human faces with the beaks of eagles or ravens, for animals could take on a human appearance at will.

In a Haida rattle (Fig. 82) the down-curving beak indicates the hawk, otherwise the motifs are those in common use regardless of what animal is represented or what the object is used for. The same eyes, the same eyebrows, the same mouth are put to many uses. Essentially, this rattle is a closely packed combination of flat bands, sharp ridges and incised lines. These curvilinear ribbons, triangular shapes and near-ovals are so compressed so as to leave nothing of the original surface of the block. The Indian artist was as attached to his stylistic vocabulary as our own artists are dedicated to an interpretation of visual appearances. Stylization using basic shapes is here developed to the utmost. One of these shapes, often the ribbon-like lips or eyebrows, is apt to appear in almost any Northwest Coast design. Such constant repetition of typical motifs makes the style easy to recognize.

The food dishes used at potlatch feasts were at times as large as small canoes. They were carved in the shape of a human figure in which the body was hollowed out to form a large bowl. Smaller bowls were carved in place of the knees and the head. The lid then looks like a large mask (Fig. 83) deeply carved to suggest eyes, mouth and cheeks. The contrasting use of color brings out the shapes and shows clearly how readily linear surface patterns were turned into three-dimensional carving. The shapes, as they appear here, must have been drawn on the surface of the log and gouged out, leaving the contours. As the lid did not have to look like a real head, this was a speedy way to get a striking effect.

Fusions of man and animal are common and reflect the basic mythology. The same basic shapes found in masks and totem poles in carved and painted details occur here also.

A carved and painted wooden model of a sea wolf with a salmon in a single small piece (Fig. 84) brings out the characteristics of Northwest Coast wood carving. These may be summarized as an emphasis of the head, a neglect of body and limbs and an allover ornamental elaboration. The significant details of the head include a large mouth with a row of teeth holding a salmon, nostrils, eyes and ears; everything else is treated in a summary fashion. Fins are attached to characterize the creature as a marine animal, and arms and legs, in man and beast, are carved in a generalized fashion, without much differentiation.

The unity of the style is also apparent in such utensils as spoons (Fig. 86) and ladles made of mountain sheep and goat horn, and in wooden bowls. The yellowish horn was made pliable by steaming and then shaped over wooden molds. Carved handles of the black goat horn were attached by copper rivets. Together, bowl and spoon are graceful in shape and contrast in color. The carved handles adapt the totem pole motifs to the small size, retaining the same largeness of scale and boldness of carving. Wooden bowls (Fig. 85) vary in shape but derive from the shape of an animal, as a frog in a bowl.

A war club (Fig. 86A) shows carved knobs and a projecting beak, all carved out of the thickness of the wood. Stylization controls the ornamental carving on such smaller objects. The relief is in lines, shallow depressions and deep, panel-like setbacks. A thunder bird and a man in relief are shown upside down on the handle. The craftsmanship is superior, the wood heavy, the appearance almost like bronze. On the back the two symmetrical sides meet in a depressed incision, almost as if a seam had been in the mind of the carver. The meaning of such detail was probably unknown to the artists, who simply perpetuated standardized designs that had been inherited from the past. By way of wish fulfillment, fat-furnishing animals, like seals, are carved on bowls, the dish itself hinting at a magical connection.

The Indians also made rectangular wooden boxes, large and small, high and low, which were used for storage. They are usually painted or carved and painted, covering fronts, sides, backs and even lids with decorations, using the familiar animal motifs (Fig. 87). The sides were made pliable through steaming, so that they could be bent and sewn together.

Occasionally a simple object like a spindle whorl—the flywheel of a spindle—was made attractive in the way it was decorated. In this case (Fig. 88) the left hand was placed on the eight-inch disk on opposite sides and traced. As one hand came over too far, not enough space was left to get the other hand on complete. The lightly engraved outlines that resulted have turned the disk into a fascinating pattern. The freshness of the cutting on the smooth surface forms a pleasing contrast repeated by the irregularity of the design contrasted against the circle, the most regular of all curves.

Prehistoric stone carvings came to light in connection with excavations on the Fraser River, as in an example of a stone mortar (Fig. 89). This heavy, bulbous shape is unlike anything we have noted in the late ornamental style. Nose, eye and chin are purposeful and individual in a style that is characterized by massiveness. How this art is connected with the art of living tribes is unknown. Another stone mortar (Fig. 90), bowl-shaped, was collected in British Columbia in 1893. A seal hunt with canoes is incised on the border in a style that seems highly simplified. The typical Northwest Coast style appears but rarely in stone. A stone pipe in the shape of a wolf's head shows the same stylistic characteristics common to wood (Fig. 91).

Indians of the Northwest Coast developed a wood carving style that was ornamental and highly unified. Motifs were derived from the animal world and objects ranged from monumental totem poles to the utensils of every day life. If there were foreign influences they were those of Asia and the Pacific area. The origins are unknown, but the styles may be presumed to have developed on the North American continent.

In spite of stylization Northwest Coast art shows vigor and adaptability. Carving and painting are so closely related that one is almost an extension of or a substitute for the other. During a century and a half of contact with the white man's civilization, this art reached its greatest development in a thoroughly original style but in the end virtually disappeared as a tribal art.

RECENT AND CONTEMPORARY ART

During the second half of the last century, the Haida Indians of Queen Charlotte Islands, British Columbia, carved argillite, commonly called slate, which occurs in this locality. Figures, small totem poles, boxes, plates and pipes were carved with dexterity and often with good taste. Though Indian motifs continued to be used, this group shows the white man's influence in the choice of motifs.

The best-known single piece of the Haida tribe of Queen Charlotte Islands is the small group known as the "Bear Mother" (Fig. 92), based on the myth of a human mother who was wedded to a bear. Her offspring, half human, half bear, showed his fierce animal nature while nursing. The expression of emotion in the recoiling figure, rare in primitive art, demonstrates the versatility of the Indian artist adapting to a foreign style. It is a striking example of how culture influences art. Except for the Haida artist's name, Skaows-Ke'ay, and the time and occasion when it was carved (1883), nothing is known about the carver. An instance of the influence of Christian iconography on Indian art is represented in a late totem pole in which Christian Biblical subjects like St. Paul are represented.

The walrus engravings and wooden masks, which have been collected by our museums, belong largely to a period before 1900. Nelson, who wrote about the Eskimo in the late seventies, tells us that even then the native ways of life were receding before the advances of the white man. The engraved ivory pipestems Hoffman wrote about in 1897 had been collected before that date. Himmelheber, who in 1936 spent time studying Eskimo art in Alaska, found no traces of the earlier walrus engravings. When the native worked for his own use, the question of sale did not enter; whatever the Eskimo made he used himself or gave away. With the appearance of the white man, first as trader and sailor and today as tourist, the Eskimo took over the white man's custom of producing objects of the crafts for sale, to add to his income.

In 1935 the Congress of the United States passed a law that created the Indian Arts and Crafts Board, to administer an educational program for the benefit of Alaskans, Indians, Aleuts, and Eskimo. At the Mt. Edgecombe boarding school run by the Bureau of Indian Affairs, near Sitka, students began to produce craft objects for sale. As in other government sponsored craft schools, standards of excellence are maintained and objects sold at prices commensurate with their quality.

This work is going on today. The craft objects produced are above the level of imported, mass-produced wares sold at popular prices. To differentiate the two groups, the genuine American-made objects bear a label which serves to protect the public against inferior imitations. The fine products that have been developed out of this planned effort to integrate native crafts into contemporary art on a level of professional competence, are bearing fruit. A graduate of this school, Ronald Senungetuk, a young Eskimo student, was enrolled at the School of American Craftsmen in Rochester, New York, and, upon graduation, stood at the head of his class. Six years after he had first started to learn English he not only held his own but took the lead among students who had enjoyed advantages that came much later to this young Eskimo. An ornamental candlestick, constructed of a section split off a curved walrus tusk for the support for the sconces, is attached to a finely proportioned hard-wood base. A native material is sensitively combined with a rectilinear block to give the piece a unique expression with a contemporary flavor. In a natural, unforced manner, a traditional and a modern element are fused, the result is highly satisfying.

This same school that brought out Ronald Senungetuk is experimenting with jade cutting to produce jewelry. The raw material is scooped up from the bottom of the sea, where the water is shallow, and brought to the shop, where individual pieces are cut for later elaboration. We may look to the future to note what this latest adventure in jade—a material that has such a distinguished ancestry in Maya art—may bring forth.

In addition to these more sophisticated works of a thoroughly contemporary approach, simpler crafts close to the historic precedent are continued in basketry. Every summer the inhabitants of King Island settle on the mainland in temporary houses where they spend the season in basket making and ivory carving. Otherwise, wood carving is the preferred craft. Carvers work in the Northwest Coast tradition. Small totem poles, usually up to a height of about eighteen inches, are made for collectors. There are still four women living today who weave Chilkat blankets in the traditional manner as a genuine continuation of the tribal craft. Considering the time, skill and artistry that goes into such a blanket, the high prices they bring are not out of proportion to their quality.

Many totem poles have rotted on the beaches, and a large number have been rescued in museums and in parks. Blankets are being made today as they were formerly, and carving and other crafts have been successfully integrated into an American market. That this development under native guidance will have a future seems to be indicated by the emergence of young artists.

A somewhat different approach to bring native Eskimo handicrafts to the attention of a buying public outside of the arctic has been started in Canada. In 1949 a test purchase of small Eskimo carvings was collected in the Hudson Bay area and shown to the Canadian Handicrafts Guild in Montreal. A painter, James A. Houston, had visited Port Harrison, on Hudson Bay, to collect the first carvings. Out of this developed a concerted effort that enlisted the support of the Hudson Bay Company and later brought a government grant in aid of the work. Purchasing agents, distributed in several places around Hudson Bay, encouraged the Eskimo to carve in stone and ivory small objects, animals and figures. They are bought and sold with no difficulty though the agency of the Guild. The natives are not taught but guided and advised. As a result, in one area over seventy-five per cent of the members over fourteen years old are actively engaged in artistic endeavors. By June, 1950, thousands of pieces had been distributed, but at no loss of individuality. Stone and ivory are the materials. It is instructive to compare these modern carvings with those found by John Murdoch in northwestern Alaska around 1885. The carvings by the Point Barrow Eskimo in stone, bone, ivory and wood, of the eighties of the last century, often show the same animals carved today, but in a more simplified version. These modern carvings appear to be advanced developments out of the native background.

Fig. 49 (above). Figure holding a bowl, Baluba style, Eastern Congo. *University Museum, Philadelphia.*

Fig. 50 (left). Two figures holding a bowl, Baluba style, Eastern Congo. *Royal Museum of Belgian Congo, Tervuren.*

Plate 2. Dance staff, Yoruba style (Nigeria).

Webster Plass Collection.
Courtesy, Time Magazine.

Plate 1. Double-headed (Janus) mask, covered with skin, Ekoi style (Nigeria).

Plate 3. Headdress, Yoruba style (Nigeria).

Plate 4. Bronze head of a king (oba), Benin style (Nigeria).

Plate 5. Mask, Bayaka style (Western Congo).

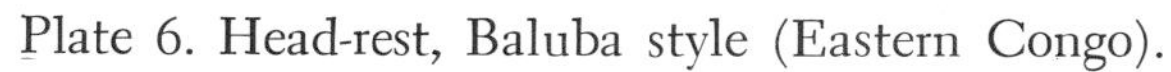

Plate 6. Head-rest, Baluba style (Eastern Congo).

Plate 7. Mask, Bena Biombo style (Congo).

Webster Plass Collection.
Courtesy, Time Magazine.

Fig. 51 (above, left). Figure (detail), Bena Lulua style, Central Congo. *Brooklyn Museum.*

Fig. 52 (above, center). Ivory head, Warega style, Eastern Congo. *Baltimore Museum of Art.*

Fig. 53 (above, right). Standing male figure, Batshioko style, Belgian Congo or Angola. H. 16 in. *Philadelphia Commercial Museum.*

Fig. 54 (left). Argillite effigy jar, Mangbetu style, Eastern Congo. *Baltimore Museum of Art.*

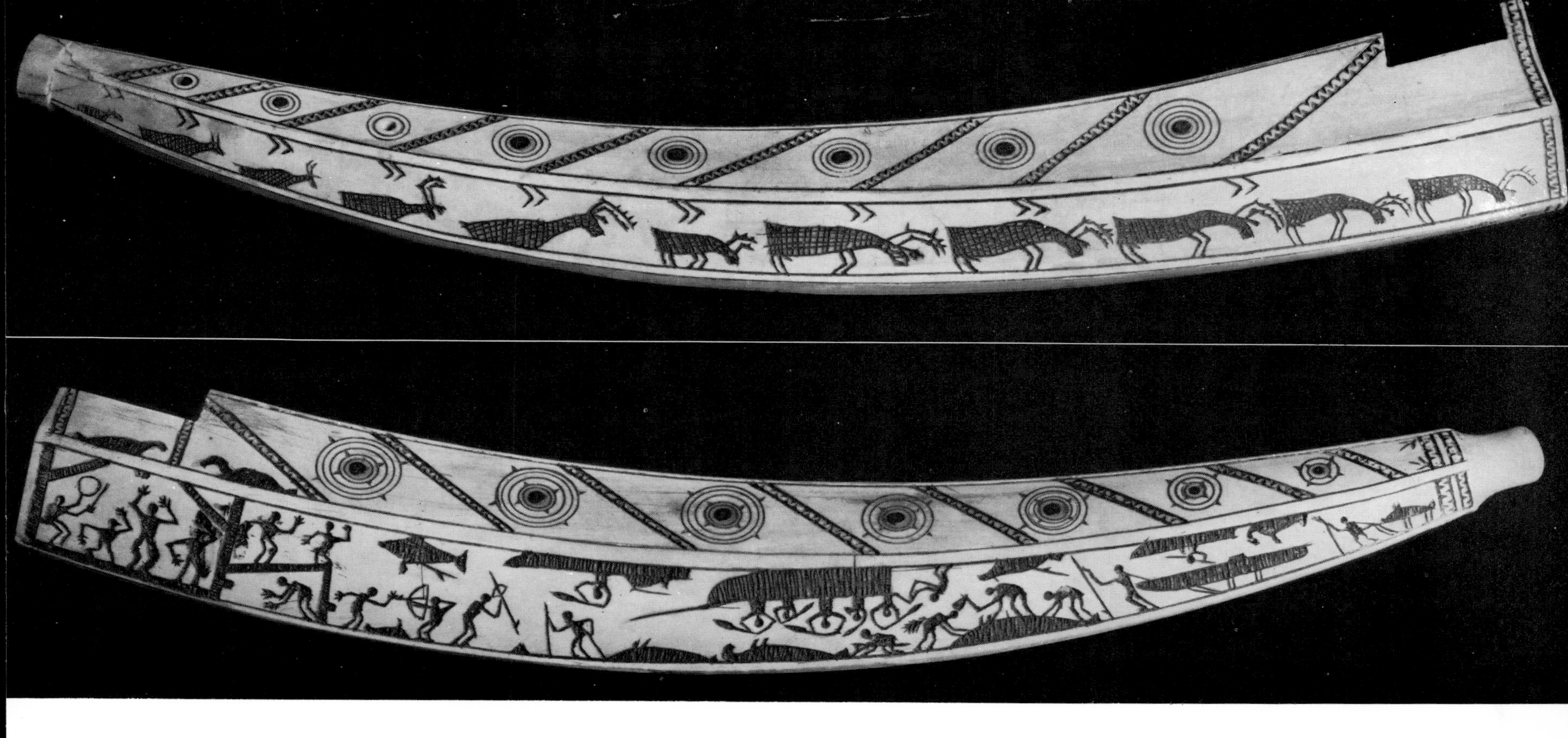

Fig. 55 (top). Engraved tobacco pipe stem, walrus ivory, Eskimo, Alaska. *Smithsonian Institution*. Fig. 56 (above). Engraved tobacco pipe stem, walrus ivory, Eskimo, Alaska. *Smithsonian Institution.*

Fig. 57 (below, left). Mask, wood trimmed with fur and feathers, Eskimo, Alaska. *Museum für Völkerkunde, Berlin*. Fig. 58 (below, center). Mask, wood, painted and trimmed with feathers. H. ca 12 in. Eskimo, Good News Bay, Alaska. *Museum of the American Indian, New York*. Fig. 59 (below, right). Mask, wood, painted. H. 18 in. Eskimo, Alaska. *Museum of the American Indian, New York*.

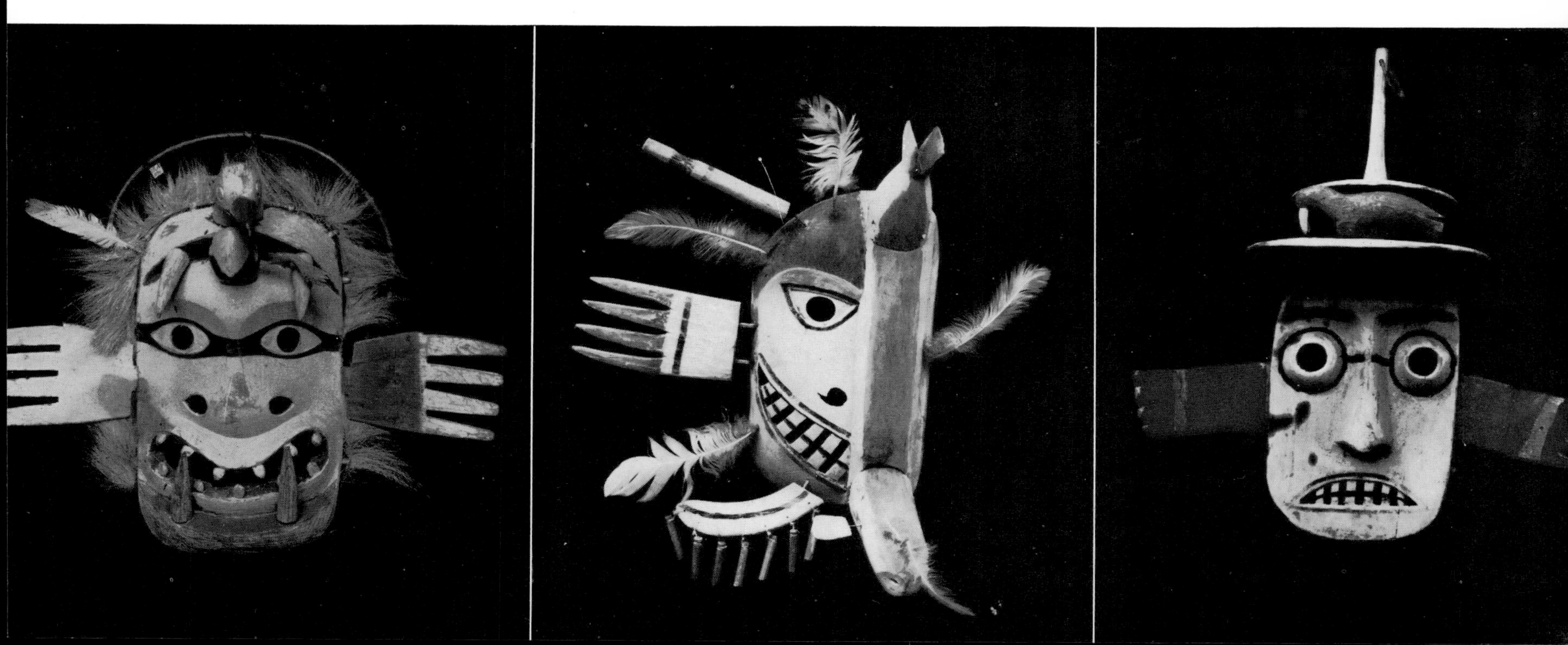

Plate 8. Composite mask representing the sun. Northwest coast. *Provincial Museum, Victoria, B. C. Courtesy, Washington State Museum and Taylor Museum, Colorado Springs, Colorado.*

Plate 9. Ceremonial shirt painted to represent a bear. Northwest coast. *Washington State Museum and Taylor Museum, Colorado Springs, Colorado.*

Opposite page: Fig. 64. Mask, Haida. *American Museum of Natural History.*

Fig. 60 (above). Totem poles. The large totem pole in the foreground is from the Haida village of Old Kasaan, Prince of Wales Island. *Taylor Museum, Colorado Springs, Colorado.*

Fig. 61 (right). Beaver pole, Haida, from Skedans, Queen Charlotte Islands. *Royal Ontario Museum, Toronto.*

Fig. 62 (second right). House post. *National Museum of Canada, Ottawa.*

Fig. 63 (extreme right). House post, Tlingit. *Smithsonian Institution.*

Plate 11. Black Ogre Kachina, Hopi style.

Plate 10. Owl Kachina, Hopi style.

Collection, Taylor Museum of Colorado Springs, Colorado. Courtesy, University of New Mexico Press, Albuquerque, New Mexico.

Plate 12. Butterfly Kachina Maiden, Hopi style.

Plate 13 (left). Maya ceramic jar, painted with a ceremony connected with the deer. *National Gallery of Art, Washington, D. C.*

Plate 14 (below). Maya mural painting, from Bonampak, State of Chiapas, Mexico; trumpeters and marine deities. *Courtesy, Life Magazine.*

Fig. 65 (above). Double mask, a crane and a bird monster, Kwakiutl. *Provincial Museum, Victoria, B. C., on loan to Taylor Museum, Colorado Springs, Colorado.*

Fig. 66 (right). Double mask, giant "Tsonoqua" and human face, Kwakiutl, Albert Bay, B. C. *Collection, Earl L. Stendahl, Los Angeles.*

Fig. 67 (left). Mask, Nootka. *Smithsonian Institution.*

Fig. 68 (below). Kwakiutl mask of Tsonoqua, a mythical spirit. H. 10 in. *Denver Art Museum.*

Fig. 69 (above). Wolf's head mask, Nootka. *Smithsonian Institution.*

Fig. 70 (right). Eagle-head ceremonial headdress, Nootka. *Denver Art Museum.*

Plate 16 (below). Olmec (La Venta) statuette, jadeite, H. ca 9 in.

Plate 15 (above). Maya clay statuette, painted after firing, H. ca 8 in.

Plate 17 (above). Toltec mask, green serpentine, H. ca 8½ in.

Plate 18 (right). Toltec frescoed clay bowl, decorated with a design representing a conventionalized plumed serpent. Style of Teotihuacán, diameter ca 5½ in.

National Gallery of Art, Washington, D. C.

Fig. 72 (left). Headdress, Tlingit. *Washington State Museum, University of Washington, Seattle.*

Fig. 73 (below). Carving of a chief (detail), Tlingit. *Taylor Museum, Colorado Springs, Colorado.*

Opposite page:

Fig. 71. Portrait mask, Tlingit. *Portland Art Museum, Oregon. Photo: Taylor Museum, Colorado Springs, Colorado.*

Fig. 74 (left). Figure, Haida, Queen Charlotte Islands. *Smithsonian Institution*.

Opposite page:

Fig. 75. Head of carved figure seven feet high, Kwakiutl. *Taylor Museum, Colorado Springs, Colorado.*

Fig. 76. Mask, Cowichan, Vancouver Island. *Denver Art Museum.*

Fig. 78 (above). House painting, Nootka. *American Museum of Natural History.*

Fig. 79 (right). Chilkat blanket, southeastern Alaska. *Smithsonian Institution.*

Opposite page:

Fig. 77. Shaman's figure. Quinault Indians (Salish), Washington. *American Museum of Natural History.*

Fig. 80. Rattle, in shape of a bear's paw and human face, Tlingit. *Indian Arts and Crafts Board, U. S. Department of the Interior, Washington, D. C.*

Fig. 81. Rattle combining figure with animal, Haida, Queen Charlotte Islands. ***Smithsonian Institution.***

Fig. 82. Rattle in shape of a hawk, Haida. *American Museum of Natural History. Photo: Taylor Museum, Colorado Springs, Colorado.*

Fig. 83. Lid for a potlatch feast bowl, Haida. H. 3½ ft. *Wisconsin State Historical Society, Madison. Photo: Taylor Museum, Colorado Springs, Colorado.*

Fig. 84 (above). Wood carving of a sea wolf with salmon. *Provincial Museum, Victoria, B. C. Photo: Taylor Museum, Colorado Springs, Colorado.*

Fig. 85. Wooden bowl in shape of a frog, Tlingit, Sitka, Alaska. *Denver Art Museum. Photo: Taylor Museum, Colorado Springs, Colorado.*

Fig. 86. Spoon, horn and wood, Tlingit, Sitka, Alaska. *Bureau of American Ethnology, Smithsonian Institution.*

Fig. 86A (extreme right). War club, thunderbird ornament, Bella Bella Indians, British Columbia. *Smithsonian Institution.*

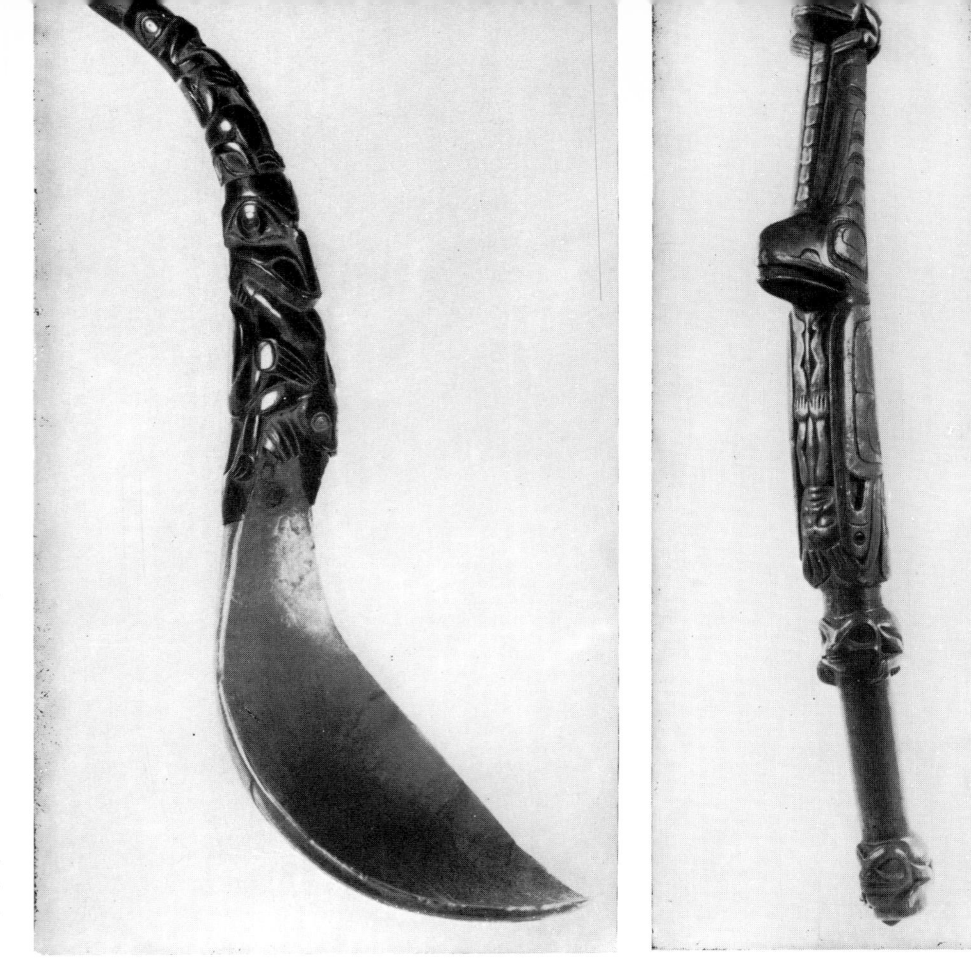

Fig. 87 (below). Wooden storage chest, decorated with sea shells, Tlingit. *Indian Arts and Crafts Board, U. S. Department of the Interior, Washington, D. C.*

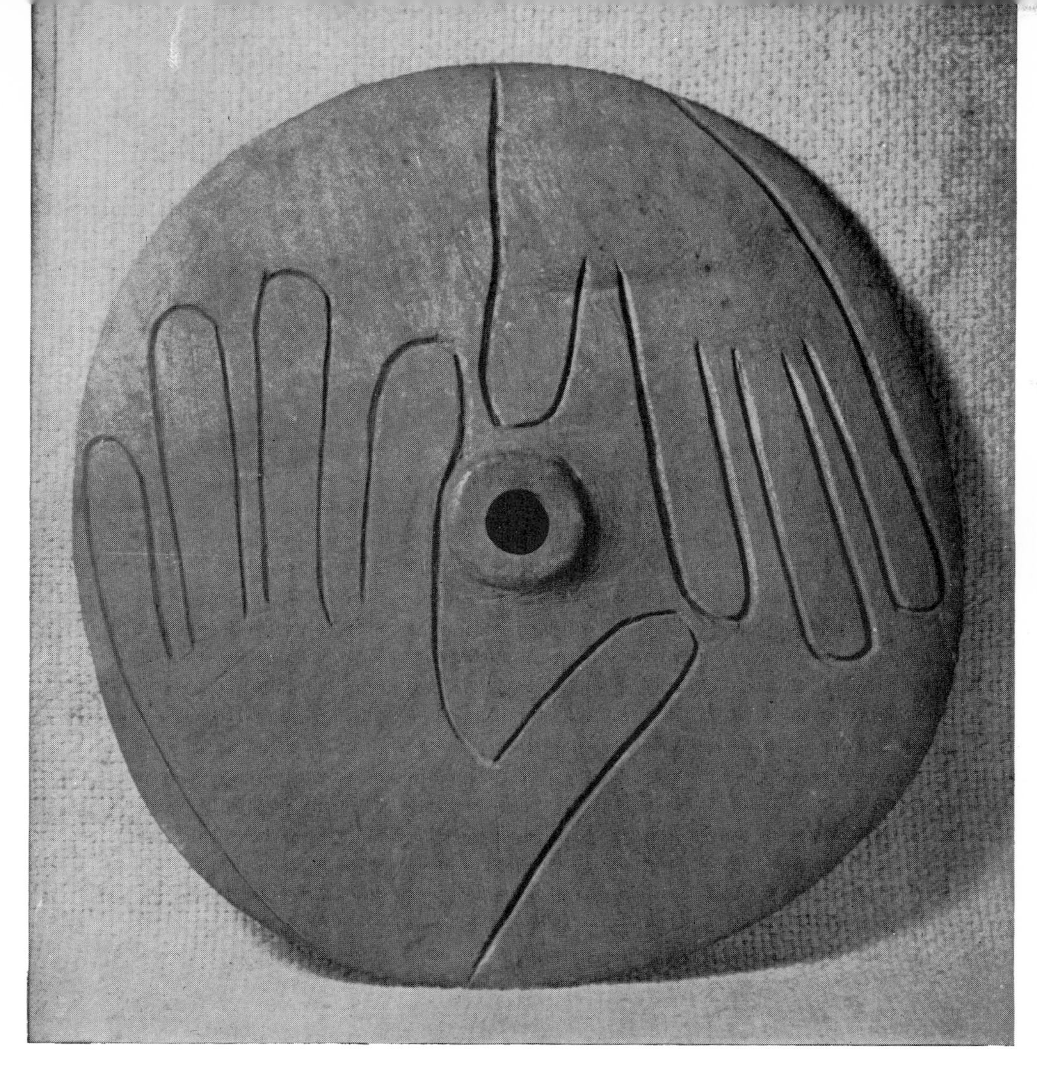

Fig. 88. Spindle whorl, maple wood. Diam. 8½ in. Salish tribe, from Nanaimo, British Columbia. *Provincial Museum, Victoria, B. C. Photo: Robert Bruce Inverarity.*

Fig. 89 (above). Stone mortar, in shape of a chieftain's head, Fraser River, B. C. *Museum für Völkerkunde, Berlin.*

Fig. 90 (left). Stone mortar. Collected by O. Jacobsen at Bella Bella, British Columbia, 1893. *Provincial Museum, Vancouver, B. C. Photo: Robert Bruce Inverarity.*

Fig. 91 (above). Stone pipe representing a wolf's head. *Collection, Mr. and Mrs. Ralph Altman, Los Angeles. Photo: Taylor Museum, Colorado Springs, Colorado.*

Fig. 92 (below). "The Bear Mother," carving in argillite, by Skaows-Ke'ay, Haida; Skidegate, B. C. L. 5¾ in. *Smithsonian Institution.*

Fig. 93. Stone pipe in form of a human figure, from the Adena Mound, southern Ohio. H. 8 in. *Ohio State Museum, Columbus.*

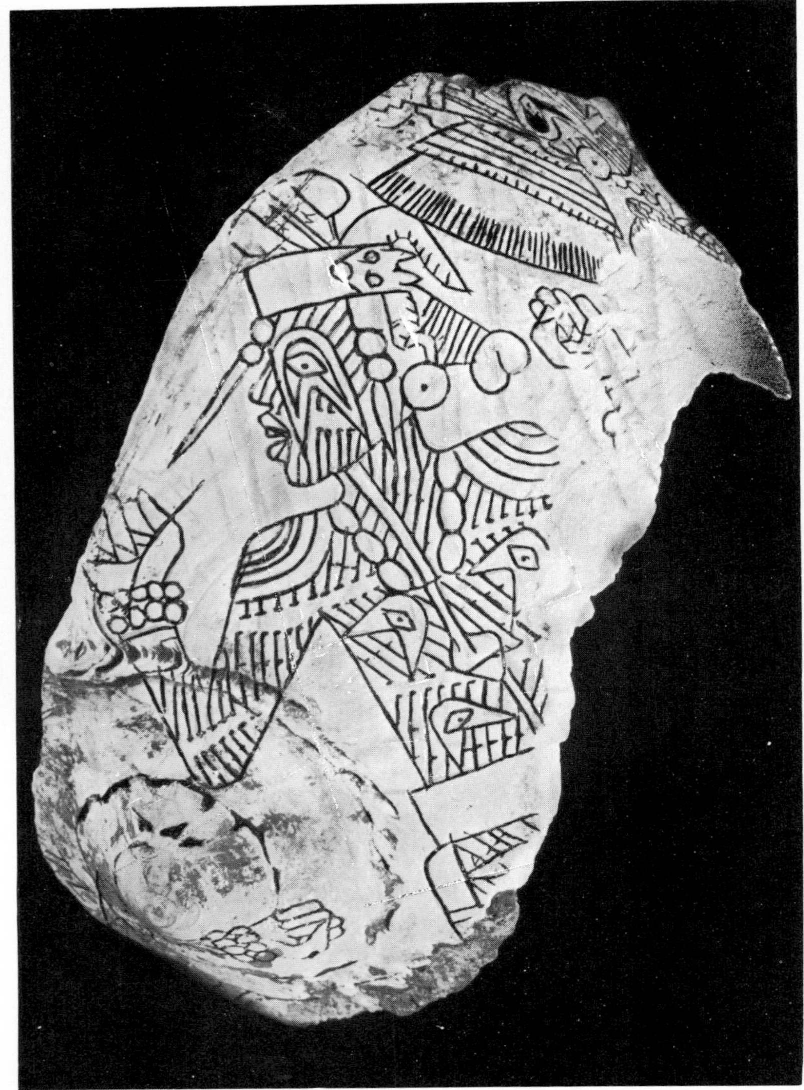

Fig. 94 (top left). Shell gorget, Sumner County, Tennessee. Diam. 3⅞ in. *Museum of the American Indian, New York.*

Fig. 95 (above). Painted shell fragment; from Spiro Mound, eastern Oklahoma. *Museum, University of Oklahoma.*

Fig. 96 (left). Stone pipe in shape of a hawk; from Tremper Mound, Ohio. L. 3⅞ in., H. 2$\frac{9}{16}$ in. *Ohio State Museum, Columbus.*

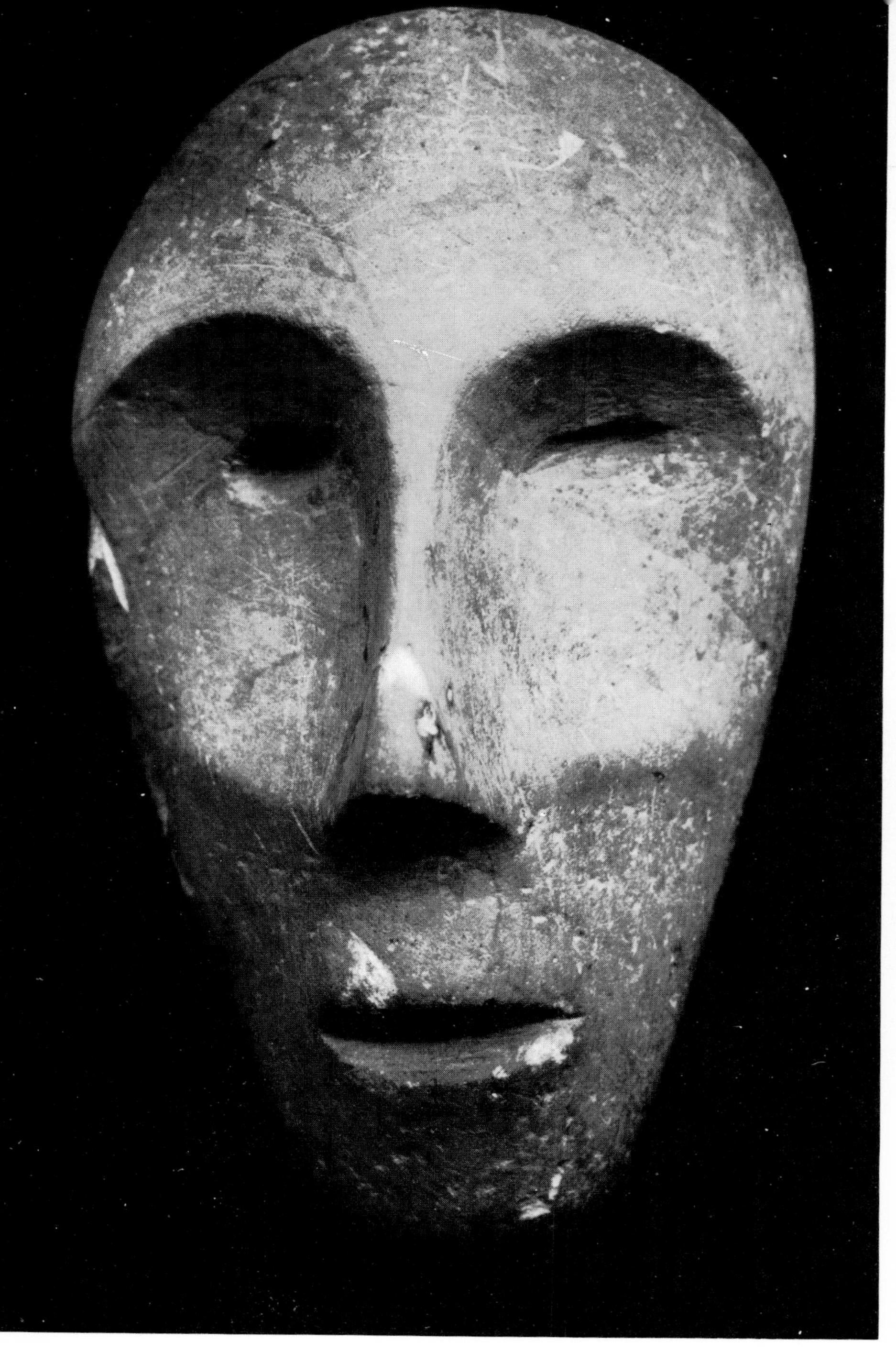

Fig. 97 (above). Stone face from Gallatin County, Kentucky. *Museum of the American Indian, New York.*

Fig. 98 (top right). Bowl of diorite with handle in shape of a crested male wood duck, from Hale County, Alabama. Diam. of rim, 11½ in.; H. (total) 12 in. *Museum of the American Indian, New York.*

Fig. 99 (right). Red stone pipe, from Moundville, Alabama. H. 4 in., W. 8½ in. *Museum of the American Indian, New York.*

Fig. 101 (above). Pottery jar, representing a seated hunchback figure, from Crittenden County, Arkansas. H. 8½ in. *Museum of the American Indian, New York.*

Fig. 100 (above). Pottery vessel from mound near Charleston, Mississippi County, Missouri. *American Museum of Natural History.*

Fig. 102 (right). Pottery jar representing a frog, from Mississippi County, Arkansas. H. 7½ in. *Museum of the American Indian, New York.*

III

THE UNITED STATES: FORESTS, PLAINS AND DESERTS

ALTHOUGH CLIMATE AND GEOGRAPHY ARE OF BASIC IMPORTANCE TO ART, THEIR INFLUENCE IS INDIRECT and not always readily apparent. The physical environment determines the way people live, and the kind of life they live affects their art.

PHYSICAL ENVIRONMENT AND RELIGIOUS BELIEFS

On the North American continent, even within the limits of the United States, there are great variations in climate and in topography. There are the seacoasts, the heights of the Rockies, the expanses of the Great Plains, the deserts of the Southwest and the wooded hills of the East. There are lakes and great rivers, mountain barriers and fertile valleys, lands where the climate is always mild and regions where there are great extremes of heat and cold. No single primitive culture could have adapted itself to such varieties of environment.

Although we may think of the original inhabitants of this continent simply as "Indians," the many tribes had different ways of life. We have the hunter of the Great Plains, with his tepee, which he moved from place to place as he rode after the herds of buffalo; the farmer of the Southwest, cultivating his plot of corn and living in his adobe hut or many-roomed apartment house; the Iroquois of New York, following the deer and living in a bark-covered house. Between these extremes were other tribes with different languages and customs.

Wherever the living conditions favored agriculture, a rich material culture is often developed. Where people depended on hunting and led a nomadic existence following their game, the arts reflected that kind of life. Agriculture allowed leisure to pursue the crafts; a settled life in one place permitted more than the minimum of household equipment and personal effects.

In the Southwest, by which is meant Arizona, New Mexico and parts of adjoining states, the arts attained an importance unmatched in other regions except on the Northwest Coast. The climate was suitable for agriculture, which made possible a secure and less strenuous way of life. It was no accident that pottery was the favored craft, since water conservation was of utmost importance. But the Pueblo Indians of the Southwest not only developed fine pottery, they also excelled in its painted decoration.

In the Southwest, the most varied developments took place in a number of crafts: basketry, pottery, mural painting, sand painting, masks, textiles, silver and modern water color painting, which cannot all be explained solely on an environmental basis, by climate, geology and geography.

In comparison with these more favored regions, the thinly populated Great Plains contributed less to the development of art. The hunter produced only such implements as he could carry. When a move was necessary, the Plains Indian woman could more easily take with her a half-finished piece of quillwork or beadwork than an incomplete piece of pottery. In the Plains, animals furnished the basic materials for art, since quill and beadwork were often done on finished skins and painting on buffalo hides.

The forested land east of the Mississippi was suitable for agriculture, and here again a more stable culture arose. In the cleared areas the Indians planted and harvested their crops, while the forests and streams yielded a part of their food. Though wood was available in great quantities, no wood carving developed comparable to that of the Northwest Coast. Large-scale wood carving involving the use of the figure was entirely absent. The forest Indians carved bows, clubs, paddles, small household utensils and masks.

Generally speaking, the Indian's reverence for the supernatural power he believed in expressed itself in ceremonies, songs and dances, through visions, fasting, prayers and sacrifice, rather than through painting, large sculpture or architecture. We know that many objects had a religious significance, but it is equally true that other objects of art were largely decorative.

The False-face masks of the Iroquois Indians and the masks of the Southwest's Pueblos represent important applications of art to ritual paraphernalia. Navaho sand paintings are still a part of a religious ceremony and were not made solely for artistic purposes. Kachina dolls were for religious instruction, and some baskets and some pottery were set aside for ritual purposes. The kind of pottery which was held sacred was often unimportant artistically. Some motifs used in pottery decoration had a symbolic-religious meaning, like clouds, frogs, insects and others associated with water. In the Southwest they were visual prayers for rain where life was dependent on moisture.

THE HISTORICAL BACKGROUND

A division between prehistoric and historic makes for a convenient orientation of Indian art of the United States. By far the greater portion of art that has been preserved belongs to the historic period.

Since the Indians had no writing, history begins for each tribe with its discovery by white men. Some tribes were discovered in the early sixteenth century, others not until Lewis and Clark opened the Northwest in the early nineteenth century, so that the length of the recorded history varies between one tribe and another according to the region.

The following areas made important contributions to art during the prehistoric period: the Southwest, with its painted pottery and murals; and the eastern woodlands, particularly in the south, with stone and ceramic sculpture, copper ornaments and wood carvings. The widely distributed petroglyphs cannot be assigned to definite periods, though many of them certainly go back to a time before the coming of the white man. Practically everything else in Indian art belongs to the historic period, and on the basis of the tree-ring calendar it has been possible to assign approximate dates to prehistoric Pueblo cultures and their crafts.

The archaeology of the Southwest is complex and of interest chiefly to specialists. For pottery, several stems have been traced back to the early centuries of the Christian era. Three prehistoric cultures may be mentioned; the Anasazi, the Mogollon-Mimbres, and the Hohokam. Modern pottery styles, with which we are here primarily concerned, grew out of one or another of half a dozen different roots comprising, perhaps, some fifty different prehistoric styles. Of these we shall discuss examples of only two; Casa Grandes and Mimbres. Though pottery takes on a special historical significance, a good deal more is known of the prehistoric Indian culture of the Southwest.

Ancestors of today's Pueblo Indians, the so-called "Basket Makers," lived in the Southwest, it is thought, between 300 and 700 A.D. They raised corn, squash and beans, developed basketry, began work in pottery and started to build permanent homes.

Probably between 700 and 1100 A.D. newcomers fused with the Basket Makers to form a new group called the Anasazi, or ancient people. They developed the primitive "pit house" into larger clusters of rectangular rooms, of which the great D-shaped apartment house at Pueblo Bonito is an example. Cotton was grown, pottery was developed and probably there was some loom weaving. Basketry was less important. Among the pottery styles of the Southwest of this period are those of the Mimbres culture, the finest of all Southwest prehistoric pottery, and the Sikyatki style developed by the Hopi and revived by them in our own period.

The period between 1100 and 1300 A.D. brought architecture, pottery, cotton weaving, work in skin and stone to their greatest development. Approximately between 1276 and 1298 it is believed that a drought of twenty-two years contributed to the abandonment of the Pueblo dwellings for new places near streams and springs. The new settlements were close to those occupied today.

Between the sixteenth and eighteenth centuries, under the rule of the Spanish, some of the Indian crafts, like pottery, declined in favor of purely utilitarian wares. However, sheep were introduced by the Spaniards, as well as wool carding, dyes, knitting, embroidery and better house building.

With the establishment of Mexican independence from Spain (1821), horses and burros formerly used by the Spaniards were acquired, and the Pueblos and the Navaho learned silverwork. The Southwest became a part of the United States in 1848 and 1853, and a new period of art can be dated from about 1880. Pottery revived, partly under the influence of American archaeologists, and weaving declined through competition with commercial textiles introduced from the East. Federal legislation of 1929 and 1932 gave the Pueblos new land, encouraged the revival of crafts and helped to make the Indians self-supporting. Weaving and silverwork were revived, and crafts were taught in government schools.

The prehistoric development of the eastern part of the United States is only beginning to receive approximate dates. Of the several archaeological areas, the Hopewell culture centering in southern

Ohio has been approximately dated from 500 B.C. to 500 A.D., though archaeologists tend to vary on such dates. The question of dating in the whole sculpture area, like the regions of New England, New York and Ontario, the lower Mississippi Valley and the Southeast has still not evolved sufficient definition in all regions for a general historical background comparable to what is known of the Southwest.

As Indians did not move into the Great Plains in large numbers until after they had acquired the horse from the Spaniards, Plains Indian art was probably not produced to any great extent until after the middle of the seventeenth century. It is known that beadwork did not develop until after 1800.

One historical factor of importance, the early European occupation of North America, has tended to preserve some remnants of these handicrafts because white men collected them as curios. A scientific interest in the artifacts of another culture, dating back to the early days of the republic, resulted in the collection of Indian articles by museums and historical societies.

GENERAL CHARACTERISTICS

In comparison with the accomplishments of the highly civilized cultures of Middle America and the Andean regions of South America, some of the major arts as practiced within the area of the United States were provincial in character. Indian art developed no outstanding stone architecture. The prehistoric communal houses, whether erected in the plain or on the sides of cliffs, represent an accumulation of small rooms involving no architectural principle that was not already inherent in the individual unit. Their interest is archaeological rather than artistic. Where sculpture was practiced, the objects carved were small in size but often vigorous in their emphasis on form and entirely satisfying aesthetically.

There is no unified style in American Indian art. Instead, we have a number of regional styles which differ widely in materials, techniques and expressions. The crafts were widely distributed as well as specifically concentrated. But although a certain craft may be associated with a particular region in which it was especially well developed, the same craft was also practiced by other tribes where it fulfilled similar needs. There is no one craft which is the exclusive property of any one tribe or region.

Indian art made use of geometric designs as well as realistic motifs based on the human figure, animal and plant forms, both during the prehistoric and historic periods.

THE EASTERN WOODLANDS; SCULPTURE AND POTTERY

Art objects of the prehistoric period have been recovered from many sites in the Mississippi Valley and southeastern states. Most of these pieces are under a foot high; a few statues are as high as two feet. The prehistoric cultures to which these works of art have been ascribed are named after important sites of excavations like Hopewell and Adena, or by geographic locations like middle or lower Mississippi.

Some carvings and engravings from the lower Mississippi and Adena cultures show a stylistic relationship to Mexico. How this is to be accounted for is not clear, whether through an influence from Mexico or through the presence of Mexicans in these regions. Except for a smaller scale and a more restricted range of materials and motifs, this style compares favorably with Mexican art.

Stone carving has been linked to the so-called Mound Builders, a name given to many different tribes who erected mounds of one kind or another. We know their cultures from excavations of the characteristic mounds, which were often burial places, though they may have served other purposes as well. Mound-building tribes have left thousands of copper tools, weapons and ornaments, and quantities of pottery, but most noteworthy is their carving in stone.

An outstanding and unique example of the Adena culture, showing the Mexican style, is a figure in the form of a pipe (Fig. 93), eight inches high. The mouthpiece is above the head, the bowl between the legs; no stem is used. It is carved of fine-grained hard clay, of a soft yellow color in front and brick red behind, and is smooth and polished; the mottled effect is due to iron in the clay. The style is mature and the treatment consistent throughout. In head, shoulders, torso, legs, hands and feet, the fully rounded forms imbue the figure with a chunky sturdiness. The rigid posture may have been taken over by the carver from larger figure sculpture, even though no examples this side of Mexico have come to light. Ear plugs, the cast of the features, the muscular build with an emphasis on shoulders and arms are characteristics also found in sculpture to the south.

A relationship to Mexico is indicated in a sandstone disk in the Ohio State Museum, Columbus. It is eight and one-half inches in diameter, engraved with two twined rattlesnakes with feathered heads, the Plumed Serpent, and is a masterpiece of design. Traces of red and white paint indicate that the grooves were filled with pigments which brought out the design; the disc may have served as a palette for a ceremonial use.

A Mexican style is also apparent in engraved shell gorgets, circular marine shells pierced to be worn as pendants engraved on the concave side. These white ornaments may be presumed to have been symbols of religious or civil authority. One shell from Sumner County, Tennessee, three and three-eighths inches in diameter, in the Museum of the American Indian, New York, is in the form of a square with looped corners and long-beaked birds projecting from the middle portion. A pierced center is placed within an engraved eight-pointed star; two holes in one bird's head suggest that these shells were worn on a cord. The design, incised with stone tools, has extraordinary vigor, a fine sense for space relations and an accomplished technique. Another shell gorget (Fig. 94) shows an engraved kneeling figure holding a severed head and a stone cleaver.

A few of the finest specimens have been excavated in Spiro Mound, in eastern Oklahoma. They are in a style different from the pipes of the Ohio mounds, but their equal in artistic quality. A choice specimen, a large pipe head in the Museum of the University of Oklahoma, shows a crouching figure with a large, forceful head and diminutive hands, a finely modeled nose and drooping mouth. Sensitiveness and force are combined in an unusual way. There is an impetuous vigor, an expression of self-confidence on the part of the artist, on a level with the best of the art of Mexico. A shell fragment from Spiro Mound (Fig. 95) is as interesting as the pipe head. The sureness of the strokes indicates the routine of the experienced draftsman. This fragment shows the upper part of a painted or tattooed man with an agitated expression. The two-pointed, hook-like motif placed around the eye has been referred to as the "weeping eye." Those who implored the gods in the festivals of the Chibcha Indians of Colombia (South America), according to Alfred Metraux, were known to have worn masks with tears to encourage the god to pay heed to their prayers. The "weeping eye" symbols might also have been used as masks, as well as isolated motifs in painted body decoration, as is here the case.

Not all stone sculpture shows a Mexican resemblance. The Hopewell culture of southern Ohio may be a regional development uninfluenced by Mexico. Fifteen different animals and twelve different birds found in Tremper Mound in Ohio represent one of the two important discoveries of the Hopewell culture. These carved stone pipes in the form of animals and birds reveal a keen observation of nature by emphasizing the individual character. A hawk carved to form a pipe (Fig. 96) shows the bird in a lifelike posture. The structure of the bird is stylized but convincingly rendered. In other pipes, an otter holds up its head swallowing a fish, a raccoon looks down, a black bear and a squirrel are represented in sitting postures and a heron and a crane stretch their long necks to drink.

The carved pipes of the prehistoric period probably also had a religious connotation, comparable with the tobacco and pipe smoking ritual of the Indians of the historic periods. It is conceivable that the blowing of smoke suggested to the Indian a means of communication between his person and the invisible deity. The reasoning for this might have been something like this: if an earthly substance, tobacco, closely identified with the person through smoking, could become invisible and one with the Supreme Being, so could prayers rise to his level and there find acceptance. Such a theory cannot be proven and ethnology may offer no evidence in its support. On the other hand it illustrates one way that sympathetic magic might have operated in the mind of the Indian.

Flat stone faces, usually under twelve inches high, have been found in a number of places. Unlike Mexican masks, they have a primitive character of their own, which grows directly out of the stone carving technique. After the pecking and grinding process had hollowed out the stone to create major space divisions, a pleasing, essentially linear pattern stood out (Fig. 97). Individual masks resemble each other in the eyebrow and nose line but vary in details.

A diorite bowl from Alabama (Fig. 98) represents, artistically, a supreme achievement. The bowl is eight inches high and has a bent handle in the form of a crested male wood duck. The contour is firm, incised lines enhance the curved form and the bowl's sturdy birdhandle is well related to its size. This bowl is one of those rare pieces that transcend periods; ageless and modern at the same time.

A large ceremonial pipe from Moundville, Alabama, (Fig. 99), four by eight-and-a-half inches, has the back hollowed out to form the bowl; the stem was attached at the base in front of the crouching figure. The pipe is of pink porphyritic sandstone, and an uneven pitted surface is sensitively carved with the head lifted in the direction of the smoker. The best view is from the side, showing the broad back and the firm profile of the long head.

Some pottery effigy jars, like one from Missouri showing a human head modeled out of the surface of the pot (Fig. 100), are delicate in total shape and in the modeled face. The vase-like shape of the jar is maintained, the face is subordinate. In a pottery jar six inches high, from Arkansas, the whole jar takes on the shape of a head, showing incised decorations, perhaps tattooing. A jar representing a seated hunchback figure (Fig. 101) suggests a mummy in the skeleton-like arms and ribs. In all three effigy jars the eyes are closed, suggesting a connection with death.

Pottery effigy jars in the shape of animals like dogs, frogs, fish, birds and other animals native to the regions have been found in stone graves of Tennessee and Arkansas and suggest the pottery dogs of the Tarascan Indians of Mexico. Some animals look as if gently inflated, perhaps to make them useful as full-bodied containers without losing their identity as animals. A frog (Fig. 102) with a wide cylindrical opening superimposed on his irregular body is a little masterpiece of ceramic sculpture. The concept of a naturalistic animal was perhaps the beginning out of which craftsmen in the course of a long tradition developed these shapes. It is also possible that the pot shape suggested the animal.

The human hand played a part in primitive art. Hands cut out of thin sheets of mica have been excavated from graves of the Hopewell culture. One from the Chicago Natural History Museum (Fig. 103), like others of the same type, emphasizes the extreme elegance of the linear pattern and neglects entirely the realistic appearance. Magic and symbolism may have been more important than any close resemblance to a real hand.

Banner stones is a name given to a large group of objects that have been found around the Great Lakes and in the states south of this region. They were symbols of authority, personal ornaments or objects of a religious significance. Their abstract shapes indicate that the prehistoric Indians were sensitive to a purely aesthetic appeal and possessed the technical ability to create beautiful objects with primitive tools.

MASKS

Two important areas of masks in North America, the regions of the Eskimo and the Northwest Coast, have already been discussed. The Southwest, including the Pueblo, Navaho and Apache Indians, and the Iroquois of New York State and Ontario also developed distinct mask styles. Various other tribes, east and west, used masks, but to a lesser extent.

The Iroquois masks have been studied by William N. Fenton, and this discussion is based on Fenton's research.

Wooden masks were carved for use by members of the False-face society, who, when a member of the tribe was ill, staged ceremonies and dances to frighten away the evil spirits who sent the disease. The evil spirit responsible was believed to be a strange creature with staring eyes and long hair. The masks were carved with staring eyes, streaming horse tails for hair and a show of teeth (Fig. 104). The masks or False-faces are portraits of mythical beings who, according to the Iroquois Indians, "only a little while ago inhabited the far rocky regions at the rim of the earth or wandered about the forests."

Masks cured ailments like swelling of the face, toothache, inflammation of the eye, nose bleeding, sore chin and earache. Certain symptoms, like red or black spots on the patient's face, were False-face symptoms. Red spots called for red face masks who must dance in the morning before sunrise whereas black spots called for black masks at night. We have here another instance of the way sympathetic magic functions in the lives of primitive people, and the close link between art and magic.

The modern Iroquois distinguish two main classes of masks: the Leader, "the great fellow who lives on the rim of the earth . . . and his underlings . . . the common forest people, whose faces are against the trees." The face of the Leader is "red in the morning as he comes from the coast, but black in the afternoon, as he looks back from the direction of the setting sun." The masks representing him are painted red or black and show a broken nose, as he was struck in the face by the mountain. The other class of mask, the "Common Faces," is less well defined and the masks are more varied.

Iroquois masks have deep-set eyes, which are emphasized by bright metal sconces; the noses are usually bent; the arched brows are wrinkled and may be divided above the nose by a crease or comb of spines. The mouth is the most variable part of the face. It may be turned up in a smile or grimace or it may be oval-shaped for blowing hot ashes, a part of the cure, and the tongue may protrude (Fig. 105). The mouth may be puckered as if whistling or it may be shaped like a spoon; it may even be straight.

Fenton distinguishes twelve different mask types: crooked-mouth; straight; spoon-mouthed; hanging mouth; tongue protruding; smiling; whistling; divided half red, half black; long nose; horned; animal and blind masks. All these were carved from living bass wood. Some represent young, some old men with white hair and wrinkled faces. Dreams, visions and the imagination of the carver could be held responsible for the styles.

Goldenweiser, as quoted by Fenton, posed the problem and suggested the answer, to quote, "Various grotesque spirits must be regarded as derived either from dreams or visions, or to be the outgrowth of the free play of the imagination. . . . Thus, it is highly probable that the False-face spirits of the Iroquois are the projections into the spiritual world of the grotesque wooden masks worn by the members of the False-face Society. . . ."

There are other societies that employ masks, for example the Society of Husk Faces or Bushy Heads. Their masks look like braided door mats (Fig. 106) on which the pile is cut off on the inside for the face, leaving a bushy fringe around the outside. Holes are cut for eyes and mouth. Husk Faces are said to be a race of agriculturalists who taught mankind hunting and agriculture. They visit the Seneca long house during two nights of the Midwinter Festival.

Southeastern Florida has contributed several fine pieces of wood carving, sensitive in their simplified naturalism, that were dug up in 1895 at Key Marco from deposits of wet muck. The few pieces that resisted the strain accompanying drying are now in The University Museum, Philadelphia. They include heads of animals, alligators, wolves and deer, showing traces of paint, shell inlays and leather hinges to facilitate movement, suggesting that they were made for a ceremonial use. The wood carvings have been attributed to the now extinct Calusa Indians of the fifteenth century.

THE GREAT PLAINS

The Great Plains stretch from the Mississippi River to the Rocky Mountains and from the Gulf of Mexico north into Canada. The tribes fall into two main groups, a western and an eastern. Those farther to the east lived a large part of the time in permanent villages of earth lodges; they depended on agriculture but also shared many of the features of the true Plains culture. The true Plains tribes that we usually think of in connection with the buffalo, on which they were so largely dependent, are the tribes of the west. As hunters, they did not develop basketry, pottery or true weaving, and had no large works in stone or wood. Their contributions to art are painted hides and quill and beadwork.

PLAINS INDIAN PAINTING

Geometric Style

During the period of buffalo hunting hides were plentiful. After the skins had been cleaned they were put to a variety of uses, among which were the covering of tepees, shields, rectangular folded containers or pouches, called parfleches, and robes for wear. They were decorated by incised designs or by painting. The painted hides fall into two groups: a geometric style painted by women, and a representational style painted by men. There was rarely a mingling of the two styles.

The robes of the geometric style frequently have borders, which more or less follow the irregular contours of the hide. A single large design motif, usually consisting of a number of smaller units, may be placed practically in the middle of this field. John C. Ewers has classified the design motifs into five basic types: rectangle within border, or border and box, hourglass within border, feathered circle, stripes and examples of symmetry. All conform to a simple system of space division, although actually they are not as monotonous as they might seem from a mere listing of the type designs. Even the border and box pattern achieves a delicacy in the way the rectangle is divided into small units; through the contrast of colors and an excellent technique, the painted hides are attractive. The feathered circle shows lines radiating like rays in several concentric circles from the center. Here, too, the use of many rays, each emanating from its own circle, adds complexity to the pattern. Feathered circle patterns on robes are believed to indicate that the robes were worn by men; border and box pattern robes were worn by women. Personal preference does not seem to have entered into the choice of pattern. An approximation of the shape of the buffalo is suggested in the hourglass pattern.

A tribal distribution of patterns has not been conclusively demonstrated. It appears that the feathered circle and border and rectangle type of designs were preferred by the Sioux (Dakota) Indians, but these types of patterns were also used by other tribes. All Comanche robes studied by Ewers showed the hourglass pattern type, though the same type also occurred in robes attributed to other tribes. Both of these types were largely limited to the central Plains tribes.

Red, yellow and blue are the colors most favored. An outstanding preference for red suggests that the exciting quality of red may have been a deciding factor, assuming that the other pigments were equally available. No symbolic meaning of colors has been suggested.

A group of Mandan buffalo hides, which Maximilian von Wied collected in 1834 and which are now in the Berlin Museum, have design patterns that are either geometric in character or are highly formalized in the distribution of the motifs. These designs are simpler than those described by Ewers. In one instance rows of arrows spread evenly across the skin, in another double pronged forks are arranged in rows, while in a third, weapons, rifles, bows and arrows are arranged in rows. There is a startling sense of freshness in the painting, even though the pattern consists only of rows of linear motifs.

Realistic Style

Painted hides representing human beings or animals have been classified by H. U. Hall as time-counts, which are records of events taking the place of calendars, records of personal achievement (Fig. 107) or imaginative records of visions. The events depicted on the buffalo robe were visible proofs of the bravery of the chief who wore it, a means of reminding his fellows of his prowess in war.

Not all pictures of battles are based on authentic events, but whether the events represented are based on reality or imagination does not affect their value as works of art, nor does the fact that many were painted for sale rather than use as early as 1877. The painted skins in the realistic style do not represent the environment in the sense of being pictorial. The human figure and the horse appear, vividly painted without indication of background or any suggestion of space. Battle scenes (Fig. 108) and horse-stealings are common; animals other than the horse are rare; the buffalo hardly appears at all and the dog never.

The technique is one of outline and flat tone filled in with solid colors, different from one figure to another. Red is the color most frequently used, followed by yellow and blue.

The realistic style adheres to tribal patterns. Different tribes draw men and horses in more or less standardized fashions which vary from the schematic types of the Cree and Mandan to the realistic, technically superior types of the Sioux and Cheyenne. All but the Sioux drawings neglect feet and leave out hands.

A painted robe was looked upon as a practical device to advance personal prestige. A painted hide was worth only two unpainted hides at a time when hides were common. Yet this does not prove that Indians were lacking in discrimination of artistic excellence but rather that robes were not collected as art objects.

Plains Indian drawings are comparable to Bushman drawings but they are less stylized. They are also different from Eskimo engravings: they are more narrow in subject matter and lack the story-telling breadth. Painting of the Plains tribes, geometric and realistic, was undeveloped and not on the level of the Northwest Coast Indians.

At the close of the buffalo era, after hides were no longer available, paintings on paper and cloth were executed by Plains Indians. This style departed from tribal tradition by representing in lively fashion battles and personal episodes reminiscent of inter-tribal exploits. An expression in painting of the individual made itself felt. Many of these early works have not been preserved as they were not yet recognized as art. Others were collected by members of the United States armed forces on duty in the western states. Some of this material is now in museums and private collections. So far nothing is known between this early period and the contemporary revival in water color painting.

QUILLWORK AND BEADWORK

Accounts of porcupine quillwork and of beadwork have been published in considerable detail by Ewers and by Carrie A. Lyford. The technical information here presented is based on these sources. Both crafts were practiced at some time over the entire northern half of the United States and in Canada, spreading beyond the area of the Plains. Porcupine quillwork is a thoroughly American craft, unknown in other parts of the world with the possible exception of Siberia. It precedes and was supplanted by beadwork. Some pieces of quillwork are of some antiquity, although most examples are more recent.

Quillwork and beadwork, like the preparation of the skins and the making of clothing, were women's work. These painstaking decorations were applied to articles of men's and women's clothing, footwear, horse trappings, bags and pouches, cradles and ceremonial objects. In some tribes they were applied to birch bark as well as to leather.

Dampened, the quills could be bent to any shape and would hold that position when dry. To decorate a slender article, like a pipestem, the quills were wound around it. In embroidery, the quills were folded and plaited over threads of sinew, which were stitched to the leather. The stitches passed only part way through the leather and did not show on the under side. Some quills were used in natural color, others were dyed with vegetable, and later with commercial, dyes. The designs were geometric (Fig. 109): stripes, bars, squares, oblongs, triangles or circles. Floral designs, where they occur, were probably influenced by white men's designs.

Quillwork placed a restraint on freedom in designs and favored straight lines although plant and animal shapes of simplified contours were not entirely excluded. The Indians must have welcomed colored beads, which needed no preparation and provided greater opportunities for decoration. The flexibility of beadwork allowed curves to be made as easily as straight lines. Beadwork began with the introduction of European beads. Indians had long made necklaces of animal teeth, bone, seeds and many other materials and the first European beads, being large, were used in the same way. It was the tiny Venetian bead known as "seed bead," which appeared about 1800 in the East and 1850 in the West, which made possible the accomplished beadwork of the Indian craftswomen. The seed beads have continued popular to the present time, but the best period of beadwork was the last quarter of the nineteenth century.

The technique of beadwork is somewhat similar to that of quillwork and was generally applied to nearly everything made of skins. The more elaborately embroidered suits or dresses, representing the work of months, were not for everyday wear but for ceremonials or special occasions. Beaded articles were saved for burial garments; they also served as a medium of exchange or as gifts to be given away on great occasions.

Methods of construction were according to tribal traditions, but designs were shared and motifs borrowed, one tribe from another. Geometric designs are impersonal, and no rigid separation into tribal styles is easy to demonstrate. Early design motifs are simple and geometric, blocks and crosses. Among the Blackfeet, floral patterns, probably inspired by white man's designs, became as popular as geometric. A double curve, as has been suggested, may have been derived from cast iron stoves. Floral designs still are popular with the Blackfeet for their own use. Among the western Sioux a sudden change in design motifs took place about 1870 when thin lines, terraces and forks appeared. Frederick H. Douglas discovered a surprising resemblance between these designs and those on common household rugs which were imported from the Caucasus and probably brought west by well-to-do settlers. Whatever the sources, the geometric shapes, pressed leaves or motifs borrowed from embroidery, were adapted to the bead technique apparently with an intuitive understanding of design.

An emphasis on craftsmanship did not exclude an aesthetic element. Even with a limited number of designs there was a choice in colors as well as in the use of line and mass and in the contrast of dark and light. The white and blue of the backgrounds made an attractive contrast against the buff color of the skin. The Indians had definite color preferences. The traders could not sell them beads in any color, but only those which were preferred. In spite of tribal patterns, there is a remarkable variation of designs in such objects as moccasins (Ewers). The earlier designs are apt to be in better taste; the more garish color combinations appeared after sale to the white man had become a factor.

The total effect of a piece of Indian beadwork is one in which artistry and practicality are happily united. The appeal is one of contrasting textures, shiny beads against mat skin, and complementary colors, light blue against soft tans, enhanced by dark areas held together against a light ground, or light areas on a darker ground. These pieces are well made of durable materials.

Beadwork is still practiced in some tribes, and is encouraged in some Indian schools. Since textiles have replaced leather and skins, a change in technique has taken place; linen or cotton thread is used in place of sinew and the sewing thread is passed all the way through the cloth so that the stitches appear on the under side.

THE ARTS AND CRAFTS OF THE SOUTHWEST

The Southwest region lying between the southern extension of the Great Plains and the West Coast includes New Mexico, Arizona, and parts of Utah, Nevada and California. It has a varied topography, ranging from mountains and plateaus called mesas to lowlands and deserts. The Indian cultures—over two dozen tribes are still living—were equally varied. Some tribes are very small today, having less than five hundred members, others have several thousand, like the Zuñi, Pima, Papago, Hopi and Apache. The Navaho, the largest tribe in the United States, number over seventy thousand, and they have produced some of the finest art. The Navaho shepherds live on a reservation in northeast Arizona. There is no single Pueblo tribe, but there are forty-four pueblos or villages in New Mexico and Arizona inhabited by sedentary agricultural Indians of four linguistic families who differ also in customs and beliefs. The Hopi of north central Arizona and the Zuñi of western New Mexico are among the best known Pueblo Indians. The Pima are semi-agricultural. The crafts are highly developed in the Southwest, certain tribes excelling in a number of different ones.

PETROGLYPHS

Petroglyphs are pictures painted or engraved on rocks, as differentiated from pictographs, a term reserved for pictures painted on skins. This terminology has been suggested by Julian H. Steward, who has most recently worked in this field.

The oldest examples of petroglyphs may date back several thousand years; others, which include such items of European origin as firearms and horses, must be more recent.

We know from the early missionaries of southern California that petroglyphs existed in the late eighteenth century. According to F. F. Latta's report about Wukchumne Indians of southern California, the immediate vicinity of petroglyphs had a supernatural or sacred significance. These same Indians said that "the paintings were generally placed at an important village site, one that was permanently inhabited, or at some place where Indian ceremonies were performed." Though some California Indians were familiar with the rock paintings in their regions, they attached no importance to them and did not explain their meaning beyond recognizing designs for which they gave the Indian names. Some California rock painting is presumably the work of Yokuts Indians, who also painted "breech clouts, bows, arrows, buckskins and even faces and bodies." Some petroglyphs may have been painted within the historic period, as Latta suggests, for the amusement of the painter, or the interest and speculation of white men. The Indians of our own day no longer understand their meaning.

Petroglyphs showing figures, animals and "magic" symbols were pecked with a hammer, or they were rubbed, or painted with a brush in red, white, black, yellow and orange (Fig. 110). Those of the West are found on vertical cliffs in California, Nevada, Utah, Colorado, Arizona, New Mexico and in many other areas. In California alone petroglyphs have been found at more than one hundred twenty-five sites. Large petroglyphs, eighty feet long and fifteen feet high, are found in canyons and caves in Texas and in Barrier Canyon in southern Utah, where large, square-shouldered figures are painted on the smooth, sandstone wall (Fig. 111).

Some petroglyphs are believed to be records of dreams or visions in connection with puberty initiation ceremonies. One of the painted designs of Carriso Rock in the Santa Barbara area shows a planned design with major and minor motifs symmetrically related. This design may be a picture of an event, or it may illustrate a myth or a vision with a mythological content. A dedication, a blessing or a thanksgiving after a triumph may be indicated. Two figures (twins) stand with arms locked and raised (in prayer) with lines (incantations) rising from their heads (mouths). The fact that the two figures stand on what looks like a centipede suggests that this may be an illustration of the Navaho creation myth, according to which twin heroes slew the great centipedes that were destroying man. Paired figures, the twin brothers of light, occur in the Navaho creation myth and in Navaho sand-painting themes, like the Sky Father and the Earth Mother. The centipede motif also occurs elsewhere, as on a Chiricahua Apache painted leather poncho in the Museum of the American Indian, New York.

Human beings in petroglyphs are highly schematic, and occasionally designs appear that suggest the human figure combined with other motifs.

MURAL PAINTING

Large murals, ten feet long and four feet wide (Fig. 112) have been found in the Pueblo ruins of north central Arizona in the Jeddito Valley, at the ruined village sites of Awatovi and Kawaika. They were painted on the walls of the kivas, the Hopi ceremonial chambers, where they formed a background for religious ceremonies which included altars, ritual objects, costumes, dances, songs and prayers. The meaning of these highly abstract designs is unknown; but the shapes, white on an orange background, are at times recognizable. A tailed quadruped stands on either side of the central circle with its open mouth overlapping the circle and with one front leg raised. A standard projects into the circle which is filled with a feather bundle; eagle feathers project out from behind each animal; a bird is seen above on the left; another, a parrot, on the right. The style of prehistoric Sikyatki pottery is here adapted to mural painting based on symmetry. A bowl excavated at Awatovi, in the Peabody museum, Harvard University, shows a design close to the scroll motifs coming from behind the legs of the animal. Cloud and corn motifs appear both in bowl and mural. The murals that have been excavated are apt to be fragmentary. This one is also restored but was fairly complete when first discovered.

From a study of the painted walls it appears that the wall was plastered with smooth brown adobe. The pigments, brownish red, yellow and white, were mixed with water. They wore off in time as they were not used in a true fresco technique, which applies the pigments to a coating of fresh lime mortar. Instead, the wall was replastered with adobe for new paintings. At Awatovi one wall had fifteen layers of paintings; at Kuaua, near Bernalillo, New Mexico, there were twenty-nine. By gluing these layers to cloth and peeling them off, each painting has been recovered. Murals at Kuaua show figures with kilts, white sashes, masks and head feathers. A bird suggests a motif still used on Pueblo pottery. A mural at Jemez Pueblo shows an arching rainbow, scalloped clouds, horned water serpents, Pueblo symbols of rain and blessing suggestive of Navaho sand painting.

According to Navaho mythology the prototypes of sand paintings were pictures made by the gods on black clouds spread on the floor. Realizing that human beings could not do this, the gods ordered the use of sand as a substitute. Each painting is necessarily ephemeral, and it is to Mary C. Wheelwright and the Museum of Navaho Ceremonial Art, at Santa Fe, New Mexico, that we are indebted for the copies, by modern artists, of the original designs (Fig. 113).

The actual production of the painting takes place in the medicine lodge and, like the Iroquois False-face dance, is part of a ceremony of healing. Every design and every ceremony is for the cure of a specific illness. "The 'Lightning Chant' cures snake bite, the 'Terrestrial Beauty' heals the spirit. The 'Big God' chant cures blindness and stiffness." Some contemporary medicine men are said to have a knowledge of over four hundred designs.

From four to twelve young men pour out the sand under the direction of the medicine man. To make the drawing the correct way is part of the ritual; though occasional details may be varied, every design is fixed and repeated each time in the same way. All lines are freehand; control and exactitude are emphasized and great skill is shown in pouring the sand in straight lines.

After a preparatory "four-day cleansing of body and mind," the patient is introduced into the painting itself and sits down on it, facing east. He is brought into physical contact with the god by having the sand touch him in the prescribed ritual. He drinks a liquid in which sand has been placed. The medicine man places pollen and white corn meal on the painting, and the patient does the same. Finally, in some cases, the body of the patient is painted with earth pigment.

The sand is believed to absorb the illness. After the ceremony is over, the sand is picked up, beginning from the center where the design started, and is placed outside, north of the lodge. Each day it is taken farther away to make it less likely that the evil will return.

Red, yellow, white and gray-blue sands are used; the colors are ground from sandstone, but corn-meal, ground flowers and the pollen of flowers, plants and trees are also used. Women are drawn with square heads, men with round; and they are also distinguished by color. Male and female gods and figures from myths are represented, together with the four holy plants, corn, beans, squash and tobacco. Different systems of color are used to designate the points of the compass.

This fusion of the arts of painting and medicine through the power of religion is unique in its variety and excellence. The ancient tradition has remained uninfluenced by the art of the white man. It has furnished a basis upon which native Indian painters of today have developed a style of their own which has gained wide appreciation.

A study of even a small number of Navaho sand painting reproductions, as they are now available, leaves one with an impression of great formality in which even the most complex patterns are under control. These designs have a crystalline clarity and an icy purity; a transparency that makes this art seem rational, calculated and imbued with a spiritual quality. Nothing is left to chance; a supreme system forces every detail into its place. But the motifs are not abstract; each is recognizable as deriving from nature and the visible world. As symbols of real things, every part has a name and performs a religious function known to the medicine man. But the principles of design, involving repetition, sequence, rhythm and balance are followed through with an unrelenting determination. The number of motifs used is limited, chiefly straight lines, zigzags, points, rectangles, circles and occasionally other curves. By variation of sizes for contrast and by using symmetry and bi-symmetry, effects of profusion are obtained, but always by new combinations of the few basic elements.

Each sand painting has about it a sense of perfection and finality, variation seems unthinkable and individuality has no place as far as any one painting is concerned. The total number of sand paintings known and recorded makes it clear that Navaho sand painting is immensely varied and rich. No other art developed by the ancient Americans is as compelling in its ability to inspire unqualified admiration.

Sand paintings were also made by the Apache, the Hopi, the Zuñi and various tribes in California, as well as by Plains tribes like the Blackfeet, but they were much less elaborate.

PREHISTORIC POTTERY

Navaho sand painting has one style, but Southwest pottery has many. In pottery we are best able to gauge the capacity of the Indian for self-expression, not only in contemporary but also in ancient pottery. Pottery began in a primitive way in the prehistoric period and has persisted to the present. Between 300 and 1540 A.D., the Pueblo group produced hundreds of varieties of pottery, but very little is known of the period between 1540 and 1800. Much of the pre-Spanish pottery has survived as pottery was placed in tombs, and fine collections exist in American and European museums. All styles, including those of the Spanish period, show a native inspiration without foreign influences. Where motifs from other sources have been introduced in contemporary pottery, they are linked to an Indian tradition.

Some early pots excavated from burial sites have a surface decoration which came from textiles pressed against the damp clay. Later, this expanded into the use of incised marks, lines and borders, which eventually led to more elaborate geometric and animal shapes, like birds and serpents. Where figures and animals were introduced they were still very simplified.

In the course of a few centuries the shapes became firm, and linear zigzags spread diagonally (Fig. *114*) in bold rhythms, black against white, as in a jar fifteen inches high attributed to the thirteenth century. A pottery effigy (Fig. *115*), dated about 1000 A.D., suggesting an animal without ceasing to be a pot, shows a small sheep head attached to the top of the neck and a linear geometric pattern in black on a white slip ground. Legs are added, stilt-like, to give the body support. No complete animal form has been thought out. An experimental approach is perhaps suggested by this kind of loose, haphazard combination of weak legs under a well-shaped body. The form and decoration have already taken on the firmness of a mature style.

Prehistoric Pueblo culture extended southward into Mexico, into the northern part of the state of Chihuahua. Several kinds of pottery have been excavated in the ruins and mounds of the Casas Grandes regions. Painted ware constitutes one of these groups of pottery. The so-called effigy vases show animal, bird and human heads as additions over part of the rim of the jar to form a kind of hood which leaves the back of the jar open. Plastic and painted decoration are combined in this style. Small ears and noses are attached through surface modeling (Fig. *116*); and in another group arms are laid on the torso in strips, and diminutive legs project out to widen the base, making the figures appear as if seated. They still look as much like pots as figures.

The character of the painted decoration is remarkable in its boldness and technical excellence. Straight lines and curves are well combined, and red and black areas are effectively contrasted against a light background. Lines are drawn with precision that shows control of the tool used, but also betrays the variation natural to the use of the human hand. A self-assured touch in the handling of the long, straight lines on a curved surface indicates that this type of design had advanced to a stage well beyond elementary beginnings. The patterns used may owe something to textile designs but do not seem to have been intended as parts of costume. The use of these effigy vases is unknown. They have been attributed to the fifteenth century of our era.

A Mohave pottery bottle from southeast California (Fig. *117*), collected about 1900, reflects a regional tradition. In contrast to the more sober and restrained geometric style of southern California, this effigy bottle has a rude, almost savage, vigor. The geometric decoration, buff on cream color, is painted in large strokes across the whole surface, in keeping with the expansive spirit of the style. Colored bead necklaces are placed around the necks of the heads. Though this example is recent, it recalls a more ancient style.

A prehistoric pottery style which achieved perfection in technique and decoration is the Mimbres ware of New Mexico. Mimbres pottery is typical only of one small region during a particular era of one period. The Mimbreños lived along the banks of the Mimbres river from about 900 A.D. to about 1150 A.D. Their potters created shallow bowls (Fig. *118*) which they painted on the inside, black designs on a white ground. Designs are both geometric (Fig. *118* and Ill. 15) and naturalistic (Fig. *119* and Ill. 16), but more than one-half of existing examples are geometric. During its development, the style changed from a heavy boldness to lightness and delicacy.

These painted decorations (Ill. 17) have a vitality that attracts attention and has an insistent appeal. They reveal subtleties of design and hint at meanings we cannot quite grasp because we are unfamiliar with the culture. A sense of energy seems to be reflected in each design. Lines and shapes are set in motion, but controlled and held in check within the circle. Zigzags flash in opposite directions and come to rest in angular scrolls. Broad bands narrow into thin stripes, and spherical triangles clamp all shapes into a close-fitting unit. All elements are integrated; there is no monotony, and symbolism may also be involved. What we can appreciate is the satisfying relationships of abstract designs and the elegance of two figures floating in light and air (Ill. 18). Liveliness and grace are happily merged with lines and shapes that grow out of the painter's brush as he modifies the border. The mechanical circle unbends to grant these tumbling figures a space of their own. On each side the rim turns in to form an attractive space filler. As if to keep the curves in balance, the artist supplies a contrast to the angular line worked into the border opposite the heads.

The art language of the Mimbreños is also our language. We react to these designs as we would to any comparable designs made in our own day. If we examine these designs critically—Cosgrove has published 740—we find they vary in artistic quality. Of the whole series, perhaps a third are definitely superior according to our standards and would be so judged by any contemporary art jury. What is remarkable about Mimbres pottery is the fact that, on an aesthetic basis, so many examples appeal to modern taste.

Ill. 15. Geometric designs from pottery bowls, Mimbres, New Mexico (Swarts Ruin). *After Cosgrove. Peabody Museum, Harvard University.*

Ill. 17 (left) and Ill. 18 (below). Designs from pottery bowls, Mimbres, New Mexico (Swarts Ruin). *After Cosgrove. Peabody Museum, Harvard University.*

Opposite: Ill. 16. Naturalistic designs from pottery bowls, Mimbres, New Mexico (Swarts Ruin). *After Cosgrove. Peabody Museum, Harvard University.*

The Pueblo potter today uses the coiling technique. She begins with a disk-shaped bottom which is pressed into a low mold. A long, snake-like roll of clay, formed with the hands, is coiled around the edge of the disk, the walls being built up to the desired shape and size. The vessel is smoothed and shaped either by the fingers and scraping tools or, among some tribes, by striking the outside with a wooden paddle against a rounded implement held on the inside. The pots are dried outside in the shade, then scraped to remove irregularities. The slip and painted decoration are then applied, and the pot is fired in a simple outdoor oven. The potter's wheel and the permanent kiln were never known to the American Indian.

The shapes most frequently made by the Pueblo Indians are jars and bowls, though new shapes have been added.

The decoration of pottery follows tribal traditions, but the designs are personal as well as traditional. One potter may not use another woman's design without asking permission. Ruth Bunzel quotes a Zuñi potter as saying: "I just sit and think what I shall paint. I do not look at anything but just think what I shall draw. . . . I always know just how it will look before I start to paint."

According to a Hopi potter: "Whenever I am ready to paint I just close my eyes and see the design and then I paint it." Potters are said even to have dreamed about the designs to be painted in the morning. The design is carried in the woman's head; use of paper and pencil seems to be exceptional. The pot is painted freehand; measuring is done only with the hand or fingers.

Though each Pueblo tends toward a style of decoration which is peculiar to it, there has been some mingling of styles. To identify a pot other factors may have to be considered, like weight and thickness, the shape and also the color of the clay. Styles varied regionally and from one period to another. A Zuñi jar made around 1875 (Fig. 120) is more severely geometric than others made since. Even so, the Zuñi have changed styles more slowly than other Pueblos.

Until recently some eighteen different Pueblo groups made pottery which was decorated more or less. Today the number is smaller as certain Pueblos, like the Zuñi, have abandoned pottery making. The well-known modern styles are of the Pueblos of Zuñi, Acoma, Hopi, San Ildefonso, Santa Clara, Tesuque, Cochiti, Santo Domingo, Santa Ana and Zia (Sia, or Tsia). So many variations have been introduced into some of the styles that only a few characteristic types will be mentioned.

Zuñi is a serviceable ware but heavy and coarse; its designs are linear and asymmetrical (Fig. 121). Overcrowding and solid areas of paint are avoided. One Zuñi potter is said to have explained: "If I use large designs, I leave large spaces between, so that it won't look dirty." (Bunzel) Crosshatching is preferred to solid paint; red is used sparingly; essentially Zuñi decoration is black-on-white. The style is characterized by uniformity and strong adherence to tradition. It is strictly limited in the use of motifs. (Ill. 19)

The Zuñi decorator divides her pot into two or four sections, each showing a bird, a deer (Fig. 122) or a rosette. The decoration on it is black with red details on a white background. The "stomachs" of the pots have their own designs. In modern Zuñi patterns, motifs like deer or spirals are confined to horizontal bands, other motifs are always reserved for vertical panels. Certain designs are characteristic for the neck and are never used on the body. The neck shows a smaller geometric pattern separated from the body decoration by a double black line left open in one place, said to be a "spirit path" so that the maker's soul will not be imprisoned.

The contemporary potter has a vocabulary of designs. One old Zuñi potter drew ninety-four motifs, her stock of patterns, of which twenty-four were explained to be old or obsolete.

In 1929 the village of Acoma produced the finest ware, light in color, hard, smooth and of almost eggshell thinness. Yet these pots are strong and watertight; "from all practical standpoints . . . the best Pueblo product." (Bunzel)

Acoma pottery has two styles; one naturalistic (Fig. 123), with bird and plant forms (a large vigorous bird with a parrot-like beak is typical), and one abstract, with patterns in complex angles and curves. The motifs of the two styles are never mixed. Acoma designs show greater variation than those of Zuñi, although Zuñi was always the larger village. Acoma geometric decoration (Fig. 124) covers the body of the jar from rim to base in a massive way. There are no horizontal or vertical divisions and the background is reduced to complete fusion with the black pattern. Background shapes count as designs just as much as do the black, red or striped areas. Triangular and leaf shapes result, also ribbons and diamonds. There are said to be no spirals or circular shapes.

Small pots show the same motifs reduced in number but not in scale. The Acoma pottery style is vigorous, but it is subject to changes like other art. Older jars do not yet show this overall highly integrated style but reveal more background, so that a black pattern is clearly painted on a white background.

Ill. 19. Painted design from Zuñi pottery, bird motif. *Denver Art Museum.*

The small bowl is characteristic for Hopi potters. Hopi bowls (Fig. 125) are low and wide and have a narrow mouth; such a shape is more easily balanced on the head. In Hopi pottery design the flat top of the shallow water jar is decorated with designs that emphasize line as a single motif or continue without subdivision of the circular rim-like surface. The attraction is also in the color of the background resulting from uneven firing.

Hopi designs are curvilinear and unsymmetrical conventionalized birds and feathers. This type of design is a modern adaptation of ancient designs found in the ruined village of Sikyatki (Fig. 126).

At San Ildefonso, several different styles were made, among them polished red and polished black, resembling Santa Clara ware, and an earlier style of black designs on cream. Contemporary San Ildefonso ware (Fig. 127) is noted for its lustrous finish in black or red with mat designs in the same color. A red slip is applied which is turned black by smothering the fire during the firing process. As the slipped surface has been polished to produce a luster, the painted designs in the same color appear dull against the polished background. The decoration is restrained and calculated to enhance the beauty of the background by contrast. It is reserved, avoids lines and complicated detail and adheres to balanced mass effects. The San Ildefonso style, so different from the other styles, brings the artistry of Pueblo decoration into sharp focus.

The Santo Domingo style (Fig. 128), black on cream, has large, white, egg-like ovals against a curvilinear black net pattern drawn thin on the sides and heavy at the ends. Bold simplicity is its character. Cochiti patterns have a delicate nervous quality. The designs show thin, thread-like birds in black against a wide expanse of cream backgrounds, while the Tesuque style has black borders in broad bands or curved elements, both based on line. This style is now rare.

The Santa Ana style of pottery favored massive angular shapes in red outlined in black against a grayish-white ground. This Pueblo no longer makes pottery. Zia design shows more variety than other Pueblos. A long-legged bird with a few long tailfeathers against white is typical. Plant sprays, conventionalized leaves and a few geometric motifs are also used. Santa Clara pottery is polished black or red all over. Five-pointed marks, called "bear paws," may be pressed into the soft clay. Santa Clara has also taken up the San Ildefonso style of lusterless designs in black against a polished background.

San Juan, Taos and Picuris pottery differ from other Pueblo styles in that instead of painting, lumps of clay are added for surface decoration. Examples of all these styles are found in several museums and collections throughout the country. The date of the Pueblo pottery is not of necessity any indication of its artistic worth. More and more the Pueblo crafts are turning from articles made for home use to those made by professionals to be sold to white people. Pots used to be made by every woman for domestic purposes; now pottery tends to be left to the hands of the more skillful and talented. Aside from commercially produced wares, that are not truly Indian, the pots are still individually made craft objects. Through the efforts of the Indian Arts and Crafts Board, high standards of artistic quality are being encouraged for the benefit of the producers and the discriminating public.

In Southwest pottery there are today, as there were in former periods, conscious revivals of ancient styles, for example at Hopi and San Ildefonso. Basic ceramic techniques have not changed, but the styles of decoration vary.

In the late nineteenth century during the Fewkes excavations of the ancient Pueblo of Sikyatki, Nampeyo (died 1942), a woman of Hopi First Mesa, became interested in the pottery being unearthed.

She began to imitate the technique, color and designs, and taught the craft to others. The Sikyatki-style pottery was made on First Mesa in quantity. Nampeyo's name has since become well known among artists and anthropologists everywhere. The pottery is still being made, though the potters no longer copy the old patterns but create new ones in the same style.

In San Ildefonso, the highly polished black pottery with dull black designs of Julian and Maria Martinez appeared about 1917. Their pottery, with its brilliant polish and perfection of technique, constituted a further development of traditional black pottery that has become world famous.

From a study of Pueblo pottery one concludes that the Pueblo artist works in ways little different from artists anywhere. There is an emphasis on good potting. We are told again and again that the Pueblo potter judges pottery from the point of view of how well it is made. The technical process receives attention primarily in the actual making, but what really stimulates the potter's imagination is the painted surface decoration. An awareness of aesthetic principles is indicated on the part of the Zuñi potters when they speak of trying to avoid "dirtiness" and to achieve a sense of light by leaving plenty of white background.

PUEBLO AND PLAINS INDIAN SCULPTURE

Several representations of the mountain sheep reflect Pueblo stone sculpture of the centuries preceding the Spanish occupation, thus paralleling the Aztec period in Mexico. A red porphyry specimen, dated perhaps, A.D. 1300—A.D. 1400, is under five inches high. It comes from the Mexican state of Chihuahua, formerly a part of the Southwest culture region. A more fully developed sculptural form is represented in a green stone effigy (Fig. 129) dated possibly 1500 A.D. and under seven inches long. Such pieces look as if they had been cut out of cylindrical or rectangular stones. In each case, perhaps, something of the original shape has been retained in the finished carving. Sioux war clubs in the shape of mountain goats (Fig. 130) of an unknown date were so carefully carved and so well finished that we think of such ceremonial objects as sculpture. These several pieces are close to certain kinds of modern sculpture in which the artist selects stones that may be changed into art forms with few modifications.

BASKETRY

Basketry is a kind of weaving in which the fibers are stiffer and harder than the soft and flexible materials used in textiles. Compared to crafts like sand painting and pottery, basketry is simple. Most aspects of basketry are more craft than art. The materials, their selection and preparation, and the uses to which the baskets were put belong to ethnology and are not necessary as preliminaries to a discussion of basketry as a form of art.

Of the four basic techniques, coiling, twining, wicker and plaiting, all but plaiting were widely distributed throughout the Southwest. Coiled baskets consist of a bundle of strands of the foundation material forming the warp or basic skeleton of the basket. This bundle, perhaps finger thick, is wrapped around with a flexible weft and fastened in place. The coil begins at the center of the bottom and forms a continuous spiral to the rim. Coiled baskets can be identified by the horizontal corrugations.

Twined baskets have vertical ribs or warps bound together with horizontal wefts. The warp is stiffer than the weft and in twined baskets the grooves or corrugations run vertically. They are the main indications of twined work. In this technique the stiff warps are laid out on the ground like the spokes of a wheel and two wefts move in and out around the spokes crossing between them.

Wicker is like twining except that only one weft is used, and in plaiting neither element is definitely warp or weft; both are active.

There are eleven different areas of basket making in the whole country, but the best baskets are from California (Fig. 131) and the Southwest. The number and variety of basketry styles, even within a single state like California, is very large. The Southwest is one of the great basket making areas of the world. Among the tribes active in coiled basket making are the Hopi, several branches of the Apache (Fig. 132), the Navaho, the Pima (Ill. 20), Papago and nearly a dozen other tribes. The Pomo tribe specialized in feather-covered baskets.

Closeness of weave is a characteristic of Southwest baskets. The Indian woman produces a basket of superior quality and beauty because she devotes much time and great pains to her work.

Craftsmanship also has an aesthetic aspect; a well-made basket is pleasing to the eye even without any pattern whatsoever. Where designs are used the artistic appeal is elaborated through the distribution of dark shapes against a light ground.

To appreciate tribal differences of style, we single out for comparison coiled baskets of the Hopi and Pima. In bowl-shaped baskets the Hopi designs have a character of their own; the darks tend to concentrate in large areas or broad bands. Pima designs in bowl-shaped baskets may also have dark areas in the center, but they are contrasted with a linear treatment. The Pima style has an elegance and an overall unity which is its chief claim to distinction whereas Hopi designs at their best are bold.

In the vertical type of Pima basket where the design is on the curving side, the effect may be due to the distribution of small dark areas or to a magnificent accent on zigzags that rise from base to rim in emphatic rhythms. No symbolism is known to be indicated in Pima baskets or in other styles. That the modern Indians are interested in design and not symbolism is suggested by the way they refer to their patterns. The Pima speak of "black centers" or "triangles locked together" by which they mean interrupted frets. What they refer to as "figured" does not mean human figures but a series of parallel dark stripes radiating out from the center. Some human figures do appear in their style, and they are believed to have been prompted by the demands of traders who suggested that the Indians use figures and animals to make their baskets attractive to white purchasers.

WEAVING

Weaving among the Southwest Indians had passed its early beginnings long before the arrival of the white man. Weaving, in one form or another, is indigenous with many tribes in many parts of the country. As an illustration of weaving in the East, the Menomini of Wisconsin at the time they were discovered in 1634 had woven yarn bags of vegetable fiber trimmed with buffalo hair. The Nez Perce wove bags of corn husks.

Ill. 20. Pima coiled basket design, "flower" pattern. *Denver Art Museum.*

There are three methods of weaving, a more elementary one-beam unstretched warp technique, and a true weaving technique with two beams with stretched warp. The triumph of the one-beam type was the Chilkat blanket, the best of the two-beam techniques is the Navaho blanket. A third type in which the warp was stretched over a roller-loom was limited to the Puget Sound region, where Salish weaving developed.

Navaho weaving goes back only some two hundred fifty years. Woven Navaho woolens are first mentioned in a Spanish document not earlier than 1706. The Navahos learned the art of weaving from the Pueblos, who had fled to the Navaho country after the Indian rebellion of 1680 to 1692. By the end of the eighteenth century Navaho blankets had become important in the Spanish colony for export. Yarns and dyestuffs have changed under the white man's influence but the Navaho loom itself is like the one used by the Pueblos, of the eighth or ninth centuries. From the male Pueblo weavers the Navaho weavers, who were women, took over the making of loomed cloth at the beginning of the eighteenth century. From the Spanish the Navaho acquired a bright red flannel cloth, *bayeta* in Spanish, *baize* in English, which they raveled to use as a weft material. This ushers in the best period of Navaho weaving, in the first half of the nineteenth century, inspired by finely woven Mexican-made *serapes*. European cloth and colors stimulated native production to achieve a high standard of excellence, so that the fine old *bayeta* blankets have become collectors' items. A fine example (Fig. 133) shows white and indigo blue zigzags on a rose-crimson *bayeta* ground, with a texture like heavy canvas. Small diamonds in the center turn to deep, large chevrons at the ends. In Navaho weaving, Indian art matched its skill against the best of European looms and produced a superior product in closeness of weave (fifteen warps and thirty-five to forty picks of weft to the inch), in color and in boldness of design.

From a design point of view, the problem was often one of bringing harmony into a pattern of contrasts, such as large scale zigzag lines against a background of fine stripes. Black stripes in a red background make the background seem darker. White diamonds in the field make a similar red background appear lighter. As if to keep the top and bottom borders from overbalancing a design, a web of diamonds was frequently placed in between.

The basic pattern developed out of the black and white stripes running crosswise, the Pueblo heritage. Out of this the Navaho developed their terraced patterns (Fig. 134). After 1863 the rectangular zigzags changed to obtuse angles and diamonds, at times even running lengthwise. Borders, in connection with rugs, are found after 1890. Essentially these are the basic changes that took place between 1800 and 1900, ignoring variations and transitions which either paralleled or succeeded these major changes.

Certain labels applying to patterns are used. In the so-called "Chief" blankets the central stripe was widened. The stripes are sometimes elaborated by addition of smaller motifs. The "Classic Period" blankets belong to the middle of the nineteenth century. "Slave" blankets combine motifs derived from the Spanish colonists with Navaho patterns. Navaho women taken in warfare between the Indians and the settlers as late as the eighteen sixties wove this type of mixed-motif blanket. Large central diamonds from Mexican serapes and other Mexican-Spanish motifs characterize this style. "Pictorial" blankets include pictures of houses, railroads, horses, cattle, birds, insects and even sand painting motifs. They are dated from the last quarter of the nineteenth century. Another elaboration of the striped type of design, called "banded-background" or "Moqui" pattern, consists of wide bands with a background of narrow stripes of black, brown or blue (indigo). "Wedge-weave" blankets show an allover array of zigzag lines arranged crosswise in uneven rows. The technique employed throws the warp out of line so that the zigzag becomes distorted and uneven. This style was popular in the 1880's and 1890's. Tișmasbas blankets are named after a locality west of Shiprock, New Mexico. Borders and swastikas were introduced into rugs by a trader of Crystal, New Mexico, in a style labeled "Crystal." Grays, whites, blacks and tans are emphasized in a type of design suggested to the Navaho by the same trader which is known as "Two Gray Hills" type.

The supply of commercial cloth threatened to put an end to woven blankets used as garments, but a demand for rugs kept the native craft alive. Reds were replaced by black, white, grays and browns, which continue to be woven at present. About 1915 the earlier colors and designs were revived, and blankets came back in addition to rugs. Native and commercial aniline dyes were used; native dyes include red, blue, black and yellow.

Here is an example of an obscure tribal craft which had its origin in the sixteenth century developing into a successful modern industry.

MASKS AND KACHINAS

Indian masks may be divided from the point of view of materials and technique into carved and constructed masks. Where wood was available, carved wooden masks assume the importance of sculpture, as among the Eskimo, the Northwest Coast and Iroquois Indians.

To the group of constructed masks belong those of the Apache and the Pueblos. The Apache mask is a cloth bag with slits cut out for the eyes. This forms the foundation for the elaborate headdress which is made of narrow strips of painted wood extending up in a great fan. This mask was derived from those of the Pueblo Indians, especially the Zuñi and Hopi. Masks in the form of leather helmets like those of the Zuñi allow for no plastic expression. Color and a great variety of materials, expressed in different mask designs, take the place of carving.

It should be emphasized that what we call art, particularly masks and costumes, is really religious paraphernalia used in connection with a rich and complex ceremonial. This is particularly true of Zuñi. The Zuñi ritual includes many things like magic, singing, dancing and offerings, in addition to a strict mode of living. The ceremonial pattern consists of a half dozen different cults, each one of which makes specific demands on citizens or priests, though not all cults involve public ceremonies.

Nearly all Pueblo tribes believe in Kachinas, or supernatural spirits. It is popularly believed that Kachinas are intermediaries between gods and men, but a controversy among experts still surrounds this point. Spirits are impersonated in ceremonial dances by human beings. The word Kachina refers to the spirits themselves, to the masked dancers who impersonate the spirits and to the small wooden dolls carved to look like the masked dancers (Color Plates, 10, 11 and 12). The Kachina cult is strongest among the Hopi and Zuñi. The Hopi Kachinas live on high mountains during half of the year, from July to January, and spend the remaining months with the Hopi tribes, living in their nine villages on the high plateaus of northeast Arizona.

The Kachinas of Zuñi live at the bottom of a nearby lake, from which they come at different times to visit Zuñi. The dancers wear costumes and masks, which are looked upon as the embodiments of supernatural power. While the dancer is participating in the dance he is controlled by the god. That fact gives an element of danger to human beings, and the masks are treated with respect. They must be appeased by regular offerings of nourishment and through silent prayer before the beginning of the ceremonies.

There are two types of Zuñi mask. Permanent, or priests', masks, which are descended from the gods, are owned by the tribes. Individual masks are privately owned, made especially for the owner, and measured to his head.

Zuñi masks are made of leather. They show a great variety chiefly because variations can be obtained by wrapping fur collars or pine wreaths around the neck, or by attaching beards, or by appending feathers, or by projecting mouths, snouts and horns. Eyes are slits emphasized by rectangular, triangular or circular painted decorations. Each variation expresses a particular Kachina and yet all conform to a pattern. There are helmet masks, bucket-shaped, that rest on the shoulders, and face masks, covering the upper part of the face, with an attached beard of horsehair to cover the lower part. Permanent masks are of the helmet type. Only the leather part of the mask is preserved; all paint and feathers are removed after each dance and the mask is painted and renovated every time it is worn. The mask is associated with an individual Kachina but does not attempt to express the character, which may be benevolent or hostile. Only one set of masks (those of the Koyemci) is individually characterized. As new Kachinas were created, new masks were invented. Once each detail had been decided upon, the character of the mask for that particular Kachina became fixed and permitted only minor variations in style.

The making of a mask is highly formalized. All tasks that go into the preparation of the pigments used on the mask as well as those used on the bodies of the wearers are performed according to prescribed ritual by persons traditionally assigned to each task. Once a mask has been completed it is given life by the kiva chief in a special ceremony. It is rubbed with chewed seeds of corn, bean, squash and other plants while the chief speaks prescribed words of blessing, requesting the spirit to call the rains when the time comes. After that the mask is painted first white and then blue. The mask has become "valuable and a person."

When the Kachinas leave, the people make little figures in imitation of the real Kachinas to teach the children what they represent (Fig. 135). In Zuñi, Kachina dolls have movable arms and garments of real cloth, while the Hopi dolls have only painted clothing.

A general characteristic of all Kachina masks (Fig. 136) is the abstract, nonrealistic design. Even a mask that is supposed to be fear-inspiring, according to the myth it represents, is as formal as every other aspect of Zuñi culture.

A mask of Saiyatasha (Fig. 137), a Zuñi Kachina, has a long blue horn on the right side "because he brings long life to all his people." One eye is long, "so that they may have long life." The benevolence of the Kachina is expressed symbolically by abstract shapes: long rectangles for eyes, and a long horn for long life. Skin and cloth combine naturally into architectural, abstract shapes, and they in turn serve well for an expression of good things "like life."

SILVER

Navaho silver making goes back about a century and a half and was learned from the Mexicans. For years the Navaho made massive and heavy silver jewelry for their own use, or for neighboring tribes, but around 1900, with the increase in travel, lighter silver was produced for the tourist trade. Much modern jewelry, hastily made and inferior, is turned out by assembly line methods, but there are Indians on reservations and in government schools who make silver according to the old traditions.

The early jewelry was made from coins melted down and hammered or cast in stone molds. About 1890, when the government prohibited the defacing of coins, the smiths turned to Mexican pesos, which contained less alloy and were more easily worked. Today the silver, supplied by the traders, comes in one-ounce slugs, alloyed with copper or brass. The contemporary craftsman largely uses modern tools which have made greater technical perfection possible.

Typical of the articles made are conchas, bracelets, rings, earrings, buckles, necklaces, bow-guards, buttons, pins, tobacco canteens and bridles. Conchas are round or oval plaques strung on a strap to be worn as a belt. They derive from Plains Indians and may originally have come through eastern tribes from white colonial silversmiths. Earlier conchas have slots in the middle through which the strap was passed (Fig. 138). When the Navaho learned to solder a loop to the back they made the plaque solid, but placed a design where the slot had been.

Up to about 1885, when die-stamped designs appeared, silver was decorated with the awl. Mexican silversmiths did not use dies, and their use must have been learned from Mexican leather workers, as the designs are often similar. By 1895 the use of the die was common, and silver designs had become more elaborate. The stamp designs fall into four basic types: crescent, the most common, triangle, circle with radiating lines, and long narrow designs with parallel edges. All have many variations, but they are without symbolic meaning.

To the Navaho, silver is valued as decoration, as a means of displaying wealth and as collateral for loans from the trader. Navaho trading posts have racks where pawned silver is stored until the Indians redeem it, which they rarely fail to do. In the spring, when their wool is sold, and in the fall, when their lambs go to market, they settle their accounts and the pawn racks are comparatively empty. During the winter the racks gradually fill again.

Of the Pueblo Indians the Zuñi make by far the most silver, and until about 1920, almost exclusively for their own use. The Zuñi learned silver making from the Navaho, and in turn taught the Navaho the use of the turquoise. The Zuñi have carved turquoise for hundreds of years, but the stones, which are mined in Colorado and Nevada, have only been common since 1920. Zuñi silver is as fine as Navaho but with its delicate set work takes longer to make and is therefore not so widely imitated. It differs from Navaho chiefly in the preference for turquoise sets rather than die work. "If a Zuñi has no turquoise to put in his silver he will not make the silver until he has the stones. A Navaho who has no turquoise, or only one or two pieces, will make the silver and decorate it with his dies . . . The Navaho is just as proud of his collection of dies as he is of his silver; to the Zuñi the die is just another tool." Silver made by the Navaho for their own use is characteristically more massive than that of the Zuñi.

Navaho silver jewelry shows a fine appreciation for the beauty of the material. However, the surfaces may be enriched by incised patterns, kept simple to form borders or central rosettes. These textured surfaces contrast pleasantly with the plain silver as in the smooth ovals of the concha belts and the flat bands of the bracelets. Cast and wrought silver with embossed designs uses essentially the same kinds of motifs: dots, scallops, zigzags. Wide flat bands are treated decoratively to emphasize surface in bracelets. In a narrow type of bracelet the lack of width is compensated for by a more varied emphasis of the cross-section, which is often triangular.

In Zuñi bracelets the silver may serve as a foundation for turquoise, forming circles or rosettes. Here the attraction is in color and each small stone is separately set in a tiny box, all closely grouped for a mass effect which is still delicate. The differences between cast and wrought work can be recognized by comparing the concha belts in Fig. 138. The second from the left is cast, the others are wrought. In the cast belt each concha is exactly like every other, as all are made from the same mold.

In wrought work, as in any kind of craftwork, the details show minor variations; the human hand does not handle the tool mechanically after a standardized pattern. That in itself is one of the attractions of the work made by hand, be it wood, clay or silver (Fig. 139).

CONTEMPORARY INDIAN PAINTING

The twentieth century has seen a remarkable renaissance of American Indian painting. A new school of painters has developed styles in opaque water color that are peculiarly Indian. Where foreign or white influences occur they have been assimilated.

An early indication of talent for graphic expression on the part of Indians came in 1903 with the publication of a series of illustrations of gods and dance rituals made by Hopi artists for Fewkes of the Bureau of American Ethnology. Another step in that direction occurred in 1917 when a young Indian, working as a janitor in an Indian school, drew dance figures of amazing realism, using bits of broken crayon. In that year Crescencio Martinez of San Ildefonso Pueblo was commissioned to paint a series of water colors for the permanent collections of the Museum of New Mexico. Other young painters—Awa Tsireh, Fred Kabotie, Otis Polelonema and Ma-Pe-Wi, who signed his work Velino Shije—were also sponsored by the Museum of New Mexico. The interest in painting progressed with the discovery of five young Kiowa painters who in 1923, under the encouragement of Dr. O. B. Jacobson of the University of Oklahoma, gained an international reputation. These events served as an inspiration to other Indian painters.

Jacobson has classified the painters into four groups with distinct styles: Pueblo, Navaho, including Apache, Plains and Woodlands. Indian painters generally do not depend on models but on strongly developed powers of observation.

From the point of view of tribal inspiration, five different sources may be distinguished, ancient murals, pottery and textile motifs, sand painting, dances and rituals and hunting. Usually one or another source of indigenous Indian art is dominant.

The artists of the Southwest paint semi-naturalistic hunts, scenes of field and home life, and supernatural representations of Kachinas and ceremonial dances. The Navaho represent the healing ceremonies of their sand paintings and the Apache warriors, rituals and dances. Among the Plains tribes are painters of the Sioux, Kiowa, Comanche and Cheyenne. The subjects painted by the Sioux are scenes with horsemen and phases of the annual Sun Dance, whereas prayers and visions are represented in Kiowa paintings. Woodland artists of the Cherokee, Creek and Onondaga tribes emphasize a decorative element in their style. The artists have been educated in American schools and colleges, and have been active in creative Indian art as developed in an Indian school. They live on or off the reservations but they are all aware of their own Indian heritage, which is strongly emphasized in their art.

The styles represent a mingling of ancient tribal traditions with elements taken over from modern painting. The Indian tribal element is at times more pronounced than the modern contributions; all paintings have a distinctly Indian flavor which easily distinguishes the style from all others. At the same time each artist has an individual manner of his own. All styles have a few general characteristics in common. The treatment is flat and decorative; there is no rendering of depth through light and shade;

and perspective is either absent or used in a decorative manner. Color may be brilliant, jewel-like, or in subdued tints and shades.

In "Shalako" (Ca'-Lako), an unknown Zuñi painter places a masked figure against a background of textile motifs. Shalako is the name of a warrior Kachina, a giant ten feet tall. Here is a very definite connection between painting and the complex religious ceremonialism of the Zuñi. The tall figure of the painting follows closely the traditional costume of the Kachina. To make the dancer look like a giant the mask was held above his head on a pole. His garments were extended by flexible willow hoops bound together.

Here, as in other Kachina costumes, the absence of any resemblance to realism emphasizes the austerity of Zuñi religion. Abstraction has become a perfect medium to bring out the sacred character of the ceremonies.

A circular design by the Hopi artist, Twoitsie, entitled "The Parrot, Sikyatki," shows curved and angular shapes found in such murals as those from Awatovi and the ancient Sikyatki pottery motifs. A balance of forms and shapes achieves a satisfying sense of perfection.

A design, "Windway," by Bennie Tilden, a Navaho painter, uses a sand painting motif, round-headed male figures holding serpent symbols of rain and blessing.

"The Delight Makers," showing a clown performing before an admiring audience, is in a realistic manner full of action, facial expression, anatomical details and costume. Though a literal, story-telling picture, it is also in the Hopi tradition. The artist, Fred Kabotie, was the first Hopi to receive national recognition.

Some of the Pueblo painters have absorbed some phases of contemporary decoration so well that the tribal elements appear relegated to choice of subjects and details. Ma-Pe-Wi's (Velino Shije's) "Hunter" would not be out of place in any one of several contemporary settings.

The Apache Indians call their masked dancers "Gan." Wesley Nash, an Apache artist, represents a Gan spirit, also called a "Devil," "Crown" or "Fire-Dancer," in a wild dance. Oscar Howe's "Sioux Warriors" should be compared with the painted buffalo hides of the nineteenth century. The modern Sioux painter still paints Indians on horseback, but the lessons of academic painting have been linked to a tribal tradition which has been largely absorbed through his great facility as a draftsman.

Modern American Indian painting is not the only case in art where an indigenous population has integrated a native tradition with a contemporary mode. The Eskimo have done the same in carving. Painting, compared to sculpture, offers a wider field, and Indian painting easily takes first place among the living arts that derive from a tribal background. Moreover, the total range of modern American Indian paintings can only be suggested by a few examples but not actually covered to do justice to all tribes involved.

The varied physical environment of the United States encouraged food gathering, hunting and agricultural economies, each producing its own influence on the style of the art. A talent for sculpture and some relation to Mexico were revealed in the stone carvings from the prehistoric period. Though small in scale and limited in materials, stone carvings and shell engravings compare favorably with the arts to the south. The simple techniques in quill and beadwork, painted hides and masks, practiced by the Plains and Forest Indians, showed a high aesthetic level.

The Pueblo styles of the Southwest developed a characteristic expression before the coming of the white man, as is seen in pottery, sand painting and prehistoric murals. Through surface decoration, using sand, textiles and pigments on clay and paper, the Indians of the United States have established for themselves a place comparable in excellence to wood and stone carving to the north and south. In these crafts they stand above a more limited expression reached in their architecture and sculpture. A religious ceremonialism used the arts to obtain benefits like fertility and health from the gods. At a later period contacts with the white man's culture developed some of the crafts in new directions. The Indian's capacity to adapt his art to new requirements without losing all of its own character is of basic importance. In Navaho rugs and silverwork and in modern Indian painting these Indian arts take their place on a professional level as regional styles in contemporary American art.

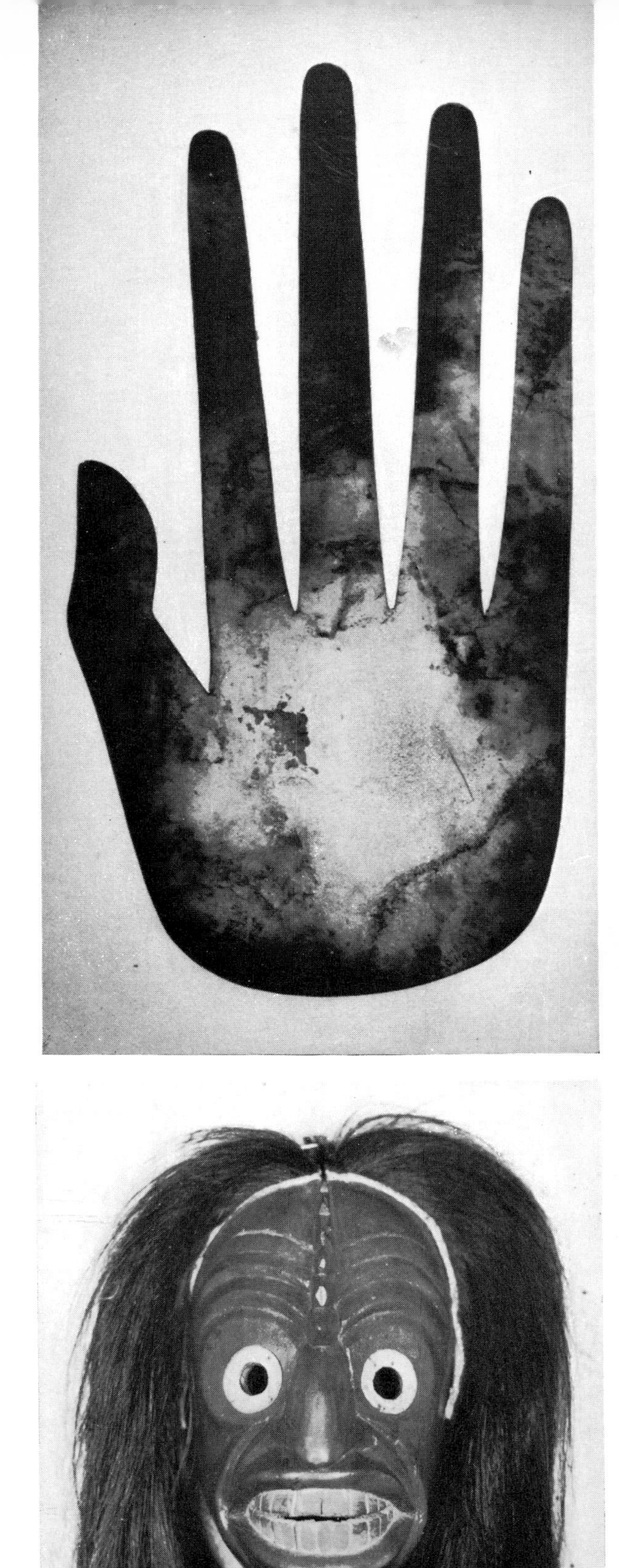

Fig. 103 (left). Mica ornament, Hopewell culture, Ohio. *Chicago Natural History Museum*. Fig. 104 (lower left). Iroquois mask, painted, with tin eyes. H. 10½ in., W. 6¼ in. *Denver Art Museum*. Fig. 105 (below). Iroquois wooden mask with protruding tongue, Onondaga Castle, New York (1888). *American Museum of Natural History*.

Fig. 106. Seneca corn husk mask. *Denver Art Museum.*

Fig. 107. Painted skin robe, illustrating the autobiography of Chief Washakia, Shoshone Indians. *Smithsonian Institution.*

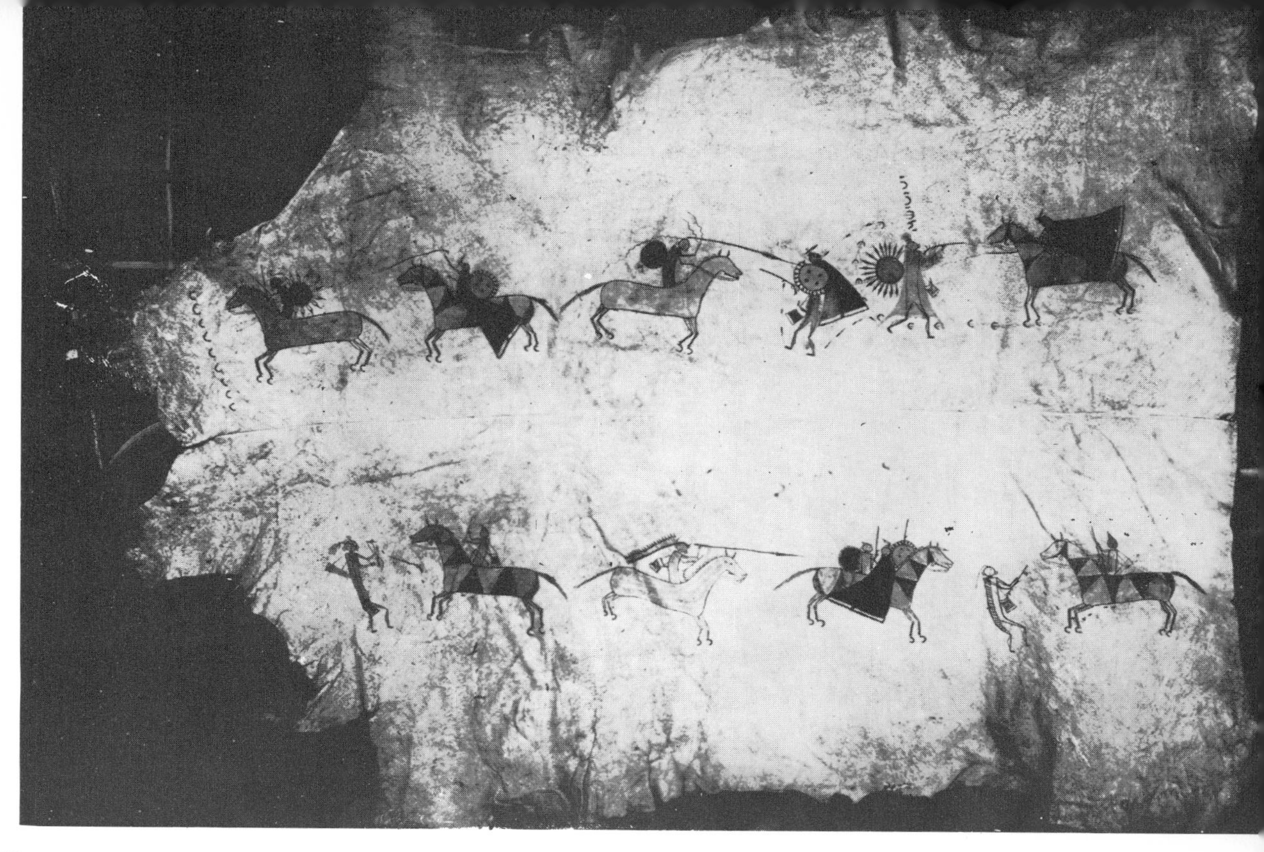

Fig. 108. Painted buffalo robe, battle scene, Hidatsa Indians. Collected by Maximilian von Wied, 1834. *Museum für Völkerkunde, Berlin.*

Fig. 109. Quill and bead pipe bags. *Indian Arts and Crafts Board, U. S. Department of the Interior, Washington, D. C.*

Fig. 110 (above). Petroglyphs in painted cave, Chatsworth, California. *Santa Barbara Museum of Natural History.*

Fig. 111. Petroglyphs, Barrier Canyon, Utah. *Museum of New Mexico, Santa Fe.*

Fig. 112. Mural from a Hopi kiva. Awatovi, Jeddito Valley, Arizona. H. 4 ft., 2 in.; L. 10 ft. After restoration by contemporary Hopi artists. Excavated by J. O. Brew. *Peabody Museum, Harvard University*.

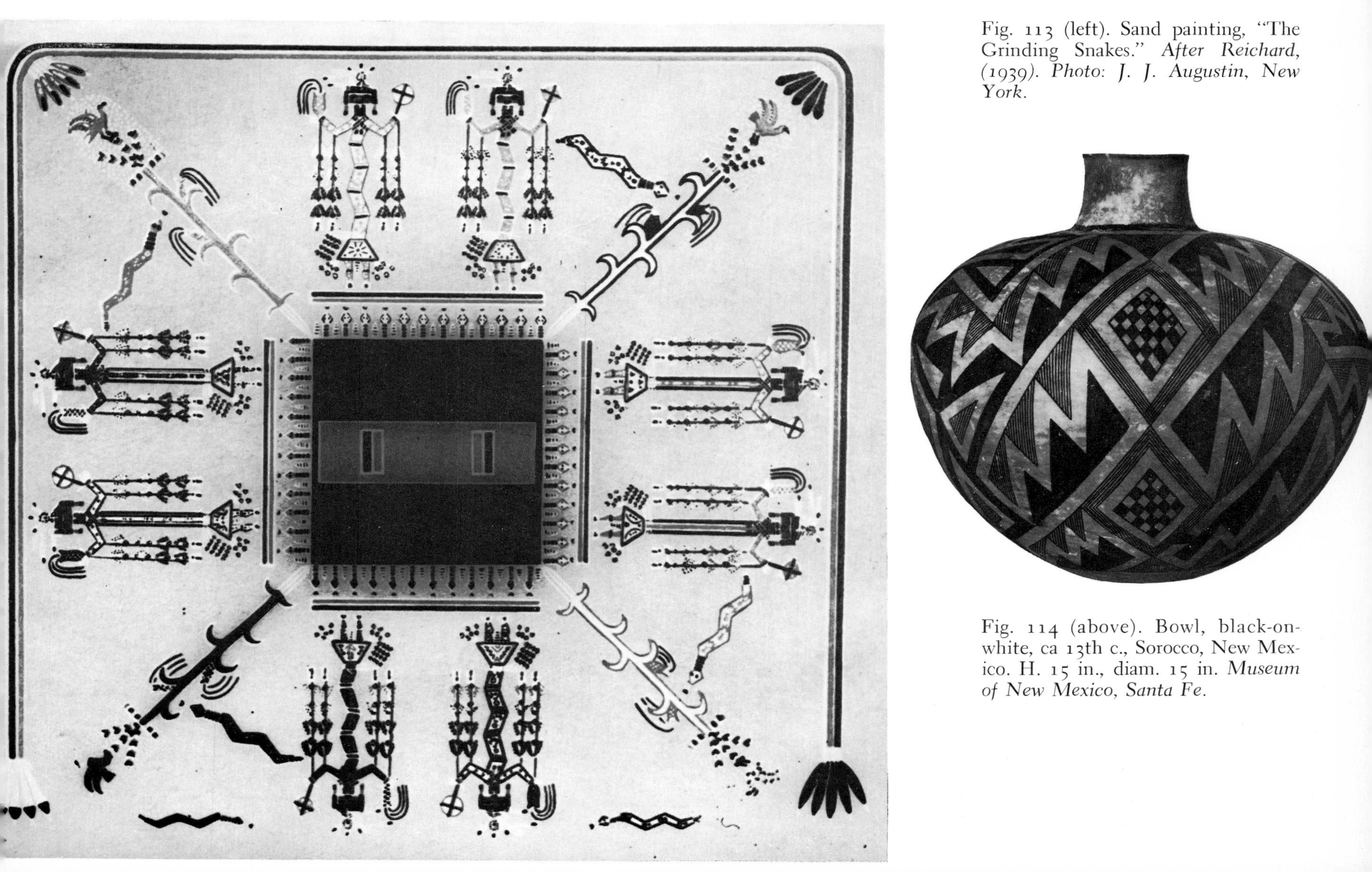

Fig. 113 (left). Sand painting, "The Grinding Snakes." *After Reichard, (1939). Photo: J. J. Augustin, New York.*

Fig. 114 (above). Bowl, black-on-white, ca 13th c., Sorocco, New Mexico. H. 15 in., diam. 15 in. *Museum of New Mexico, Santa Fe.*

Fig. 115 (left). Pottery effigy, ca 1000-1200 A.D. *Museum of New Mexico, Santa Fe.*

Fig. 117 (above). Mohave pottery bottle, southeast California. H. 11 in. *Denver Art Museum.*

Fig. 116 (left). Painted effigy vase, ca 15th century, from northern Mexico, State of Chihuahua. *Museum of New Mexico, Santa Fe.*

Opposite page:

Fig. 118 (top left). Pottery bowl from Mimbres, New Mexico. *Collection, Mr. and Mrs. Ralph Altman, Los Angeles.*

Fig. 119 (top right). Pottery bowl from Mimbres, New Mexico (Swarts Ruin). *Taylor Museum, Colorado Springs, Colorado.*

Fig. 120 (bottom). Zuñi pottery jar, archaic style. *Smithsonian Institution.*

Fig. 121 (above). Pottery jar, Zuñi Pueblo, New Mexico, about 1875. *Smithsonian Institution.*

Fig. 122 (right). Zuñi pottery drum. *Smithsonian Institution.*

Opposite page:

Fig. 123 (top left). Pottery jar, naturalistic style, Acoma Pueblo, New Mexico. *Smithsonian Institution.*

Fig. 124 (top right). Pottery jar, abstract style, Acoma Pueblo, New Mexico. *American Museum of Natural History.*

Fig. 125 (bottom). Pottery jar, Hopi Indians, Arizona. *Smithsonian Institution.*

Fig. 131 (opposite page, lower left). California twined basket. *Indian Arts and Crafts Board, U. S. Department of the Interior, Washington, D. C.*

Fig. 132 (opposite page, lower right). Western Apache basket. Diam. 23 in. *Indian Arts and Crafts Board, U. S. Department of the Interior, Washington, D. C.*

Fig. 126 (above, left). Pottery jar from Sikyatki, Arizona. *Bureau of American Ethnology, Smithsonian Institution.*

Fig. 127 (left). Pottery jar, polished style, San Ildefonso Pueblo, New Mexico. *American Museum of Natural History.*

Fig. 128 (above). Pottery jar; from Santo Domingo Pueblo, New Mexico. *Denver Art Museum.*

Fig. 129. Greenstone effigy, ca 1500 A.D. *Museum of New Mexico, Santa Fe.*

Fig. 130 (above). Ceremonial war club, stone, carved with mountain goat head and turtle, Sioux Indians. L. 29¼ in. *Joslyn Art Museum. On loan from Public Library, Omaha, Nebraska.*

Fig. 133 (right). Navaho blanket. Bayeta, a coarse woolen cloth, flexible and close-woven. Colors: Indigo blue and white on bayeta red ground. Size: 54 in. by 72 in. *Museum of New Mexico, Santa Fe.*

Fig. 134 (extreme right). Navaho blanket. *Collection, Mary Cabot Wheelwright. Photo: Exposition of Indian Tribal Arts, Inc., New York.*

Fig. 135 (right). Hopi (Arizona), Kachina doll, representing Chaveyo or Ogre. H. 19 in. (to top of feathers). *Denver Art Museum.*

Fig. 136 (extreme right). Hopi, Kachina doll, mountain sheep showing mask. H. 15½ in. (to top of horns). *Denver Art Museum.*

Fig. 137 (below). Zuñi (New Mexico) mask of Saiyatasha. *Brooklyn Museum.*

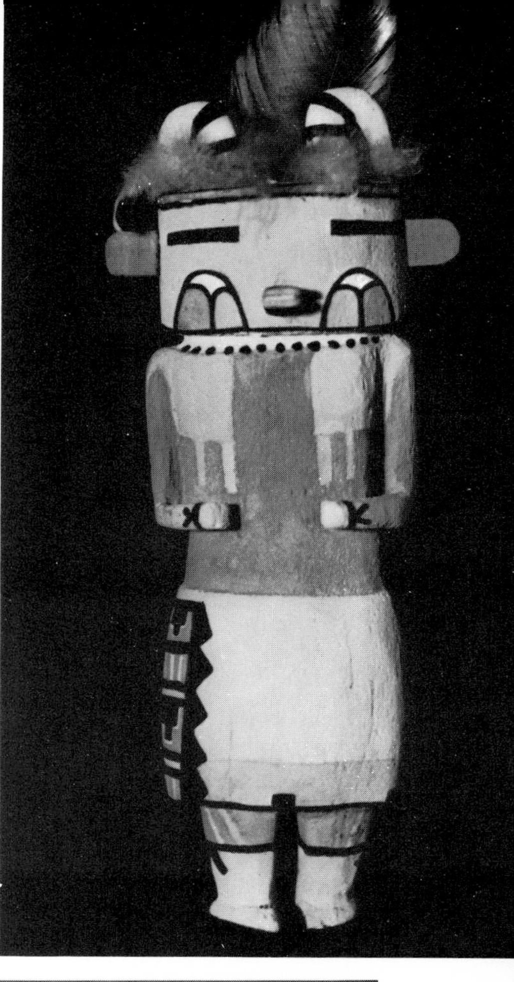

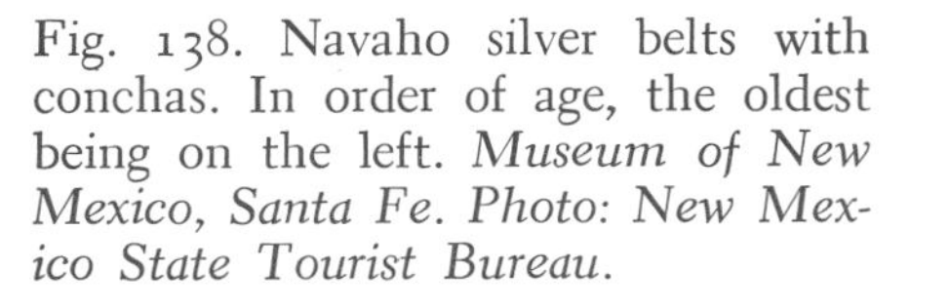

Fig. 138. Navaho silver belts with conchas. In order of age, the oldest being on the left. *Museum of New Mexico, Santa Fe. Photo: New Mexico State Tourist Bureau.*

Fig. 139. Navaho silver necklaces with pomegranate and crescent designs. *Museum of New Mexico, Santa Fe.*

Fig. 140 (left). Clay figure from western Mexico, Tarascan. *Museo Nacional, Mexico, D.F. Photo: Taylor Museum, Colorado Springs, Colorado.*

Fig. 141 (below). Clay figure from western Mexico, Tarascan. *Museo Nacional, Mexico, D.F. Photo: Taylor Museum.*

Fig. 142 (lower left). Clay figure from western Mexico, Tarascan. *Museo Nacional, Mexico, D. F. Photo: Taylor Museum.*

Fig. 143 (right). Clay head from Colima or Jalisco (fragment). *Philadelphia Museum.*

Fig. 144 (above). Broad pottery bowl, from western Mexico. *Museo Nacional, Mexico, D.F. Photo: Taylor Museum, Colorado Springs, Colorado.*

Fig. 145 (below). Maya stone relief (Relievo Hermoso), from Palenque, State of Chiapas, Mexico. *Museo de America, Madrid.*

Fig. 146 (right). Maya lintel 17, from house F, "A Worshiper Making a Blood Offering." From Yaxchilan (Menché), State of Chiapas, Mexico. *British Museum.*

IV

MEXICO AND THE ANDEAN REGION

THE ART STYLES WE ARE CONCERNED WITH HERE ARE THOSE OF THE COUNTRIES FROM THE RIO GRANDE to the south coast of Peru. This is a mountainous region, with the great chain of the Rocky Mountains continuing southward into Middle America and connecting with the Andes of South America. Mexico, Colombia and Peru have plateaus at high altitudes, fringed with mountains and narrow coastal strips on the Pacific side. In Mexico the mountain ranges descend steeply toward the west and more gradually toward the Gulf coast, turning into lowlands in southern Veracruz, Tabasco, Yucatán and in parts of Oaxaca.

Climate everywhere is affected by altitudes as well as by latitude. Mexico combines the characteristics of the northern temperate zone with those of tropical Central and South America. The highlands north and south have moderate temperatures while the coast is hot and humid. In Peru the coast is hot and dry, and in Ecuador it is a tropical jungle. The dry climate preserved the textiles in the burial grounds of the south coast of Peru, and moisture led to their destruction in Mexico.

The natural environment was favorable for grazing and agriculture; cities developed with advanced cultures, in which the arts flourished. Of the varied fauna some animals, like serpents, jaguars, eagles, lizards, crocodiles, frogs and bats, were reflected in the arts. Other species equally spectacular, like butterflies, were hardly represented, and the rich flora was largely ignored as a source for motifs in art. Vegetables like maize or potatoes were used in pottery design in Peru; it was not their natural beauty which inspired the artists, but these plants were useful to man and for that reason were personified as protecting spirits. The fact that plant and insect life were used sparingly where nature was lavish shows how subject matter was limited to certain fields. Nature was not so much a source of inspiration for design as a source of materials for the crafts: feathers for blankets, plant fibers for mats and baskets, cotton for textiles in Mexico, wool from llamas, alpacas and wild vicuñas for woven fabrics in Peru, clay for ceramics and wood and stone for carving in many places.

Here, as elsewhere, topography and climate determined culture and affected the arts only indirectly. What related to the heavens and the earth found expression in beliefs and in art. Sun, moon, stars, thunder and rain were symbolized in major gods; the earth was the great mother goddess, and lakes, rivers, springs and caves became local spirits. Animism, growing out of man's relation to the unseen forces in nature, contributed to his sense of security. The favorable environment in these middle and lower sections of the Americas made for an elaboration of culture and an enrichment of the arts, but it did not necessarily produce better art. Mimbres painted pottery and Eskimo ivory engravings were as fine in their fields as the stone architecture and sculpture of Mexico or the textiles and ceramics of Peru.

COUNTRIES AND PEOPLES

Of the countries of Central America we deal only with what are now Guatemala, British Honduras, Honduras, Costa Rica and Panama. Of the South American countries, Colombia, Ecuador and Peru are here represented by examples of their ancient art, although the Andean culture area is much larger, extending north to the Caribbean Sea and south to include portions of Bolivia, Brazil, Chile and Argentina.

Pre-Columbian archaeology in Mexico may be identified in different ways, by countries, states, archaeological sites or by Indian tribes. In art, tribal names are used to designate styles, like the Toltec, Maya, Totonac, Tarascan, Huasteca and Olmec, because particular works of art to which these names apply were found in regions known or believed to have been inhabited by these tribes. The styles are well defined, but the tribal names are at times printed in quotation marks to indicate that the link of style to tribe is not necessarily based on positive historic evidence.

At the time of the Spanish Conquest, the Aztecs dominated the tribes of Mexico and the Inca ruled Peru, but not all pre-Columbian art in Mexico was Aztec and much Peruvian art was not Inca.

The Aztecs, the best known of the tribes of Mexico, lived at the time of the Conquest in central Mexico, in the valleys of Puebla, Taluca and in the fertile valley of Mexico. Their capital, Tenochtitlán, the Mexico City of today, was located offshore in the great salt Lake Texcoco. Before the appearance of the Aztecs the valley of Mexico had been held by the Toltecs, a tribe associated with the most impressive architectural monument of central Mexico, at Teotihuacán, a few miles northeast of their capital city. The pyramids of the sun and the moon are the most impressive remains of this important Toltec religious ceremonial center.

The Mixtec lived to the south in the southern part of the state of Puebla and in northern Oaxaca and the Zapotecs in the central valley of Oaxaca and the Isthmus of Tehuantepec. A great historical and archaeological center of south Mexico, second only to Teotihuacán, is the Zapotec site of Monte Alban in Oaxaca. In western Mexico the Tarascans were located in the present states of Colima, Jalisco, Michoacán, Guanajuato and Querétaro.

Olmec art has been excavated on the Atlantic coast in the western part of the state of Tabasco on the archaeological site of La Venta and in the state of Veracruz at Tres Zapotes. Olmec, one of the un-

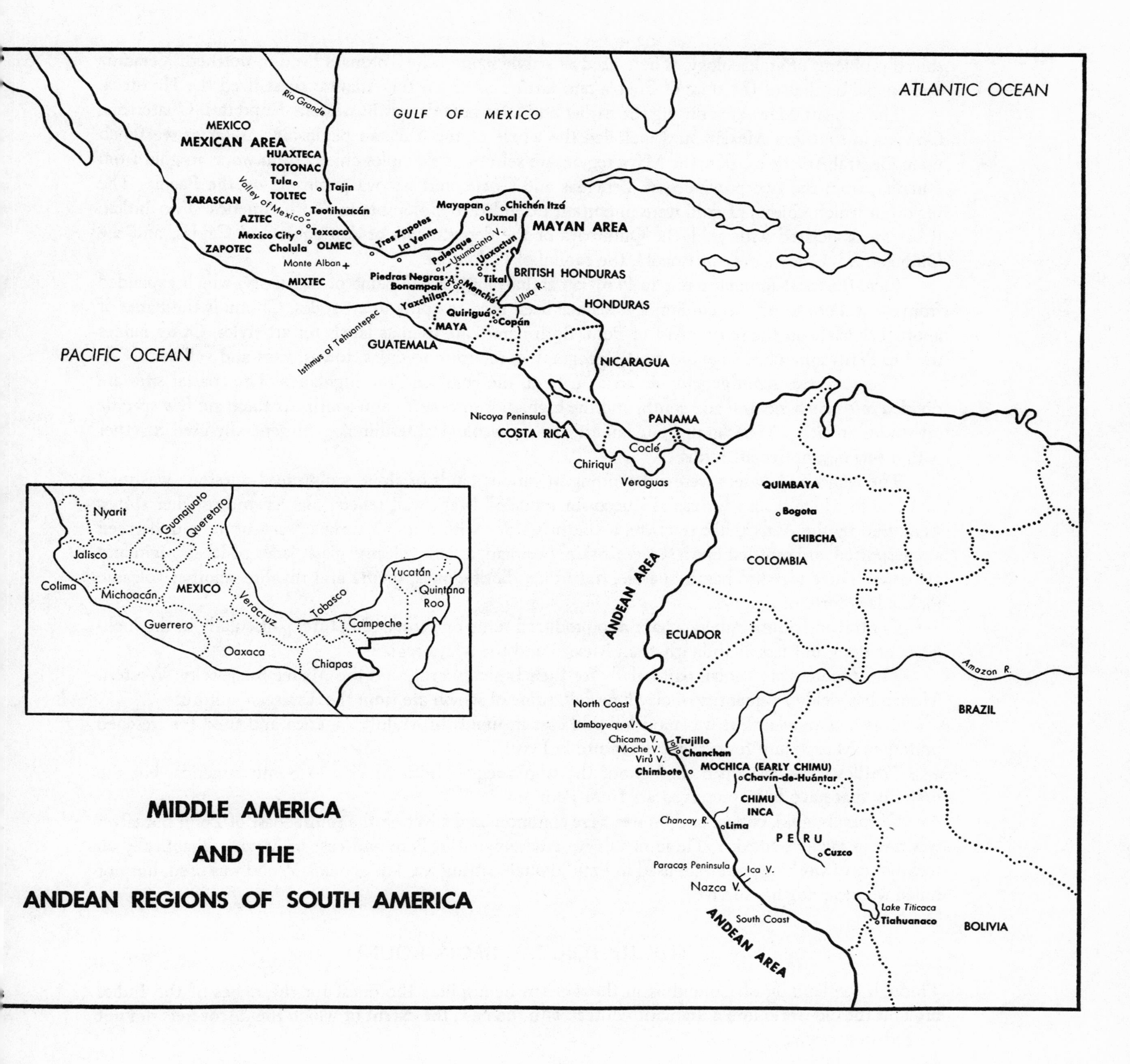

MIDDLE AMERICA AND THE ANDEAN REGIONS OF SOUTH AMERICA

solved problems of archaeology, is here used as a style name. The Totonacs lived in northern Veracruz and on the borders of the state of Puebla and farther north on the Atlantic coast lived the Huasteca.

The ancient Maya area during the earlier and later periods was in western Honduras, Guatemala, Chiapas in southern Mexico, and included the whole of the Yucatán peninsula. As far as we touch upon Central America, below the Maya region, we select our examples chiefly from works in gold from Panama; from the two provinces of Veraguas and Coclé, and Nicoya peninsula on the Pacific. The region in which objects of gold were important extended to Colombia in South America. Two Indian tribes are associated with gold, the Quimbaya of the departments of Antioquia and Caldas, and the Chibcha, from the vicinity of Bogotá, the capital of Colombia.

Inca, the most familiar name in Peruvian archaeology, is the name of a dynasty, which expanded from south Peru to rule an empire; it has since been used to apply to art styles. Chimu is the name of another dynasty on the north coast of Peru. Both names are used as labels for art styles. Other names used in Peruvian archaeology are mostly geographic, referring to cities, towns, sites and valleys.

There are two main geographic areas in Peru, the coast and the highlands. The coastal sites are divided into north, central and south, and the highlands into north and south. As there are few specific art studies in either Mexican or Peruvian art, the archaeological terminology is generally used together with a few descriptive art terms.

The Maya and Aztecs were outstanding in various kinds of stone sculpture. Limestone was used in Yucatán where it also furnished stucco for modeled Maya wall reliefs. Harder and tougher stones were used by the Aztecs, like trachyte, a volcanic stone with a rough surface; serpentine, a dull green stone spotted and mottled like a serpent's skin; obsidian, a dark volcanic glass; jades of local origin and alabaster. There was also basalt, marble, travertine, diorite, onyx, quartz and rhyolite, another volcanic rock, a lava form of granite.

Central and South America have also produced some fine stone sculpture, particularly in the highlands of Peru, but less abundantly than Mexico and the Maya regions.

The Zapotecs are known particularly for their funerary urns, and the Mixtec for jewelry. Western Mexico has yielded a quantity of clay figurines, some of which are from the Tarascan culture.

Clay was universal; it was modeled and cast in molds in Middle America and used for frescoed pottery in Mexico and for ceramic sculpture in Peru.

Textiles were developed throughout the whole region from Mexico to South America, but the majority that have been preserved are from Peru.

Of metals, gold, copper and bronze were common, and silver on the south coast of Peru; but silver was rare in ancient Mexico. These metals were hammered in Peru and cast in Mexico. Practically all techniques of working gold were used in Peru, though casting was less general. Wood was used, but not much woodcarving has survived.

THE HISTORICAL BACKGROUND

Through the landing of Columbus in the western hemisphere the quest for the riches of the Indies brought the old world into a dramatic contact with the new, the extent of which the discoverers did not immediately realize.

When Cortez stepped ashore in Veracruz in 1519 A.D., European and Indian faced each other in sharp contrast. It has been well said that the clash could not have been more amazing had Cortez appeared on the banks of the Nile at the time the Pharaohs were ruling Egypt, thousands of years before his day. Here were iron-clad warriors on horseback and armed with firearms in the midst of processions of gorgeously clad natives plumed and decorated. Carrying colorful standards, they could have suggested a gay carnival to the stern warriors from Spain, still unaware of the years of struggle that were to follow.

A few years after Cortez had conquered Mexico, "a lieutenant of Pizarro, in north Peru in 1526, met with an Indian bark" . . . "laden with merchandize," including "beautiful wool and cotton cloth, articles of gold and silver, bronze (?) bells and mirrors." Having heard of a temple covered with plates of gold and silver, Pizarro, accompanied by an advance guard, pushed on to see with amazement populous towns, tilled fields, temples of the sun with their adjoining convents (Lehmann-Doering, 1924).

These first impressions were followed by the Conquest that destroyed and plundered everything above ground. Fortunately, ruins and excavations left something for later scientific explorations; the tombs of the coast of Peru have yielded pottery and textiles wrapped around the mummies; and a great "Well of Sacrifice," the Cenote at Chichén Itzá in Yucatán, many fine objects of jade, gold, wood, copper, copal and pottery which had been cast into the murky waters as a sacrifice to appease the gods. Human beings were also thus sacrificed.

A few frescoes have been copied, like those of the Temple of the Jaguars at Chichén Itzá; others at Bonampak and a small number of Maya and Mexican illuminated manuscripts have come down to us from the pre-Conquest period. Fray Bernardino de Sahagun, a Franciscan monk, had Indian artists prepare for him Aztec picture-writings (after 1529) which he compiled in a manuscript of twelve books now in Florence. His *History of Ancient Mexico*, on which he worked for a quarter of a century, finishing it about 1569, is our best literary source, as it was written by a scholar who obtained firsthand information directly from the Aztecs.

Native American art was temporarily forgotten after it had excited the admiration of sixteenth-century Europe. The impression the Spaniards received from Mexican art and architecture when it was still complete and fresh the world has since been obliged to regain for itself from ruins and the results of excavations.

Two Americans, John Lloyd Stephens, a consular officer from the State Department, and Frederick Catherwood, an artist, rediscovered Maya sculpture in 1839, when Van Buren was president. They were the first from the outside world to lay eyes on the ruins of Copán, in Honduras, of which Catherwood made some magnificent drawings. Some forty years later, between 1881 and 1894, an Englishman, Alfred Percival Maudslay, in seven expeditions brought a collection of original works of sculpture, cast and stucco reliefs to England which are now in the British Museum. The most important archaeological discoveries are subsequent to Maudslay's expedition. This includes the Maya calendar with its eighteen months of twenty days each and a nineteenth month of five days to make 365 days of the year. The most famous calendar is now in Mexico City; it is of stone, weighs about twenty-four tons, and has the surface carved. In the calendar art is linked with astronomy, for each day had its individual pictograph, often in the form of an animal.

A few of the works of Middle American art can be dated in the Maya calendar, especially the

Maya stelae; some Aztec works also have dates inscribed in the form of glyphs which can be read and which have been related to our calendar. The Indian tribes had no true writing, but early Spanish scholars made careful accounts of the life and history of the Aztecs. Indian authors, a generation after the Conquest, added to these records, but their accounts are so mingled with myth that no clear historical picture resulted. To an extent these literary sources have been corrected through archaeological research. Time sequences have been worked out for the Aztec, Toltec, Maya and other cultures.

Little is known about Maya history, in its early part, before the twelfth century of our era, as there are no documentary sources. There are, nevertheless, important architectural ruins and stone monuments, the dated stelae or time markers of the Maya. Frescoes and ceramics have added material for archaeological research. On the basis of these remains the Maya history has been outlined.

The art historical relations between Mexican, Mayan and Peruvian styles are hardly sufficiently clear to contribute anything definite to an approach that emphasizes appreciation. The Toltecs, Maya and Zapotecs developed important styles in the Mexican area. The early Maya, perhaps through contact with the Zapotecs, may have influenced the Toltecs. There is historical and archaeological evidence that in the tenth century tribes from central Mexico migrated to Yucatán, where they eventually took a leading role in the New Maya empire. Here the Toltec leader Quetzalcoatl, under the name of Kukulcán, became the founder of the new dynasty and was later perhaps deified as the Feathered Serpent and patron deity of Chichén Itzá, the great Maya-Mexican center.

A broad historical outline has been suggested by George Kubler. Basing his sequence of periods for Mexico on the results of the Carbon 14 method for dating organic archaeological specimens, the following time table results: (1) Early period to the beginning of the Christian era, with the invention of pottery, placed about 900 B.C. Olmec art and pyramid temple architecture fall toward the end of the Early period; (2) Middle period, first century A.D. to 800 A.D. The dated Maya monuments, as well as Teotihuacán and Monte Alban are contemporary and fall into the Middle period; (3) Late period, about 800 A.D. to about 1300 A.D. The Toltec of Tula and the Totonac culture of Tajin belong to the late period; (4) Terminal period, 1300 A.D. to about 1500 A.D. The Aztec culture is of this period.

Two styles, Tiahuanaco and Inca, covered all Peru, coast and highland, at different times. The Tiahuanaco was roughly contemporary with the period of the Romanesque and early Gothic in Europe; the Inca, with the period of the Renaissance. Of the important styles of the north and central coasts, the Chavin corresponds roughly with the period of European antiquity of the first millennium B.C. up through the end of the Roman Empire. The Mochica, on the north coast, parallels the Byzantine and Romanesque, and the Chimu parallels the late Gothic and Early Renaissance periods. On the south coast, the Paracas Necropolis style was about contemporary with Greek and Roman, the Nazcan with the Byzantine and Romanesque, and the Inca with the Gothic and Early Renaissance. These comparisons of periods should not be taken to suggest that there was a parallelism of development with Europe, which of course there was not.

RELIGIOUS BELIEFS

The gods of the Aztecs were represented in stone sculpture, and often a religious meaning must be presumed even though the particular god represented in art may be unknown to us. The number of

Aztec gods was so large that it is possible to divide them into groups. The reason for their great number is that the Aztecs were in the habit of including the gods of the tribes they had subdued among their own. The great gods were the God of War (Huitzilopochtli), the Sun God (Tetzcatlipoca), the God of Water and Rain (Tlaloc), Huchueteotl, the Old God, who under another name (Xiuhtecuhtli) was known as the Fire God and "Lord of the Year." To an extent, all tribes had some of the gods in common. Statues of the gods were placed in temples on top of stepped pyramids. Art was closely linked to a concern for rain to assure good crops, and to a desire to appease the god on whom the crops depended, and to human sacrifice, as the gods were conceived as depending on human blood for sustenance. Periodic sacrifices of human beings kept the universe going, for the gods lived on human hearts. These bloody rituals were represented in manuscripts and occasionally in sculpture. There are statuettes of Aztec priests clothed in the skins of flayed victims who had been offered to the god Xipe, "Our Lord the Flayed One." This was done to symbolize spring, "The new covering of vegetation with which the earth clothes itself each year." The ritual was in origin an act of sympathetic magic to encourage nature to cover herself with a new garment of vegetation.

A mere listing of the gods by name and attribute would indicate how closely Aztec religion and art are interwoven with ritual. We get this also from the works of art themselves and from the accounts of writers like Sahagun. He describes some rituals which immediately preceded the sacrifice of a man to a god on the altar of the temple. "The slaves who were about to die went to the houses of the masters to bid them goodbye . . . They dipped their hands into the bowl of paint or of ink and put them (the hands) on the lintels of the doors and the posts of the house, leaving their imprints in colors; the same they did in the houses of their relatives."

This incident brings in another facet of the culture, primitive law. According to Huntington Cairns: "Property is basically conceived as part of the personality or self, it is a relation between the person and the thing. Something that the individual has touched or handled becomes imbued with a portion of his personality." This would then mean the houses became the property of the gods to whom the slaves were to be offered in sacrifice, for the gods ate the hearts of the slaves, who thereby became one with the gods. The sacrificial victims were looked upon as sacred property of the gods; they were well treated by being feasted and entertained and given much attention; to an extent they were willing victims. The houses bearing the imprints of the gods would enjoy their special protection. The sacrifices took place in the temples, the houses of the gods. Thus art merged with ritual, law, and religion into a service to honor the gods and safeguard public welfare. We can no more separate such rituals from ancient Mexican art, than we can ignore the part played by the church service in mediaeval cathedrals.

Human sacrifice against a background of architecture and sculpture had a practical bearing on the daily life of the Aztec people. This is demonstrated by another excerpt from Sahagun. "Then he (the priest) ascended to the temple once more and upon reaching the top they just killed the captives so that these should precede the slaves in death and then sacrificed the latter. After killing one they at once blew horns and shells . . . After having killed the slaves and captives, everybody went home and on the following day the old men and women performed marriages and the chieftains drank pulque . . ." This means the gods have been appeased by food, human hearts; hence they are in a good mood, and the time is auspicious to embark on important things like marriage. How art participated in another way we learn from Sahagun when he tells us that the priest going to the slaughter carried in his arms the statue of Paynal, the messenger of the god Huitzilopochtli, sun god and chief god of Tenochtitlán, as a witness to the sacrifice. For the Aztecs a human sacrifice honored a god; a statue of a god—a work of art to us—is used as a witness, so that Paynal, the gods' messenger should take note that man had done his duty by the god in whose honor a slave had been sacrificed.

Aztec religion did not make it easy for sculptors. Coatlique, "Our Lady of the Serpent Skirt," the Earth Goddess, is represented in the well-known statue in the National Museum of Mexico. Here we have concepts taken from myth, serpent heads, skulls, cut-off hands, hearts, writhing snakes, a jaguar head and claws, all symbols of aggression. We may assume that a realistic presentation of these symbols in stone was to appease the Earth Goddess by a perpetual offering in the form of a statue to obtain from her some favorable consideration. Hence she wears a human skull, the symbol of death, because the earth receives the dead, and human hearts, because human hearts nourish the gods.

How religion stimulated art is evident from the imaginative combinations of earth and sky symbols, which at Teotihuacán and in Yucatán artists translated into stone. The serpent was the symbol of the earth, as the bird was the symbol of the heavens. Together, in the feathered serpent, they formed a symbol of the universe.

In Maya carving and manuscripts, jaguars, water lilies, feathers and various species of birds appear. Originally, Maya religion consisted of a personification of forces of nature presumably without priests. When corn was introduced and when later the calendar, chronology and hieroglyphic writing were invented, the number of gods was increased. To take care of these cultural additions, a professional priesthood seems to have evolved which helped interpret the many gods to the people, and Maya worship and ritual became complex.

There were, according to Morley, few statues of gods in the Old Empire. The human beings represented in Maya reliefs are worshippers, priests, rulers, warriors and captives. Gods in Maya art are part animal and part human, and serpents became progressively anthropomorphic. Nose and earplugs were added to serpent heads and human heads were placed in serpent mouths.

The Inca religion of Peru had many gods, headed by the Sun God, a large priesthood and a complex ritual. The Inca emperor opened ceremonies by rendering homage to the sun and made offerings of precious vessels or images to the god. Gold was not economically of value to the individual Peruvian, but it was collected and delivered to the temple of the Sun God. According to their belief, gold was from the sun, lost to the earth when the sun set and to maintain the sun's power the lost gold had to be returned.

The Creator, or Great Ancestor, was the ruler of the Land of the Dead and was connected with funerary practice and beliefs. He ruled over the shadows at the end of the world, which was in the west. Known as Viracocha, in the abbreviated form, meaning: "The Ancient Foundation, the Lord and Instructor of the World," he made the earth, sky, stars, and mankind, and taught man agriculture and the arts. Viracocha was worshipped in temples and represented in anthropomorphic images. Originally a culture hero, he was elevated in rank by the priesthood and became even greater than the powerful Sun God, but less popular with the people.

In a creation myth relating to Viracocha, the story is told that Viracocha, having risen from Lake Titicaca, created heaven, earth, sun, moon and stars, and then man. Interesting for art is that part of the story which relates that Viracocha made stone patterns for man and woman, to be created, including a pattern for a ruler, of pregnant women and of mothers with children. He then ordered his companion, who had risen with him out of Lake Titicaca to populate the country with human beings, after the patterns made in stone, and to name the people according to the names of the stone statues. The people were also to come out of mountains and caves. Wherever Viracocha went he created man in the same manner. Only people familiar with sculpture could have imagined this detail about stone patterns for the creation of man.

Coniraya was a solar god on the coast of Peru; Pachacamac, also revered on the coast, was a god associated with a famous temple; and the Earth Mother, Pachamamla, was a major deity. In addition there were other gods and minor deities. The living desired to placate the dead and facilitate their journey to the land of the dead. Hence, in funeral rites ancestral mummies were taken in processions and were offered sacrifices.

Any account of the relation of art to religion in ancient Peru must remain sketchy and incomplete because sources of information no longer exist. In the case of the Aztecs we have stone sculpture to demonstrate how the gods were represented in addition to traditions about Aztec religion. In regard to Peru we know something of the religious beliefs during the late Inca period, but we are without corresponding representations of the gods in art. Where we suspect religious meanings in the art of Peru these relate to earlier periods, before the time of the Inca state religion. For the earlier local religions we find some correspondence between beliefs and actual works of art in the ceramic representations of the spirits of animals and vegetables. Many gods and demons were associated with nature, and plant spirits were symbolized by large ears of corn or oddly shaped tubers, and had their own cults. Spirits representing animal or vegetable species could take on a human form and marry human beings, but something about their aspect was monstrous. They had two heads or protruding eyebrows, or may have been linked together like Siamese twins.

Among the Chibcha Indians of Colombia a religious ceremony took place in which men covered with luxurious ornaments of feathers and gold, disguised as animals and wearing gold masks went on a raft to the middle of Lake Guatavita to honor the Snake God. The chief was covered with gold dust and gold objects were thrown into the lake as sacrifices. In modern times gold objects have been recovered from the lake. The Andean region also had human sacrifices, including children, to propitiate the gods.

MAGIC VERSUS ART

Where an animistic religion, as in Mexico and Peru, personifies the Universe, and represents spirits in animal and even vegetable form, almost any representation in art could presumably be religious in nature. There was perhaps no decoration in these styles without a religious meaning; even what had been abbreviated and appeared to be purely ornamental could still be religious in origin.

As we are here discussing art rather than religion and magic, as such, it may be permissible to use the terms magic and religion interchangeably; magic may be looked upon as a primitive type of religion. In view of such emphasis on magic in art one may wonder, had art in primitive cultures any validity of its own? Where craftsmanship and the religious aspect of art received so much attention the question arises, can we attach any importance in primitive art to decoration and a sensuous enjoyment? The inference seems to be that primitive people valued craftsmanship but not individual expression; the personal element making a work of art different and unique, resulting in its being valued as art by some later collector, was ordinarily absent.

But it is difficult to explain away entirely decoration and sensuous enjoyment, even as a factor in the mind of the artist, whether we call him primitive, preliterate, or civilized. We should not assume that there was any basic difference of attitude toward art on the part of the artist merely because some cultures are called primitive because they were preliterate whereas others are not so designated. A relation of magic to art was inherent where art was created for a religious use. The difference between primitive and contemporary attitudes lies in the fact that we can separate magic from art, and do so with a degree of discrimination which was probably foreign to primitive attitudes. Wherever we can detect an element of artistic interest we may be certain it did not appear as a result of magic or the workings of priests but out of the endeavors of artists.

This aesthetic trend crept into the artist's work as something he desired for its own sake. It may at times seem slight, but less so in the larger perspective of stylistic changes. It is important when we consider that a desire for perfection in craftsmanship is aesthetic in itself.

As culture matured the magical element in art lived on, but did not become more powerful. The hoped-for gifts of the gods with the passing of time continued to be a factor, but art increased in elaboration. If art had been no more than a device for magic, once a style had proved effective, it need not have developed beyond a primitive stage. Otherwise, one would have to assume that the better the art the better the magic, which would be difficult to prove. The fact is, primitive peoples tended to cling to their older images as more efficacious.

Art and magic were not always equally important. Not all deities were represented in an artistic form. The famous idol of Pachacamac, in Peru, was a roughly sculptured post, and Viracocha was represented in anthropomorphic images, as well as in an oval, golden plate. Many idols were rudely carved and had no particular form. Some German scholar, with European art in mind, coined the phrase, "Wundertätige Bilder sind meist schlechte Bilder." (Magical pictures are mostly poor pictures.)

Art may have grown out of magic, as magical powers were attached to objects found in nature. As these were improved by the hand of man, art and magic were bound together. Eventually some art developed without a magical connection, as secular art. This stage of evolution is also present in the art of some primitive cultures.

GENERAL CHARACTERISTICS

In spite of the wide range of pre-Columbian art, a few characteristics apply more or less to all styles. In fact, differences between styles could be considered as variations of one style. In addition, there are a few unifying elements that differentiate American art in one way or another from the arts of other preliterate cultures outside the western hemisphere. They may be characterized in four ways: (1) all arts were practiced, including architecture, sculpture, painting and the crafts; (2) architecture was dominant; (3) the human figure, though of major importance, was still merged with other elements and (4) there was a basic trend toward realism.

Though this all-inclusiveness of the arts exceeded anything attained in either Negro Africa or Oceania, the several branches of the arts were not developed to the same degree. Painting, outside of frescoes, was backward, and sculpture and the crafts were advanced. Practically all basic materials, except bronze and iron, and all techniques that were used in the Old World, had their parallels in the New World.

Though architecture is not a part of our subject, it should not be left unmentioned. Architecture was important in its own right, and an architectural character was apparent in sculpture, ceramic decoration, and textiles. These arts showed a preference for geometric forms, straight lines, and angles, and an emphasis on mass, all characteristics of architecture. Examples are so numerous it is unnecessary to point out particular ones. As in mediaeval Europe, much of sculpture was also part of architecture, mostly in the form of reliefs, in connection with the decoration of monumental staircases, of walls of stepped pyramids, of columns, altars, panels, lintels and stelae, at times covering the surfaces completely with carved stone or stucco work. For freestanding stone sculpture much of the original rectangular block was preserved in the finished piece. Even where figures and animals were used as motifs they were simplified to bring out straight lines and simple curves. Whatever may have been responsible for this trend it deserves to be called architectural rather than natural or pictorial. Had certain Peruvian textiles been inspired directly by nature they might not have developed the angularity and severity so characteristic of that style. Actually, the stone block, as much as the human figure, has left its imprint on the arts.

Pre-Columbian art showed little interest in the human figure as such. Though the figure was basic to sculpture, and was used in pottery and textile decoration, it was obscured by an elaboration of motifs that originated in ritual. This tendency to combine the figure with ornamental detail made for confusion, so that in the reliefs often little of the background shows. In the case of Maya sculpture Philip Drucker has suggested that the filling in of background space "with secondary design suggests habits of composition acquired in painting." The figure was also subordinated in another kind of sculpture in the round. Wherever the figure was made part of an object such as an incense burner or a ceremonial ax blade, it was only a part of the object with which it was combined. From our point of view such objects are accepted as sculpture, for we value them for their sculptural form. Carvings in jade may suggest a human figure but were used as pendants to serve as talismans. The freely posed unencumbered figure occurs in stone sculpture but is less frequent. When carved in relief, the figure became part of an ornamental setting. The figure could be long and slender as in some Maya reliefs, or short and squat as in some Chimu tablets. Accessories of costumes, weapons or implements were often as important as the figure, and at times were made so large that they compete with the figure for attention.

Such conventions did not favor freely detached figures. Each style has its own artistic objectives, and no style should be evaluated aesthetically by the absence of qualities foreign to its spirit. Pre-Columbian art used the figure, but neither the study of anatomy nor the scientific pursuit of realism were major problems, even though the Mochica portrait vases and some Maya stucco reliefs went far, even in that direction. Only Greek sculpture reveals the gradual unfolding of the freestanding figure from static immobility to dynamic expressiveness. Outside of Greek art, there is no parallel in art history for an equal preoccupation with the figure.

But Mexico and Peru had a tradition of realism that found expression in various ways. A fairly standardized mask-type of head is known in Mexico from the archaic period on. Peg-noses, oval-shaped eyes and parted lips represent a pattern that prevailed from early terra cottas to late stone carvings. In modeling and carving the pattern increased in skill, in refinement and expression, but it retained an undisguised human aspect. The Mexican artist differentiated clearly between human beings and gods, who could be human, part human and part animal or wholly animal. Emblems characterized the gods in human form. The god of water and rain, Tlaloc, had circles around his eyes and huge teeth or fangs. The goddess of the earth, Coatlicue, had a serpent head (Fig. 192), or a skull as goddess of death. In such cases the variations from the human form merely indicated specific gods, grotesque though they may seem to us. Indigenous American art does not show the variability of form of Negro African masks. Aztec art may seem grim and repellent, but it is basically sober and not given to extravagant fancy. Peruvian ceramic sculpture even produced portraiture, and portraiture was perhaps approached in some Maya sculpture. A definitely realistic expression was realized in the Totonac laughing heads and in the Olmec baby-face heads. It may be that these were isolated instances prompted by religious motivations rather than by a general trend toward realism.

To appreciate the significance and character of the American achievement in art, we must keep in mind how the continent was settled and what, in broad outlines, these achievements were. At an early date, a part of the human race became isolated from the larger and more populated land mass of Eurasia. After the two portions again came into contact through the Spanish Conquest, it became clear that, in the field of art, ancient America had pursued about the same objectives and had developed the arts in all major fields, somewhat parallel to those of the Old World.

Mexico developed architecture and sculpture, but drawing and painting remained static over long periods of time after a stage of development toward naturalism. Drawing and painting are linked to illustration on paper, to books, a written language and literature. Mexican picture writing was still too clumsy to express abstract ideas. There was less need for thinking, the acting out of religious ceremonials took its place. Art flourished where it served religion, but it did not exist as a free and independent creative activity of the individual. Through religion the culture emphasized art, but minimized the artist. A comparable situation existed in mediaeval Europe but in Mexico the dependence of art on religion may have been even closer.

These ancient American styles compare favorably with those of Europe and the ancient Near East, but fewer works of art have been preserved. Wood carving is inadequately represented, Aztec gold is known only from a few examples, actual textiles, with minor exceptions, are known only from Peru and painting in manuscripts and frescoes from the few examples that have been preserved. But what has survived or has been recovered from ruins and tombs is sufficient to rank ancient and mediaeval American art alongside the arts of Europe and Asia.

REGIONAL STYLES

The order in which the regional styles are here presented does not imply historical relationships, except in a broad sense. The Maya appeared at an early date, and the Olmec likewise. For that reason Maya and Olmec art are taken up first and the Aztec as the last of the Mexican styles, as they ruled the country at the time of the Conquest. The other styles are placed between the major styles, all represented largely by stone sculpture. The Andean styles of Central and South America are treated according to the materials used, gold, stone, pottery and textiles.

Any discussion of artistic qualities must necessarily deal with individual works of art. Even a single work of art often conveys a good deal of the spirit of an era, and the artistic problems the style was dedicated to. Regional styles did not always develop at an even pace; some were retarded and others were advanced. This makes the dating of pre-Columbian Mexican sculpture difficult and a matter for archaeology to deal with.

In a broad survey of pre-Columbian styles, three stages of development can be distinguished: a primitive, a stylized and a realistic stage. Each of these stages does not exclude entirely admixtures of the other two. They appear rather as dominant trends and are unevenly distributed among the several tribes. A primitive tendency is characteristic for the Tarascan and a realistic for the Maya style and for some phases of the styles found in Peru. The others fall largely into the stylized stage. As the Tarascan clay figurines also stand out as a group that is easily differentiated from all other styles, we shall take them up first.

TARASCAN CLAY FIGURINES

Small clay figures, often female, have been found in tombs throughout the whole area extending from the southwestern United States as far south as Colombia. Among those showing the greatest variety in modeling are the Tarascan figurines, which reflect the daily life of the people in contrast to much of pre-Columbian art which appears to represent the interests of officials and priests, as representatives of the state. Some of the Tarascan figurines may be closer to what might be called folk art. There are no gods and no traces of human sacrifice; the spirit expressed is entirely one of the world of man. We can only guess at their religious significance and assume that they were intended to contribute to a pleasant existence.

They vary from a flat and truly primitive painted "gingerbread" type with necklace and bracelets, of which thousands are known, to others fully modeled and largely undecorated. This more fully modeled type with which we are here concerned ranges in size from five to twenty inches and is baked, unbaked, solid or hollow. The human form appears in different postures and proportions, rotund or rectangular, pot or disc-shaped and occasionally sharp and angular, but more often massive and soft as if inflated. Noses are pinched on and mouths and eyes scraped out. Even where feet are slighted and where there are no real hands the figure still looks human.

Of all Mexican arts, these Tarascan figurines are the liveliest. The figures may be standing, reclining, crouching, sitting or engaged in some action like holding a child, vase, staff, utensil or weapon, or playing a musical instrument. Acrobats, warriors, children, animals and houses are also represented, and there are couples and groups of dancers arranged in a circle and attached to a base.

The abbreviation of the figure, like placing the head on amorphous leg-like extensions or combining two uplifted arms with a cylindrical vase, is typical. A free way of dealing with the natural proportions of the figure may seem to give these figures an infantile character, as if these shapes had been arrived at playfully. But the resemblance is more apparent than real and contradicted by an unchild-like gravity and sedateness. These figurines have a character that is strangely adult and a technique that is often accomplished. Regardless of styles, figures are made to stand or sit solidly, even to the extent of making feet into prongs or points that could be pressed into the ground. Other feet are broad, as in standing postures, to give figures a solid support. Arms were not needed to balance the figure and they could be thin, whether kept free of the body or laid on top of the torso. Heads are small or large and seem to depend for size on how securely the figure would stand up. In a seated figure with a broad base, the head is comfortably large (Fig. 140). No action seemed to be too difficult for the artist to attempt. Clay was easily manipulated to assume whatever action was desired. Even a seated pose with legs stretched out sidewise (Fig. 141), or one leaning forward, with arms resting on the knees, was convincingly solved.

In a rectangular standing type of figure in the Charles Laughton Collection, the box-like torso is overlaid with tattoo marks and the woman wears a nose ring, a necklace, shoulder ornaments and arm bands. Another example shows a more slender male version with the same jewelry but no body paint. A lordly expression, reposeful and dignified, is clearly indicated in a seated figure (Fig. 142) with half-closed eyes. This may represent the master who is perhaps awaiting his translation to a world after death. In another figure a musician furnishes entertainment in the manner he was accustomed to on earth. Abstract forms and shapes suggestive of vegetables are curiously combined, as in a lady with a turnip-like head and arms that grow out of the body like roots. As an exercise of balanced forms and contrasting movements this is a superb example; it comes from Nayarit, and is now in the Portland (Oregon) Art Museum. Compared to this classic composition a mother and child in the National Museum of Mexico is in the vein of an impressionistic sketch, a momentary pose with the mother tenderly supporting the head of the crying infant. In a group of a hunter crouching on the ground, panting under the load slung over his shoulder, the primitive mode has been left behind. In this figure, in the form of a jar, from Colima, now in the Robert Woods Bliss Collection on loan at the National Gallery of Art, Washington, we find a stylistic peculiarity that occurs in different Mexican styles. Developed traits of naturalism, as in the posture and the modeling of the head, combine with undeveloped sketchy hands and lumpy feet and a generalized treatment throughout the figure. A highly stylized version, in which traits suggested in some of the preceding figures have fused into a sophisticated mature expression, is shown in a figure from the National Museum of Mexico. A fisherman with a cane in one hand and leaning forward, is balancing himself on a double-headed fish. An impressive clay head, eleven inches high, from Colima or Jalisco (Fig. 143), has been attributed to the middle period (Kubler). This head combines monumental power with a particular physiognomical trait, the mouth drawn down on one side. In that grimace we seem to recognize the expression of one who is putting his whole personality behind a command, this is perhaps virtually a cartoon in stone of a rugged character who talks out of the corners of his mouth. Realism and stylization in the same work is not uncommon in Mexican art, and different from a grotesque element expressed in a conventionalized style. Here the expression is not grotesque, but realistic.

Ceramic vessels from western Mexico in the National Museum of Mexico show pottery in choice examples. A little dog-vase, recalling pottery from the southeastern United States, and a broad bowl (Fig. 144), with a face delicately modeled out of the surface, are shapes that are aesthetically most satisfying. They combine boldness with elegance and refinement.

MAYA ART

Each of the four general characteristics previously discussed as applying to pre-Columbian art applies with particular emphasis to Maya art. Maya architecture ranks at the top in complexity and decoration, though the Toltecs of Teotihuacán surpassed the Maya in the size of their pyramids. The Maya are the only group here represented by mural painting. In sculpture the Maya were preeminent in carved stone and modeled stucco reliefs, and in pottery they excelled in a painted ware showing religious ceremonies, but also developed decoration in relief and in the round. That the Maya were probably the first painters of mediaeval America is indicated by painted manuscripts, notably those in the Codex Dresdensis.

Descendants of the ancient Maya are still living today; over one million people continue to speak dialects of the Maya language. In Mexico, in the states of Chiapas and Yucatán, and in the mountains of Guatemala, Maya Indians plant corn and live in palm-thatched houses. The Maya held out longer against the Spaniards than other Mexican tribes, but after the ruling classes, who alone understood the writings and controlled the arts, had been destroyed, the whole civilization came to an end.

OLD EMPIRE SCULPTURE

Wherever Maya civilization may have had its beginning, on the coastal plain of Veracruz or in northeastern Guatemala, stone sculpture produced its finest work in Copán, in Honduras, close to the border of Guatemala, and in Quiriguá, in southeastern Guatemala, as well as in the Usumacinta River valley, in Piedras Negras (Guatemala), and in Yaxchilán (Menché) and Palenque (Mexico, State of Chiapas). Piedras Negras is best known for various kinds of stone sculpture, Yaxchilán for stone lintels, Palenque for stucco modeling. The first stone records of the first century, or early part of the fourth century of our era (depending on which correlation is used, the Spinden or the Goodman-Martinez Hernandez-Thompson, a difference of 260 years) are from Uaxactun and Tikal in northeastern Guatemala. The finest Maya wooden carvings that have been preserved are also from Tikal.

The Maya used relief carving for the decoration of temples, for ceremonial chambers, for monolithic stone stelae and, at Quiriguá, for stone blocks and boulders to represent mythological animals. The largest stone stela ever quarried by the Maya, one at Quiriguá, was thirty-five feet long, five feet wide and about four feet thick. Stelae served primarily as time markers and were erected about every five years. They stood in paved courts or plazas more or less related to architectural monuments such as temples, staircases or altars.

For the stone stelae, quadrangular blocks were quarried, transported to the site where they were to stand and there erected. They were then carved from a scaffolding with figures in relief on one or both of the broad sides, with hieroglyphics on the narrow sides.

The human figure, as represented in Maya reliefs and paintings, does not conform to a single type as far as proportions are concerned. Long, slender (Ill. 21), as well as short, massive figures occur

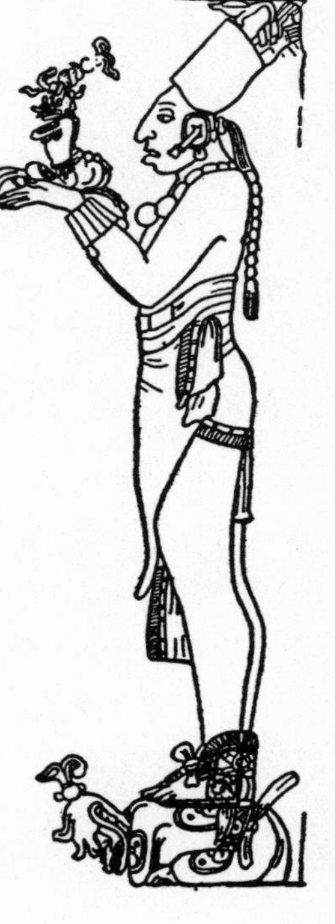

Ill. 21. Maya triple slab in the "Temple of the Sun." Drawing of a presiding priest at Palenque, State of Chiapas, Mexico. *After Joyce.*

(Fig. 145). Others approach the normal proportions freely rather than in an attempt to obtain scientific accuracy. Eventually the Maya artist could handle the figure with some ease as to reasonably correct proportions and a sense of freedom to express action. The final stage reached in figure drawing goes well beyond archaic restraint but is still bound to representations of types.

Tatiana Proskouriakoff points out in her study of classic Maya sculpture that there are about 400 major pieces of monumental sculpture in the classic style available for study, of which 160 can be dated, covering a span of five and a half centuries. The classical monumental style seems to have occurred during a long period which was not subjected to outside influence. The style developed a formal serenity in composition and in the design of stelae featured a single human figure, standing or sitting on a throne or in a niche, or holding a ceremonial bar, shield, spear, scepter or staff. Where action is represented, it may be presumed to refer to a ceremonial gesture, as the scattering of grain or the letting of blood (Fig. 146) or the capture of prisoners. Such scenes occur on lintels more often than on stelae.

The motif of the figure developed postures from the early Maya through the classical Maya into the late Toltec-Yucatán period. In the subtle changes which single motifs have undergone, Tatiana Proskouriakoff sees an aesthetic development in the Maya style. In the early side-view posture, both feet point in the same direction and do not overlap, nor do knees overlap, and the shoulders are in front view. Nine different kinds of posture represent the development from an early, static type of figure to a late type showing movement (Illus. 22).

Stelae in the late classic period show the figure facing front with both feet turned out. At first the hands remain unchanged but gradually they are raised or lowered, point out from the body and at times are freely detached. Eventually motion is suggested, feet are raised from the ground and the body may be slanted sidewise, out of its perpendicular position. A comparable development took place with the seated figure. Legs may be in side view or crossed in front so that both knees are visible. The seated posture is rare on stelae but occurs on other monuments.

The figure is treated in many ways and with more restraint in the stone stelae. But even in stelae several figures were combined, one above the other, or several figures were freely grouped as crouching prisoners beneath their conquerors, at Piedras Negras, stela 12 (Fig. 147). Lintels offered better shapes for combining figures on the same level. Some of the most effective monumental compositions belong to this group. The freest and most intricate figure compositions occur on full-figure numerals, as on those carved on stela D at Copán (Illus. 23). They represent elaborations of the simpler face numerals to which bodies have been attached. The middle row, with the hand attached to the face, is recognizable as zero, but others are less certain, as they show no easy correspondence to face numerals. For invention and skill in turning figures into ornament, these small designs are masterpieces. Though the originals are carvings, even the line drawings convey an impression of the power and control of the artist. There is here more variety of facial expression than is usually found in Maya art.

In the use of the human figure Maya art is more nearly comparable to the mediaeval stage of European art; adherence to a typical expression is evident in Maya heads. The forehead slants back, the nose is prominent, the mouth open, the chin receding. The receding forehead, where it occurs, is due to artificial flattening, a characteristic not ordinarily present in the modern Maya.

In the representations of prisoners Maya art reached its most realistic stage in relief carving, as

Ill. 22. Maya sculpture. Standing figure with both feet pointing in the same direction; from the early to the late classic period. *After Tatiana Proskouriakoff. Carnegie Institution of Washington, D. C.*

in stela 12 at Piedras Negras, where individual heads show an uncommon degree of individualization. Here the fifteenth century Netherlandish school offers a parallel from European art. Even an expression of a mood is suggested in the sullen, dejected heads (Fig. 147).

The figure shows torso and arms in full front view and heads, legs and feet in profile, on a carved jade pendant, now in the Leyden (Netherlands) Museum. This so-called "Leyden Plate," a celt-like object eight and a half inches long and three inches wide, is the earliest known dated object from the Maya area. The engraved date corresponds to 60 A.D. (or 320 A.D.) and represents the date the plate was actually engraved; with minor changes this profile position was continued throughout Maya art. The full front view was used on stelae in standing and seated postures. In the most developed stela design the seated figure appears in a niche; three-quarter views are usually avoided.

Greater action in the delineation of the figure occurs in small reliefs, codices, ceramics and mural painting. Here vivacity, complexity and a degree of invention go beyond the reposeful dignity of the larger compositions in stone relief, even where a number of figures are used.

Drapery plays a small part in Maya sculpture, animals and the ceremonial elaboration of the figure were more important than the figure itself. But there are exceptions where drapery is elaborated and well defined. An example is a standing figure at Palenque (Ill. 24). Spinden has shown that in the place of drapery the Maya developed a system of ornamentation based on the animal gods, like serpents, jaguars, birds, dragons and also bones, which were symbols of death, as well as on maize, on various divinities and astronomical symbols and ceremonial objects. To this group belong the so-called "ceremonial bars" and the "manikin scepters" held by the figures in stelae and on altars.

The importance of the serpent may have been even greater in art than in religion, for there was no serpent god as such. The serpent motif was based on the rattlesnake, modified in appearance and turned into ornamental designs. Plumes of the quetzal bird were added to the serpent to form the feathered serpent. Art further idealized this creation of myth and religion by adding scrolls, spirals, circles, and other undulating flame-like lines. A human head with nose and earplugs was added to the serpent body to turn the serpent motif into an anthropomorphic being, the human head protruding from the serpent's jaws.

The curved serpent body was turned into angular scrolls, and by elaborating, simplifying, eliminating and substituting details the serpent was changed in many ways. Parts like head, fangs, eyes, spots and others were used symbolically to suggest the basic motif so that a serpent became so simplified as to be barely recognizable. Even plant and vegetable forms were combined with serpent-like details.

Such a fusion of an animal body and a human head was developed by the Maya in an original manner. A mere increase in size of the animal body to suggest divinity was not sufficient, the god had to be imbued with intellect, hence, human heads appeared within serpents' mouths (Spinden). In some examples the human head is more important than the serpent mouth, suggesting that the head was not a victim, but part of a symbol of divinity. In other examples this head in a serpent's mouth may have been intended as a victim.

Maya architecture and sculpture were painted—in some cases a whole building or monument with a single color. Traces of pigments have survived. Carved surfaces were painted in contrasting colors, red for the nude portions of the figure and for animals; blue and green for ornaments; green for feathers; blue for garments. Color in some variety was used for stucco ornamentation at Palenque. Color may have brought an element of repose into the ornamental details which often seem confusing now that the color has disappeared.

A remarkable work of sculpture, and one of the best preserved, is zoomorph P, at Quiriguá (Guatemala) (Fig. *148*). This huge boulder, seven feet high and over eleven feet in diameter, is one of several. The front view, showing a seated figure within the mouth of a two-headed serpent or dragon, represents the composition at its best. The serpent body coils across the surface of the boulder, dividing into separate motifs, each one attractive by itself but lost in the total design.

This carved boulder, perhaps the most ambitious sculptural work of the Maya, resists easy comprehension. It is not a simple matter even to recognize the motifs. The recessed spherical shapes are the two eyes, each engraved with a cross, beside a row of conventionalized feathers. The saw tooth border, seen more clearly on the right, represents teeth. The figure, surmounted by an elaborate headdress, holds an emblem in his right hand, the "manikin scepter," an object known only from its appearance in art. Angular scrolls are parts of serpents and leaf shaped motifs are feathers. The figure is defined in head, torso, arms and knees and in its pattern of small-scale surface enrichment. The contrast of delicate, low relief against bold, high relief, setting small-scale shapes against large bulging forms, accounts in part for the artistic effect. Added to this is a basic unity, the figure dominating the animal parts on either side.

Ill. 23 (right). Designs of full figure numerals, from Copán, Honduras, Maya stela D. *British Museum.*

Ill. 24 (extreme right). Maya triple slab in the "Temple of the Sun." Drawing of a figure at Palenque, State of Chiapas, Mexico. *After Joyce.*

A combination of figure, ornamental elaboration, a sumptuously displayed feather headdress and hieroglyphics achieved the utmost in stela F at Quiriguá. The quadrangular block has been modified, so that the plane of the figure stands in front of a receding hieroglyphic enframement, and the figure itself is concealed beneath an unusually elaborate pattern of carved stonework.

One of the most elaborately carved figures is stela H at Copán, 522 A.D. (or 782 A.D.). It is twelve feet high and over three feet wide (Fig. 149) and projects out in high relief from the stela. The rectangular block has disappeared completely under a maze of projecting ornamentation. The head, the arms holding the ceremonial bar and the feet are the only recognizable parts of the figure which otherwise has been turned into a piece of jewelry-like stone decoration. The headdress consists of a serpent head from which carved feathers and tassels spread out fan-like; a skirt, overlaid with masks and pendants, is carved in flat, medium and high relief. Stone is treated with a lace-like delicacy comparable to the late Gothic cathedrals of Europe.

Among the outstanding stelae at Piedras Negras are stelae 12 and 14. On stela 12, 535 A.D. (or 795 A.D.) the style is pictorial. In the upper part of the now broken stela a seated figure, perhaps a Maya territorial ruler, is represented in a combined full-view torso and profile view of head and legs. The conventional pose is expressed with an easy naturalness in the downward bend of the head and the position of the arms. Three officials and a supplicant are represented in the middle section and the before-mentioned squatting prisoners with their arms tied behind their backs.

In stela 14, 501 A.D. (or 761 A.D.) (Fig. 150) the seated figure is in the half-round and placed within a deep niche. The conception of a single surface that has been cut into to bring out relief has been abandoned. Instead, there is a considerable variation in the depth of the relief, several planes are used, one is set back of the other, before the seated figure in the niche is reached. The outer planes of the stela are in low relief but varied slightly in depth to detach details and differentiate between levels. There is no adherence to absolute symmetry, as in the scrollwork of the frame flanking the niche. The most precise carving is in the headdress of the seated figure; the lower right corner, said to be occupied by a third figure, has disintegrated beyond recognition.

Stela 10 from Seibal of the upper Usumacinta River region is of the late period, dated 589 A.D. (or 849 A.D.), and is in low relief (Fig. 151). The main contours are sharply drawn, with the background cut away, after the manner of the *champlevé* technique, so that the large design stands out by contrast. By carving the surface of the original slab a flat and shallow relief is created. The effect is close to drawing on stone, except that details are given a slight relief with sharp and soft contours.

In spite of an overwhelming richness, the pattern is clear. The human head is placed opposite the presumably divine serpent head, which is so highly ornamentalized as to be barely recognizable. For invention of linear rhythms and effects of texture, for variety and elaboration and an all-over exquisite preciousness, the relief is unsurpassed. The sweep of the feathers in the headdress, in the way they are grouped, recessed and curved, gives a subtle impression of vigor. On the opposite side, the elements of the serpent head break up the space in ever-changing curves. On the same side, the section immediately above the vertical row of glyphs is a masterpiece of refinement. At the feet, blossoms with spiky leaves burst forth, and to the right, more freely disposed curves fill in a broad rectangle. The profile head is joined in a gesture of convincing naturalness with the bent arm holding the ceremonial bar beneath a broad necklace. Grace, delicacy and impeccable taste are characteristic of this Maya stela of a period which archaeology classifies as decadent.

Stone lintels from Yaxchilán (Menché) now in the British Museum (Maudslay Collection) reveal Old Empire relief carving at its best. Each lintel represents probably a priest before a kneeling figure, richly costumed. In lintel 24, about three and one-half feet high, the kneeling figure offers his own blood by drawing a cord through his tongue; in lintels 15 and 23 (Fig. 152) the kneeling figures, about three and four feet high, hold a basket with the implements of penance, used for ceremonial blood letting. The spirit is the same in all three reliefs and so are the compositional schemes, major figures arranged on either side of a diagonal and inscriptions, or glyphs, fitted in around the edges and into vacant spaces. Each lintel has a quality of its own. One (24) shows an expression of power and dignity, accomplished through a balanced design contrasting curvilinear elements in bold relief against a solid mass carved in a smaller scale. The other (23) is extravagant in its expression of movement. Two gods are indicated, the upper god shows a head and shoulders armed with spear and shield as coming out of a serpent's mouth, and the lower god a head with the emblems of Sun and Death. The low relief of the figure clings to the corner in contrast to the bolder convolutions of the god which expand in energetic movement. Each lintel has an individual style and every detail is consistent with its style.

Lintels 15 and 24 have a good deal in common; stylistically, all carry through their own technique to the utmost perfection in the shaping of the edges and in the carving of the details.

In an oval-shaped relief from Palenque (Fig. 153) two seated figures are represented, an official on a jaguar throne beside a subordinate figure holding up a crown. Here the pattern is emphasized and the background is related to the carved portions, so that every detail takes its place. More simplified in technique and drawing than the three rectangular lintels from Yaxchilán, this oval shaped panel is its equal in rhythm.

In another stone relief (already illustrated in Fig. 145) attributed to Palenque, now in the Museo de America, at Madrid, a chief, or priest, is admirably fitted to the enclosure. He holds a religious symbol in his right hand, perhaps a serpent with a water lily. A combination of mass and weight in the figure, with an easy graceful posture, constitutes the particular attraction of this panel. The head, conforming to the Maya-type, reflects nobility. Maya figures are usually devoid of much expression, but lordly priests and high officials look commanding by their action, just as supplicants look meek.

A ball-court marker dated 331 A.D. (or 591 A.D.) in the National Museum of Mexico (Fig. 154) is a disc-like stone slab carved with a central figure surrounded by a border of dots and bars and face numerals containing the date of the carving. The ball player is carefully spaced within the circle, between a disc and two engraved panels. The upper portion of the ball player shows a strong profile, under a headdress of feathers, bars and a small figure supporting water lilies. The ornamental pattern of the player with his padded knees and elbows, the contrast of smooth and textured surfaces, the relationship of surface to background, are well studied. Against the smaller scale of the center, the border is carved in broader style. The interest is on the accessories and on the figure chiefly to the extent that the figure supports the emblems. The extended arm receives less attention than any one of the down-curving feathers.

Though movement is already present in the classic period in carving as in painting, in the late period of the New Empire relief carving became lively in the action of the figures, as Tatiana Proskouriakoff has shown in her comparative study. In a door jamb of a structure at Kabah the figure has become free to the extent that action is convincingly expressed though not anatomically correct.

Maya stone sculpture in the round is known from some figures and heads which are fragments taken out of their architectural setting. Among the finest known examples are a part of a head from Louisville (British Honduras) now in the collection of the Institute for Middle American Research at Tulane University, a so-called maize-god head and maize-god bust from Copán, now, respectively, at the Peabody Museum of Harvard University (Fig. 155) and the British Museum. Though badly weathered, the Tulane University head is appealing in its delicate modeling and the better preserved maize-god head of the Peabody Museum is in the same style. In this head pre-Columbian art reaches the level of the best of Greek and Gothic sculpture, though actually the style recalls Oriental rather than European art. Maize leaves form part of the headdress and earplugs add a note of firmness beside the ethereal quality of the features. The Maya type of head appears here in its most spiritual version, and without the excessively receding forehead and chin.

The same general character is apparent in the more complete maize-god bust from Copán (Fig. 156). Comparison with other heads from Copán suggest that this slightly emaciated type may have been the personal style of one artist. The calm resignation expressed in the features is reinforced by the gesture of the hands, one raised as if to restrain, the other lowered as if to encourage. That a message of some import is being conveyed seems evident. Serenity here presumably expresses some lofty aspirations, different from the usual involvements with a heavy ceremonialism linked to animal symbolism. We cannot be certain of the interpretation of this beckoning gesture, but it seems removed from the grosser expressions of primitive magic.

An outstanding example of marble sculpture is a vase under ten inches high from the Ulua Valley of northern Honduras (Fig. 157). A surface pattern of scroll elements represents a central mask between four profile heads so combined with the scrolls that the profiles merge into the pattern; ornamentation becomes playful and perhaps symbolical. Such play of line, where scrolls and faces unite into an ornamental design, also occurs in European art where such ornamental motifs are known as arabesques. The scrolls also bear a faint resemblance to early Chinese art, but neither Europe nor China had any influence on these patterns which are wholly indigenous. Two animal-carved handles in their compact solidity are well related to the massive character of the style.

WORK IN STUCCO

In stucco reliefs and stucco sculpture in the round, Maya art reached another high point, as illustrated in some fragments from Palenque. In one of the best preserved wall panels a central figure stands between two kneeling attendants. The costumes elaborated with feathers, masks, emblems and net-like skirts recall the stelae. The technical competence is equal to the lintels of Yaxchilán, but in addition the spaciousness of the background is unique. Delicacy and refinement are here carried further than elsewhere in Maya sculpture, which may be due in part to the more plastic medium. The style reflects the spirit of the stelae but is more elegant and more graceful.

Two Maya heads in the round, one modeled in stucco over a prepared armature, from Piedras Negras, now in the National Museum of Guatemala City (Fig. 158) and the other cut in limestone from Honduras, now in the Middle American Research Institute of Tulane University, represent other versions of the Maya style. Both have the parted lips, the protruding eyes, and the calm expression in common with the maize gods' heads of Copán, but otherwise each head reflects its own type of realism. Suppleness and grace characterize the stucco head, whereas the limestone head is imbued with a sturdy vigor. Traces of parts of a serpent are still recognizable in the fragmentary headdress.

Clay figurines, so amply developed by the Tarascans, also occur in the Maya region. A figurine in the collection at Tulane University (Fig. 159) represents a woman holding a child by one hand and a dog under the other arm. Primitive traits in thick feet and thin arms combine with a head that reflects the classic manner. Eyes, mouth and the modeling of the cheeks is close to the stela style. The little dog with his legs drawn up to his body is obviously based on observation, and the heavy-set figure may also be from life. In contrast to such realism, the small figure is most unchildlike. This is another example in which primitive conventions and classic and realistic details are found in the same work, a trend which is characteristic for pre-Columbian Mexican art.

NEW EMPIRE SCULPTURE

In the New Empire sculpture in the round, independent of architecture but as a part of the architectural setting, was continued at the large centers as at Chichén Itzá. It included four types: (1) the so-called Chac Mool figures; (2) jaguar thrones; (3) standard-bearers and (4) Atlantean figures. Chac Mool figures, of which about a dozen have been located at Chichén Itzá, are reclining figures beside temple doorways holding stone plates probably used as receptacles for offerings. Jaguar thrones are stone benches in the form of jaguars, carved with jaguar legs and heads. Standard-bearers are supports of masts used for feather banners, in form of seated figures, and Atlantean figures are shaped rectangular pedestals for altars carved in relief to suggest a supporting figure. In each of these applications of human and animal shapes to an architectural use, the motifs are simplified and subordinated to the utilitarian object. The massive character of the stone is emphasized, which is in keeping with the massive character of the surrounding buildings to which these objects related.

The artists responsible for these late works were no longer purely Maya since the arrival in Yucatán of tribes from Mexico. This Mexican-Maya culture left its imprint on sculpture. We see this difference clearly when we compare a well-known example, like a head emerging from the mouth of a serpent from the house of the magician at Uxmal, Yucatán, with the maize god heads from Copán. A sterner type of human being is here reflected, different from the gentler expression of the Copán maize gods. The style of carving has hardened to an ornamental pattern, firm, static and accomplished, but also without the vitality of the Old Empire style.

PAINTING

We know Maya painting particularly from painted ceramics, from fresco wall paintings and from illustrations of manuscripts or codices of which the Codex Dresdensis is the best.

Richness of color is noteworthy in an outstanding vase from the later period (Color Plate 13). In a loose, angular style of brush strokes a figure in jaguar skin skirt or kilt holds an antler and two javelins. A hawk-like bird, a deer with crossed bones indicated on its blanket, together with other figures are believed to represent a ceremony held in March when the deer shed their antlers. But beyond that, the real meaning is not clear. Compared to Greek vase painting, these differences stand out: in subject matter, a closer involvement with the animal world; in design, a tendency to fill the space without depending on the background to aid the effect; and in technique, a painterly approach emphasizing color rather than line.

To an extent, painting is a measure of the cultural and artistic maturity of a people. The Maya, like the Greeks, developed monumental painting and both nations were the leaders in art in their respective regions and periods.

A well-preserved Old Empire painting is a fresco from the wall of a chamber in structure B-XIII at Uaxactun, excavated by the Carnegie Institution in 1937. Twenty-six figures are arranged in two rows, one above the other, presumably representing a ceremony. Figures from this painting show the grace and charm of the drawing which depend on elegant profile postures and a careful rendering of costume. Like most of the world's drawing and painting outside of Western European art, the Maya also used the modes of line and flat tone and sought its effects largely within profile postures arranged in a frieze-like manner. It is only partially dedicated to realism and combines primitive characteristics with others that are advanced. Tiny hands and board-like legs appear side by side with expressive gestures, well-placed feet, an appreciation for sweeping lines in the contours of figures, and a love for ornamental detail. More attention is paid to costume than to anatomy, and differences of sex are hardly noted.

Fine Old Empire wall paintings were discovered (1946) in eastern Chiapas (Mexico) on the interior walls of a temple on a site named Bonampak, a Maya name meaning "painted walls."

The walls of three separate chambers are covered with many nearly life-size figures, some seventy in the first chamber. Gorgeously attired Indians are arranged in two and three friezes one above the other; masks and glyphs complete the decoration. The subjects represented are ceremonies, processions, battle scenes, presentations of captives, dances and groups of seated figures. The composition by friezes is varied by another scheme using steps, on which the figures stand or sit. This represents a device to overcome the lack of other methods to indicate space and was probably suggested by the real steps of Maya architecture. The temple in which these murals were found stands on a terrace approached by steps.

The subject matter of the Bonampak murals has been defined tentatively in a recent publication by the Carnegie Institution of Washington (1955). The main scenes are thought to represent: (1) preparations for a dance by impersonators of gods of the earth (Room 1); (2) a raid, capture, and arraignment of prisoners needed for sacrifice (Room 2); (3) sacrificial ceremony and dance (Room 3).

The representation of the figure combines a conventional element with realism. The chief convention consists of profile heads combined with front or side view figures. Figures overlap to suggest that they exist in space, and in the battle scenes they are massed three or four deep. In the processions, individuals turn to each other as if engaged in conversation. Arms are raised and hands hold trumpets or grasp objects; there is also the pointing finger, or the hand pleading for mercy. The skill with which the hands are drawn varies with the painters who worked on these frescoes. The same lively expressiveness is not found in the drawing of the heads; they conform to a type, even though there is some variation in profiles and some noses are larger and more aquiline than others. Expression is not in the features but in the action of the figure, in the use of masks and in fantastic disguise.

Costumes and accessories contribute to an effect of great splendor. The leading figures have jaguar pelts thrown over their backs or wear close-fitting jaguar jackets, collars, belts, sashes and various kinds of elaborate animal and feather headdresses. Individual groups are of great beauty, like the scene of the costuming of the chief, in the upper level of the first chamber, where attendants place the last finishing touches. The attendants holding conversation on the same level and a group of water gods (Color Plate 14) beneath this level are among the most attractive. The masks of the water gods include animal and vegetable motifs, like water lily, crocodile (or cayman) heads and crab claws. There is a wealth of ornamental pattern that holds one's attention throughout the whole fresco cycle.

In the realm of figure drawing there are fine postures that suggest the military valor of the Maya, but the most involved example of difficult foreshortening occurs in one of the captives. A sprawling figure with head fallen back and one arm hanging down limp is on the step beneath the Maya chief in the second chamber. The motif is unique and is perhaps unrivaled by any other.

Composition, drawing, ornamentation all contribute to the total effect, but less so than color. The over-all effectiveness depends mostly on a contrasting color scheme, glowing and sumptuous dark browns and even black against backgrounds of blue and yellow. Other colors, red, green, purple and white, as well as blue, are used in smaller areas. This impression is gained from the modern copies made by Augustin Villagra Caleti, but we assume they are based on a scientific study of the remains of actual color that was still visible on the walls in spite of the damaged and fragmentary condition of the originals.

Since the publication of the Villagra copies, the copies in color of all frescoes made by the well-known Guatemalan artist, Sr. Antonio Tejeda Fonseca, in 1947 and 1948, for the Carnegie Institution of Washington, and now at the Peabody Museum of Harvard University, have appeared. These copies are said to be accurate and without any restoration that would have involved seriously damaged sections. Only minor uncontroversial portions that were damaged in the originals have been restored in the copies. Reproductions printed on paper show a good deal of variation; our illustration strikes a medium range of brilliance between the very pale and the most intense.

The frescos of Bonampak are triumphs of Maya painting. They demonstrate how far Maya art could go when released from the restraining influence of stone. Here the art of the stelae found expression in a flexible medium representing Maya painting on a level with the reliefs of the bound captives of stela 12 at Piedras Negras. The fact that individual figures are without modeling in light and shade may be in part due to the difficult medium of fresco. But of greater importance was probably the fact that there was no compelling reason for the inclusion of this particular element in Maya painting. What Altamira achieved in that respect Bonampak might have accomplished had the Maya painter thought it essential.

The two artists, who worked side by side on the copies, believe that the originals were painted on the damp plaster in true fresco style.

Bonampak itself was a small site, outclassed by at least twenty Maya cities; it flourished about 600 A.D. to about 825 A.D. (Thompson correlation). The discovery of these outstanding frescoes by Giles G. Healey in 1946, while engaged in making a film "The Maya Through the Ages" for the United Fruit Company, constituted an event of major importance in Middle American archaeology. What made the discovery possible was the fact that a local Lacandon Indian, a descendant of the ancient Maya, had led Mr. Healey to the structure which was so well concealed in the tropical jungle that it had escaped detection (Carnegie Report).

A complete New Empire wall painting, a battle scene, is represented in the Temple of the Jaguars at Chichén Itzá (Ill. 25). It covers a wall space of one hundred square feet with the small figures averaging ten inches in height. The figures increase at the top to about twice the height of the figures at the bottom. A person seated before the painting would be able to "read" the picture more clearly all the way from bottom to top. At the top is the Maya village, which is being defended by Maya warriors against an attacking Mexican tribe. The Mexican standard, the feathered serpent, is seen at the lower right; the lowest zone is occupied by peace negotiation.

The painter gives us figures in action without confusion. Each figure is represented in outline filled in with a flat tone. No depth, perspective, air or illumination are indicated. The figures float, so to speak, against a flat green background. With no space to give a unified effect, the painter had to create a pattern to keep his groups in order. In a group of defending Maya at the top of the mural, shields and spears repeat shapes and lines to produce a rhythm that unites the group. It should also be noted how the artist places a foot or draws a hand grasping a spear. All details are apparently based on observation.

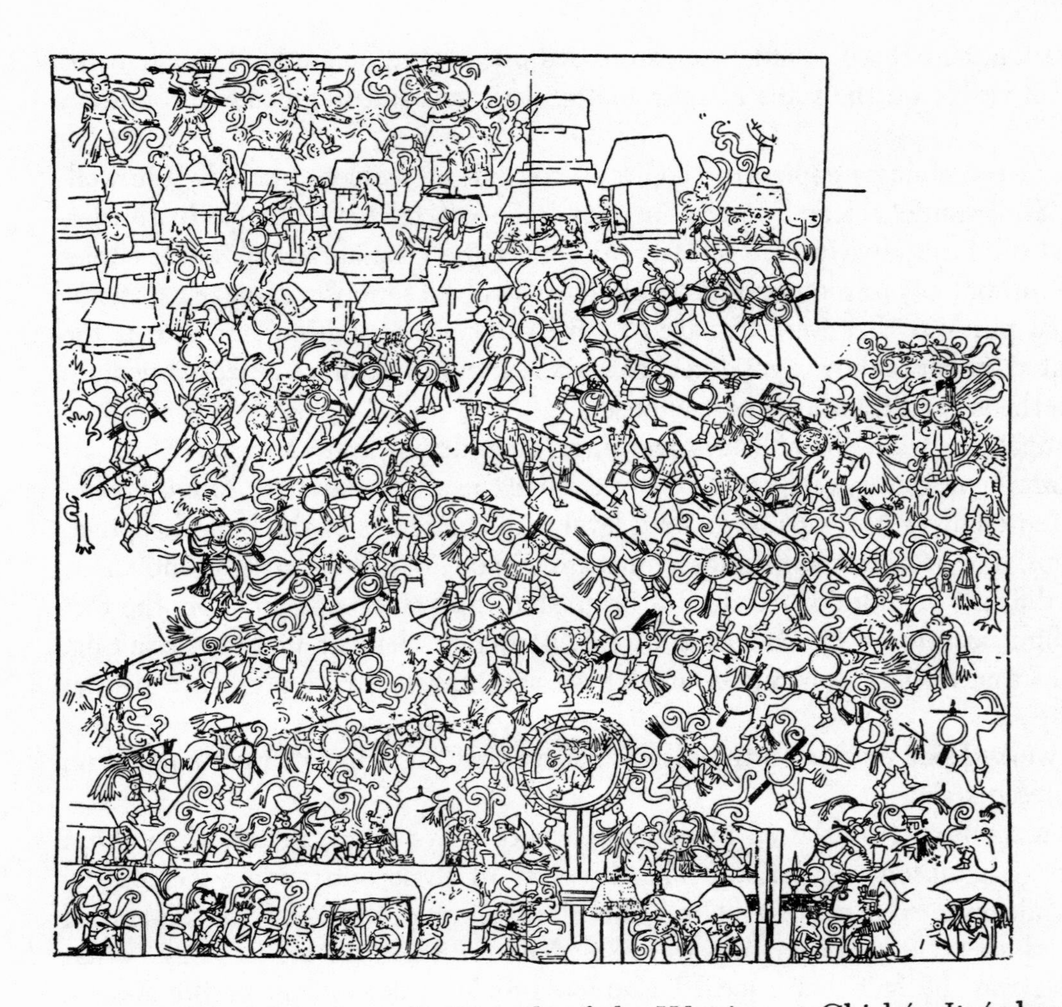

Ill. 25. Maya New Empire mural painting, battle between Maya and Mexicans, Temple of the Jaguars, Chichén Itzá, Yucatán, Mexico. *After a copy by Jean Charlot and Mrs. E. H. Morris. University of Minnesota.*

A wall painting from the Temple of the Warriors at Chichén Itzá shows a fishing village in the upper and a water scene in the lower register. This one, as well as another battle scene in the same temple, is more primitive, but both have their own individual styles and represent figures as animated types. New Empire wall paintings have been found in a number of other places in addition to Chichén Itzá. The corbel-vaulted chambers of the New Empire were roofed over by capstones, which sometimes were painted with figures in a style resembling the Codex illustrations.

DRAWING

Of the Maya illustrated manuscripts or codices only three have survived, hardly sufficient by which to judge Maya book illustrations. Pictorial representations of Maya gods from the codices show a unity that give an impression of one phase of graphic art (Ill. 26). The gods are represented by seated or standing figures in action in profile. Heads are typical of the god represented; they may be grotesque like the wind god (K) holding a bird and decorated with feather headdress, a feathered tail and a projecting nose, or old, like god D, the chief god Itzamna, or youthful, like god E, the corn god.

A pictorial and a decorative character are often combined as in god A, the death god, including a skeleton back and showing a bone for a lower jaw, or in the goddess of suicide (Ixtab) (Ill. 26, J). Representation and decoration may combine to form an ornamental design or to give a confused total effect. Profile, hands, feet and action each contribute to make these figures seem alive. But liveliness is dominated by an over-all ornateness. Headdress, implements and costume details impose themselves on the figures to obscure action at the expense of decoration. Judged by standards of design all but three are decidedly attractive, the corn god is perhaps the finest one of the group.

POTTERY

The Maya developed pottery for domestic, ceremonial and funerary uses in many shapes and techniques. At times, smaller works, executed apparently spontaneously, have a freshness and suggest the range of expression of which a style was capable. This is so in the incised drawing of a seated warrior on a Maya cup under five inches high. With deft strokes sharply delineating the figure the artist emphasized the headdress and the action of the figure with the sole of one foot turned out. A Maya painted clay statuette about eight inches high (Color Plate 15) shows us a figure of normal proportions. All artistry has been lavished on features, headdress, ear plugs and necklace, and

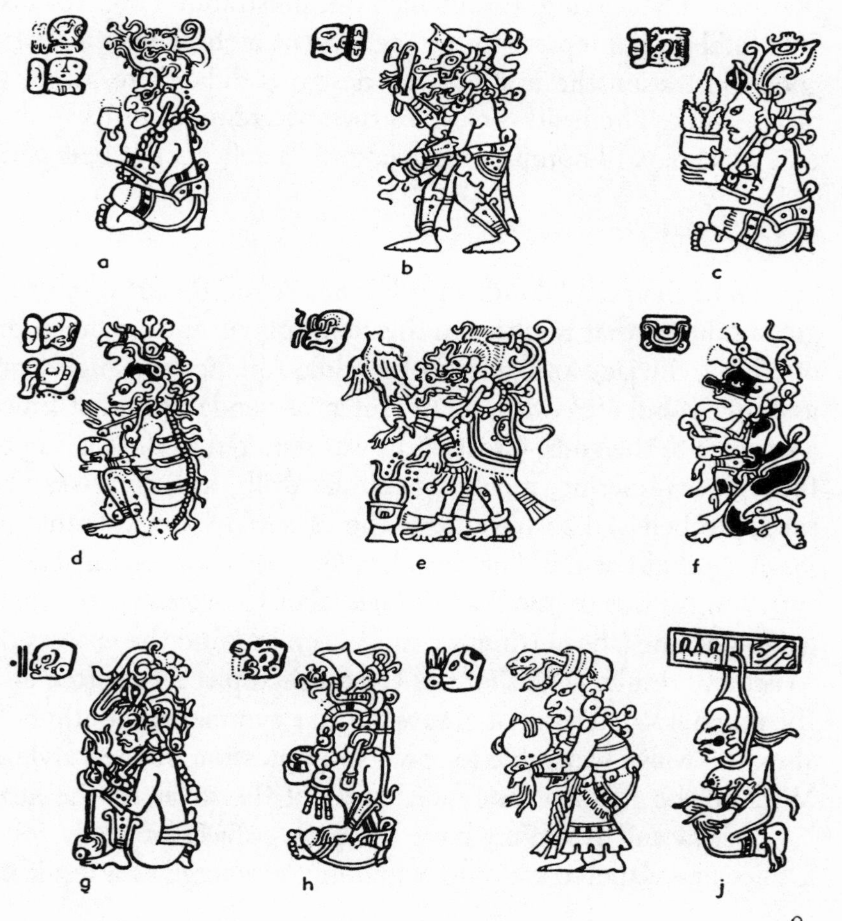

Ill. 26. Principal deities of the Maya pantheon, as represented in the codices. (a) Itzamna, head of the Maya pantheon (God D); (b) Chac, the rain-god (God B); (c) Yum Kax, the corn-god (God E); (d) Ah Puch, the death-god (God A); (e) the wind-god, perhaps Kukulkan (God K); (f) the war-god (God L); (g) the god of sudden death and of human sacrifice (God F); (h) Xaman Ek, the North Star god (God C); (i) Ixchel, wife of Itzamna and the goddess of childbirth and weaving (Goddess I). (j) Ixtab, the goddess of suicide. *After Morley. Stanford University Press—Oxford University Press.*

the posture is formal and dignified. The contrast of the careful head and the summary treatment of the figure indicates that personality and rank in such figures as these were more important to the ancient Maya than any interest in a realistic development of the figure for the sake of art. Culture quite universally determines where the artist is to place his emphasis.

In addition to the painted vases are those decorated in low relief, as in a well-known red-orange vase from Quiché, Guatemala, now in the University Museum, Philadelphia. Its attraction is in its technical perfection, less in linear rhythm, in which Mimbres painted pottery has set such a high standard of achievement.

Another outstanding Maya piece is a bowl about seven and a quarter inches high, carved in deep relief, in sharply contrasting levels. Coming from Quiriguá it shows a style reminiscent of the involved convolutions of zoomorph P. (Fig. 160). Relief carving, whether carved directly or impressed through use of a mold, shows many styles.

WOOD CARVING

Wood carving achieved great distinction in the Old Empire. A few door lintels from the great pyramid temples of Tikal have been preserved though in fragmentary condition. These lintels were made up of from four to ten beams of sapodilla from seven to over seventeen feet long, depending on the span. The carving, from which our illustration (Fig. *161*) is taken, is one of extraordinary richness. The total design represents a huge serpent arching over a central niche with a seated figure. Even in a good illustration the unity of the design is difficult to grasp. Fortunately, a detail reveals the quality of the work. The head is close to the style familiar to us from stone sculpture. As this lintel has been dated 751 A.D. (Thompson correlation), it reflects the best period of Maya sculpture.

JADES

Several of the pre-Columbian tribes developed the art of cutting hard stones, especially jades, a bluish-green mineral that is native to this hemisphere, and occurs in different regions (Fig. *162*). Like the jade of China, the jade and jadeite of Middle America was highly priced, surpassing gold. Jades were carved as amulets and were worn by the rulers as pendants and at times placed with the deceased or offered as a sacrifice to the gods. Great effort was required in the carving of this hard mineral. Copper, made hard through hammering, including tubular drills, and abrasives like emery and sand, using plant fibers as saws, are believed to have been the essential tools available to the carvers. Straight lines and circles leaving a slight central knob were, comparatively speaking, easier to produce than curves and modulated surfaces. All this required additional labor to overcome the marks left by drills and saws. For an appreciation of fine jade cutting, we must keep in mind the endless drilling, abrading and polishing necessary to achieve results. The shape of the finished piece was often allowed to remain irregular as the shape of the original stone was not always cut to a symmetrical outline. Due to their highly perfected craftsmanship, the Maya were able to leave an impression of their style even on this most resisting of materials. We find the characteristic facial types of the stelae on the heads of carved jades.

Maya and Aztec art have been the subject of study for a considerable time, but such styles as Olmec and Zapotec are only beginning to emerge as a result of more recent excavations. The Toltecs, who are associated with the pyramids at Teotihuacán, had an important culture and eventually migrated from central Mexico to the south and east, one branch settling in Yucatán. Each tribe, in fact, developed a style in its own region during the first millennium of the Christian era and even up to the time of the Conquest.

THE OLMEC STYLE

Very little is known about the gifted and civilized Olmecs. According to Indian legends, the Olmecs were believed to have been the oldest civilized inhabitants of Mexico. The name Olmec means "citizen of Olman" (from olli, rubber), the tropical lowlands of the south of Mexico, and particularly the southern Gulf Coast (Covarrubias). Some scholars believe that Olmec art came after the early Maya due to the fact that their calendar, patterned after the Maya calendar, contains errors which give a false impression of antiquity. Others hold to the opinion that early Olmec sculpture was of an early date, and that the inscriptions are of the same early period. That could make the Olmecs a center, from which influences diffused to the Zapotecs and Maya.

Matthew W. Stirling, chief of the Bureau of American Ethnology, discovered a number of colossal stone heads near the coast at Tres Zapotes and La Venta (1939-44), and fifty miles inland at San Lorenzo and Potrero Nuevo (1945-46). The sites are located in the states of Veracruz and Tabasco, in the region where the Spanish conquerors first landed. A colossal basalt head, one of several, measured eight and a half feet in height with a circumference of twenty-two feet. The largest head, at San Lorenzo, is over nine feet high and has been estimated to weigh close to fifteen tons. One monolithic block of basalt is carved on top with the representation of a jaguar skin and on one side with life-sized figures placed in niches. A second altar shows a relief carved with figures holding infants. In all, twenty stone monuments were found at Tres Zapotes and La Venta during the earlier expeditions, some mutilated, suggesting that the Olmecs were conquered by invaders. La Venta was the regional center of the classic Olmec area and the place of residence of the Olmec rulers. In addition to four colossal heads, the La Venta site yielded stone altars, carved stone stelae, an earth pyramid, an area enclosed with stone columns, numerous caches of buried jades and a mosaic floor with a design suggesting a jaguar mask, buried twenty-three feet below ground.

The basalt heads with bands and ear flaps show broad and massive features, with thick lips and wide nostrils. The impression is one of grim, forceful realism and softness in the treatment of the flesh, with a suggestion of wrinkles between the eyes. A different individual is represented in a head (San Lorenzo) over five feet high (Fig. 163). The helmet shows jaguar claws, one over each eye, and circular earplugs, whereas a horizontal piece pierces the ear lobe on the larger San Lorenzo head.

In this head the nose is more normal but recedes behind the protruding lips. The eye is recessed, and the carving around the cheeks and the corners of the mouth, the curving of the lips and the treatment of the chin are anatomically convincing. Grooves on top of the heads suggest that they were intended for inserts. Realism in carving and restraint in the use of decoration differentiate the Olmec stone heads from the Maya, Zapotec, Toltec and Aztec styles, which are usually more conventionalized and elaborated with ornamental masks and feathers. These heads are the most realistic, the least stylized, of all Middle American styles. Only Totonac sculpture, also of the Gulf Coast region, shows a comparable realistic trend less given to ornamental elaboration.

At San Lorenzo, Stirling discovered fifteen major stone monuments, of which six were colossal heads. The carving on all sites suggests the same school of art. Upon closer study, a resemblance between heads proved to be due to the racial type akin to the modern Indians living in these regions today. Within this general racial similarity the heads showed individual differences, leading Stirling to conclude that we have here portraits of individual rulers. From vestiges of color discovered on a protected fragment it was revealed that originally the heads were painted red.

Olmec art presents unsolved problems, artistic and cultural. Thus, a carved stone figure on the side of an altar at La Venta (Fig. 164) protrudes from a niche-like hollow holding an infant in outstretched arms. Another aspect of Olmec art that is not well understood, and perhaps related to the infant-holding figures, is an emphasis, in stone sculpture and in jade carving, on infantile characteristics. In another altar at La Venta (Fig. 165), two child figures or dwarfs are represented holding up the projecting slab above their heads. Of grim facial expression, these figures are broad and massive; conventionalized jaguar eyes are incised on the rim of the ledge they support. Realism is also apparent in a less well-preserved relief from an altar at San Lorenzo where the figure is holding the end of a rope. Even in this rougher carving the mouth is emphasized and there is a suggestion of fleshy features. Among the pieces of stone carving found at San Lorenzo was a fragment representing a copulation scene between a jaguar and a woman. Whatever myth or belief this fragment may refer to, it seems to accord the jaguar a high place in Olmec culture. The jaguar, rather than the serpent, was the leading Olmec god. Infantile characteristics merged with a jaguar resemblance stand out in some of the carved jadeite masks and votive axes. They range in size from a few inches to a height of seven to eleven inches, and have been found in many places throughout southern Mexico and beyond.

Typical features show flaring nostrils, in some examples a hoop-like appendage below the nose or an open mouth pulled down on either side. Where the lips are outlined, as if "everted," a resemblance to an infant, or "baby-face," is suggested, and in some examples the human expression is replaced by an animal or "tiger face" type, as on a six-inch head in the Bliss Collection and on a blue-gray, eleven-inch jadeite ax in the American Museum of Natural History (Fig. 166). This baby-face type Clarence W. Weiant also found in certain ceramic heads of Tres Zapotes that seem to foreshadow the later Totonac smiling type face as if the "smiling type" might have developed out of a baby face.

In addition to the realism of the stone heads, and the baby-face jaguar character of small carvings, jadeite statuettes, standing or seated, further define the Olmec style. The standing type is well represented in a statuette eight inches high of blue-green jadeite in the Bliss Collection, on loan at the National Gallery of Art in Washington (Color Plate 16). The figure shows an elongated head, and the outstretched arms suggest that they originally held an emblem. The head, not of the baby-face type, in mouth and nose shows something of the realism of the stone heads. The eyes, made for inlay, slant toward the nose as do the eyes on the San Lorenzo head. In shoulders, arms and thighs this statuette has the plumpness characteristic of the style. It is found in statuettes even where the heads differ, as in a jade figurine about four inches high in the Cleveland Museum of Art. Here the mouth is turned down in the baby-face manner, the head is elongated and the extended arms hold emblems. A small, reclining figurine of a greenish stone (Fig. 167) shows the crying baby-face.

A jaguar-mouth, baby-figure god, in the American Museum of Natural History, combines the ferocity of the jaguar in the snarling mouth set in a human head with pudgy, baby-like arms. Baby characteristics fuse with those of a jaguar, suggesting again a close connection between infants and jaguars in Olmec mythology. In the combination of these contrasting elements, the style reveals vigor, determination and great technical skill. Simplicity in carving heads and figures without ornamental elaborations seems to reflect a culture in which art was mature and free from ostentatious ceremonialism. Olmec art was capable of realism on a monumental scale and great vitality in small pieces. In fact, if monumentality, simplicity and realism are measures of achievement, Olmec art might claim first place in the pre-Columbian styles of Mexico.

The problems connected with Olmec art are historical—where did it originate, how does it fit into the development—and cultural—what does it mean from the point of view of myth and religion. Some students have pointed out its resemblance to Chinese art. On the cultural side, speculation has linked up with the anthropomorphic significance of the jaguar, as indicated by jaguar masks, faces, claws and pelts used in Olmec art. The Olmecs may have thought of themselves as related in some way to the jaguar by descent. The altar at La Venta, where a figure within a niche holds an infant, may point to a belief in an origin from caves or from the earth. A jaguar mosaic mask found at La Venta buried in a deep pit may support a view of the earth as the seat of fertility. Colossal stone-carved heads resting flat on the earth have been thought to emphasize an earth connection. Monuments that address themselves to men usually stand upright to be seen. Even on a boulder, a figure can be carved to face an audience, as in the Maya zoomorph P, at Quiriguá (Guatemala). If the heads originally stood up against a wall, as Stirling suggests, the fertility idea may lose its significance. It is a question whether the advanced artistry of the carving fits in with a seemingly paleolithic notion of fertility through contact with the earth.

There is one other explanation to account for the baby-face type. According to this view the infants are represented as crying and shedding tears. They are taken to be sacrifices for rain, as tears, through sympathetic magic, were believed to bring rain.

We know that the Aztecs practiced infant sacrifice in honor of the rain god Tlaloc to produce rain. According to Sahagun, "If the children who were to be killed cried a great deal and shed many tears, they (the priests) were glad of it, for they took it as a prognostication of a great deal of rain for that year." The altars of La Venta carved with infants have been interpreted as pointing to infant sacrifices. The weakness of this argument is the fact that infant sacrifices are known in the Aztec period, but not at this early period. Moreover, rain magic belongs to the highlands, the tropical coast presumably could dispense with rain magic as the climate was moist to begin with.

There is hardly a well-defined historical order of Mexican styles, where one style is known to be definitely related to another. We must therefore proceed geographically and go on to the Zapotec style.

THE ZAPOTEC STYLE

The Zapotecs developed a high civilization contemporary with the Maya, but less comprehensive in its artistic expression. The Zapotecs also formed a link between central Mexico and the Maya region. The Toltecs are believed to have conquered the Zapotecs in the twelfth century, and the Mixtecs took over Monte Alban at a later period. The Zapotec language is still one of the languages spoken in the provincial capital of Oaxaca, and art treasures from the explorations at Monte Alban are housed in the Oaxaca Museum. This hill, dominating the city, retains the ruins of mounds, terraces and ball courts from the time when Monte Alban was the ceremonial center, and perhaps the capital of the Zapotecs. Archaeologically, the site is important as here the undisturbed earth makes it possible to differentiate five distinct layers which together constitute a complete record of cultures from the early centuries of our era to the time of the Conquest. The Zapotecs had a calendar, hieroglyphics and a system of writing taken over from the Maya, but their writing has not been deciphered. Not all objects of art found in the Zapotec region are necessarily of Zapotec origin. Some of the works here included are tentative attributions. Other works may be pre-Zapotec, like large stone slabs of an architectural frieze carved in relief with about life-size dancing figures.

The stone slabs show nude figures in leaping and seated postures with bent knees and drooping hands, as if engaged in some dance mimicking animals. They have wide-open, thick-lipped mouths; they wear ear plugs and occasionally a necklace. The style is massive and loose in its broadly grooved outlines, which leave the background largely uncut. An early type of realism is here carried through on a monumental scale, representing the primitive stage of pre-Columbian art (Monte Alban I).

The great period of Zapotec art, according to Alfonso Caso, was Monte Alban III, between the sixth and eleventh centuries of our era; this was also the period of the ceramic funerary urns.

A funerary urn consists of a cylinder for the ashes applied to a standing or seated figure which conceals the cylinder attached back of it. Except for head, hands and feet, the dwarfed and squatting figure is also concealed, as it is entirely overlaid with modeled and molded decoration (Fig. 168). The featherwork headdress is of great splendor, overpowering in size, broad and massive and sharp and precise in details. The head, with its large, heavily lidded eyes, its aquiline nose and open mouth, has an intensity also found in Toltec and Aztec masks. This sculpture is architectural in spirit.

Except for minor differences, heads seem to follow standardized patterns, repeating the same features with the open mouth showing teeth (Fig. 169). Differences are in the placing of the hands and in the elaboration of the headdress, collars, necklace, ribbons, knots, tassels, cords and masks, and other objects not easy to identify. In another urn from the Stockholm Museum, a mask is shown on the the upper part of the face. In some urns the rain god or the jaguar god is clearly indicated. Where such emblems of divinity are absent, chiefs or priests may be represented. The characteristic neglect of the figure as such is emphatically brought out in these funerary urns, which are essentially heads overwhelmed with ceremonial detail. Realism is incidental; we have here pre-Columbian art in its stylized stage of development.

But this same period, Monte Alban III, was also able to dispense with stylized ornamentation and represent the figure in more nearly natural proportions, as in a seated clay figure thirteen inches high (Fig. 170). The head is but a variation of the heads of the funerary urns, and the hands and feet are treated in the same sketchy fashion which is typical for many pre-Columbian styles. A basalt figure of a god with twisted serpents for nose and eyebrows, over eight inches high (Fig. 171), and a prehnite pendant four inches high (Fig. 172), may also be Zapotec. The loosely scratched granite slab (Fig. 173) suggests a relationship to the dancing figures of Monte Alban I, and seems to be of an early date, at the primitive stage of development. The prehnite pendant shows several influences, including a suggestion of stone sculpture from central (Toltec) Mexico (Fig. 172). These smaller pieces belong to the stylized stage of development.

(continued on page 209)

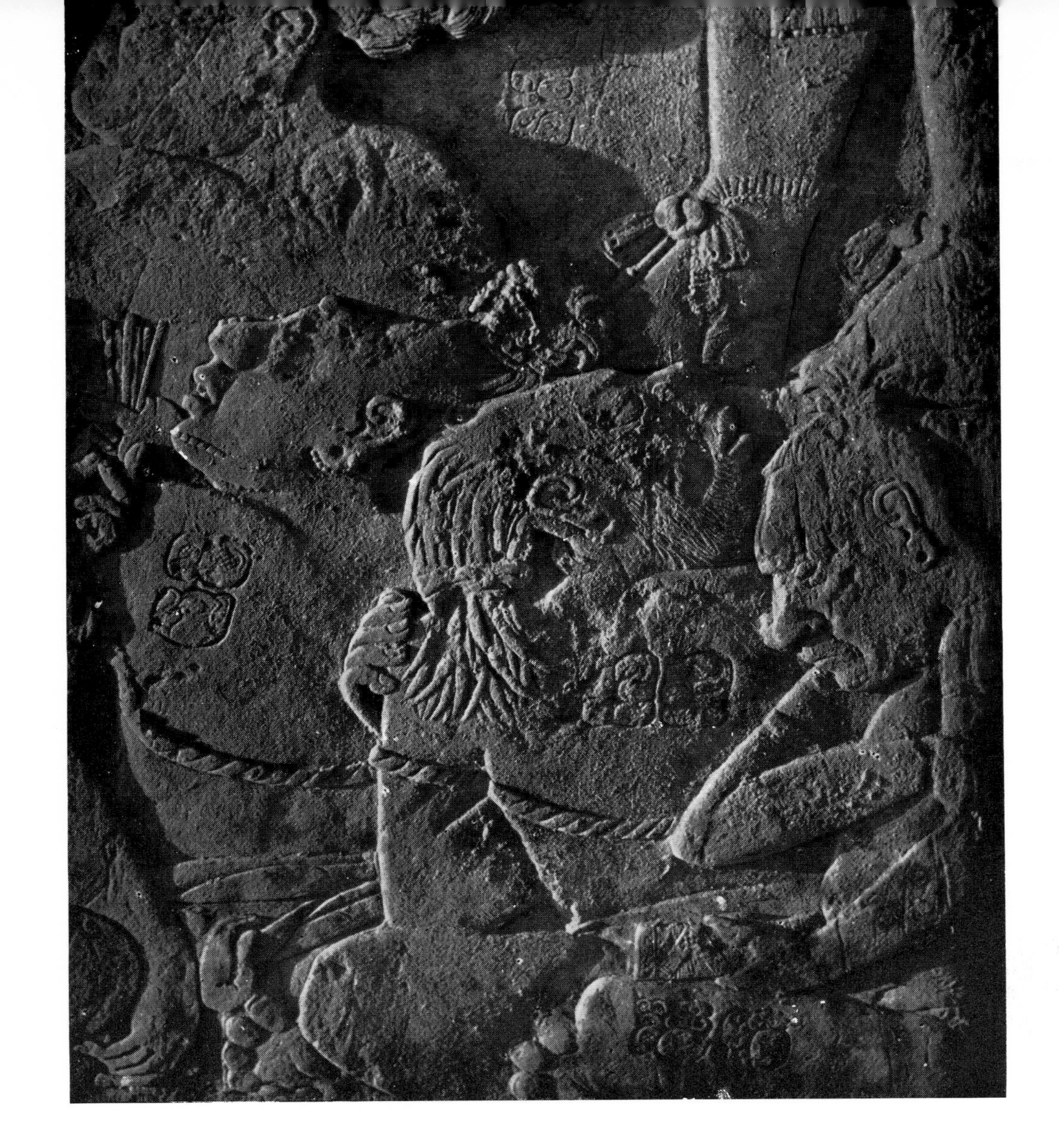

Fig. 147 (top left). Maya stela 12, dated 535 A.D. (or 795 A.D.), from Piedras Negras, Guatemala. Details of heads of prisoners. *Museo de Arqueologia, Guatemala. Photo: Peabody Museum, Harvard University.*

Fig. 148 (lower left). Maya, zoomorph P, carved stone boulder, at Quiriguá, Guatemala. *Photo: United Fruit Company.*

Fig. 149 (right). Maya stela H, at Copán, Honduras, seen from northwest. *Photo: United Fruit Company.*

Fig. 190 (left). Aztec goddess of corn, stone. H. 5 ft. *Philadelphia Museum of Art.*

Fig. 191 (right). Aztec stone figure of Xochiquetzal, Goddess of Flowers, H. ca 20 in. *Photo: Musée de l'Homme, Paris.*

Fig. 192 (lower left). Aztec stone figure of the Earth Goddess, Coatlicue, front view. H. over 8 ft. *Museo Nacional, Mexico, D. F.*

Fig. 193 (below). Aztec seated stone figure. H. over 2 ft. *British Museum.*

Opposite page:

Fig. 159 (left). Maya clay figure, woman with a child by her side and holding a little dog, from Zona Sala, Zupa, near Palenque, State of Chiapas, Mexico. *Middle American Research Institute, Tulane University, New Orleans.*

Fig. 160 (top). Maya sculptured bowl, from San Augustin, near Quiriguá, Guatemala. *Museum of the American Indian, New York.*

Fig. 161 (bottom). Maya wooden lintel, detail of a fragment from Temple 4, Tikal, Peten, Guatemala. *Museum für Völkerkunde, Basel, Switzerland.*

Fig. 162 (right). Jades, pre-Columbian, Mexico and Guatemala. *University Museum, Philadelphia.*

Fig. 163 (top left). Colossal head, stone, from San Lorenzo, Veracruz (Monument 5), Olmec style. *Photo: Bureau of American Ethnology, Smithsonian Institution, and National Geographic Society.*

Fig. 164 (above). Stone altar, showing figure in niche presenting an infant (Altar 5), from La Venta, Tabasco, Olmec style. *Photo: Bureau of American Ethnology, Smithsonian Institution, and National Geographic Society.*

Fig. 165 (left). Stone altar, showing two atlantean figures in relief, from Potrero Nuevo, Veracruz (Monument 2), Olmec style. *Photo: Bureau of American Ethnology, Smithsonian Institution, and National Geographic Society.*

Fig. 166 (below). Votive adz, jadeite, Olmec style. *American Museum of Natural History.*

Fig. 167 (right). Olmec figurine, serpentine. *National Gallery of Art, Washington, D. C.*

Fig. 168 (lower right). Zapotec clay funerary urn. *Smithsonian Institution.*

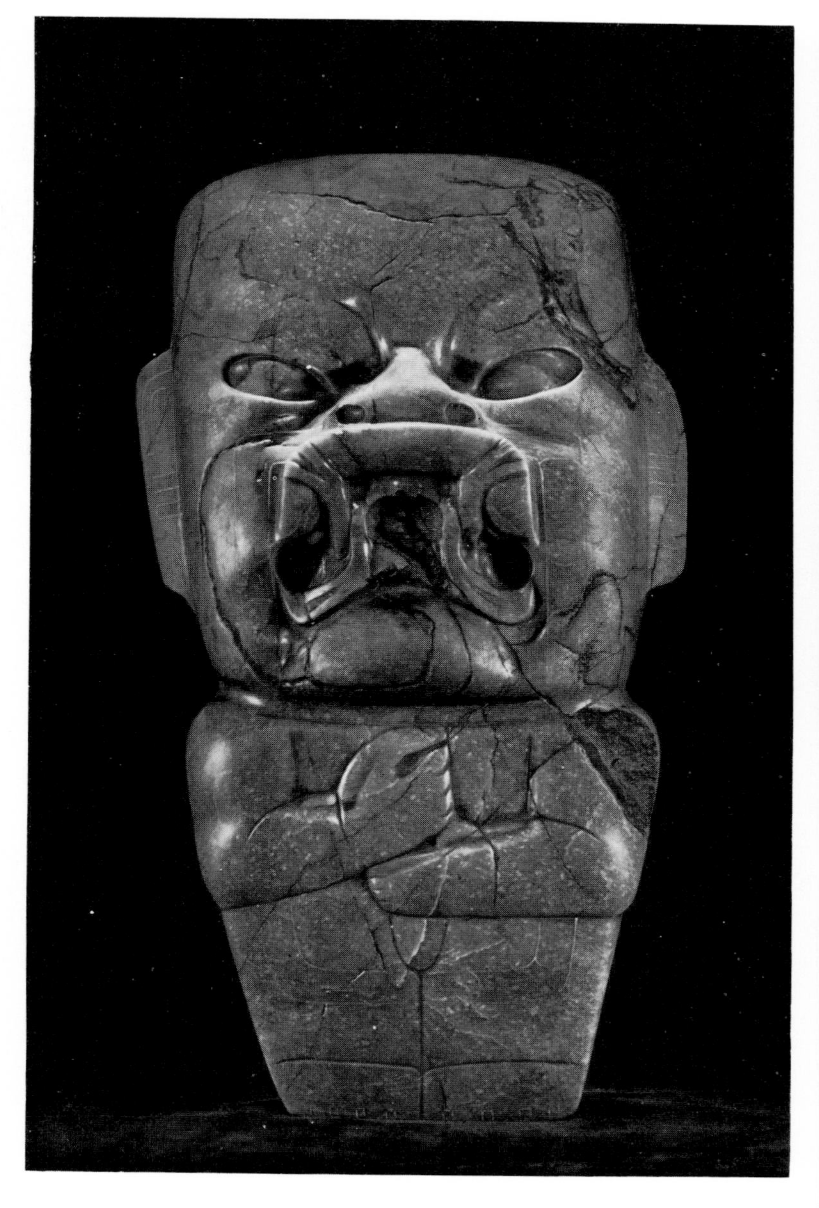

Fig. 169 (top left). Zapotec clay funerary urn (detail) from Oaxaca, Mexico. *Statens Etnografiska Museum, Stockholm, Sweden.* Fig. 170 (left). Zapotec seated clay figure, from Oaxaca, Mexico. H. 13 in. *American Museum of Natural History.* Fig. 171 (above). Zapotec (?) basalt figure. H. 8⅜ in. *National Gallery of Art, Washington, D. C.*

Fig. 172 (above). Zapotec (?) prehnite pendant. H. ca 3 in. *National Gallery of Art, Washington, D.C.*

Fig. 173 (top right). Zapotec granite slab. H. 10 in. *National Gallery of Art, Washington, D. C.*

Fig. 174 (right). Jewelry, nose ornament, Mexican, Mixtec-Zapotec. *Museum of Art, Rhode Island School of Design, Providence, R. I.*

Fig. 175 (extreme right). "Totonac" head with crest. H. 5¾ in., basalt. *National Gallery of Art, Washington, D. C.*

Opposite page:

Fig. 176 (top left). "Totonac" marble head with crest. H. 6⅜ in. *National Gallery of Art, Washington, D. C.*

Fig. 177 (top right). "Totonac" head, jadeite. *Peabody Museum, Harvard University. Photo: University Museum, Philadelphia.*

Fig. 178 (lower left). "Totonac" gray marble ceremonial ax head, representing a diving god, Hilzin. *National Gallery of Art, Washington, D. C.*

Fig. 179 (lower right). "Totonac" palmate, stone, Veracruz, Mexico. H. 16 in. *American Museum of Natural History.*

Fig. 180 (above, left). "Totonac" smiling head, clay, Veracruz, Mexico. H. 6 in. *American Museum of Natural History.*

Fig. 181 (above). "Totonac" smiling figure, clay. H. ca 8 in. *Museum für Völkerkunde, Berlin.*

Fig. 182 (left). "Totonac" porphyry yoke. *National Gallery of Art, Washington, D. C.*

Fig. 183 (left). "Totonac" slate mirror back. Diam. 6 in. *American Museum of Natural History*. Fig. 184 (below). "Totonac" head, limestone, late, east coast. *Philadelphia Museum*. Fig. 185 (lower left). Maya head, bird pecking at human skull, basaltic rock. H. 9 in. *Philadelphia Museum.*

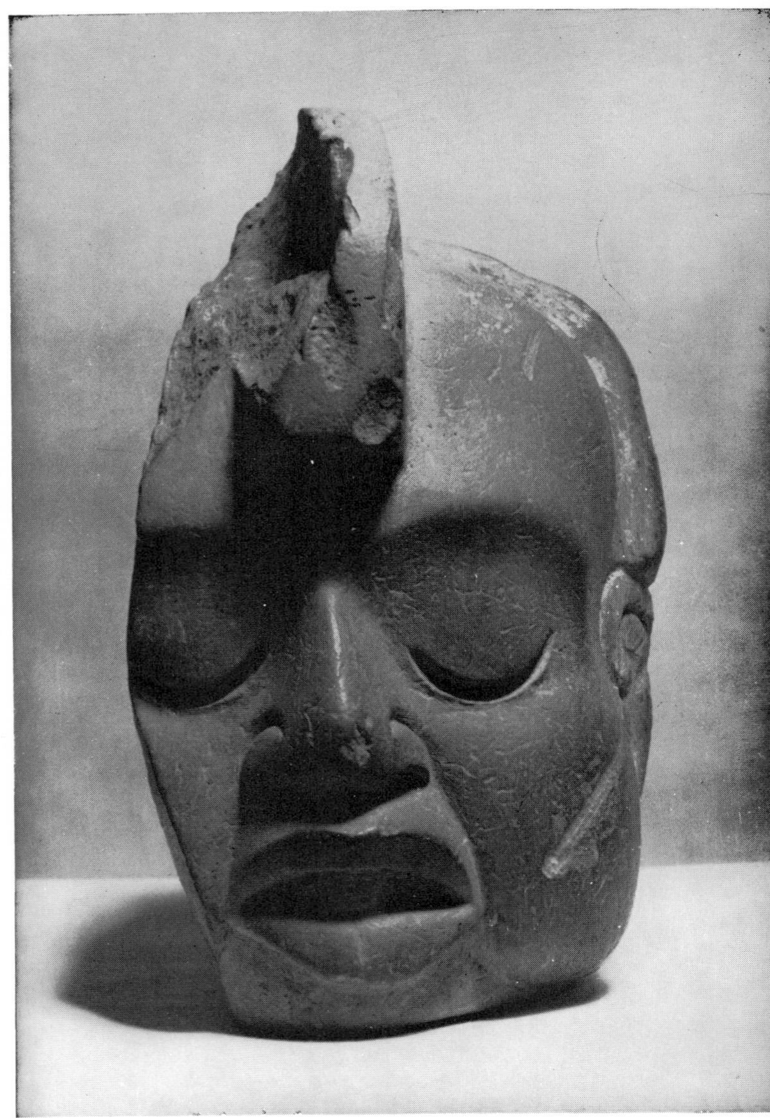

Opposite page:

Fig. 186 (left). Huasteca, seated female figure, stone, probably from Veracruz, Mexico. *American Museum of Natural History*. Fig. 187 (top right). Toltec serpent head, stone, from Temple of Quetzalcoatl, Teotihuacán, Mexico. *Photo: Instituto Nacional de Antropologia y Historia, Mexico*. Fig. 188 (lower center). Toltec goddess, stone, from Teotihuacán, Mexico. *Museo Nacional, Mexico*. Fig. 189 (lower right). Toltec style of Teotihuacán, small seated serpentine figure. *National Gallery of Art*.

THE MIXTECS

The Mixtec contributions to art are associated with the temples at Mitla and the discovery of the greatest of all treasures, found by Alfonso Caso in tomb 7 at Monte Alban. Gold and silver jewels, jades, turquoise mosaics, necklaces of amber and rock crystal, pearls by the thousands and engraved jaguar bones are part of this collection, which is now at the museum at Oaxaca.

Mixtec jewelry is unmatched in delicacy; Italian Renaissance jewelry looks clumsy in comparison. A necklace of beads in the Bliss Collection cast by the *cire perdue* process has three tiny bells attached to each bead, and an ear ornament in the same collection represents the head of a humming bird on a filigree disc. In addition to casting, soldering and molding techniques, repoussé work was also practiced.

One of the most spectacular single pieces is a small pectoral plate of gold, four and a half inches high in the Oaxaca Museum. Although it looks as if it were made of gold filigree work, it was actually cast by the *cire perdue* process. The fine threads formed a part of the wax mold which the gold replaced when the molten wax escaped from the form. The head is covered by a tiger or serpent helmet, and wears a mask in the form of a fleshless jawbone in the manner of the god of Maya codex; quetzal feathers and paper decorations make up his headdress.

The Mixtec metalworker showed his superior taste also in comparatively simple objects like gold nose ornaments (Fig. 174). Pre-Columbian art in Mexico and Peru developed the type in a variety of designs based on abstract and on animal motifs. In this piece it is less craftsmanship that attracts attention—the design is not well-centered and the cutting is uneven—than a sense of design indicating a well-developed tradition. Small spirals are placed for effect, embossed subdivisions do not obtrude on the unadorned middle section. Only styles that have matured have this kind of sensitive regard for the function of line, contour and surface.

THE TOTONAC AND HUASTECA STYLES

These two groups were settled in Veracruz on the Gulf north of the Olmec. At the time of the Conquest the Totonac were among the tribes that sided with Cortez to liberate themselves from Aztec rule.

The archaeological past of the Totonac is vague. Their great period, as illustrated by the stone pyramid of Tajin, the name which has been attached to this archaeological site, is believed to fall roughly between 800 and 1200 A.D. Some of the finest sculpture of Mexico in stone and clay has been found within the Totonac region. This includes large stone heads over six feet high showing strong features beneath a tall headdress, and stone masks and small heads also expressing tremendous power.

A most vigorous expression in stone, based on the human countenance without infusion from the animal world, is represented in a basalt head of a reddish tint (Fig. 175). It dramatizes form in almost geometric abstraction. Only five and three-quarter inches high, this massive head with its crest stands as a supreme achievement of sculpture. Whether we analyze this head for its fusion of a linear pattern with round, bulging forms and flattened rectangular shapes or dwell upon its brooding expressiveness or admire it for texture or for its effect in light and shade, it is equally satisfying. For self-contained concentration and a sense of inwardness, due to its averted gaze, this head is perhaps unmatched by any other work.

Another Totonac head, of marble, six and three-eighths inches high, exhibits a quality of another kind (Fig. 176). This one is less gripping and more suave; no indentations cut deeply into the stone to disturb its calm reticence. Light is not trapped in sharp contrasts but envelopes the surface in soft gradations. Marble is here treated as fits its smooth grain and light color. The differences in the carving of stone in these two heads demonstrate that the Totonac sculptor was sensitively attuned to his material.

A jadeite mask from Papantla combines parts of an animal with an essentially human head (Fig. 177). Its middle section, in the short nose and the projecting snout, suggests the jaguar, whereas forehead, chin and total head shape are human. The Totonac sculptor merges god with man in a well-considered, plausible form, recreating the jaguar in the image of man presumably to give the god human intelligence. The artist of the Pacific Northwest Coast used animal motifs as symbols; and the Maya artist superimposed a realistic human head on a conventionalized serpent, and having a serpent to humanize he could do no more. This Totonac head is a man-like tiger god. Without being grotesque, the animal is built into the human skull. From our point of view this is an imaginative creation of the highest order. Compared to the Olmec tiger-face god, the emphasis is on the human element and on an intimate fusion of man and animal.

There are four other categories of Totonac sculpture, all of which command respect for Totonac art. These categories are: (1) ax-head gods, (2) so-called *palmas* or oarblade-shaped carved stones, (3) stone yokes, and (4) ceramic "laughing heads."

A white marble ceremonial ax with traces of red paint about eight inches high, in the Bliss Collection represents a jaguar, stylized but without the human element. Angular serpent scrolls typical of Maya art reappear here as part of the carving of the forehead. From the scroll above the eye to the chin the lines sweep down in boldly carved relief.

Totonac art was varied in its resourcefulness, and found ever-novel combinations on the theme of the ax-head god. A ceremonial marble ax ten inches high, in the Bliss Collection, and another marble ax a foot high representing a diving god are both massive; one is a solid blade, the other is perforated (Fig. 178). In the diving god ax the richly detailed head is relieved by the open shapes. We do not know the precise meaning of the ax heads, but the ax, as a religious symbol, occurs in cultures outside the Americas.

Palmas or palmate stones are carved reliefs, usually of basalt, and are blade- or bird-shaped in contour. Their meaning is unknown, but a ceremonial-religious use, perhaps in connection with the funeral, has been suggested. Since we have no knowledge of how these stones were used or what symbolism was involved, they speak to us solely as works of art. In a *palma* (Fig. 179) we recognize earplugs, belts, angular scrolls, all characteristic of the Mexican-Mayan styles. Often the motifs on Mexican reliefs are so compressed that the effect is one of texture rather than of related shapes. Such is not the case here where the artist has differentiated between major and minor motifs and related them to the background. The roughness of the stone sets a limit to the delicacy of the carved detail, which in scale is comparable to that found in rugs.

Ceramic "smiling heads" and figurines from Veracruz are referred to as "Totonac," using the term Totonac loosely, rather than in an archaeologically defined sense. The heads are broad, intentionally deformed, and the expressions vary from smiles to laughter; in some the eyes slant up at the outer corners (Fig. 180) and others show two large upper teeth (Fig. 181). A tubular extension on the back of the head suggests that such a head was set into a wall as a votive offering to a god. A few hollow ceramic figures with smiling heads have also been found. Beyond surmises that smiling heads or figures with smiling heads may represent dancers or persons selected for sacrifice, nothing definite is known as to their meaning.

Realistic as these expressions may seem, they are still stylized, and not momentary impressions caught from direct observation, the way a modern artist will model a portrait from life. Though based on the study of models, each has eyes, noses and lips stylized as to shape and combined artfully into a semblance of nature.

Stone yokes, of which several hundred are known in collections, were common on the Mexican Gulf coast in central and southern Veracruz and elsewhere. Samuel K. Lothrop and Gordon F. Ekholm have demonstrated that stone yokes are ceremonial replicas of pieces of equipment that were worn by ball players and made of lighter materials. Throughout Mexico ball courts were part of the religious centers; the games were played with a large solid rubber ball and had a religious significance. According to Caso, yokes may have had a mortuary-religious connection, as they have been found in burials. In the yoke illustrated in Fig. 182, the upper parts of serpent masks, symbols of divinity on corners not visible in the illustration, hint at a religious connection. A human head in front is connected to arms reaching back in the manner of an acrobat.

Earplugs, discs, scrolls, water lilies, serpents and other motifs link Totonac art to the art of central Mexico and to Maya art, but the Totonac sculptor compressed the features so that eyes, mouth and chin are narrowed down to proportions different from the usual Mexican ones. Refinement is not an exclusively Totonac characteristic, but it is present in Totonac carving to a marked degree. Totonac art also shows considerable variety in the kinds of objects carved, and in the styles of carving, even though no large stone sculpture is known.

In a slate disc carved in low relief with a profile head (Fig. 183), various influences deriving from a wider area seem to converge. This comes close to a portrait relief, carved with details for their decorative value, and suggesting vaguely a Spanish warrior portrayed in native style.

A carved limestone head, seven inches high, representing a dead man (Fig. 184) is partly stylized, partly realistic. The features have a unity of style and expression. Well-defined edges of eyes and mouth contrast with the softness of the cheeks and the firmness of the forehead; sagging eyelids and parted lips are brought together by the well-shaped nose. The Mexican sculptor has dealt with an expression of death in a restrained, sensitive manner. Though only a fragment, this head is still effective as a work of outstanding merit. It has been attributed to the east coast of the late period (Kubler), otherwise known as "Totonac" style.

Some of the qualities of Totonac sculpture, like well-defined masses, linear emphasis and subdued realism, reappear in a head found in the Maya area (Fig. 185). A nine-inch basaltic rock, carved into the shape of a human skull, is surmounted by a crest-like bird pecking at the skull. Stylistically, this head fits in with the east coast Totonac manner and is different from the Maya style, as represented by the stelae.

The Huasteca Indians of eastern San Luis Potosi and northern Veracruz are believed to be related to the Maya of Yucatán in language and appearance, but to have become separated from the main tribe early in history. For that reason they did not participate in the Maya culture. A kneeling Huasteca figure (Fig. 186) clearly shows in its form how it was carved. A front and a profile drawing were made on the front and sides of the original stone block which was then cut back. Symmetry, simplicity and a compact cubical form result from this method of production. This style with its rounded forms and sharp edges in place of an anatomical rendering is attractive and contemporary in spirit. Early sculpture, in Mexico as in Egypt, often reveals a similar derivation.

TOLTEC ART

During the nineteenth century it was not uncommon to attribute any archaeological discovery in the Valley of Mexico to the Aztecs. But their rule in central Mexico belongs only to the last two centuries before the Conquest. Before the Aztecs the Toltecs had created a civilization of greater antiquity and longer duration. Their history was surrounded with myth and conflicting traditions that made their identification difficult.

This Toltec style is centered at their great religious center of Teotihuacán, with its pyramids and the so-called Temple of Quetzalcoatl, or the Citadel, renowned for its remarkable architectural stone carving. Its raised platforms are decorated on one side with projecting heads of conventionalized plumed serpents with obsidian eyes, the serpents' rattles spreading out into carved reliefs on either side. Alternating with the serpent heads are heads of the rain god Tlaloc. They are carved in a massive, rectangular style, with circles for eyes and teeth below the upper jaw of the mouth (Fig. 187). Carved shells, suggestive of water, symbolize the rain god. Originally the carved stonework was painted green for the feathers of the quetzal bird and red for Tlaloc. For boldness of form and for decorative effect this façade ranks as one of the world's achievements of architectural sculpture. Toltec art reached its greatest development during this so-called classic period of Teotihuacán, between the eighth and ninth centuries of our era. Monumental figure sculpture was closely related to architecture, and also belongs to the earlier Teotihuacán period.

In the carving of a single statue, Toltec sculpture hardly advances beyond the basic block form. Toltec statues are essentially massive stone piers, sub-divided and shaped barely to suggest the figure (Fig. 188). A few motifs, like faces and hands, are carved in relief on the surface of one side of a more or less rectangular block. Within a restricted range an expression of great power is achieved, as in this goddess of agriculture in the National Museum of Mexico (Fig. 188), or the fire god, the "Old God" of Teotihuacán, in the same collection. In this stone block a figure has seemingly been contracted into a head. Age is expressed by a formalized pattern of lines for wrinkles and by a half-open, drooping mouth and a furrowed chin. In both the architectural character is pronounced; this is virtually sculptural architecture, rather than architectural sculpture.

The architectural character of Toltec art is also apparent in frescoes, a severe, almost geometric pattern forming a framework in two dimensions for color, reds contrasting effectively with light greens and yellows. In a fragment of the Bliss collection a priest, richly dressed with feathered headdress and plumed scepter and holding a scroll representing his speech, kneels before a painted structure symbolizing a temple. A road marked by footprints leads from the figure to the door of the temple, with an elaborate, presumably thatched roof. In other Toltec frescoes the figures exist as isolated ornamental details not integrated into a major composition involving action and a setting in space as in the Maya frescoes at Bonampak.

After Teotihuacán was abandoned in the tenth or eleventh century the ensuing centuries between 1100 and 1300, the so-called Chichimec period in Toltec history, named after an invading tribe, were a period of confusion. The Toltec settlement of Yucatán and the contributions to art the Toltecs made at Chichén Itzá were discussed in connection with Maya art.

Cholula, near Puebla, was a sacred city, and had a large pyramid. Cholula was still famous at the time of the Conquest for its pottery and Tula, the ancient Tollan, was the Toltec capital, where, according to tradition, the Toltec culture-hero, king and priest, Quetzalcoatl, ruled. He appeared as the peace-loving bringer of civilization, who eventually wandered to the seacoast and departed by way of the sea, promising his disciples to return someday to reoccupy his throne.

Excavations at Tula from 1940 on brought to light from the debris of the ruins of the pyramid a number of stone columns, separate sections of caryatid figures, including legs and heads. These were again set up in front of the pyramid. A re-erected column, perhaps some twenty feet high, shows a Toltec warrior in full regalia. These figures are believed to have served as supports of the temple, which stood on top of the pyramid. The hollow eyes and open mouths were originally inlaid with mosaic. The style is geometric, ornamental and cubical, and cylindrical shapes make for a total effect that is massive and severe, but also calculated in its refinement. All details are treated as surface decoration, more architectural than sculptural.

The pyramid at Xochicalco, near Cuernavaca, is, like Tula, later than Teotihuacán. Its base is carved with large reliefs of figures, plumed serpents and hieroglyphics, and shows Maya influence. In these carvings on a gigantic scale the Toltecs reveal themselves as bold decorators in keeping with their monumental architecture.

We see this same kind of angularity in smaller architectural fragments, where the cubical form is rounded off along the edges and details tend to geometric shapes. Even on a small scale the cutting is bold. In a small seated figurine, about two and a half inches high, a large smiling head is placed on a small body (Fig. 189). This piece shows how much regional styles have in common. The sketchy treatment of the body with its stumpy feet and undeveloped hands, only grooved for fingers, is an archaic survival, common in Tarascan clay figures. The smiling face recalls Totonac types but is more stylized and more vigorous; comparable seated poses occur in Zapotec clay figures. This figurine is believed to be Toltec in the style of Teotihuacán.

Almost any regional work reveals something also found in other Mexican styles. A Toltec mask (Color Plate 17) reflects general characteristics in several ways. The total impression is one of strength, which is also typical of Aztec art. The parted lips indicate an interest in expression, but coupled with restraint. This, too, occurs in Toltec, Zapotec and Aztec art. The formalized, undistorted features emphasize man as being different from the gods, and this is a theme maintained throughout Mexican and Maya art. Though formal and without individualization, this mask, which is really a solid head, could be an idealized portrait. Whether intended as a magic symbol, as a part of the tomb furnishings, or as a memorial of a person, the style is unmistakably Mexican.

A comparison of any two Toltec masks, carved in a hard stone like jadeite, shows the similarity characteristic of the type, and a close observation reveals subtle differences.

The architectural character of Toltec art is well illustrated in its ceremonial pottery. Setting a bowl on blocks and shaping it with nearly vertical sides shows a preference for shapes that could be constructed like walls, even though the plastic material would have permitted more freely modeled shapes.

A baked clay bowl, a tripod (Color Plate 18), shows the plumed serpent painted on a white plaster slip surface. The conventionalized style is mature and the execution fresh and sketchy; the brush lightly touched the surface in sure, quick strokes. Such vessels, dated 800-900 A.D., were widely distributed, but are best known at Teotihuacán.

AZTEC ART

The Aztecs were one of several tribes who, according to their own records, left their original mythical home in 1168 A.D. After "long wanderings," they arrived in the early fourteenth century in the Valley of Mexico and settled at Tenochtitlán in 1325 A.D. In the course of another century the inhabitants of this community conquered the surrounding settlements and established themselves as the dominant tribe of Mexico. After Cortez had taken Tenochtitlán, the city was destroyed and the ruins used to fill in the canals. From this debris underlying the modern city stone carvings and pottery have been unearthed in the past and continue to be found in our own day.

Architecture, sculpture and pottery have contributed to Aztec art. It is particularly in these fields that Aztec art has survived, as in architectural carving, in statues of volcanic stone, in animals carved in granite, in masks of serpentine, in alabaster jars and obsidian bowls, in ceramic pots and incense burners. The human figure, animal and vegetable motifs and conventionalized designs are all represented. Much has been recovered, even after the destruction of most of the work in gold and perishable materials, as in textiles, featherwork and manuscripts.

The custom of sacrificing prisoners of war made the Aztecs feared by other tribes. Though human sacrifice earned them a reputation for brutality, such practices had no evident effect on their art, which reflects sternness and vigor rather than brutality. Where we mistakenly see brutality, we project into Aztec art our ideas of the Aztec character, and thereby make art a vehicle for our own feelings.

Aztec sculpture is at times hard to distinguish from Toltec sculpture, but there is a difference between Aztec and Maya art. The Aztecs carved statues of their gods, like the maize goddess or the goddesses of water and of the earth and death. In large statues the rectangular form is conspicuous; the human figure hardly emerges from the block. Small figures that one can hold in one's hand tend to be compact and rounded off at the edges and corners. Surface ornamentation is used sparingly, and then as a flat pattern in low relief. Attention is given to the head, hands holding an emblem are large, legs are minimized, and feet, where they occur, are often slighted in the carving of details.

The technical difficulty of carving stone with stone tools has influenced styles in sculpture. The laborious process of chipping and smoothing down the surface encouraged simplification. The fact that realism was not carried beyond a rudimentary stage also set limits to an expenditure of effort. In spite of these trends toward simplification, complexity of form and refinement in details are not entirely absent in Aztec art. On occasion the elaboration of detail is considerable, as in the carving of jades and other hard stones, indicating that carvers did not always avoid technical difficulties. This fact should caution us not to interpret a style exclusively on the basis of the part played by tools and materials; other influences also contributed to the formation of styles.

In Aztec stone sculpture the rectangular block or the rounded boulder bring out the figure in a simplified form which was incised with flat relief (Fig. 190). The original surface of the block was cut into to define heads, hands, feet and ornamental detail. Contours emphasize straight lines or simple curves, and a sense of bulk is retained. Huge hands and massive feet, and heads that grow directly out of the torso without transitions, give an effect of weight. A large Aztec stone carved figure looks like a piece out of a stone structure (Fig. 190). Even figure sculpture made to stand freely is architectural. This goddess of corn is bounded by flat planes. The face, the only portion that is carved with some semblance of rounded surfaces is in low relief. The figure appears here in its most architectural version, essentially a stone block, somewhat modified to indicate the figure. Out of this flat structure, a headdress made of paper was used in the ritual, the head of the goddess peers out with a penetrating gaze, the only living part in the midst of a ceremonial setting.

In another stone figure (Fig. 191), a more intense inner feeling is expressed. Projecting out slightly in front of the torso, the head seems to advance in a forward thrust. We are made aware of an eagerness on the part of the carver to infuse life and give to his statue intensity. The shapes are extremely simple, only scratches are used for toes and fingers and rounded forms for head and torso. What delights the eye is the reticence with which the artist treats his material. This build-up of effects from the rectangular feet and the curved surface of the skirted body to the bulky hands, which once held emblems, and broadly modeled head is carried through with a sense of fitness that is calculated to get the utmost out of what skill the carver possessed and out of the coarse stone he had to work with.

The standing monument achieved a spectacular development in the earth goddess, the Coatlicue of the National Museum of Mexico to which we have referred before. Simplicity is here elaborated. We are confronted with different effects, depending on the direction from which we view this monster. From the front (Fig. 192) all emblems are visible: claws, intertwining serpents, skulls, hands and hearts. Two serpent heads turned toward one another form a unit on top. The rear elevation is more unified; a skull above the center dominates the design, a long massive scarf brings out height in a reposeful and unified manner. The side view shows up the complexity of the total mass and makes it clear that the figure was designed to be seen from the front. The lines converge toward the top in a slightly pyramidal fashion.

Overflowing with symbolism, replete with meaning, the Coatlicue is massive and powerful. Along with zoomorph P of Maya sculpture, this Aztec earth goddess is one of the original sculptural creations of this hemisphere, for what has been carved in the Americas since the Conquest stemmed from European traditions. As a stone monument, the mother of the gods is intensely alive, seething with a turbulence which still adheres to the surface of the stone block. The sculptor could not go beyond his place in the development of his craft. Within these limits he expressed in one tremendous effort the awe Indians must have felt before the inexorable powers of nature. As a concept the Coatlicue is a proud statement of man's courage to accept his fate, which was pain, suffering and death, so tellingly symbolized by skulls and hearts.

The mother goddess carved in stone was also represented with a human skull in place of serpent heads. In other stone-carved figures the absence of any easily recognizable emblems makes identification difficult. Such is the case in the seated figure of volcanic stone (Fig. 193) which adheres to the cubical block. There is a living quality in the sharply delineated features, and in the individualized chin. The eyes are suggested by a hollow beneath the overhanging brow, the same technique that was used in the small Totonac head (Fig. 175). Compact mass and a forward thrust of the head, as if peering into the distance, suggest latent energy. Realism in the general effect and stylization in details are combined in a manner common in Mexican art. Simplification in seated postures varied from the statue of the well-proportioned, freely posed god of games, festivals and flowers (Xochipilli) in the National Museum of Mexico, and the seated corn goddess of the American Museum of Natural History to the numerous figurines of water goddesses (Chalchihuitlicues), earth goddess (Coatlicues) and others which are heads, with figures compressed into a base that serves as an arm rest.

Mexican art shows little awareness of sex. For a young goddess (Fig. 194) the interpretation is more stern and solid than feminine and graceful. Breasts are attached to a muscular torso, timidly, like emblems, as a concession to the fact that a goddess was represented. Though hard and muscle-bound, this statue represents Aztec art in a gentle mood. Mexican artists serving a fierce religion under a priestly class had little occasion to express any joy of life in their work.

Small seated figurines of coarse-grained basalt about six inches high (Fig. 195) may seem hard in their thin-lipped ungainliness. All show the same expression, but they are not alike in design. Dark slits for eyes and mouth contrast with broadly modeled surfaces in which incised head bands, necklaces and hands stand out. Even these lesser works have an attraction in the relation of the shapes, as in the oval face placed between spherical knobs ending in cones and terminating in horizontals parallel to the base line. The triangle formed by the necklace completes the pattern to give unity to the composition. Thus, formal qualities of art counteract associations that might adversely affect appreciation.

Aztec carvers were most successful with animals, birds and insects, like serpents, jaguars, dogs, frogs, turtles, eagles and grasshoppers. The general shape of each one is brought out, but all take on something of the character of the material, which is often stone. They have a roundness and firmness that does not always correspond to the character of the species represented. To an extent the forms of nature were interpreted to suit an Aztec preference. We may explain the Aztec style in carving solely in terms of materials and tools, or we may search for other contributing causes. A muscular fleshiness in the Indian physique may have predisposed the Indian carver to carry a preference for mass and weight into his carved figures. Once such habits had been established, the same heaviness could have been carried over into animal carving.

A feathered serpent, emblem of Quetzalcoatl and symbol of divinity, (Fig. 196) carved in diorite, about a foot and a half in diameter, was once surmounted by a crest, now broken off. Massiveness makes the coil look larger than it is, and a monumental character is preserved in the shape of the original boulder. An ornamental surface pattern in low relief uses the bars and dots of the time count. Snakes of this type, (Ziuhcoatl), were associated with time and the new year. The glyphs on the base denote the year "2 Reed" corresponding to 1507 A.D., and the name Montezuma II. This was the date of the last cyclical ceremony celebrated by the Aztecs, for Montezuma II was later captured by Cortez.

An eagle's head with open beak, perhaps devouring a human heart, is engraved in a stone disc in the Bliss Collection. Eagles, as symbols of the rising sun god, had a divine significance. A priest placed the heart of the human sacrifice in a bowl or jar, but the use of this disc (or lid?) is not known.

A combination of animal and human heads constitutes another sculptural group of statues, masks and pendants. In a jadeite pulque god (Fig. 197), a human head within a parrot's beak is smaller than the rabbit's head, the emblem of the god of intoxication. On the other hand, the rabbit crouches like a human being and the proportions of the body are more nearly human than rabbit-like. Elements from three species are made into a new form. To dignify the god the rabbit's head is over-large; to give him intelligence the human face is added.

The relation of man to animal takes on a different expression where the serpent is involved because the mythology is different. As the sun god each night sinks into the earth goddess, so man after death is received by the earth. The serpent is the symbol of the earth; the orange spots on the serpent reflect the sun shining through the serpent's body after having been devoured. This symbolism of man's dying is perhaps expressed in part in a terra-cotta mask in which a man's head with half-closed eyes and open mouth is enframed within a serpent's jaws (Fig. 198). The style is different in the case of a hard stone selected for its shape to fit, as nearly as possible, the final form envisioned by the artist. Preliminary cutting was thus reduced to a minimum. This undoubtedly happened in the case of a pendant, under five inches in height, of an oyster-gray polished stone with orange and blue veins, a choice specimen technically and aesthetically (Fig. 199). The human head dominates the design when seen from the front, and the bulging forms flatten out in the serpent's head; but when seen from the side the two heads merge. Serpent heads swallowing human heads were represented convincingly and with dignity, with no suggestion of the grotesque. Realism is subdued; there is no sense of horror, but an emphasis on tragedy and pain. Indians, who to us appear so brutal in human sacrifices, by comparison retained a surprising measure of reserve in art.

Travertine marble jars were made as a specialty in a few places, such as at Técali, in the state of Puebla and on Isla de Sacrificios, off Veracruz, probably not long before the Conquest. They were carved with animals like rabbits, jaguars and monkeys that projected out of the jar (Fig. 200), as if they grew out of the material itself. In one, about a foot high, showing a monkey, the animal shape disappears into the body of the jar, and the carver has used the monkey's tail to unify animal and bowl.

An Aztec head (Fig. 201) shows individual features: a long, thin nose, an overlapping upper eyelid and a raised upper lip with teeth showing. These realistic traits are combined with primitive traits, conventionalized ears and eyes placed unnaturally high.

A specific motivation may explain a diorite mask, about four and a half inches high (Fig. 202), showing a twisted mouth and tears out of one eye. Sahagun, speaking of a belief held by the Aztecs, suggests that a person's "mouth would twist to one side as a punishment of his sin." His sin was to have taken pulque, or "even to have dipped the finger in to taste the wine previous to the fourth day," when the newly brewed pulque would be tasted officially in a special ceremony, all this relating to preparation for festivities. We do not know whether or not such carved faces with twisted mouths relate to what Sahagun describes, but it is reasonable to presume that the twisted mouth had some sanction in folklore.

An obsidian head or skull, over four inches high (Fig. 203), is a carving of great distinction. A blend of realism and abstraction represents a strange mingling of effects, based on a balanced relationship of lines, shapes and textures. Preoccupied as the Aztecs were with death, they represented the symbols of death with all the refinements of which their artistry was capable.

The Aztecs, like the Maya and other pre-Columbian tribes, valued works in jade, in beads, earplugs, pendants and miniature works of sculpture. Various greenish stones like serpentine and porphyry, which were softer than jade, were also used for pieces of jewelry. The most difficult material to work was rock crystal, on account of its excessive hardness. A few beads and pendants are known, a fine vase from Monte Alban, a few rock crystal skulls in the National Museum of Mexico, the American Museum of Natural History, and the most famous of all, a nearly life-size skull in the British Museum.

Mosaic work, in the form of masks, weapons and ceremonial objects of various materials ornamented with small flecks of turquoise, jade and shell, was a skillfully executed, highly prized technique throughout the Mexican and Maya regions. Such objects were recovered from tombs, from a cave, and from the Sacred Well at Chichén Itzá. The development of mosaic art has been attributed to the Toltecs as well as to the Zapotecs.

In a wooden mask, believed to be Mixtec (Fig. 204), the carving is in accented planes that join in ridges and thereby provide the flat surfaces to which the flakes could be glued. Contours are emphasized by borders made up of the larger pieces. Variations due to color and polish make for a scintillating effect. Such masks may be replicas of others used in dances to represent the gods. Several mosaic masks are in the National Museum of Mexico, in the Prehistoric Museum in Rome, and a fine example is in the British Museum.

CENTRAL AMERICAN STYLES OUTSIDE THE MAYA AREA

JADE, STONE SCULPTURE, CERAMICS

The fully developed art styles of Mexico, based on architecture, did not continue across Central America. No monumental stone masonry buildings occur south of San Salvador until we reach Peru, but pottery and works in jade and other semiprecious stones were of excellent quality, especially in the Nicoya peninsula of Costa Rica. This region was inhabited in the sixteenth century by a branch of the Chorotega, and central Costa Rica by the Guetar Indians. Pendants of jadeite in the form of celts are highly attractive, with their polished surfaces and perfect shapes. These same celts of hard stones were carved in relief with masks, diminutive arms and hands, and notched and grooved for use as pendants (Fig. 205). Stylistically, these so-called "ax gods" seem related to South America. Other pendants of a greenish chalcedony are less elaborate than the highly perfected Maya jades, but are not inferior artistically.

Some of the regional cultures of the tropical highlands of Costa Rica and Panama produced stone sculpture. The pieces here illustrated are medium size, hardly exceeding three feet in the largest dimension. The styles seem related to South America, and they have been referred to the Guetar and Chorotega Indians, and designated by archaeologists as "late." This attribution is for reason of the stylistic development rather than as an indication of a specific date. The stone subjects include grinding stones (metates), jaguars and figures.

The province of Chiriquí, in western Panama, near Costa Rica, is one of the regions where these stone monuments have been found. William H. Holmes published them as early as 1888. Grinding stones, also known as hand mills or metates, consist of a concave or sometimes curved tablet, a common household implement used for grinding grain, seeds and spices. The finest examples are works of art above the purely utilitarian level and may have served in some religious function. The coarse surface of the volcanic rock was well suited for grinding maize.

A fine example (Fig. 206), 38 inches long, attributed to the Guetar Indians shows typically slender proportions. Legs and tail partake of the functional form of the slab; the stylized jaguar head, still fierce in expression, has shrunk to the size of a projecting handle. A conventionalized incised pattern on the outer surfaces may reflect the markings of the jaguar's pelt. A Chorotega metate, in the Philadelphia Museum of Art, with a projecting head in the form of a bird, is of a different style; the shaped sections used as supports are slab-like. A comparable thinness, which is vigorous at the same time, relates the Chorotega metate stylistically to the Guetar type. A granite slab figure, about fifteen inches high (Fig. 207), may seem primitive, but is too highly stylized to be an early piece. How this type otherwise fits into a style development is unknown. A sandstone mortar (Color Plate 20) represents the same style in its most attractive version. The arms of the figure, as well as the legs of the puma, are attached like ornaments to the sides. The grinding stones have often been found on the surface, as they remained in use by succeeding generations.

Some extraordinarily rich ceramics have come from the graves of Costa Rica and Panama in early (De Zeltner and Holmes) and recent (Lothrop) finds. Guatemala and Nicaragua have contributed incense jars and lids modeled in the shape of animals, animal effigy jars with negative painting and polychromed tripod bowls. These pieces are often involved in shape, in which a bowl or vase is combined with animal heads and legs. The combination is accomplished in a forthright manner. Neither pot shape nor animal form concede any priority of expression, one to the other. Though stylized animal heads are fantastically bold, they are also fierce in expression. Where painted decoration is used (Fig. 208), the motifs are equally strong and closely packed to form an allover pattern. The inside of a bowl (Ill. 27) on top of a stand combines an alligator head with the body of a man or monkey. (Such animals have been called alligators in the literature, though according to the zoologists the living

Ill. 27. Design from the inside of a bowl-shaped vase, Province of Chiriquí, Panama. *Peabody Museum of Natural History, Yale University. Illustration: Smithsonian Institution.*

alligator did not get into Middle America.) The colors are red and black on a white ground. Nothing is known of the use of the piece in regard to its mythological or religious meaning, but artistically the design is easy to appreciate. In comparison with this fantastically elaborated, vigorous pattern, in its expression of a fierce vitality, even the Mimbres designs appear sober, and most Peruvian pottery decorations quite tame. As if to court confusion, the pattern is complex but this artist still controls his motifs with no loss of energy.

A vase (Fig. 209) combines two female figures with a box-like container, terminating in a beaker-shaped top. The figures are modeled in a free, unconventional and almost grotesque manner; the flaring top and the curved rectangular sides are of the utmost reserve. Contrasting expressions, classic purity and primitive playfulness are brought together in an extraordinary way. We may be certain that such a piece had a long preparatory development.

WORK IN GOLD IN CENTRAL AND SOUTH AMERICA

The story of gold in ancient America is associated in our imagination with the reports that have come to us from the days of the Spanish Conquest of Mexico and Peru. The quantity, quality and variety of the objects of gold sent to Spain to be melted down and turned into coin incited the Spaniards to extravagant praise. Even before Cortez set foot on the mainland, the first of the invaders, who came into contact with the Maya of Yucatán, were amazed at the sight of the gold that reflected from the ornaments of Maya warriors. In later reports dealing with Montezuma, we hear of his golden sandals and thick slabs of gold and silver that covered the walls of the oratory of his palace. The Aztecs, like the Incas, were believed to have made full-scale gold and silver models of plants, like maize, which at seeding and harvest times were set out in rows in the sacred gardens of the gods. This lavish supply of gold objects varied from every kind of personal jewelry to life-size golden statues of the rulers of Peru, which stood in the palaces or temples and were tended to by being clothed and fed as if they were living persons. Of this vast treasure, only a few incidental objects have survived.

Fortunately our knowledge of pre-Columbian gold is not dependent solely on the accounts of the past. Objects of gold recovered more recently from graves and other places are now in many public and private collections. The richest collection of all is the Gold Museum of the Bank of the Republic, in Bogotá, the capital of Colombia. To date this museum has 6,726 pieces from Colombia, over four times the total number of gold objects from Colombia in all other museums the world over.

Gold was probably the first metal known and worked by man in the western hemisphere and in the Old World. It was found in a native state in river sands and in mountain veins, and by its color gold was related to the sun god. Gold is malleable, a gold nugget could be easily worked. Most American Indians had some knowledge of metals at the time of the Conquest, but only the more primitive hammering techniques were generally used. The higher skills, based on casting, were confined largely to the territory between Mexico and Peru. About two dozen cultures produced metal works of outstanding artistic quality. According to a table prepared by Dr. J. K. Lothrop, cast gold was typical only in central Mexico, in the Isthmus and in Colombia, but was known also in Peru in the Chimu and Inca periods. Hammered gold was known in the major cultures from Mexico to Peru, but was common in Peru.

The development of metallurgy, as in Peru and Colombia from the early periods to the Conquest, falls within the special province of archaeology. In the early Chavín culture of Peru, around 700 B.C. according to the Lothrop table, the major techniques of working gold, except casting, were practiced. The working of gold in Colombia may antedate the Christian era by several centuries, according to Dr. José Perez de Barradas of the University of Madrid.

For casting gold two methods were used, the *cire perdue* method, and the method of using carved stone or clay or charcoal molds. Plating was used, and wire was soldered to plates, metal was inlaid with metal or lacquer, as bronze with copper and silver. Repoussé was a technique in another type of decoration in which stone matrices or molds were used to bring out designs in relief or impress them into the metal. Decorations were also cut out of flat sheets of gold and bangles were attached with rings or links to other objects. The native gold of Colombia contained some silver in varying percentages, from less than one percent to twenty percent, and some copper in addition. This alloy, called *tumbaga*—a word derived by the Spaniards from a Malay word *stembag*, meaning copper—may be of either a low or a high grade, depending on the amount of copper in the mixture. Objects with a high copper content were gilded in various ways, but with no intent to deceive. Copper facilitated the casting process.

Pre-Columbian works of gold cannot be classified with certainty in any fixed chronological order. Instead, styles are related to geographic areas, in Panama to the provinces of Veraguas and Coclé, and in Colombia to the Quimbaya and Chibcha Indians, and to the styles of the Tairona, Sinu, Darien, and Calima cultures, each in its own region in the north and western parts of the country. Peruvian objects of gold are classified by periods, as Chimu, Inca, or by geographic site names, as Lambayeque, named after a river valley on the north coast of Peru. Two classification names might be combined in objects of gold, as being from the Lambayeque Valley of the late Chimu culture.

At the time of the discoveries, the Indians of Costa Rica, the "rich coast" were seen wearing gold eagles (Fig. *210*) around their necks. As early as the fourth voyage of Columbus (1502), graves with deposits of gold ornaments were discovered and have been searched ever since. The province of Veraguas, in Panama, was a manufacturing center from which gold was traded as far north as the Maya of Yucatán. Veraguas was selected as their Duchy by the Columbus family on account of its wealth.

Eagle pendants vary in size—those from the Bliss Collection measure up to four and a half inches in width. They also vary in craftsmanship, some are rougher than others. A bird god with a small animal in its beak, from the Bliss Collection, shows a vigorous design in which the solid parts are well co-ordinated with the perforations. Frogs (Fig. *211*) with round bodies are polished and reflect the light from the head, back and edges, and absorb the light from the flat legs. The soft mellow glow that results greatly enhances the beauty of the piece.

To the east of Veraguas lies the province of Coclé, where expeditions of the Peabody Museum of Harvard University, and one in 1940 by the University Museum, Philadelphia, uncovered gold ornaments and pottery vessels.

The embossed gold plaques in the University Museum, Philadelphia, eight inches in diameter, and worn on breast and back, are of superior quality. In one, a fierce monster, baring teeth and claws, holds a staff in either hand. The design, stylized and separated into many parts, is remarkably vigorous and vibrates with energy. In another plaque (Fig. *212*) its equal artistically, the representative element is more disguised. These plaques demonstrate the high level of the art of this culture.

Some of the finest of pre-Columbian objects of gold were produced by the Quimbaya tribe of Colombia. At the time of the Conquest this tribe occupied approximately the regions of the present departments of Antioquia and Caldas, but the gold objects, to which the Quimbaya name has been applied, are believed to be earlier than the sixteenth century. The Quimbaya used *tumbaga* in solid and hollow castings as well as in hammered, repoussé and cutout work. The objects they made were mace heads, masks, human and anthropomorphic figures, scepters and vases, and ornaments like necklaces, bracelets, earrings, nose rings, pendants, pins and beads. These are largely cast, but objects like diadems and breastplates were hammered. Crocodiles and birds were used as motifs and presumably had a religious significance.

A pendant of twin animals, under three inches long, represents the style at its best (Fig. 213). The long, smooth shapes of the animals show off the beauty of the metal. Lines of threadlike thinness fringe the plain surfaces, coil into headdress ornaments and form spirals in place of tails; the contrast of round, solid forms with flat, spiral ornaments is particularly effective. This same appreciation of breadth of surface contrasted with a concentration of ornament is evident in staff finials, which were also cast. Spiral motifs seem to have had a particular appeal, for they were often used. Spirals are held like emblems in the outstretched arms of a seated nude female figure, nine inches high, in the University Museum, Philadelphia. In its elegance and economy of ornamentation this figure is unique, as different in the style of the head from the Maya and Mexican types as from those of South America, and suggestive of affinities to styles across the Pacific. But such resemblances, where they occur, may also be incidental, as other Quimbaya heads are closer to the Andean type. A type of bottle, oval-shaped and fluted in the lower part and highly polished, constitutes one of the best known achievements of the Quimbaya style. Upper and lower parts, which in some bottles look like parts of a fruit, were cast separately.

The Chibcha Indians lived in the vicinity of Bogotá, the present capital of Colombia. They had the same metal-working techniques used by the other tribes of Colombia and the Isthmus, but their castings are often rougher. The style uses cast plaques overlaid with linear surface patterns. Typical Chibcha pieces consist of stylized votive figures, in which head, torso and legs are reduced to near-geometric shapes, chiefly ovals and rectangles (Fig. 214). This technique is embroidery-like, as if threads had been applied to a background. This type of design does not lend itself to precision and results in a certain primitive character. Where the design in Chibcha gold objects looks infantile, it is due to isolated details, like hands, drawn with five strokes emanating from the end of a straight line. Aside from such mannerisms, the drawing is stylized, as in the Chibcha cast gold ceremonial knife which interests us chiefly as a design. In the example in Fig. 215, solid areas are strikingly set off against delicate lattice work, and curves and straight lines together produce a closely knit profile. The design has firmness and delicacy; one enhances the other. The art historical significance escapes us, and we do not know what part such objects played in ritual or which gods are represented.

The most abstract of pre-Columbian works in gold are pendants and pectorals in anthropomorphic form combining separately cast parts soldered to a sheet of gold. A symbolic figure is recognizable in the eyes, suggesting screwheads, a nose composed of four spirals above the mouth, which holds a serpent. Semi-spherical breasts and spirals of uncertain derivation complete this highly abstract design. The religious meaning is not known, but the artistic significance is clear.

Hammered gold was also known in Colombia, as in a diadem in the Calima style (Fig. 216), but was common in Peru. A plaque with designs cut out and embossed with discs, used as bangles over the eyes (Fig. 217), is of the late Chimu culture of the north coast of Peru. The many holes indicate that the piece, in the form of a face with headdress, had attachments, or was itself attached as masks were to the wrappings containing the mummies. Technically this represents the simplest kind of gold work, as if sheet gold had been used as easily as a child might cut out paper dolls. But there is an awareness of pattern and a desire on the part of the artist to create a style. This is noticeable in the embossed corners of the face, which bring out rectangular shapes, emphasize horizontals and verticals, so that the details fit into these rectangular shapes. The design is by no means as haphazard as the unevenness of the technique might lead one to believe.

The gold diadem from Colombia, in the Calima style (Fig. 216), cut and embossed, uses basically the same techniques in an object that may have allowed the artist more scope. In a richly indented profile, curves are used freely, dots are punched out of the metal, thin strips and discs are suspended along the edges, and a nose ornament, like a mask, forms part of the embossed head. A simple technique is here elaborated, but remains all wiggle and dazzle; classic perfection is outside its sphere but not beyond the style itself. In a much simpler object, a Calima style spoon, the design is compelling and final in the form in which the artist left it. We can imagine a more functional spoon, but not through tampering with this particular oval shape, which as a design is wholly satisfying as it is.

A Peruvian mask, from the Chimu culture, embossed out of a thin sheet of gold, now in the University Museum, Philadelphia, came from a mummy bundle, where it was attached to the textile wrappings. In a hollow silver alpaca (Fig. 218) of the Inca style, the last of the Peruvian periods before the Conquest, a realistic head and realistic feet protrude from a formal pattern of channels hammered out of the metal to produce a corrugated surface. As in other instances, the technique helped to determine the style. Embossing led the craftsman to stylization and ornamental effects, and away from realism. The same emphasis on preserving the beauty of the material, sheet silver, appears in a hollow figure of a man, under nine inches high, in the Inca style (Fig. 219). With the least interference with the attractiveness of the sheet metal, the figure is only approximated. This is virtually a cylindrical form modified to bring out head and limbs.

Bronze implements, presumably sacred and for ceremonial use, of the southern highlands of Peru, were even inlaid with silver and copper, as in a chopping knife with a handle terminating in a llama head and an adz in the shape of a bird, both in the Bliss Collection. The utilitarian and the ornamental are fused to bring out an emphasis on pleasing form.

Having entered the domain of Peruvian art through its use of metal, we shall now deal with Peruvian pottery, textiles and wood carving.

PERUVIAN ART

SCOPE

The major arts of architecture and sculpture that played such a part in the arts of Middle America existed also in Peru from early to late periods. Magnificent ruins, monumental in their cyclopean masonry and precise in the working of stone, are in the highlands of Peru in the Urubamba Valley at

Machu Picchu, in and near Cuzco, the ancient Inca capital, in the region of Lake Titicaca, at Tiahuanaco in Bolivia, and in north Peru at Chavín de Huántar, noted for its engraved stone monoliths. Among the remains of brick architecture are the ruins of ancient cities and fortresses on the north coast of Peru, particularly those near Trujillo, on the site of the ancient city of Chanchan. The remains include walls, staircases, terraces, watch towers, fortresses, pyramids and tombs, but few major structures left today attain any great height above ground. A mass platform at Chavín, the highest structure and principal building, is forty-five feet high. As archaeological sites these places are well known to archaeologists, but hardly at all to the general public. Stone sculpture exists in Peru on the original locations and in museums and private collections. Ancient Peruvian art, as it has reached the museums, consists largely of ceramics and textiles, in addition to works in metal. Peruvian art is also known in objects of wood, bone, stone beads, shell carvings and shell and stone mosaic. A mirror from southern Peru in the Bliss Collection has a surface of hematite (iron ore) in carefully fitted and polished blocks. The back side shows a Tiahuanaco style face with tears—the weeping eyes—terminating in feline heads and angular frets, all encrusted with shell mosaic, stone and mother of pearl.

Peruvian art has been dealt with from the scientific point of view by archaeologists who have carried on the excavations and described, named and dated what has been recovered from the earth. Archaeological labels are retained, as they describe the styles and differentiate periods. A discussion of works of art from an aesthetic point of view necessarily places less emphasis on sites, horizons and relationship of one culture to another. Sculpture, ceramics and textiles are presented separately but, as far as possible, chronologically within each group.

ANDEAN STONE SCULPTURE

Peruvian sculpture can be illustrated only by a few examples, because ancient Peru apparently did not produce sculpture in quantity comparable to Middle America. These works in stone belong to three different periods, the Chavín period (c. 1200-400 B.C.), the Tiahuanaco period (c. 1000-1300 A.D.) and the Inca period (1438-1532 A.D.). These dates are according to Bennett, but roughly they appear to be acceptable also to other archaeologists. During these three periods these cultures were dominant over wider areas, the Chavín on the coast from north to south, the Tiahuanaco and Inca over most of the region of the Central Andes.

A carved granite slab, six feet high, the so-called Stela Raimondi (Ill. 28), found at the site of the village of Chavín de Huántar, now in the National Museum of Peru, Lima, is an important monument of the early period. The incised low relief covering the whole surface represents a standing figure, a cat-like deity, holding a huge staff in either hand. A cat head with two deeply drilled nostrils and lightly engraved eyes, mouth, teeth and two fangs can be made out. The upper two-thirds of the relief consists of a headdress, in which scrolls and serpents project out at an angle on either side. Serpents, scrolls and teeth make up the center of the headdress. The human figure is used as a support for religious emblems, cat or jaguar heads, and serpents. The meaning of the emblems is unknown, but claws and teeth suggest aggression and the repetition of motifs may indicate a desire for prestige or for the working of magic; the serpent motif is repeated perhaps eighteen times, counting only one side. Artistically, this is a cultivated product, ornate and highly formal. Its apparent complexity is controlled by

Ill. 28. Stela Raimondi, H. 15 ft., from Chavín de Huántar, Peru. *Museo Nacional de Arqueologia y Antropologia, Peru. Courtesy, Frederick A. Praeger (New York).*

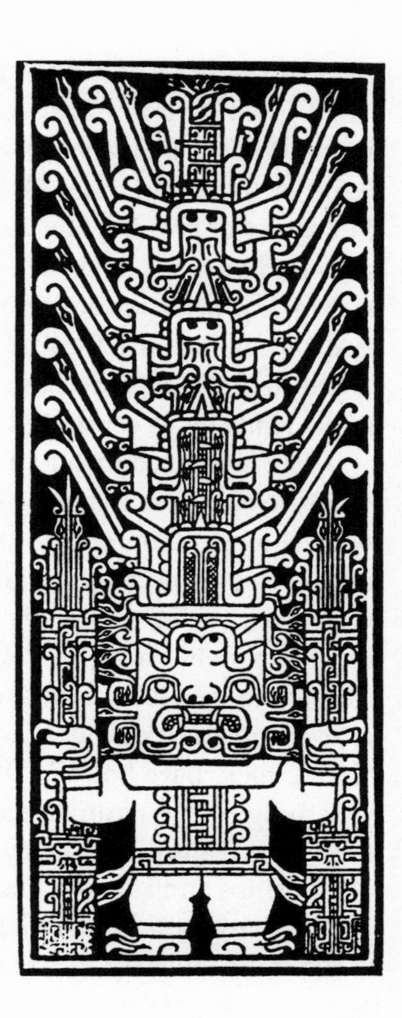

the application of the principles of dominance and subordination to bring out an orderly relationship of parts. Technically, the relief shows the background cut away and the details engraved on the original surface as a linear pattern. It is superior in craftsmanship. The same feline head with the large mouth showing fangs and square teeth and the same eyes and nose appears in metal work and stone sculpture.

The second of the Pan-Peruvian styles is found in Peru and Bolivia in the Titicaca basin, at an altitude of 12,500 feet. The style is believed to have been centered in Bolivia at Tiahuanaco. In this bleak and forbidding country, which is too high for tree growth, the influence of Lake Titicaca, the largest body of water in the Andes, made the cultivation of corn possible on its shores. A large area was once covered with structures, the largest one being a stepped and stone-faced pyramid, the Acapana, about fifty feet high. Erosion and the use of the land for agriculture have greatly reduced the ruins.

Many stone carvings are still standing, huge blocks in the form of kneeling and seated figures. One column, monolithic, like the seated figures, and at least twenty feet high, the Stela Bennett, was discovered by Wendell C. Bennett in 1932. It is a quadrangular shaft carved in relief with designs to suggest a textile pattern, and resembles a figure with head, bent elbows and hands clasped in front, each holding an emblem. This stela shows stylistic affinities with the Toltec caryatids of Tula, which were constructed in sections, but the Tula caryatids, in refinement, surpass the Tiahuanaco stela. The carved frieze of the lintel of a monolithic doorway, called the "Gate of the Sun" has a central figure holding a staff in either arm, thrust out to the sides, and engraved with condor heads (top) and puma heads (bottom). The square head shows round eyes, each with three smaller round circles below, perhaps meant as tears, and a headdress of rays engraved with puma and condor heads. A frieze on either side shows rows of running figures bearing staffs, carved in relief in heraldic style. The contour of each figure is squared off to fit its panel. The significance of this relief lies less in any outstanding artistic merits of its own, but more in the fact that the motifs used appear as the characteristic motifs of the Tiahuanaco style throughout the Central Andes, particularly in ceramics and on textiles. A finer quality is represented in a clay incense burner in the shape of a llama under twenty inches long (Fig. 220). Though hardly realistic, its severity of shape reflects something of the vitality of living forms.

The artistic contributions of the Inca period were in stone construction and stone cutting; stone sculpture is known only in a few examples, but they are very fine. A low ceremonial stone vessel, over two feet long, composed of one large and two smaller circular bowls, in the University Museum, Philadelphia, shows serpents clinging to the exterior and resting their heads on the rim. The massive solidity of the bowl, which hugs the ground, stands out in contrast to the writhing serpents. A stone vessel, under five inches high, in the shape of a llama head (Fig. 221) reveals the Incas as sensitive artists, on a level with the Aztec animal carvers. Peruvian carved stone animals are as stylized, and reveal, perhaps, an even greater dependence on geometric shapes. Small llamas, from three to four inches long, of basaltic rock, have holes in their backs, presumably for offerings. In spite of simplification, they retain something of the naturalness of the living animal. Raised heads and open mouths clearly suggest an interest in realism, not favored by tools and techniques. Artists instead applied themselves to formal relationships and superior craftsmanship and produced the artistic qualities we admire today.

The attribution of isolated stone carvings of unknown provenance must remain uncertain. One of two stone tablets (Fig. 222) engraved with short, stocky-figured warriors, shows a general resemblance to running figures on painted Mochica pottery. The artist was clearly interested in costume, weapons and implements, resulting in a descriptive kind of engraving in which the figures are spread out laterally. The demands of space, and a desire for clarity to illustrate the warriors fully, together with the art tradition of the period, may explain this particular example.

PERUVIAN CERAMICS

General Characteristics

The place occupied in ancient Mexico by sculpture was taken in Peru by ceramics. Pots that were buried with the dead include many shapes: flasks, bowls, beakers, jugs and vases, varying in techniques and styles of decoration. In the course of the millennium before the Conquest, which is less than one-half of the time span allotted to the archaeological periods of prehistorical Peru, pottery took on something of the character of sculpture or of painting, or combined the two. And yet the modeled figure and the painted decoration were subordinated to the requirements of pottery. The modeled portrait head remained a vessel that could be filled through a spout, and a modeled figure with head and limbs was basically a pot. Within the field of ceramics, sculpture came closer than painting to establishing an independence for itself. On the other hand, painting on pots also adapted itself to curved surfaces and produced brush drawings excellent in their own right.

In examining Peruvian pots of many styles, we get the impression that decoration was given meaning beyond the sensuous, artistic appeal. Motifs were selected, not primarily for the sake of their beauty, but for their religious and mythological significance; yet they were developed artistically. Some examples are poor in design and slovenly in execution, but others are superior, ranking with Greek and Chinese pottery. Peruvian pottery is also remarkably inventive in creating unusual forms, especially by fusing vegetable and animal forms with human ones.

In ancient Peruvian pottery, spirits and demons take on the guise of living creatures, often fantastic and distorted. That may explain the pots which are shaped like animals, birds, fish, or beans, peanuts and potatoes. Human-headed pots with vegetable bodies undoubtedly had a religious motivation.

The Peruvians had no writing, and what we know of their life from eyewitness accounts of the Spaniards relates largely to the Indians with whom the conquerors had come in personal contact. Information gained from pottery in some instances fills a gap in our knowledge by furnishing us with facts on earlier cultures, often not known from other sources, so that conclusions can be drawn to enlarge the evidence of archaeology. We have in mind representations of costumes, weapons and other objects, as well as battle scenes, real and mythical, that appear on the vessels of the Mochica style. This fact holds true where the pottery has been retrieved under the controlled conditions of scientific excavations. However, the contents of collections are often of unknown origin due to the fact that ceramic specimens came into the trade through "pot hunters," who began looting graves for pots and textiles during the nineteenth century, after the precious metals had been exhausted.

Techniques

Great as the stylistic differences are, the basic techniques were much the same everywhere. In the simplest method a lump of clay was molded or pinched into shape by the hand, a method that was adequate for small pieces. For larger pieces, the coil and the paddle techniques were used, the same methods employed by the North American Indians. On the north coast of Peru pots were cast in molds. Presumably some mold-made pieces were also finished by hand, as no great number of exact duplicates has been noted. The pots were fired to produce a light color, or they were made to come out dark-colored or black by reducing the amount of oxygen in the firing. The surfaces were decorated by incising, by pressing carved relief stamps into the soft clay, by applying clay to the surface in form of pellets or strips, and by painting in one of two methods. The surface was covered with a coat of thin clay (slip) which served as a background for the painted decoration. This was the more usual method, where many colors were used, as in the Nazca style.

A simpler kind of surface decoration was obtained by covering the design with a resist material like wax. With portions of the surface thus covered, the whole pot was dipped into the pigment, so that the design, when free of the wax, would show up in the natural color of the clay. In pottery this type of resist is called "negative painting."

Another method used modeling, either for the whole vessel or for a part of the vessel. This method, in which the figures were modeled in relief or in the round, is essentially ceramic sculpture, as it was used in the Mochica style. Much of the ceramic ware found in graves was made in molds which had to be made from an original piece that had been modeled. The stirrup-spouts, so commonly used in the Mochica style, were added to the vessels. Whatever luster shows in Peruvian pottery was obtained by polishing; no glazes were used. From the occurrence of well-rounded pieces, it is believed that some simple device to produce rotary motion may have been used, although the potter's wheel was unknown.

Actual samples of pigments have been found in different containers such as shells, stone jars, gourds or leather bags. Shells certainly were used to prepare pigments for use, and hair and bristle brushes that have come down to us look much like our brushes today.

Periods, Regions and Styles

It is possible to illustrate Peruvian ceramics with examples from each of Bennett's six periods. A cylindrical steatite vase (Fig. 223), in the Chavín style of the highlands of North Peru (1200-400 B.C.), is engraved with two figures, wearing masks and feather headdresses. The design is highly ornamental; the flat, ribbon-like band which each figure clasps is only slightly modified to serve also as arms and legs (Ill. 29). On one figure, visible on the drawing, a serpent head protrudes from underneath the band next to the hand. The massive proportions and the flat relief, firm and precise in cutting, are typical of the Chavín style. The relief is admirable in its breadth and vigor; the pattern is large in scale, studied in its refinement and skillfully adapted to the curved surface.

Strength, so characteristic of the Chavín style, is also present in pottery from the south coast of Peru (c. 400 B.C.-400 A.D., style of Paracas Cavernas). A severely simple design on a bowl in the University Museum, Philadelphia, shows incised and painted serpent heads within rectangles. Though well adapted to the bowl, the rectilinear pattern may have originated in textile designs. A bowl in negative painting (Fig. 224) shows a spotted feline with round eyes and square mouth with teeth reminiscent of the favorite Chavín motif. In a double-spout flask, red angles or chevrons suggestive of tattoo marks combine with curvilinear motifs on a dark yellow ground. The savage expression of the animal, with its half-closed eyes and grinning mouth with bared teeth, suggests that this trophy head was meant to convey strength (Color Plate 19).

The pottery styles, of which there are many examples available, are the Mochica, on the north and the Nazca, on the south, coast (c. 400-1000 A.D.). These two will be described at some length after a survey of the whole development. Mochica architecture included pyramids built of sun-dried bricks, and walls that were painted or decorated with reliefs. The graves have yielded pottery in quantity, as well as objects of wood, bone and metal (Color Plate 21). Though the textile arts were highly developed, they have been less well-preserved here than on the south coast. Its realistic pottery has helped to make the Mochica culture one of the best known of pre-Columbian Peru. Among the examples of this period are some fine jars decorated in negative painting, such as one from the Recuay culture of the highlands of north Peru, now in the American Museum of Natural History. The stylized animal designs suggest the Coclé style of Panama.

The Highland Tiahuanaco style (c. 1000-1300 A.D.) developed a few standard shapes painted with abstract designs, based on puma, condor, and human face and figure motifs. A fine example is a beaker six and a half inches high with flaring sides and painted decoration of conventionalized animals and masks (Fig. 225). The Tiahuanaco culture also spread to the coast of Peru, where it is called Coastal

Ill. 29. Drawing of a steatite vase engraving of figures wearing jaguar masks, style of Chavín de Huántar. *National Gallery of Art, Washington, D.C.*

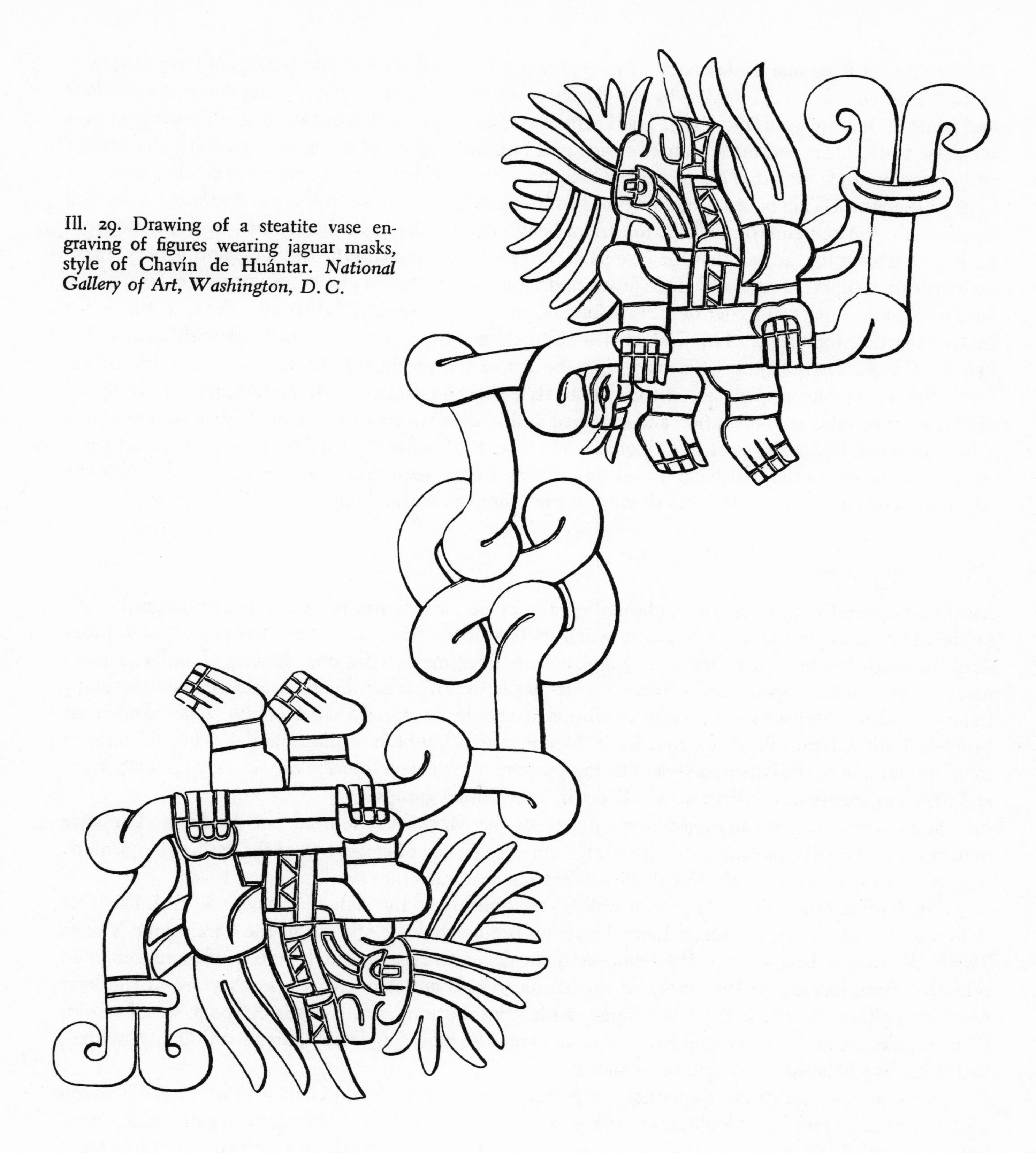

Tiahuanaco, or Epigonal Tiahuanaco. A large, thick urn is described in archaeological terminology as "Coast Tiahuanaco-A, represented by the Pacheco site in the Nazca Valley." The colors are in black and white on red slip base (Fig. 226). The Pacheco cemetery, where this urn was found, became known for these thick, U-shaped urns, painted inside and out with representations of Viracocha, the creator god of the pre-Inca period. This painted Viracocha design follows the engraved stone relief from the Gate of the Sun at Tiahuanaco in posture and emblems. The headdress on the urn also has condor and puma heads, the belt ends on the side in condor heads, and trophy heads hang down in front and from both eyes. Except for the fact that the vase painter in places skimped on the details, painting only seventeen instead of nineteen rays, and three heads under the belt instead of six, the correspondence is of the kind one would expect in a coat of arms belonging to the same family. Artistically, the urn painting is better than the stone relief. The Tiahuanaco culture was followed by local cultures with local styles, like the Chimu, the Chancay (Fig. 227) and the Ica of the north, the central and the south coasts. Some black-ware stirrup-spout jars of the Chimu style show an impressed decoration, perhaps of spirits or demons, fantastic as to invention and dignified and reserved in style. The Chimu style (c. 1300-1438 A.D.) continued the traditions of the Mochica style, after the Tiahuanaco style, which came in between. As a continuation of the Mochica, in a strictly chronological sequence, the Chimu should follow the Mochica. The Chancay and Ica periods are also contemporary with Chimu.

The Mochica Style

Mochica pottery has been classified chronologically by periods, or has been referred to geographically by the main valleys of the north coast, in which pottery of the Mochica culture has been found. From north to south the principal valleys are Lambayeque, Pacasmayo, Chicama, Moche, Trujillo (a place name), Viru, Santa, Nepena, and Casma. The names in use by archaeologists to differentiate the many Peruvian cultures are many. To avoid confusion it should be noted that Mochica is also known as Muchik, Early Chimu, Proto Chimu, Early Moche, and Chimbote (a place name). They all refer in some special way to the Mochica style. For the purpose of a general orientation, we may ignore periods and sites and adhere to subdivisions by shapes in a few broad groups.

The question of the origin and development of the Mochica style need not detain us. The style may have developed in one more or less uninterrupted sequence of stages out of the earliest Cupisnique style (Color Plate 22), with the so-called Salinar style as a transition (Collier).

The Cupisnique style has a certain stylistic relationship to the style of Chavín de Huántar. This style was first discovered by Rafael Larco Hoyle on the north coast of Peru in the Cupisnique Valley. This archaeologist believes that the feline motif in decorative art radiated from a religious center in primitive Peru, located on the coast. Stirrup-handle vessels are characteristic as they are in the later Mochica culture, to which the Cupisnique made contributions. On the stirrup-spout vessel (Color Plate 22) a feline face is combined with a human face. The modeling is bold, broad and highly stylized, and religious symbolism may well be involved.

According to another interpretation, the pottery styles of Salinar and Gallinazo, which fall between early Cupisnique and late Mochica, are the result of invasions of the Cupisnique region, which were later repulsed (Bird). For our purposes we may accept the Mochica style as a unified group in which, according to archaeology, early, middle and late stages are included. Setting aside the Cupisnique, Salinar and Gallinazo styles, we proceed to a discussion of the Mochica.

Often more than one motif is used and the human figure may be included in one or another way. Using the most prominent motif in each case, we arrive at groups composed of fruit and vegetables, animals, human figures and portraits, houses, temples, musical instruments and other objects, and globular stirrup-spout vessels. Modeling and painting often combine, but in the portrait group modeling is predominant, and painting subordinate. In the globular stirrup-spout vessels painting is often of the greater interest, and modeling may be entirely absent.

Stirrup-spout vessels in the form of a potato, a peanut (Fig. 228), and a squash (Fig. 229), are representative of the vegetable group. Symbolizing fertility, these pots were presumably dedicated to the spirits who watched over the crops. Good will is at times reflected in the facial expression of their humanized heads, for as deities they took on a human aspect. In the broad smile of the peanut woman (Fig. 228) there is a closeness to life based on observation of real persons uncommon in early art. These heads are individualized to an even greater extent than the "smiling faces" of Totonac art. In the squash vessel (Fig. 229) an aloof sort of dignity is expressed in the combination of an owl with the face of an old lady, assuming the spirits of nature deities to have been female.

Among the animals represented in modeled form are birds, including parrots and vultures, crabs, llamas, pumas, apes, foxes, seals, turtles, cuttle fish, snails, dogs, frogs, serpents, fish and rats. Some of these have been found on central coast sites, where the styles tend to become more geometric.

A fragment of a handle-spout (Fig. 230), painted red on cream and about four inches high, represents a jaguar (?) head. Here is an example where Peruvian and Romanesque art pursued a parallel course. Had twelfth century Europe modeled jaguars in clay, instead of lions, to be cast in bronze, they might have shown a fair resemblance to this type of head.

A more fully modeled stirrup-spout vessel of the middle Mochica period shows a seated deer, virtually a human figure with a deer head (Fig. 231). In typical Mochica fashion, the form is full and massive, the head alone is treated to differentiate each part, and arms and hands are made a part of the pot-shaped body. Judging from a kneeling warrior attributed to middle Mochica, the development was toward increased naturalism (Fig. 232). Here the limbs have detached themselves from the pot. The parts of the figure begin to function, especially details like helmet, club and hands and painted costume.

The most spectacular examples of Mochica pottery are the portrait heads in the form of stirrup-spout vessels. Their highly individual styles make it certain that they are portraits. In the development toward naturalism, they stand ahead of anything achieved in Middle America.

Mochica portrait heads represent individuals modeled from life, probably members of the ruling caste. Most of them are men (Fig. 233), but some could be women (Fig. 234). Each one reflects a personality often forceful, with head erect and of proud bearing. They vary as to age, some are youthful, others show lines in the face, or have a double chin, but they are not senile. They still show the person at his best, in a style that is simplified without being stylized. The sculptors understood anatomy but differed in skill, the most talented ones were quite able to bring out refinements in the modeling of details, as in the overlap of the upper eyelid and the rendering of the inner corner of the eye (Fig. 233), whereas others did not give up entirely the use of some standard forms. Painted decoration, perhaps of a social or religious meaning, was used in the head band and on the face itself (Color Plate 23). In some examples the face shows half dark and half light. Though realistic, these portrait heads also show an idealizing trend, as if to memorialize individuals for the desirable qualities they possessed.

The balance and poise in the treatment of the figure was but one phase of Mochica art; another more emotional element was also represented in human heads of another type. Some represent fantastic combinations of human and animal form, grotesque in shape and irregular in outline, others vary from serious and thoughtful types to expressions of suffering, and to persons afflicted with features ravished by disease, with misshaped noses, split lips and protruding teeth. Along with these physical ailments, other head and figure vessels represented drunkenness, sex perversions and scenes of punishment, of decapitation and death. Mochica pottery reflects a culture that had some of the social and psychological problems we still have today.

A group of miscellaneous objects is of a cultural rather than an artistic interest. Gable roofed houses, stepped pyramids and temples with a spiral ramp leading to a shrine at the top, boats (balsas) with fishermen, and jaguar-headed trumpets belong to this category. Wherever a figure is represented in connection with inanimate objects, the figure is believed to represent Ai-Apec, the chief Mochica god. Some are from Chimbote and Trujillo and others of unknown origin.

Perhaps the most characteristic Mochica shape is the stirrup-spout vessel, a few examples of which we examined earlier. About half of all Mochica ceremonial vessels belong to this group. The basic shape is globular with two arched tubes on top, which join in a single cylindrical spout. In the animal and vegetable shapes one tube of the stirrup-spout connects to the head or figure on top of the container. The globular shape, with or without superimposed figure, was best suited for painted decoration. A stirrup-spout vessel with a modeled figure on top, seated cross-legged and tying on his bonnet, is shown in Fig. 235. He wears a nose ring and his headdress shows a modeled and painted animal, perhaps a bat. The same figure reappears on the painted frieze below, recognizable by the headdress. On the left figure his face is half dark, half light—as in the modeled figure on top, but the third figure shows a "weeping eye." The drawing is fresh and spontaneous, the action of the runners convincing. The effect depends on the decorative treatment of the whole frieze, especially on the interweaving pattern of lines and dark accents against a light background. An over-all pattern is used in a stirrup-spout vessel showing only the spout above a globular pot with an energetic parabolic profile (Fig. 236). A battle of bean warriors armed with javelins and shields is represented. The humanized beans assume a variety of postures and are drawn with a remarkably free precision. Both sides in the battle use the same weapons and are alike in other details. This suggests that this mythical battle may be a ceremonial demonstration within the bean warrior group. The same type of runner holding the same emblem is seen as a single figure on a stirrup-spout vessel in the Minneapolis Institute of Arts. In this case a bird's head and wings are combined with the figure, representing another god.

In the example in Fig. 237, a crab demon, believed to represent the ranking Mochica god Ai-Apec, threatens a fish demon. For design and brushwork this extraordinarily rich pattern shows Mochica art at its best. The blind spout, to which the stirrup-spout connects, is in the form of a war club. Painted black, it gives a note of balance to the lively pattern below. In contrast to its complexity, another stirrup-spout vessel from the Art Institute of Chicago, with a spider design, reverts to simplicity. The bold rendering of the spider goes well with the sturdier handle, which is left undecorated.

Like the Tarascan figurines of Mexico, the Mochica pottery of Peru has a human interest in addition to its artistic significance. From that point of view, these two styles of pre-Columbian art are unique.

The Nazca Style

The Nazca culture of the south coast, contemporary with the Mochica culture of the north coast, developed primarily textiles and ceramics, which have been recovered from Nazca graves in large quantities. The style is limited to south coast valleys. Less is known of Nazca than of Mochica culture, partly due to the fact that fewer excavations have been carried on, and partly due to the style itself, which does not depict the life and customs of the peoples. The shapes include bowls, cups, beakers, bottles with handle-spouts and vessels with two short spouts connected by a low bridge. In some vessels this bridge connects to a spout modeled in the form of a head, animal or human. Vessels resembling the human figure with a globular body and a large head are also known. The preferred decoration here is painting rather than modeling, in as many as ten colors, including several reds, yellow, violet, cream, buff, brown, gray and black and white.

The painted motifs include seeds, vegetables, fruits, bats, birds, fish, llamas, human heads and human figures, demons and mythical scenes. The colors are applied flat and are often outlined in black, and the vessels are polished. The technique is excellent, the painting is executed with care in sure strokes in a professional, workmanlike fashion. Stylistically, Nazca pottery has great unity, devoid of personal expression. Designs differ, but there is uniformity in the technique that links one pot to another. Eyes and mouths on human heads, and outlines and borders repeat according to a standardized pattern. Color values are used in striking contrasts, often dark against light, but also light against dark. The scale is large, the shapes are broad and massive. A mechanical precision is characteristic of the examples illustrated, but a loose and spontaneous technique, in the manner of free brushwork, also occurs. No generally accepted division of styles by chronological periods has been worked out.

It may be that shapes can be correlated with motifs. Birds and plant forms are used on bowls (Fig. 238), demons and mythological scenes on globular-spout vessels, human figures on taller vases, but there are also exceptions. Though motifs are recognizable, they are conventionalized, not realistic; each detail is simplified and approaches the geometric.

A bell-shaped bowl (Fig. 239) shows trophy heads turned sideways with long hair hanging down in a striking effect. In another such bowl the heads are placed in horizontal rows to form a closely knit pattern. The lowest band at the bottom of a pot is often painted black. Trophy heads seem to point to a practice of taking heads of slain enemies in order to assure the victor, through possession of the head, of qualities possessed by the man defeated in battle.

On a beaker (Fig. 240) with a broadly conventionalized decoration, eyes and claws of a quail are fitted into a pattern of stripes and rectangles. A modeled beak between the eyes and two projecting ears are kept small; by being inconspicuous these additions interfere little with the smooth contours. The fact that such details, perhaps necessary for the sake of magic, were absorbed into the pattern shows that the feeling for style was strong. You cannot make a beaker look like a quail if it is a beaker you strive for. For that reason function came first, after which symbolism served the needs of magic by merely suggesting resemblances.

A boldly conceived contrast appears in the design of a spout-handle vessel (Fig. 241). Two arms reach out from underneath a poncho and rest on the geometric pattern of a mantle. As the spout lent itself to being modeled into a head, a closer adaptation to a human figure resulted.

In some of the globular two-spout vessels of Nazca pottery the greatest width is near the bottom, and painted decoration varies from realism to near abstraction. In one example, a fisherman holding a net in realistic fashion is obviously meant to show a man at work, even though an incident from mythology is probably represented. Action is restricted to posture, the huge, paw-like hands making no pretense at grasping the net. On another vessel of the same type (Fig. 242), a cat demon carries an ax in one hand and two trophy heads in the other; there are heads on the tail and a frieze of heads in the lower register. The cat head motif, recognized by its whiskers, appears with the same emblems, but simplified and in a larger scale on a double-spout vessel in the Bliss Collection. Aesthetically, one of the most satisfying of all Nazca vessels is shown in Fig. 243. Long, tapering spouts connected by a thin bridge project sideways and contribute vitally to the total effect. The painted designs, circles, smooth curves and wavy contours are used to suggest a skull in a formal, unrealistic manner.

Nazca design explores a considerable range, but even where it depends on painting, it is unlike the Mochica style. It is further removed from the Maya and totally different from the Mimbres style and the more recent pottery styles of the southwest of the United States.

The Inca Style

The Incas excelled in ceramics, textiles, metallurgy, weaving, and architecture. The crafts increased in production, stimulated by the Inca state (c. 1438-1532 A.D.). Techniques, largely inherited, improved under a system of mass production. Fewer designs were repeated on more objects. Motifs were geometric, but were also drawn from plant and animal life. The Incas emphasized structure; function and utility were stressed, rather than expression for its own sake. Their magnificently strong and simple stone architecture expresses their art in its purest form. The Incas were able organizers, who profited from the developments made by the people they had conquered and incorporated into their empire. The subjugated tribes were absorbed into a unified system of governmental control, which included taking over the Inca language. Trends aiming toward a basic reorganization of many tribes into a single state were continued by the Spaniards after the Conquest.

A good deal is known about Inca culture, but not much information has come down to us in regard to Inca pottery. We are largely dependent on the objects themselves, which are known in many shapes. Of these, two shapes are common; a shallow plate, with one or two handles and a jar (aryballos) with a pointed foot, a long neck and two handles placed low. The fish and vegetable pattern on a plate (Fig. 244) uses shapes nearly alike, though not identical, that look like freely spaced patterns of virtually the same fish. Each fish on the outside is turned toward the rim. An apparent freedom was obtained by still adhering to order, even where a suggestion of variety was intended. A spout-vessel of Inca (coastal Inca) black-wear in the Gaffron Collection represents the modeled llama and two figures in a sturdy, structural manner with little of the freer pictorial manner of Mochica modeling. Verticals are repeated and any divergencies from simplicity, which a group might have suggested, are avoided. The use of modeled figures links the style to the Mochica, and more recently this piece has been assigned to the earlier Chimu style (c. 1300-1438 A.D.).

In some examples, ceramic and textile patterns have the same rectangular character and geometric motifs are repeated in rows. In a small jar (Fig. 245), under six inches in diameter, the design seems eminently expressive of the Inca genius for organization. The foregoing represent the best known ceramic developments of the western hemisphere. There were others, such as Panamanian (Ill. 27), and Chilean, which we have no room to illustrate in this present survey.

The relation of the cultures of the Peruvian highlands to the Amazon basin to the east are as yet imperfectly understood. Archaeologists have pointed to a number of similarities between Andean-Amazonian cultural traits during the early periods and have even suggested that the Chavín culture was Amazonian, and that its curvilinear style of stone carving was derived from wood carving. From the few known sites objects have been recovered, such as burial urns and effigy vessels from Marajão, and richly decorated clay bowls on stands with incised decorations and molded figures, as well as effigy vessels, from Santarem, Brazil. The one illustrated in Color Plate 26 represents a hunchback with a rattle in one hand and a bag hanging from his shoulder. Though there may be here no close stylistic relationship to most of the Peruvian styles here discussed, there is some resemblance to the Mochica style in its more primitive version. The vessel is seventeen inches high and may be presumed to have had some use in ritual.

As the South Seas and Australia have little to offer us in pottery, the American styles can be said to represent best the ceramic achievements within our field.

TEXTILES

Peruvian textiles were found in tombs wrapped around mummies to form conical shaped bundles about five feet at the base, and five feet high. The mummy and, with it, the offerings of food constituted the least part of these huge bundles, which were wrapped around with layers of cloth and bunched at the top to suggest a head on which a hat was fitted. This first bundle was then supplied with additional layers of cloth, again tied in a bundle bunched and tied at the top and given a hat, as before. The same process was repeated several times. One bundle at Paracas consisted of as many as four separate wrappings. The textiles of Paracas Necropolis consisted of wearing apparel, ponchos, skirts, shawls, breech clouts, hats and mantles. Some pieces were too large for wear and had been woven apparently for funeral uses only. Julio C. Tello in 1925 removed over four hundred mummy bundles from Paracas Necropolis.

One bundle might contain fifty or more fabrics. The labor of salvaging these fabrics is so time-consuming that today, a quarter of a century after the first discovery, several hundred of these bundles remain yet to be explored. The term Paracas Cavernas refers to subterranean tombs in the same region from which Tello obtained, in addition, some 250 mummy bundles. Archaeologists incline to disagree as to the relative sequence of Paracas Necropolis, Paracas Cavernas, and Nazca, but Junius Bird, who has most recently brought the problem up to date, accepts the above time sequence. Nazca graves yielded cloth-wrapped mummies, but not in the form of bundles. The people who wove these fabrics must have spent a large amount of their time in the making of textiles for funeral and burial purposes.

Chiefly wool and cotton were used in the weavings, coarse, strong wool from the llama, and fine threads spun from the wool of the alpaca, which varied in color: white, bluish gray, light and dark brown, orange and black. The finest wool came from the vicuña in hues of brown. The same materials were used during all periods; flax and silk were unknown.

Pre-Columbian Peruvian textiles have been found in practically all weaves known to European antiquity from very heavy to very light.

A gauze with a pattern of flying birds, from the Textile Museum of the District of Columbia, represents the very light weave. Through embroidery over the net the weaver accomplished a striking pattern, dark on light, simple and remarkably solid in appearance. In technical perfection, in size and richness of color Peruvian textiles are among the finest the world has ever produced (Color Plate 25). An excellent quality of hand-spun yarn was produced with simple tools, and the wide range of colors is proof of the skill of the dyers. In Paracas Necropolis dyed yarns, a hundred and ninety hues have been distinguished. But the number of colors in any one of the so-called Paracas Cavernas group of textiles is ten to twelve, and larger in the Paracas Necropolis series. The excellence of the weavings must have been due to the skill of the weavers, rather than the looms, for the backstrap loom they used was a simple device. It limited width to the convenient reach of the hands. As weavings close to fifteen feet wide have been found, three women must have worked together as a team. The important techniques include: plain webs embroidered and sometimes painted, tapestries, sheer voile-like fabrics and feather work. Of these the embroidered Paracas mantles and the later tapestries are the essential fabrics. The embroideries were done with a needle on the finished weft on one side, and in rare cases on both sides. There were many experimental techniques in between these main groups that defy classification and present problems for specialists.

Tapestries are distinct from weavings in the fact that the weft covers the warp completely. Hence the design is carried by the weft threads which stop wherever the color changes. In weavings both warp and weft are carried across the loom. Technically, Peruvian tapestries are superior to European tapestries of the same period. As many as 327 weft threads are used to the inch, but in some details of the pattern the weft threads are crowded together at a rate of 500 to the inch. In that case a cotton yarn was used for the warp. Such Peruvian weaves were used for wear and not for wall hangings, as in Europe, and had to be finely woven.

The textiles come from the south coast, from Paracas peninsula near Pisco, and from Nazca, south of Paracas, famous for its ceramics. Both places had burial grounds each representing its own culture. Paracas, known as Paracas Necropolis (c. 400 B.C.-400 A.D.) in the Bennett chronology preceded the Nazca culture (c. 400-1000 A.D.), but not all scholars agree on this sequence; some believe that the Paracas Necropolis and Nazca cultures were contemporary.

Weavings do not have the range of styles from realistic to abstract found in ceramics. In comparison with painting, the technique of the loom restricted the weaver in his use of line. Though motifs were often derived from the human figure and animals, they were simplified in later tapestry styles often to a degree of unrecognizability. A straight line character is typical of tapestries; curves take on an angular contour, and motifs placed within rectangles and borders are common. Nevertheless, as far as they have been studied, a few styles stand out and can be recognized. They are chiefly Paracas Necropolis, Tiahuanaco and Inca. Mythological monsters of a type found on pottery also occur in textiles, as the cat, the bird, the centipede demon, and the multiple-headed god.

The cat demon motif (Fig. 246) is either part human or part bird, carries severed human heads, and appears as a ferocious monster, with either claws or hands, in three, four or five parts. The bird demon shows no human attributes, is often highly conventionalized, and appears as unfriendly to man. A multiple-headed god motif in a Paracas mantle of the Bliss Collection appears in a creature with a head fantastically elaborated, with realistic arms and legs, and three additional heads. The centipede motif, human or animal-like, holds decapitated heads. In textiles, as in pottery, gods or demons have attributes; one or several may be used in the same figure (Fig. 247). They are: the protruding tongue, the mouth mask, headdress, face-painting, ear ornaments, and weapons. Actual metal mouth masks have been found on early Nazca mummies. They consist of a semilunar shape, that hangs down from the nose and has extensions to either side, suggesting cats' whiskers. Circular objects, or rings, cover the ears, as ornaments. Emblems in the form of weapons include spear-throwers, war clubs, ceremonial staffs and chopper-shaped knives.

Though the total range of colors in Peruvian textiles is considerable, the number of colors in any one piece is restricted. A large Paracas mantle, like the one in the American Museum of Natural History, may show a dark blue or purplish red background, with rectangles and border motifs applied through embroidery in red as the dominant color. A Nazca tapestry from the Nelson A. Rockefeller Collection, showing about the same red background, has an allover pattern of four to six colors.

One of the peculiarities of Peruvian weavings is in the way colors are repeated. In a Paracas mantle from the Bliss Collection, we find demons within embroidered rectangles repeated in rows, checkerboard fashion. The color distribution differs in each of the first seven demons of any row. With the eighth, the color scheme of the first is repeated; the ninth is like the second, and so on to the last in the row. The same scheme repeats in the second row lengthwise; again one and eight are alike in color distribution.

To discover the plan of the over-all pattern one may choose a single detail, the head, which appears at the top left corner of the figure in the top row. In the second row this head appears at the bottom left corner of the figure, in the third at the top right corner, in the fourth at the bottom right corner, and in the fifth and last row the head returns to the position of the first row, the top left corner. This shows how monotony was avoided by turning the same motif in various ways.

For a Paracas Necropolis mantle in the Textile Museum of Washington, it required three detailed charts in the museum's catalog to describe accurately the color distribution, in addition to an explanatory text. In the central row of this magnificent fabric, the colors in the seven winged men are repeated across the width in this fashion 1-2-3-1-2-3-1. This means that the first, fourth and seventh are alike in color, and the two's and three's are alike in color, and diagonal rows are alike in color. Where fewer colors are used, as in the birth scene fabric of the Gaffron Collection (Art Institute of Chicago), the same principle is used. The corner figures, with some variation, correspond diagonally as to color distribution; the upper left and lower right have blue bodies and brown heads, the upper right and lower left have brown bodies and blue heads. The demons have the same design, but do not look alike, because position and color change pattern. As a result, Peruvian textile patterns seem complex, in spite of their basic simplicity. This may be chiefly for artistic reasons to obtain rich complexity.

Aside from color, pattern in woven Peruvian textiles is characterized by (1) a tendency to straight lines and angles, (2) a preference for motifs in the form of rectangles and borders, (3) an emphasis on the motif as a separate element without fusion or overlapping. The self-contained spot is more in evidence than the moving line. This does not completely eliminate linear rhythms, but a static balance is more typical than strong movement.

The large mantles show rows of motifs of irregular outlines (Fig. 248) or of rectangles embroidered in a checker board pattern to fill the whole mantle. In a section of a Paracas Necropolis textile four different personages are represented. The systematic color variation comes out even in the black and white reproduction in the variations of the color values. As far as the skill of the needleworker and the precision of the technique permitted, design follows a pattern in the rendering of legs, feet, arms, crowns, trophy heads. Where the motifs become complex with many trophy heads, paws, hands, tails, rays, eagle heads, all fused into one design, an embroidered rectangle looks like a patchwork of emblems. This impresses one as a kind of pictorial script, a mosaic of prescribed emblems, in which one motif is as important as another. Only the monster's head stands out as being of greater importance. What seems conventionalized to us was perhaps still meant to be realistic. There is no expression of the artistic personality, for which neither the technique nor the culture were suitable.

A cat demon, a centipede god and trophy heads are combined in a fragment of an embroidered shawl in the Paracas Necropolis style, now in the collection of the Boston Museum of Fine Arts. Formal qualities of design are brought out in a striking fashion, but here, too, color cuts across pattern regardless of balance and unity.

Textiles were sometimes painted, as in an example in the Cleveland Museum of Art. A cat demon with a fierce expression holds a trophy head and an obsidian knife, and his tail ends in a trophy head. The sacred animal walks like a man, and wears a headdress, mouth mask, collar and loincloth. His front paws are five-fingered and the hind foot has four claws, like a cat's. Bared teeth suggest aggression. The Peruvian cat and condor take the place of the Mexican jaguar and eagle as symbols of strength.

In the Paracas style, motifs like cats, birds, fish, centipedes may appear conventionalized, but they are not turned into geometric shapes. Motifs are not only recognizable, but lines and shapes retain some sense of freedom and different types of gods or demons may be included in one textile. How movement may be involved, even in a figure that stands still, becomes apparent if the eye follows the irregular and jerky outline of a figure. The artist, with a realistic effect in mind, was restrained by the embroidery technique and was bound to the style of his period.

To the extent we can speak of free expression in Paracas style textiles, this freedom gave way to a stiffening and hardening of shapes, to symmetry and simplification, in which slanting lines run at angles of forty-five degrees. These characteristics, when expressed in pumas, condors, human heads and human figure, recall the motifs from the "Gateway of the Sun," at Tiahuanaco, and constitute a coastal Tiahuanaco style. Wherever this frontal figure of Viracocha, with both arms stretched out holding staffs, the side view running figures, or the fret-like bands from the lower "Sungate" relief appear in textile designs, there a Tiahuanaco influence is in evidence. It is believed that this stylistic change in art reflects a contact of peoples, and is of an historical and cultural significance. What political events were responsible for these influences, which seemingly spread from the highlands to the coastal regions, is unknown.

An embroidered figure (Fig. 249) from Paracas, shows a faint resemblance to the Viracocha of the "Sungate" relief, in the squared-off figure, and the tear track under the eyes, but this may still belong to the Paracas period. Here the single staff, a spear thrower, ends in a monkey, the other hand holds a "chopper" type knife, and a banderole carries trophy heads.

A Tiahuanaco contribution is more pronounced in another fragment, perhaps a sleeve from a tapestry garment, in the Boston Museum of Fine Arts. In an abbreviated form, the posture suggests the original "Sungate" figure. The several borders contain disconnected frets, and the whole design has a geometric character. The same figure appears simplified, without the characteristic details in a fragment (Fig. 250) which may be a late piece. In a red garment tapestry with white birds, the large figure retains the typical pose and the details are simplified. In another fragment, found in southwest Peru, hands, eyes and frets combine with octagonal panels that have a feeling of stone masonry (Fig. 251). In its most abstract version, the original meaning of the shapes is no longer apparent. Black octagons that have white spots and connect to rectangles have been interpreted as jaguar eyes, spirals as tails, and S shapes as mouths (Fig. 252).

Ancient Peru also practiced feather work (Color Plate 24). Each feather was tied to a string and then bent underneath a second string, so that the well-secured feathers could be sewn to a textile in rows, one feather overlapping another. The richness of the colored feathers and the softness of the finished cloak gives them a sense of preciousness. This technique is well represented by an Inca feather cloak with a bird and puma design (Fig. 253) and by a feather hat in the coastal Tiahuanaco style in the Brooklyn Museum. Even in this difficult technique there are animal heads with the characteristic bared teeth and glaring eyes.

Peruvian feather capes and Paracas embroidered weavings in color and texture are probably the richest and most decorative fabrics we have in the realm of pre-literate art. Ancient Peru also produced works in metal and small stone carvings. Of ancient Peruvian art even some wood carvings have been preserved locally.

WOOD CARVINGS

Carved panels, in the form of leeboards, that may have had a ceremonial use have been found in graves of the coastal regions. The handle of such a board from the south coast is decorated with a row of freestanding figures, above a pattern of perforations, made up of rows of zigzags and step designs. In another example, the broadside of the board shows an allover pattern of conventionalized birds, and a carved joist from the north coast has a row of demons. Such patterns bear a resemblance to architectural reliefs of Chanchan, the ancient Chimu capital, or they suggest textile patterns. There are, also, mummy masks (Fig. 254) that are carved of wood, painted red and have eyes inlaid with shell. The style of these wood carvings resembles the late Tiahuanaco style. The front of a wooden litter shows five figures chiseled out of the plank in flat outlines. The style is essentially like the Tiahuanaco stone carvings and textile designs, only simplified. Wood carving does not appear to have equaled the textile arts in richness and complexity. These, and other small wood carved objects, inlaid with shell or shell inlaid with silver, are of a local significance, hardly comparable in importance to pottery and weaving.

The arts of the southern Andes of Chile and Argentina are in part related to the northern and central Andean arts, and in some instances have an artistic individuality of their own. Objects of ceramics and in wood from these areas have not as yet received the attention that has placed ancient Peruvian art in the center of interest.

An aesthetic evaluation is out of place if it is used as a yardstick with which to measure the artistic achievements of continents, the Americas against Africa or Oceania. Each style is unique, yet all are of the same essence, making their appeal to our sensitivities. Man was no more artistic in the eastern than in the western hemisphere; both provided settings capable of bringing out his artistic capacities to the fullest. The diversity of opportunities in the Americas was more nearly like that of Europe and Asia.

If there is any single factor that seems particularly emphatic in the arts of this middle section of ancient America, it is often a sense of vitality conveyed by individual pieces. Our response to a Baulé mask might be "how refined," "how elegant," or "how beautiful"; before an Aztec stone figure we would be more tempted to exclaim "how strong."

Fig. 194 (above). Aztec goddess of corn. *American Museum of Natural History.*

Fig. 195 (top right). Aztec Water Goddess, Chalchihuitlicue. H. 6¾ in., basalt. *National Gallery of Art, Washington, D. C.*

Fig. 196 (right). Aztec feathered serpent, diorite. H. ca 17 in. *National Gallery of Art.*

Fig. 197 (extreme right). Aztec pulque god in form of a rabbit, jadeite. *National Gallery of Art.*

Plate 19. Pottery jar in shape of a trophy head, H. ca 7½ in., Paracas Cavernas, Peru. *Museum für Völkerkunde, Munich.*

Plate 21. Copper figure, painted with cinnabar, Mochica style, H. 9 in. *Peabody Museum, Harvard University.*

Plate 20. Carved stone mortar in shape of a puma, H. 6½ in., Chavín de Huántar, Peru. *University Museum, Philadelphia.*

Plate 22. Pottery stirrup vessel in form of feline and human faces, Cupisnique style, Peru.

Courtesy, Time Magazine.

Plate 23. Pottery head jar, Mochica style, Peru. *Courtesy, Museum of Modern Art.*

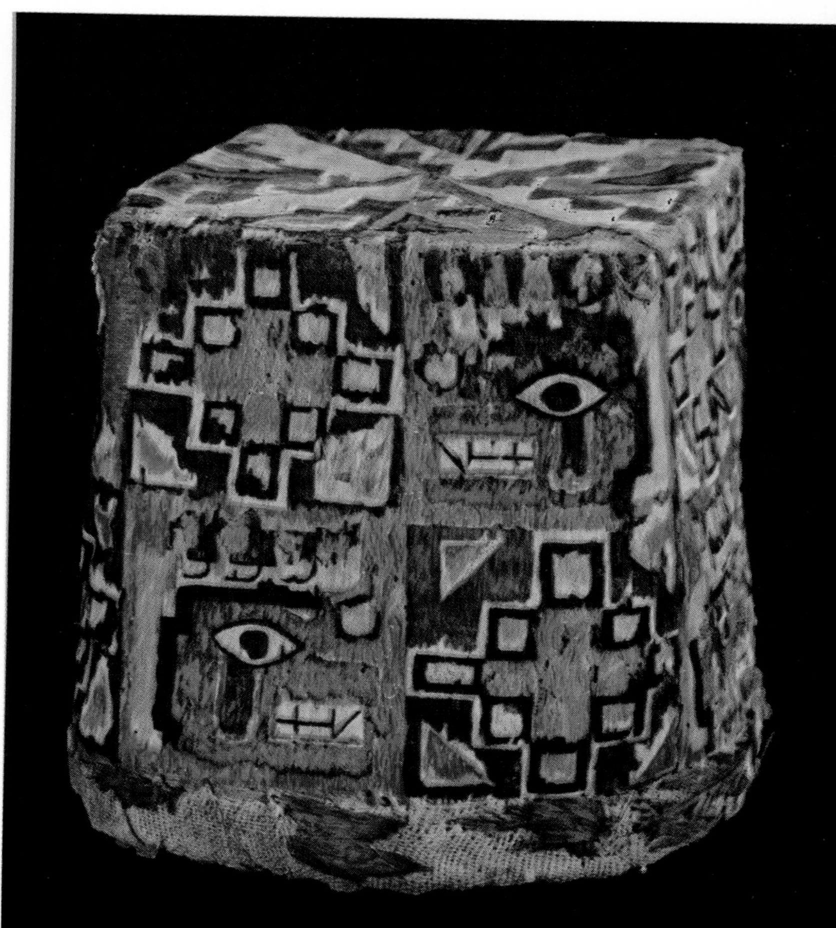

Plate 24. Feathered hat, Tiahuanaco style, Peru. *Brooklyn Museum.*

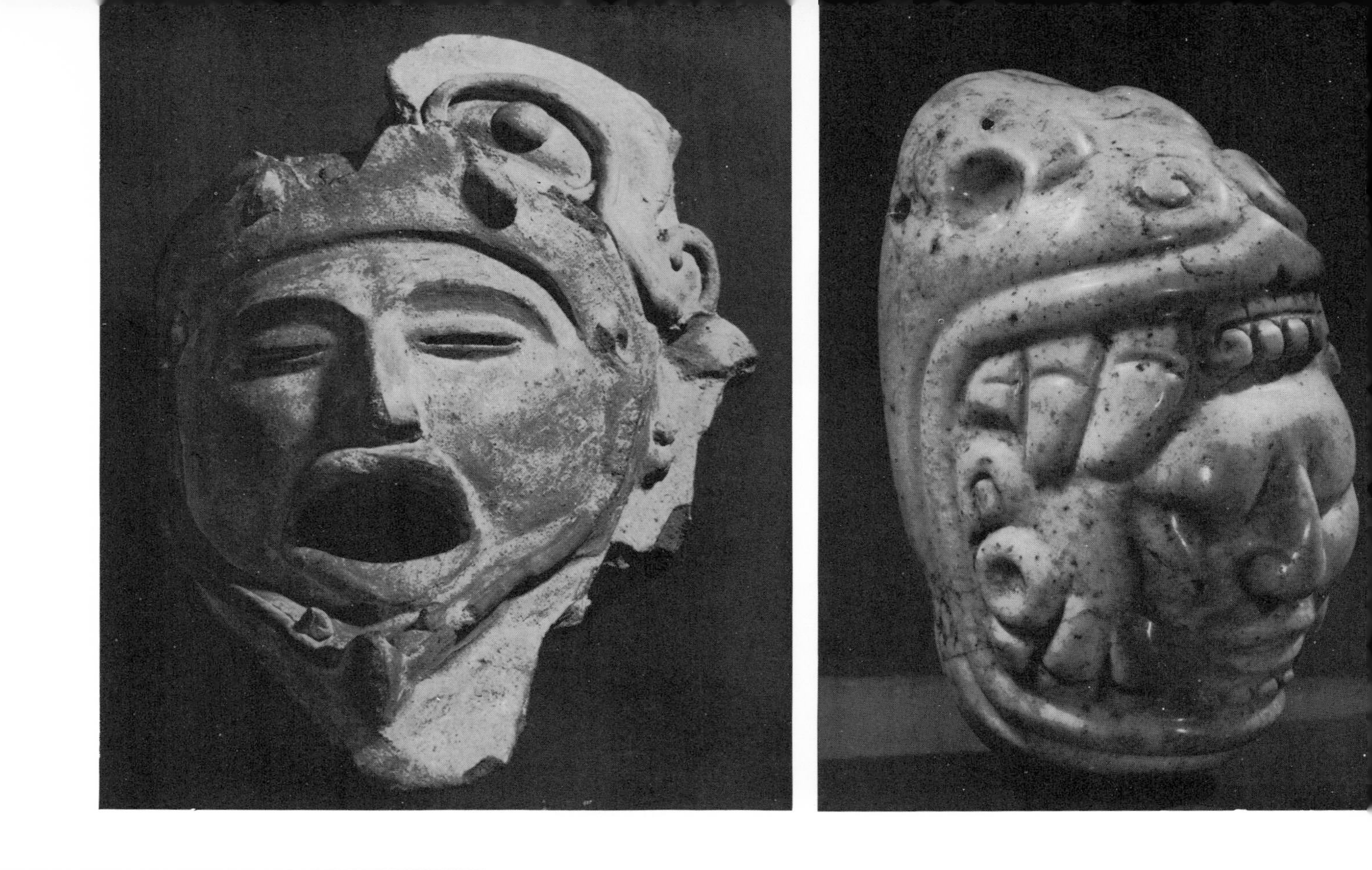
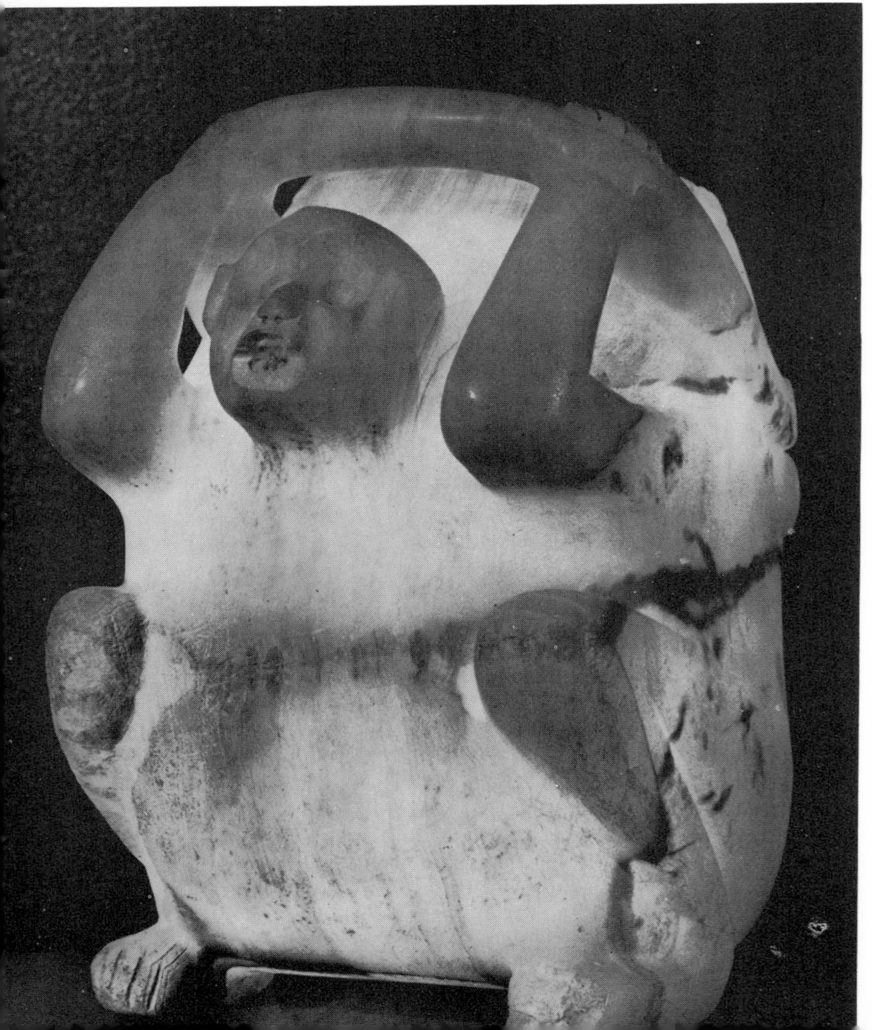

Opposite page: Fig. 198 (top left). Aztec terra-cotta mask.

Fig. 199 (top right). Human head within a serpent's mouth (side view), stone, Mexican. H. ca 2½ in.

Fig. 200 (lower left). Travertine marble jar representing a monkey, central Mexico. H. 12½ in.

Fig. 201 (lower right). Aztec mask, a man with a decorated turban, with date 1507 on the back, diorite.

Fig. 202 (above, left). Aztec mask, showing a twisted mouth, diorite. H. ca 4½ in.

Fig. 203 (above). Aztec head or skull, obsidian, H. ca 4 in.

Fig. 204 (left). Wooden mask covered with turquoise mosaic, Mixtec.

National Gallery of Art, Washington, D. C.

Plate 25. Mantle border (detail), mythological people, Paracas style, Peru. *Textile Museum, Washington, D. C.*

Opposite: Plate 26. Pottery effigy vase, in shape of a hunchback, from Santarem, Brazil. *University Museum, Philadelphia. Courtesy, Time Magazine.*

Fig. 205 (left). Ax god pendants, jadeite, Nicoya, Costa Rica. *National Gallery of Art, Washington, D. C.* Fig. 206 (below). Metate in jaguar form, volcanic rock, Guetar Indians, Costa Rica. L. 38 in. *Philadelphia Museum of Art.* Fig. 207 (lower left). Figure, granite, Costa Rica, late (?). H. 15½ in. *Philadelphia Museum of Art.* Fig. 208 (lower right). Polychrome tripod bowl, Nicoya ware, probably from Alta Gracia, Ometepe Island, Nicaragua, top view. *University Museum, Philadelphia.*

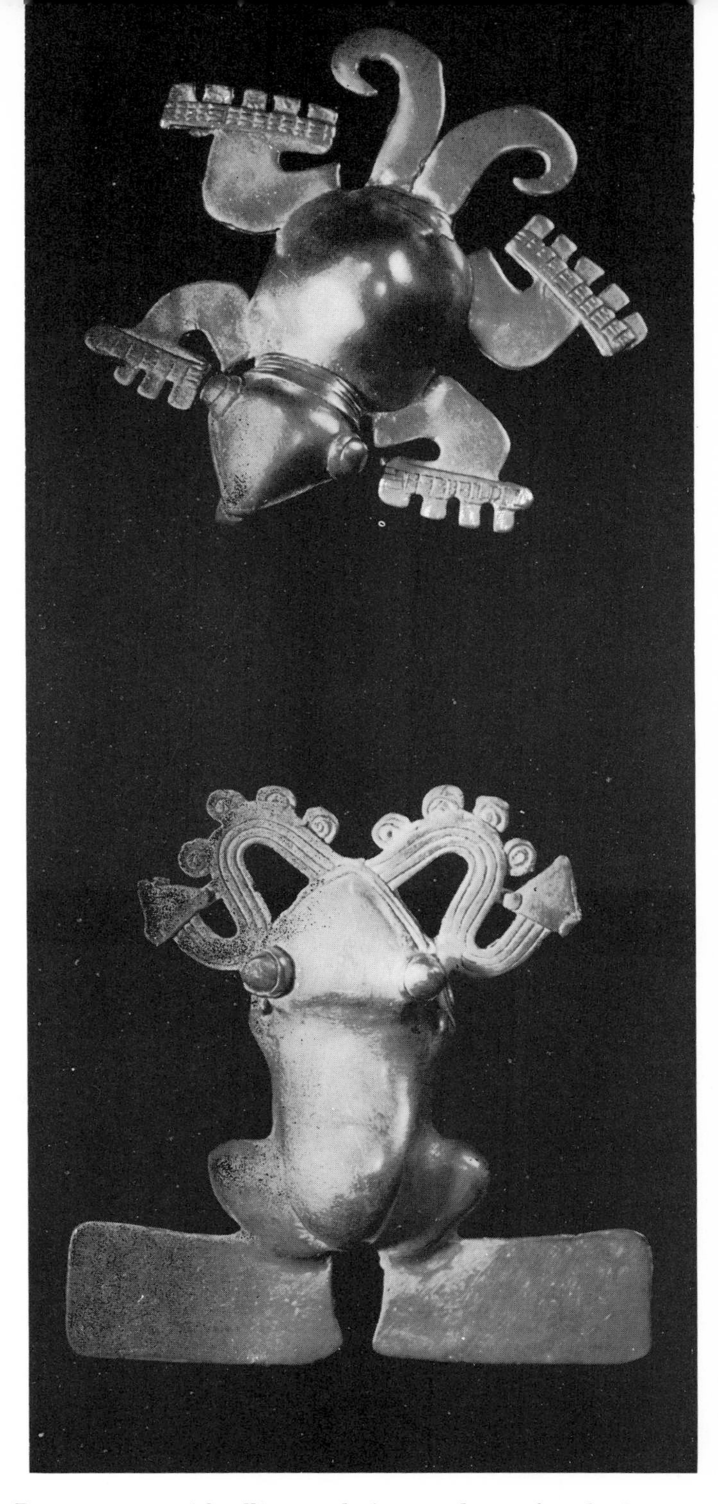

Fig. 209 (top). Pottery vase, with alligator designs and two female figures, province of Chiriquí, Panama. *Peabody Museum of Natural History, Yale University*. Fig. 210 (left). Gold ornaments representing birds, "eagles," style of Veraguas, Panama. *National Gallery of Art, Washington, D. C.* Fig. 211 (above). Gold pendants representing frogs, style of Veraguas, Panama. *National Gallery of Art, Washington, D. C.*

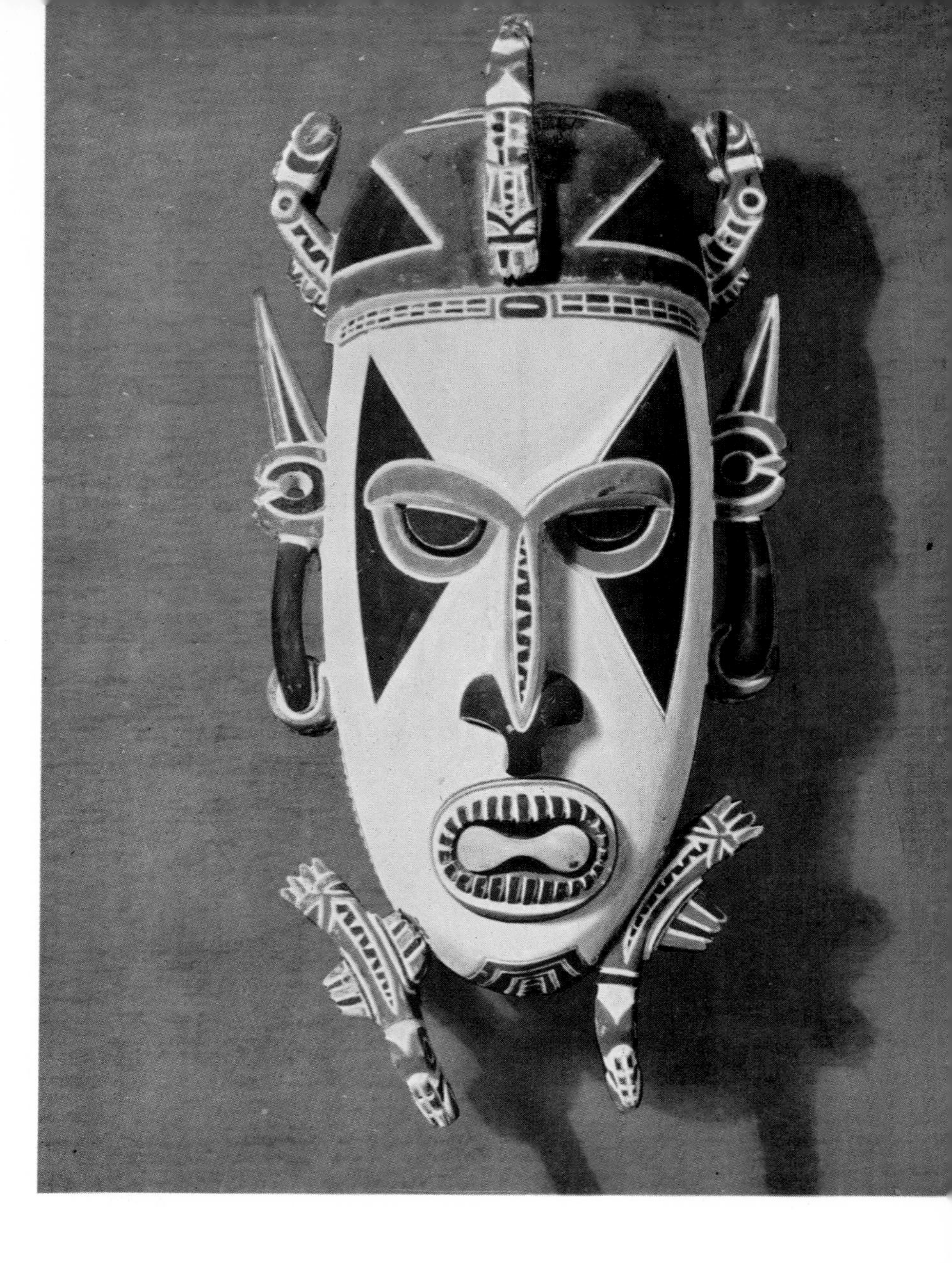

Plate 27 (above). Melanesian dance mask, *tami* style, H. 24 in. Huon Gulf, New Guinea. *Chicago Natural History Museum.*

Plate 28 (left). Melanesian dance mask, Sulka tribe, New Britain. *Collection, Chicago Natural History Museum. Courtesy, Museum of Modern Art, New York.*

Plate 29. Figure carved from inverted tree-fern trunk. New Hebrides. *Courtesy, Life Magazine.*

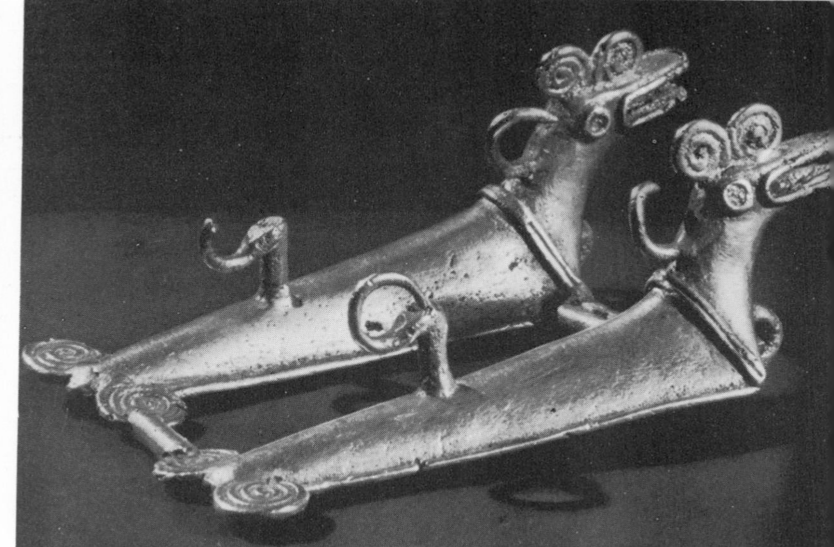

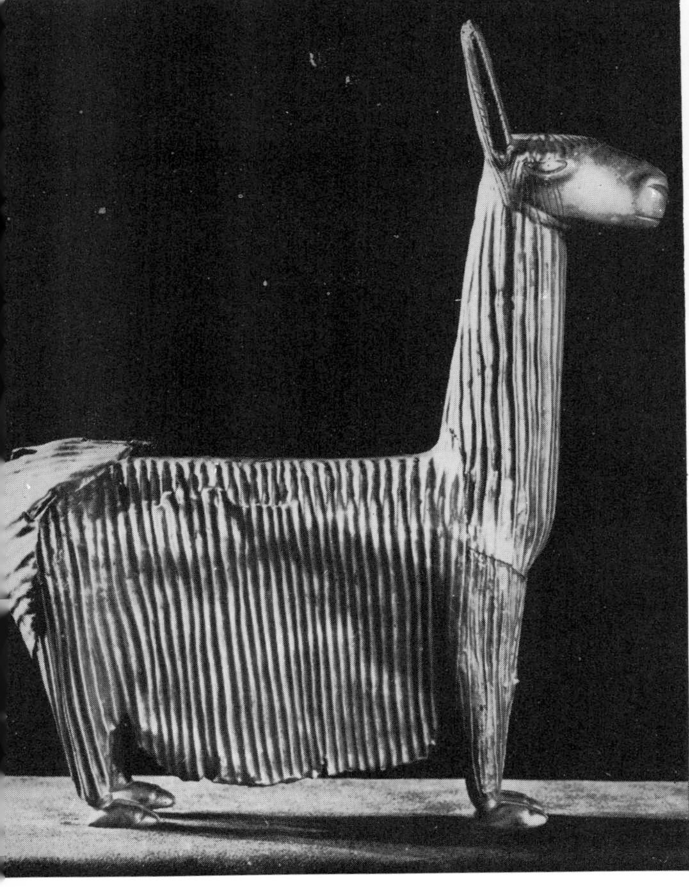

Opposite page:

Fig. 212 (top left). Gold plaque, embossed with a design showing two bird-headed monsters, Coclé style, Panama. *University Museum, Philadelphia.* Fig. 213 (top right). Gold pendant of twin animals, Quimbaya style, Colombia. *National Gallery of Art, Washington, D. C.* Fig. 214 (lower left). Gold figures, cast, Chibcha style, Colombia. H. ca 4 in. to 5 in. *Cleveland Museum of Art.* Fig. 215 (lower right). Gold ceremonial knife, cast, Colombia. H. 7 in. *University Museum, Philadelphia.*

This page:

Fig. 216 (above, left). Gold diadem, hammered, Calima style, Colombia. *Gold Museum of the Banco de la Republica, Bogotá, Colombia. Photo: National Gallery of Art, Washington, D. C.* Fig. 217 (above). Gold plaque, cut and embossed, late Chimu style, Lambayeque Valley, Peru. *National Gallery of Art, Washington, D. C.* Fig. 218 (left). Silver alpaca, hollow, Inca style, Peru. *American Museum of Natural History.*

Plate 30. Melanesian female figure, Abelam tribe, Sepik River region, New Guinea. *American Museum of Natural History. Courtesy, Museum of Modern Art.*

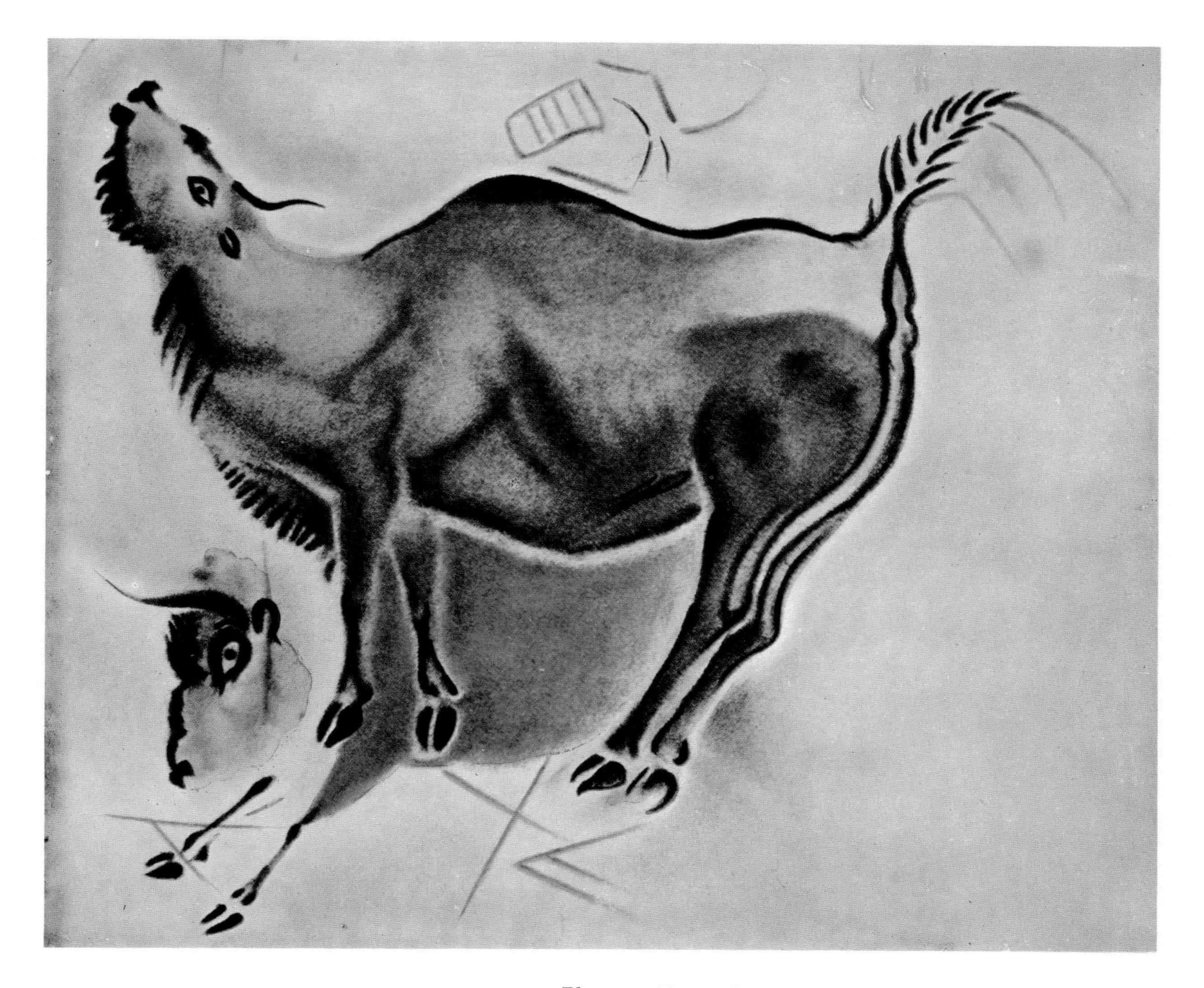

Plate 31. Young bison, cave painting from Altamira, Spain.
After Breuil. Courtesy, Transatlantic Arts.

Fig. 219 (left). Silver figure, hollow, Inca style, Peru. H. ca 9 in. *National Gallery of Art, Washington, D. C.* Fig. 220 (above). Incense burner in the shape of a llama, clay, Tiahuanaco, Bolivia, L. 19¼ in. *American Museum of Natural History*. Fig. 221 (lower left). Inca stone vessel in the shape of a llama head. H. ca 4½ in. *Chicago Natural History Museum*. Fig. 222 (below). Engraved stone tablet with running warriors, Mochica style, Peru. *American Museum of Natural History*.

Opposite page:

Fig. 223 (top left). Steatite vase engraved with figures wearing jaguar masks, style of Chavín de Huántar, Peru. *National Gallery of Art, Washington, D. C.* Fig. 224 (top right). Pottery bowl with stylized cat motif, in negative painting, style of Paracas Cavernas, Peru. Diam. 6 in. *Montreal Museum of Fine Arts*.

Fig. 225 (lower right). Pottery beaker, Highland Tiahuanaco style, Peru. H. 6½ in. *University Museum, Philadelphia.* Fig. 226 (lower left). Pottery vessel, painted with six main figures of Viracocha, the Creator God; Coast Tiahuanaco style, Peru. H. 29 in. *American Museum of Natural History.*

Fig. 227 (right). Pottery urn, from Chancay, Peru. H. 15½ in. *American Museum of Natural History.*

Fig. 228 (above). Stirrup-spout pottery vessel in form of a peanut, Mochica style, Peru. *University Museum, Philadelphia.*

Fig. 229 (right). Stirrup-spout pottery vessel in form of a squash with a humanized owl head, Mochica style, Chimbote, Santa Valley, Peru. *The Nathan Cummings Collection, Chicago.*

Fig. 230. Pottery vessel, fragment, head of a jaguar (?) painted red on cream, Mochica style, Peru. H. 4¼ in. *Art Institute of Chicago.*

Fig. 232. Stirrup-spout pottery vessel in the form of a kneeling warrior holding a war club, painted orange, earth-red and cream, Mochica style, Chimbote, Santa Valley, Peru. *The Nathan Cummings Collection, Chicago.*

Fig. 231. Stirrup-spout pottery vessel in form of a seated deer, painted red-brown on cream, Mochica style, Chimbote, Santa Valley, Peru. *The Natham Cummings Collection, Chicago.*

Fig. 233. Pottery stirrup vessel in form of a portrait head, painted red across the forehead on natural clay, Mochica style, Chicama region, Peru. H. 14 in., W. 9½ in. *Art Institute of Chicago.*

Fig. 234 (above). Pottery stirrup vessel in form of a portrait head, showing traces of slip, Mochica style, Chicama region, Peru. H. 10¾ in., W. 7⅝ in. *Art Institute of Chicago*.

Fig. 235 (top right). Stirrup pottery jar with seated figure on top and a painted frieze of warriors on the body, Mochica style, Peru. *Art Institute of Chicago*.

Fig. 236 (right). Stirrup-spout pottery jar with painted decoration of a mythical battle of bean warriors, Mochica style, Peru. H. 10¼ in. *Art Institute of Chicago*.

Opposite page:

Fig. 237 (left). Stirrup-spout pottery vessel with a blind spout in form of war club. Painted decoration, earth-red on cream, showing Ai-Apec as a crab-demon approaching a fish-demon, Mochica style, Chicama Valley, Peru. *The Nathan Cummings Collection*. Fig. 238 (top right). Bowl, with painted decoration of hummingbirds, Nazca style, Peru. H. 2½ in. *Art Institute of Chicago*. Fig. 239 (lower left). Pottery bowl painted with trophy heads, Nazca style, Peru. *Art Institute of Chicago*. Fig. 240 (lower right). Pottery beaker with a painted quail decoration, Nazca style, Peru. *Art Institute of Chicago*.

Fig. 243. Double-spout globular pottery vessel with skull decoration, late Nazca style, Peru. *National Gallery of Art, Washington, D. C.*

Fig. 241 (top). Single-spout pottery vessel with figure decoration, Nazca (?) style, Peru. *Art Institute of Chicago*. Fig. 242 (above). Globular two-spout pottery vessel with cat demon and trophy heads, Nazca (Ica?) style, Peru. Diam. ca 5½ in. *Museum für Völkerkunde, Berlin.*

Fig. 244. Pottery tray, Inca style, Peru. W. ca 9 in. *Art Institute of Chicago.*

Fig. 245 (below). Low jar with handles representing jaguars, Inca style, from Island of Koati, Lake Titicaca, Bolivia. Diam. 5⅜ in. *American Museum of Natural History.*

Fig. 246. Painted border of a mantle (detail), Paracas style, Peru. *Cleveland Museum of Art.*

Fig. 247 (above). Embroidery (detail), Paracas Necropolis style, Peru. *Boston Museum of Fine Arts.*

Fig. 248 (left). Embroidered mantle (detail), Paracas Necropolis, Peru. *Boston Museum of Fine Arts.*

Fig. 249 (left). Embroidered figure (detail), Paracas, Peru. *Boston Museum of Fine Arts.*

Fig. 250 (above). Textile showing Tiahuanaco influence, Peru. *Museum of International Folk Art, Santa Fe, New Mexico.*

Fig. 251 (extreme left). Fragment of Tiahuanaco tapestry, Peru. *Museum of International Folk Art, Santa Fe, New*

Fig. 252 (left). Tapestry poncho, Tiahuanaco style, Peru. *Art Institute of Chicago.*

Fig. 253. Feather cloak with puma and bird design, Inca period. *M. H. De Young Memorial Museum, San Francisco.*

Fig. 254. Mummy mask, wood and fabric, Inca style, Peru. *Philadelphia Museum of Art.*

Fig. 255 (top left). Indonesian ancestor figure, Nias. *Collection, Mr. and Mrs. Ralph C. Altman, Los Angeles.*

Fig. 256 (left). Melanesian carved drum, painted red and white, showing a hornbill on a conventionalized human head, Middle Sepik River region, New Guinea. H. 23 in. *British Museum.*

Fig. 257 (below). Melanesian memorial board, New Ireland. L. 41½ in. *M. H. De Young Memorial Museum, San Francisco.*

Fig. 258 (top left). Melanesian painted bark, worn by women at festive occasions, and also used as a grave cloth, Sentanimeer region, New Guinea. *Kon. Instituut v/d Tropen, Amsterdam, Netherlands.*

Fig. 260 (right). Melanesian lime tube stopper, polychromed wood, Sepik River, New Guinea. L. 16½ in. *Honolulu Academy of Arts.*

Fig. 259 (bottom). Melanesian lime spatula handles, Anchorite Islands. *British Museum.*

Fig. 261 (top left). Melanesian bowl with double volute, Admiralty Islands. *Chicago Natural History Museum*. Fig. 262 (top right). Polynesian design, Fiji Islands tapa (cloth). *Smithsonian Institution*. Fig. 263 (lower left). Polynesian sculpture, New Zealand whalebone club. *Chicago Natural History Museum*. Fig. 264 (lower right). Melanesian carved coconut cup, Huon Gulf, New Guinea. *Chicago Natural History Museum*.

Fig. 265 (above). Melanesian carved wooden drum. *Brooklyn Museum*. Fig. 266 (right). Carved canoe prow ornament, Trobriand Islands, Massim area, New Guinea. *Chicago Natural History Museum*. Fig. 267 (below). Melanesian neck-rest with frigate bird design, Massim area, New Guinea. W. 20 in. *Royal Ontario Museum of Archaeology, Toronto*.

V

THE SOUTH SEAS AND AUSTRALIA

THE ART OF THE SOUTH SEAS SHOWS AN EXTRAORDINARY VARIETY AND EXTRAVAGANCE OF INVENTION. For fantastic elaboration and weird combinations the figures and masks of the Sepik River tribes in New Guinea hold first place, but they have their rivals in the *uli* figures and *malagan* figures of New Britain and New Ireland. This variety becomes even more impressive if we consider the whole Pacific area; and the many variations represented by the local styles of each island or region.

THE ISLANDS; SETTLEMENTS AND RACES

Of the innumerable islands, 2,650 have been listed as main islands. They may be divided into groups and for our purpose we shall use the familiar classification, based upon the distribution of native populations as they exist today, of Micronesia (from the Greek *micro*, small, and *nesos*, island), Melanesia (*melas*, black) and Polynesia (*poly*, many). We also touch upon the East Indies or Indonesia to the west of New Guinea and upon Australia to the south. In both these regions man has had a long history, suggested by the fossil bones, remains of one of the earliest and most primitive type of man, found in Java and considered by many scientists to be the progenitor of man. The aboriginal culture of Australia is also very old. Though the material culture of the aboriginal Australians is meager—they are hunters and food-gatherers, rather than raisers of food—it is recognized today that their culture as a whole is not on a uniformly low level, as formerly believed.

The migrations, which gradually populated the Pacific Islands, go back to an early date when the Indonesians came over from southern Asia. The Australians belong to an even earlier period. Migrations continued eastward and penetrated Melanesia. Out of Indonesia came the Micronesians and the Polynesians in an earlier and a later wave. Thus the Polynesians were the most recent of the prehistoric colonists of the Pacific, and they spread the farthest. It is believed that by the tenth century the

Polynesians had reached the Marquesas, and by the beginning of the fourteenth century, New Zealand, though the traditional date of the first discovery of New Zealand is 950 A.D. The Polynesians, the unexcelled navigators of the Pacific, may even have reached the Antarctic and the west coast of America. Though some of the later settlements antedate the discovery of America by Columbus by a few centuries only, the migrations began perhaps somewhat before the beginning of the first millennium B.C. Many races mingled in these regions, but two contrasting groups are readily distinguishable. In Melanesia and Australia are the dark-skinned and woolly-haired tribes; in Indonesia, Micronesia and Polynesia are light brown people with wavy or straight hair. One of the native races, the Papuan, is sometimes referred to as a separate race. Compared to the early settlement of the Americas, the South Sea Islands received their population comparatively late in history.

REGIONS

For the arts, Melanesia is the most important group, and of these islands, the art of New Guinea is outstanding. Art has often been affected by isolation. High mountains are barriers to communication, but rivers are highways of commerce; New Guinea has both. Uniformity of design was encouraged and counteracted at the same time. Today the island is divided politically between the western Dutch part and an eastern part mandated to Australia.

Various regions of the island have their own individual styles. Of special interest for the native arts are the following regions: on the north side, belonging to the Netherlands, is Geelvink Bay; to the northeast, in the Australian mandated section, are the Sepik River region with its wealth of sculpture; and the Huon Gulf area with the small Tami Island known for its geometric style of decoration. The Massim area with its curvilinear style and frigate-bird motifs is in the east. Close by is the small group of the Trobriand Islands.

Of the Melanesian Islands outside of New Guinea, New Britain and New Ireland developed the most original wood carved figures. These two islands, together with the Admiralty group, famous for its carved bowls, are known as the Bismarck Archipelago. South of New Ireland is the large group of the Solomon Islands with Bougainville and Guadalcanal, the historic Guadalcanal of the landing of the marines in the Second World War. Carved wood figures, painted or inlaid in mother of pearl and figure-carved prows of canoes are among the characteristic art expressions of the Solomon Islands. The smaller group of the New Hebrides lacks the material wealth of New Guinea and the Solomons, and art reflects the more modest scale of their resources. In New Caledonia, at the southern end of Melanesia, wood carving is the particular achievement in the arts. The Fiji Islands at the eastern end of Melanesia, at times grouped with Polynesia, are represented by bark cloth, called tapa.

Polynesia includes, among many other groups, the Hawaiian Islands, the Marquesas and Easter Island, which is off to the southeast, and New Zealand. Between them there is perhaps one and a half times the distance of the greatest diagonal extension in the United States, the distance between the state of Washington and the extreme tip of Florida. And yet the total land area of all Polynesian Islands together amounts to only the land area of Vermont or Maryland. This amount of land is scattered over an ocean area about four times the size of the United States. Polynesia is known to lovers of art because it includes Tahiti, the island to which Gauguin retired, and Typee, the island about which Herman Melville wrote.

From the point of view of the arts, the Polynesian Islands may be divided into a central group which was practically without sculpture, but had decorated tapa, and a peripheral group, in which sculpture was highly developed. The western and central groups include Samoa, Tonga, Cook, Society and Austral Islands; the peripheral group, the Hawaiian Islands north of the equator and the Marquesas, Easter Island and New Zealand in the South Pacific.

Many islands of the Pacific are rough and mountainous, ranging in height from 3,000 to 4,000 feet in the Fiji group, to ice and snow covered peaks, over 15,000 feet high, in New Guinea. There are a number of active volcanoes and many hot springs; earthquakes are common. Dense tropical forests cover the islands, except in places where the natives have made clearings for their villages, or where valleys and hillsides have some open grassland, as in parts of New Guinea. The most impenetrable jungles of the world are on the Solomon Islands, where giant trees and buttress-like roots make midday seem like twilight. There are few wild animals in Melanesia; wild pigs are the largest. There are lizards, crocodiles, and especially birds on New Guinea. Fish, crustaceans, shellfish and turtles are not only important as food, but also furnish materials for the crafts.

Australia, with its ancient population, forms an art region independent of Oceania. Indonesia is here touched upon with incidental work from Sumatra, from the small island of Nias, and from Celebes. It is from these western regions that some of the basic forms traveled east.

BELIEFS AND CUSTOMS

The religion of the South Sea islanders shows some of the same ideas found in other primitive cultures, such as veneration of sun and moon, ancestor worship, a belief in magic and spirits, totemism and even monotheism. Totemism was strong in Melanesia, less important in Micronesia and almost absent in Polynesia. There was usually no organized theology, and no priesthood, except in Polynesia. Deities were often less important for art than ancestors.

Some ancestral figures are interesting primarily as scientific objects. This type is made of sticks covered with fiber and has attached skulls modeled of clay and sap, as in south Malekula, to create a resemblance of the deceased. These figures are feared by relatives and friends, for the ghosts of such persons are believed to have great power over the living, and must be appeased by prayers and offerings. This mysterious power called *mana* is possessed by spirits and ghosts, and may be acquired by human beings from the spirits. Wizards and sorcerers, or anyone else who is successful in an undertaking, may have *mana*, and this power may also be possessed by inanimate objects.

Much, if not all, of artistic creation was based on an acceptance of the supernatural. Art was concerned with secret societies, initiation ceremonies, dances and festivities; the spirits of the ancestors were impersonated by dancers wearing masks. The veneration of ancestors led to statues, and in some cases parts of utensils and weapons were given a human aspect. Thereby such utensils and weapons could be endowed with a force which increased their performance.

A decorated drum had a better sound than a plain drum, an arrow engraved with an eye ornament had a more certain aim, a face or figure at the end of a spear representing its spirit guided the

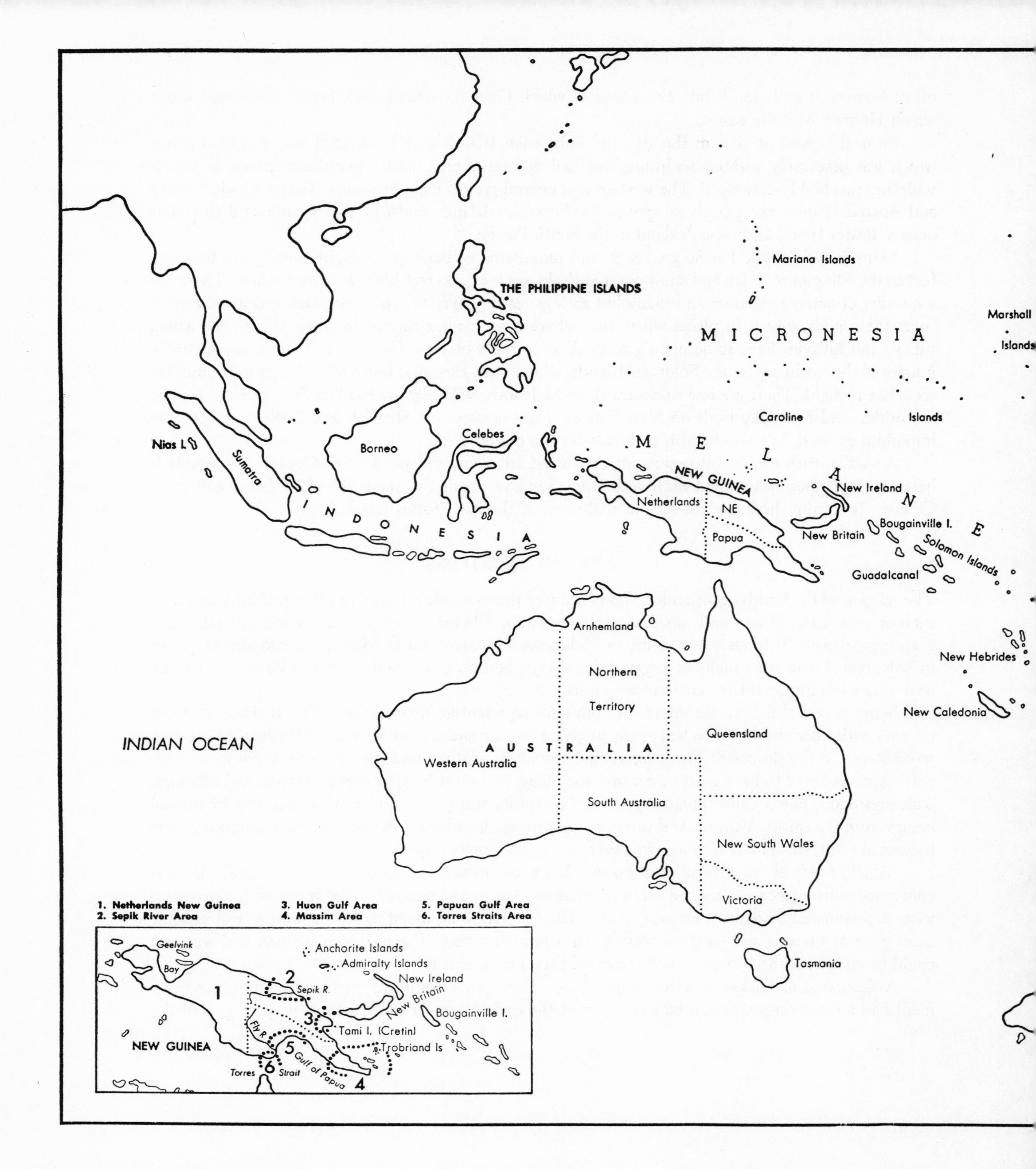
Mariana Islands
THE PHILIPPINE ISLANDS
Marshall
Islands
MICRONESIA
Caroline
Islands
Nias I.
Sumatra
Borneo
Celebes
MELANESIA
NEW GUINEA
New Ireland
Netherlands
NE
INDONESIA
Papua
New Britain
Bougainville I.
Solomon Islands
Guadalcanal
Arnhemland
Northern
Territory
New Hebrides
New Caledonia
INDIAN OCEAN
Queensland
AUSTRALIA
Western Australia
South Australia
New South Wales
Victoria
Tasmania
1. Netherlands New Guinea
2. Sepik River Area
3. Huon Gulf Area
4. Massim Area
5. Papuan Gulf Area
6. Torres Straits Area
Geelvink
Bay
Anchorite Islands
Admiralty Islands
New Ireland
Sepik R.
New Britain
Bougainville I.
Tami I. (Cretin)
Fly R.
NEW GUINEA
Trobriand Is
Gulf of Papua
Torres
Strait

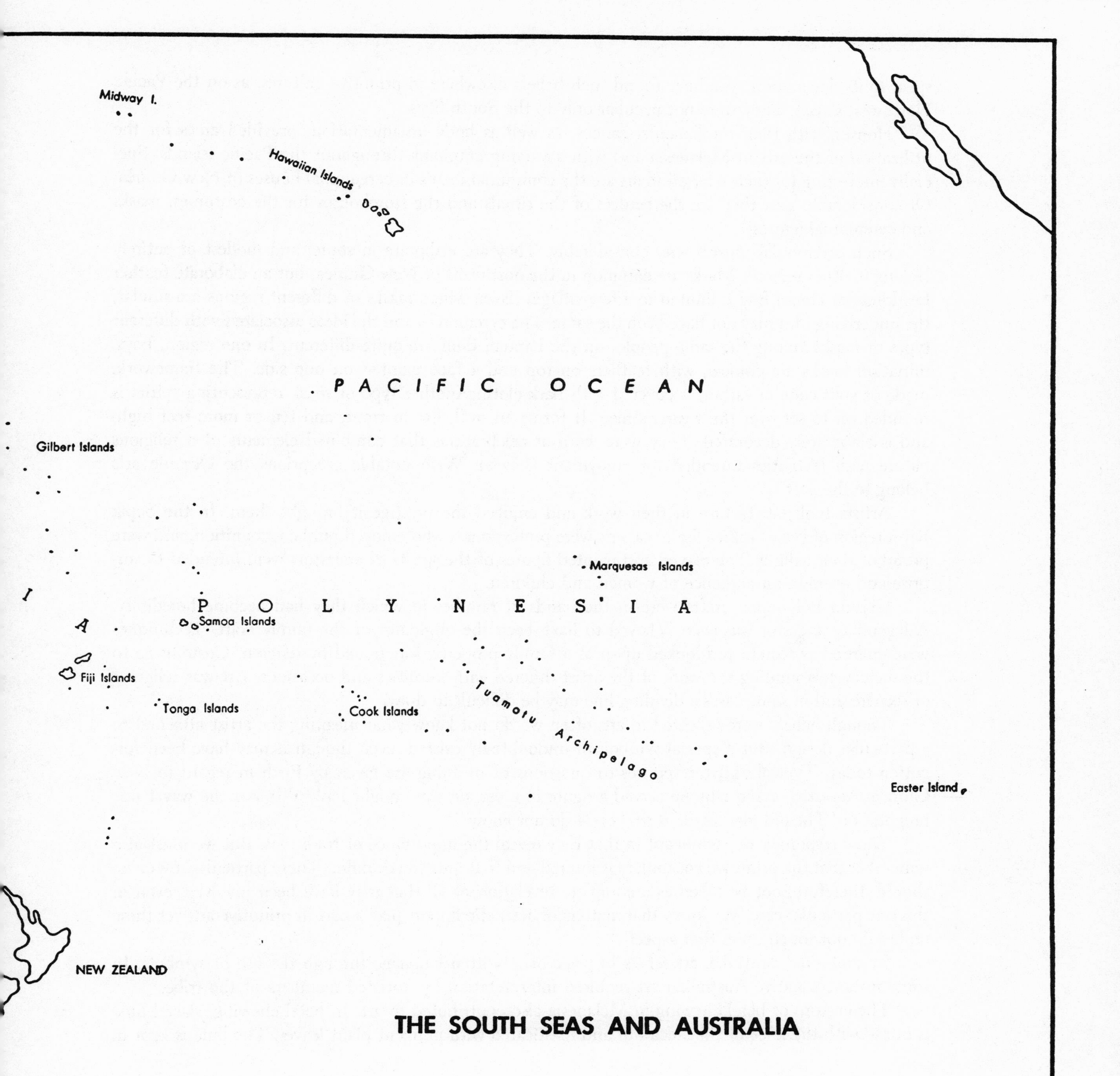

THE SOUTH SEAS AND AUSTRALIA

spear to its destination. We have found such beliefs elsewhere in primitive cultures, as on the Pacific Northwest Coast. They were not peculiar only to the South Seas.

Houses, with their implements, canoes, as well as body ornamentation, provided areas for the utilization of the arts in Melanesia and with a varying emphasis throughout the Pacific islands. Specially interesting for their relation to art are the communal men's or ceremonial houses of New Guinea. Of considerable size, they are the centers of the rituals and the storehouses for the costumes, masks and ceremonial figures.

Such ceremonial objects vary considerably. They are elaborate in some, and modest or entirely lacking in other regions. Masks are common in the northwest of New Guinea, but an elaborate feather headdress of Hansa Bay is limited to a few villages. Even where masks of different regions are similar, the underlying idea may not have been the same. The ceremonies and the ideas associated with different types of masks among the same peoples on the Papuan Gulf are quite different. In one region, boys' initiation masks are conical, with feathers on top and a face painted on one side. The framework, made of split cane or rattan, is covered with bark cloth. Another type of mask representing spirits is rounded off to set over the wearer's face. It forms an oval, flat in front, and ten or more feet high, and is elaborately decorated. They were worn at celebrations that combined elements of a religious nature with festivities intended for enjoyment (Lewis). With notable exceptions the Oceanic arts belong to the past.

Artists took satisfaction in their work and enjoyed the prestige it brought them. In the Sepik River region of New Guinea figure carvers were professionals who enjoyed public recognition, and were proud of their calling. The carved and painted figures of the spirits of ancestors were intended to surprise and overawe an audience of women and children.

Certain Polynesian crafts were in the hands of families in which they had become hereditary. A legendary ancestor was even believed to have been the originator of the family craft. Techniques were guarded as secrets and looked upon as a family property, sanctioned by religion. Customs as to the secrecy surrounding the work of the artist differed with localities and occasions. Art was religious or secular, and in some cases a dividing line may be difficult to draw.

Though beliefs were reflected in art, often we do not know what meaning the artist attached to a particular design. But a special symbolism undoubtedly existed, even though it may have been forgotten today. Typical native responses to questions of meaning are given by Firth in regard to New Guinea. An artist, asked why he carved a figure in a certain way, might reply: "It was the way I was taught," or "The old man made it so," or "I do not know."

These responses are significant in that they reveal the importance of traditions. But we must also remember that the primitive vocabulary is limited and that individuals differ. These particular responses should, therefore, not be taken as a complete revelation of all that may have been involved, even in this one particular case. We know that matters of aesthetic import play a part in primitive art, yet these replies do not touch upon that aspect.

In aboriginal Australia, art serves in place of a written language through the use of symbols. In some instances native Australian art required interpretation by initiated members of the tribe.

The custom of betel chewing in Melanesia also contributed to art. In betel chewing, slaked lime is mixed with the juice of the areca nut and masticated with pungent plant leaves. The lime is kept in bamboo containers or in gourds. The handles of the spatulas, with which the lime is taken out of the containers, are carved with intricate designs.

Oceanic designs may appear fantastic and even grotesque to us, but it seems entirely plausible that somehow these strange shapes were meant to give impressions of the invisible world of ghosts, spirits and supernatural beings. To the South Sea islanders these spirits were as real and as normal as the manifestations of saints and devils in mediaeval Europe. As represented in art, they were the products of historical developments, and not the results of momentary inspirations of individuals. What any single artist added may have consisted of variations, but not of novel inventions due to individual inspirations of an abnormal kind. Fear was part of the normal human existence; more so than with us, and art was a part of the culture, but not the outgrowth of mental ill health. Emotionally unstable individuals may well have played a part in primitive cultures, but they were not responsible for art unless they were artists to begin with.

CRAFTS, MATERIALS, TOOLS

South Sea art consists chiefly of ancestral figures and memorial tablets; ceremonial objects, like masks, drums and bull roarers; utensils, like bowls, scrapers and neck-rests; and weapons, like shields and clubs. These objects were carved of wood, constructed of split cane or rattan or made of bark cloth. In addition, there are specialties used for jewelry and ornamental wear made of shells, tortoise shell, human hair, and feathers, used for shields, and feather coats and capes. Each region excelled in a kind of artistic production peculiar to its own talents.

Monumental stone architecture is entirely lacking, but stone structures and stone sculpture occur in limited areas as in the Marquesas and on Easter Island. Oceania had no writing, and painting in our sense of the word was unknown. However, decorated tapa is a type of painting. New Guinea and Australia had rock pictures, and Australia bark and ground painting. Pottery was restricted largely to New Guinea, and weaving to Micronesia. Because of isolation and the limitations of local resources, larger works of art and such techniques as the arts of metal were never developed. Materials were unevenly distributed and there was no great variety; even wood was scarce on Easter Island.

Except for Indonesia, all objects of art and utility were made with primitive tools before the coming of the white man. Axes and chisels were of stone, shells and bone; scrapers and files of coral, shells and shark skin; knives of obsidian, bone and teeth. Earth pigments and plant juices provided color. Generally speaking, the best work was done before contact with the white man, and before iron became available. Nevertheless, important collections have been formed in more recent times and during the early part of this century. Wood carving in the old style was continued into our own period in New Zealand.

STYLE GROUPS

There are perhaps a hundred different styles in the Pacific area. Though some might be called substyles or variations within styles, each one is sufficiently individual, so that it can be identified in major examples.

On a formal-aesthetic basis, Paul S. Wingert (1953) has suggested five major categories of Oceanic art forms as follows: (1) contained form expressed by its own sculptural shapes (Fig. 255); (2) expansive polychrome form; (3) related forms expressing an assemblage of shapes and ideas (Fig. 256); (4) aerial form in which the wood is pierced or cut away to form a cage-like structure (Fig. 257); and (5) two-dimensional surface decorations, incised or carved in low relief. Wingert's classification includes the whole Pacific area; it is objective and all-inclusive.

The great diversity of styles in Oceania is due in a measure to the fact that small groups lived on many islands in isolation for long periods. Many of the styles may have been developed on the islands, merging traditional motifs introduced by the colonists with new ideas developed locally. The power of tradition was so strong that designs at times betray a stylistic relationship to Indonesia and southeastern Asia. A few examples from Indonesia suggest connections between Oceania and the westerly regions from which these tribes originally came.

In Melanesia we may differentiate between styles that are ornamental and those that are sculptural, using animals and figures carved in the round or in relief, combined with painting. As this is a division for convenience, no rigid consistency is here intended.

MELANESIA

ORNAMENTAL STYLES

A house gable decoration from Sumatra, with a mask-like face worked in beneath the lowest scrolls, so reminiscent of a classical acroterium, is said to be purely Indonesian.

A bark cloth painted with crocodile motifs, from Geelvink Bay, north New Guinea, is interesting ethnologically and artistically (Fig. 258). Similar lizard or crocodile shapes on New Guinea rock paintings are believed to relate to sun worship and may include a fertility symbolism. They are perhaps not exclusively artistic innovations; a magic intent was probably also originally involved. A spiky, linear character is related to the body shapes, and a consistent style, suggestive of a nervous energetic quality, carries through the whole design.

Middle Celebes bamboo flutes are engraved and painted or burned. The simplest of motifs are used; bands, zigzags, loops, chevrons and the like. Incised bamboo was also used for lime containers in the Sepik River region of New Guinea. Gourds were decorated by the individual user, and this type shows a greater invention in the decoration. Delicate carvings are to be found from the Anchorite Islands (Fig. 259). There the lizard-crocodile motif appears in carved lime spatula handles and spiral forms combine with open zigzags.

A fantastically beautiful creation is a lime tube stopper from the Sepik River region (Fig. 260). This carving of a flying bird has a light and aerial quality, achieved through perforations. The wave-like shapes of the wing are united with a severely rhythmic sequence of crescents of the body of the bird. The open and solid shapes above are separated from the crescents below by the thin, blade-like wing. This is wood carving carried to the point of virtuosity.

In the Admiralty Islands round wooden bowls occur in different types, as in a bowl with handles in double volutes (Fig. 261). However, the handles usually end in a single curve. These Oceanic bowls

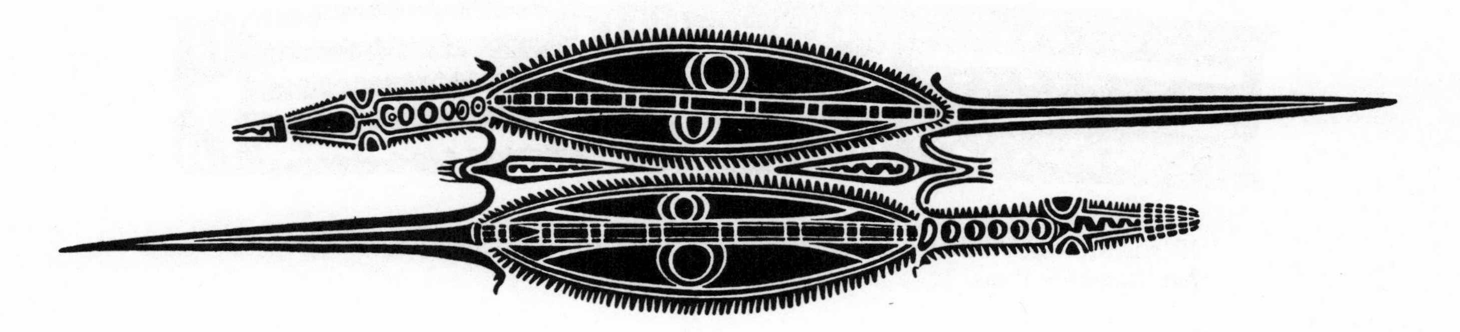

Ill. 30. Melanesian design, *tami* style. *After Reichard (1953). Columbia University Press.*

compare with ceramic Greek vases, combining elegance with sturdiness. What is noteworthy is the firmness of the contour, the solidity of the legs, carved of the same block and set in contrast to the delicate, perforated handle. Within this basic design the artists invented variations. The bowls vary in size from about ten inches to over four feet in diameter. The larger ones were used at wedding feasts. The purely ornamental handles are gummed on; they were made of extremely hard wood, and many show an excellent finish. The hollowing out was done by burning. Tami Island, also, is known for its wood carving, which includes here, as in other parts of Melanesia, bowls, lime spatulas, neck-rests, drums, canoes and house beams. The bowls are long in shape, and are carved in low and high relief. Specialization was highly developed and every carver used patterns owned by his family.

Styles in the South Seas were as localized as they were in Africa. Melanesian design used elements like lines, dots and triangles in low relief for surface enrichment. The Fiji Islands developed bold, geometric designs as in tapa (Fig. 262). Of six style regions of Polynesia, the Tonga and Samoa Island styles are made up of zigzags, straight, and dentated lines in the carving of wooden bowls, whereas New Zealanders in their wood carving specialized in curves and spirals (Fig. 263). The *tami* style—named after the island Tami (Cretin), in the Huon Gulf, off northeast New Guinea—used sharply pointed triangles (Ill. 30); in the Admiralty Islands the triangles are more nearly equilateral (Ill. 31). Isolation was never so complete as to exclude all exchange of ideas between islands.

Two carved coconut cups (Fig. 264) from the Huon Gulf area of New Guinea, represent this style in its extravagant brilliance. For sparkle and vitality, for variety, richness and invention, these designs are perhaps unsurpassed. Long curves, set with spiky saw-tooth edges contrast with black eyes and bold scrolls. There is enough symmetry and repetition within the larger elements to give an allover sense of unity. Within the general design, details introduce an element of discovery and surprise. Two

Ill. 31. Melanesian design, Admiralty Islands style. *After Reichard (1933). Columbia University Press.*

sides are never identical and the variations seem to increase in complexity as the pattern is studied.

In his study of the art of New Guinea, Alfred C. Haddon (1895) pointed out that decoration was often based on bird, crocodile or fish-hook designs. In a wooden drum (Fig. 265), the reptile-headed handles were very likely intended as crocodiles. Human heads are carved in relief on the ends of the supporting crosspieces.

The frigate bird appears in a highly developed design, in the Massim area of New Guinea. These motifs were carved on shields, drums, canoe prow ornaments, lime spatulas, lime gourds and also on neck-rests, which were used wherever the hairdress had to be preserved.

A canoe prow ornament from the Trobriand Islands (Fig 266), which belong stylistically to the Massim area, combines the frigate bird with other shapes in which the bird character has practically disappeared. Long sweeping curves terminating in scrolled ends, and borders enriched by incised carving, contrast with unadorned surfaces. Curves and straight lines unite to give firmness and clarity; strength and precision are as emphatic as elegance and refinement. The whole design is imbued with a vital energy, and entirely free of any weakness or confusion.

A canoe prow ornament in the Buffalo Museum of Science, from the Louisiade Archipelago of the Massim area, shows the style in a bold version with a minimum of elaboration. The same motif was carved with greater elaboration and more elegance in a neck-rest (Fig. 267). Note how the curves relate, one taking up where the other leaves off in a smooth, rhythmic sweep. This neck-rest is one of the superior examples of Oceanic design.

In a painted version of the bird motif, from the Middle Sepik River region, the birds are seen seated back to back combined with blossoms of the areca palm (Fig. 268); black and red are contrasted against white. Such paintings in large sizes were used to cover the walls of the men's houses, dance places or the sites of initiation ceremonies (Wirz, 1954). The frigate bird motif is seen again, carved and inlaid with mother-of-pearl, in a Solomon Island float (Fig. 269).

Breast ornaments from New Ireland (Ill. 32), New Britain and the Admiralty Islands (Ill. 33), called kapkaps, were made of discs ground out of the tridacna shell, over which a thin disc of tortoise shell was placed, to form a fine openwork design. The spiderweb-like designs of concentric rings are extremely delicate. The larger ones are rare and highly valued, as they required a larger shell and skillful work. Those four to five inches in diameter were worn by men only; the smaller ones, two to three inches in diameter, could be worn by women.

Ornamental designs in Melanesia were applied to other objects of utility and to house construction. Ceremonial ladders, richly carved and not intended for use, were sometimes set up in new houses. Bullroarers, noisemaking instruments used ceremonially, were carved with variations of face designs; they were common with the many tribes of the Purari delta, of the Papua Gulf. The finest canoe paddles were painted in the Solomon Islands with figures in white and black. The north coast of New Guinea, so rich in masks and other ceremonial objects, also developed ornamental objects and utensils, like ladles, carved pestles, carved flutes and carved and painted suspension hooks. Canoe prows were carved in the shape of crocodile heads on the Sepik River, and in the shape of birds and in panels perforated with curvilinear designs, in the Dutch section of the north coast. Posts and beams on Lottin Island, between New Britain and New Guinea, were carved with shapes of animals; carved wooden figures were set up in pairs on either side of the house doorway on the Admiralty Islands; and carved wood spires were placed on the roofs of houses in New Caledonia.

Ill. 32 (left). New Ireland kapkaps. Ill. 33 (right). Admiralty Islands kapkaps. *After Reichard. Columbia University Press.*

Figures and masks in Oceanic art fall into styles, which according to Felix Speiser (1937) are in part related to the migrations of cultures from west to east. The styles suggested by Speiser are recognized in head shapes and masks. He distinguishes the following styles, mainly in Melanesia: *korovar*, *tami*, *uli*, triangular and oval, which apply to heads; and curvilinear and beak, which have a more general application. The beak style may also be described as an elongated nose style, and is really a variation of the curvilinear style. Diagrams may be used to describe the basic shapes of the above-mentioned head-style series (Ill. 34).

The *korovar*, *tami* and *uli* styles apply to wood carving. The *korovar* is essentially unpainted; the other two emphasize color. The primary, curvilinear and beak styles used bark cloth over a lightly constructed frame, or braided fiber, and depended heavily on paint, often white, black and red. At an earlier date (1929), Augustin Kraemer called attention to the difference between wood-carved styles of permanent figures and painted, bark cloth or braided fiber masks made for one-time use at special ceremonial occasions. The wood-carved figures may conceivably be due to Malay-Indonesian influences; the bark cloth and braided fiber styles are characteristic of the Papuan-Melanesian regions.

The *korovar* takes its name from a wooden casket or shrine which was used for the preservation of the skull of an ancestor. It takes the shape of a squatting figure, as shown in Fig. 255 combined with other motifs, all carved in one piece. The *korovar* style (Ill. 34a) is cube-like and is terminated by a horizontal at the base of the head. This style appeared in Indonesia, spread to parts of New Guinea and can be traced as far as the Solomon Islands.

The *tami* style (Ill. 34b) has little relief; it is flat and massive, and uses painted geometric decorations, the *uli* style (Ill. 34c) has a broad mouth, a pointed chin, and is often pointed on top. According to Speiser, the triangular (Ill. 34d) and round or oval styles (Ill. 34e) represent primitive stages that never developed an emphasis on straight lines and firm contours, but not all rounded and oval shapes belong to the primary style. Even if it should not be possible to demonstrate conclusively that the historical development followed such a course, a grouping by stylistic details helps to bring order into a multiplicity of styles.

One type of *korovar*, twelve inches high (Fig. 270), from Dutch New Guinea, shows a short figure with a large head holding a pierced shield in front. The mighty head conceived as a huge block, is still linear in the treatment of the features. This ornamental character finds its expression in the pierced shield. The pattern, showing an affinity with a pierced gable ornament found in Sumatra, illustrates the movement in art forms from west to east.

Another example of the *korovar* style is a wooden mask from central New Britain (Fig. 271). The wide mouth, horizontal and placed low, and the rectangular outline of the head are typical. The head is sculpturesque in treatment, strong and powerful in the shaping of the planes and unusually effective.

We recognize the *korovar* influence in the rectangular type of head in a Trobriand Islands female figure (Fig. 272), and in a more emphatic form in a Solomon Islands canoe prow (Fig. 273) with its horizontal base line terminating the head, which is pushed forward. In an Admiralty Islands male figure (Fig. 274) the head has elements of the *tami* style in the mouth set low and in the hairdress, and the primary style, in the pointed triangular shape of the face. In the mature *tami* style the face is fully

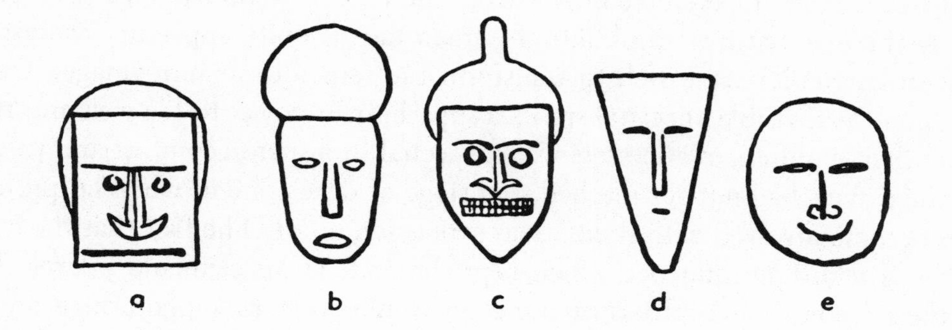

Ill. 34. Melanesian sculpture, designs, head styles: (a) *korovar* style; (b) *tami* style; (c) *uli* style; (d) triangular style; (e) round or oval style. *Zeitschrift für Ethnologie, Berlin. After Speiser*

rounded and massive. Though carved in wood, all three have tube-like limbs, and heads terminating in sharp edges. The use of inlay occurs in the Admiralty Islands figure, but the incised patterns are not the same on the Solomon Islands canoe prows. Both styles show legs that look like posts doweled to flat plates. Incised ornaments make up for a lack of sculptural form on the Admiralty Islands figure. Sharp ridges, a forward thrust of the low set mouth, pipe-like arms and legs with hands that fade out to points, are more or less common to all (Fig. 275).

The *tami* style is well represented in the mask in Color Plate 27. The flat carving offers a surface for painting, and red and black triangles on white are used in this instance. There are curved horns for ears, and carved lizards attached to headdress and chin. The incised motifs on the ridge of the nose, "streamers," are widely used in Melanesia. The *tami* style is bold, massive, self-assured but somewhat static. Note the shape of the low placed mouth, and the rounded hood or cap indicative of a particular type of headdress, perhaps actually worn by the islanders.

The influence of the *tami* style with its geometric ornament in New Britain, (formerly Neu Pommern), is illustrated in the painted eyes, nose, and mouth of a mask of the Sulka tribe (Color Plate 28). This mask, shaped like a hat, is constructed of pith fastened to a bamboo frame. Such masks, often larger than the human head, have raffia attached to conceal the figure. Another well-known example, in the Chicago Natural History Museum, is an ancestral figure from Malekula, in the New Hebrides. The bent limbs suggest the crocodile motif so common in South Seas art, and the boar tusks protruding from the corners of the mouth recall the important place occupied by the pig in New Hebrides economy. The effect depends on color, red and blue, with painted borders and zigzags around arms and legs. Ancestral figures of this type were used at initiation ceremonies at which individuals were promoted to a higher social rank. This comparatively simple type was not made by professional artists but by those who sponsored the candidate for promotion.

As in the case of the smaller New Hebrides figures, huge heads carved from the trunks of fern trees were made by those who were to be advanced to a higher social grade. Some of these tree-fern figures are full, others only half figures. (Color Plate 29.) They are often twelve feet in height and the original tree is more apparent than is usually the case in wood carvings. The effort to subdue nature by turning the inverted tree trunk into a human face is quite apparent. Fantastic shapes, well over life-size, in striking color serve well to transform the fern into a spirit image. Tremendous eyes seem to confer upon the invisible ancestral spirits a superhuman power to see well and thereby to keep better watch over their children, as ancestors were expected to dispense comfort and reassurance to the living. Perhaps the carvers had not yet reached that stage of development when, as professional artists, they might have become involved with styles as an expression of art. The fact that the carvers were laymen may point to a retarding influence which kept the craft at an elementary level. The neglect of the figure and the pronounced emphasis of the head would seem to support such an interpretation.

The third basic type of head, the *uli* type (Ill. 34c), is also illustrated by a central New Ireland (formerly Neu Mecklenburg) *uli* figure (Fig. 276), which gave the name to other heads of this style. Two characteristics are the broad mouth, perhaps derived from the skull, and the shape of the top, a way of wearing the hair, stained yellow, to indicate mourning. The meaning of the side supports is not known, but a possible serpent connection has been suggested.

At least a dozen different *uli* type figures are known. They appear to symbolize the power of the ancestors, an apotheosis of fertility, an affirmation in the wake of death, which the primitive mind refuses to accept. The ancestors, through these images, were forever maintaining an active connection with the living. Funerals were occasions for festivities and were not dedicated to mourning alone. The *uli* figures represented ancestors for whom gigantic celebrations were staged, lasting with interruptions for as long as two years. A number of chiefs combined to pay for these funeral celebrations, at which the *uli* figure occupied the center of public interest. The rivalry among them, the endeavor to stage celebrations worthy of a great chief no doubt stimulated the artists to give their best. That may explain the variations within the same style.

Wood carvings comparable to the *uli* figures were the even more complex funeral figures of northern New Ireland, the so-called *Malagans*. They combined superimposed and intertwined openwork carvings of figures and birds as an impersonal memorial for a chief and his contemporaries. In the *Malagans* much of the wood was hollowed out, so that a thin structure and a few solids were left freely standing in space. The block lost its solidity by having the wood cut out. A parallel from European art in stone, or at least an affinity of spirit, is the late Flamboyant Gothic architecture. In New Ireland, as in mediaeval France and Belgium, solid matter was made light, almost as if there had been an unconscious desire to turn the weight of the wood into something suggesting the lightness of the invisible spirit.

The open perforated style carries over into New Ireland masks (Fig. 277). Eyes, nose and mouth are severely defined by the large openings related to one another as a design. Even the huge mouth loses some of its fierce expression, due to stylization. The effect, from our point of view, depends less on fantastic shapes or on size—the total height with fiber top is only about eighteen inches—but more on the skill of the wood carver to obtain a well-defined design out of the complex shapes of an elaborate style.

Another type of wood carving from northern New Ireland is represented by memorial boards.

They are carved partly in high relief, and partly perforated, and are painted chiefly in red-orange and white. As they are carved out of light-weight wood, a whole beam is finished in a comparatively short time—Kraemer suggests it was a matter of a few hours. Birds, serpents, fish, are the motifs used, as well as small figures said to represent the ancestors. A hornbill devouring a serpent forms the center in the carving shown before in Fig. 257. The bird, with its large beak, wing and tail, is inscribed in a rich pattern of curved and scrolled plumage. Such complicated designs were carved directly out of the wood without drawings, and the finished carving was set up in a fenced-in place.

The Chicago Natural History Museum has a splendid collection of about 150 pieces of New Ireland wood carvings on exhibition, including many of this perforated-openwork type. There are nine different kinds of carving; carved figures, dance masks, dance ornaments, prepared skulls, carved planks, memorial totem bird carvings, sacred figures, house and memorial masks.

Ancestral figures from southern New Ireland, two to three feet high, in the same museum, are cut from a soft oölitic limestone in the interior. The cylindrical figures, with semi-oval disc heads, incised eyes and mouths, tattoo marks, projecting noses, conical breasts and prominent sex organs, stand pole-like in stiff frontal positions. These figures are kept in a special house in the village before which the women stand in mourning, but which they are forbidden to enter. There is no question of these statues being preserved as works of art. They serve their religious purpose and, having served, are removed and destroyed.

The beak and curvilinear styles take us back to New Guinea. The beak style has received its name from the long, projecting nose, which is more bird-like than human. One of the characteristic details is the slant of the eyes. The style is essentially surface-covering. Curves flow in various directions, in ovals and spirals, in saw-tooth patterns, and in smooth lines. Concentric rings surrounding the eyes are related to a long nose. Small pinpoint eyes are contrasted with large whites. In the example shown in Fig. 278 the carved and painted figure is part of a ceremonial stool from the Sepik River region.

These ceremonial stools combine a standing male figure as a back, with a stool, both carved in one piece in a weirdly dramatic style. Like masks, the heads of the figures are kept flat. The stools are covered with a brown earth-like pigment over which the face is given a linear pattern in white; red is also used as a third color. Stools have been traced to a dozen or more villages on the middle and lower Sepik River and vary in the shapes of the heads, in proportions and in the use of color. The variations may be due also to the fact that each figure was meant for the spirit of a particular ancestor. Such stools served at council sessions held in the ceremonial houses. They were not used as seats, originally, but were sacred as symbols, if not as the actual seats of the ancestral spirit. In one case, it is reported that an ancestral skull was placed on the back of a stool, presumably as a symbolic act to indicate participation of the ancestor in the deliberations.

The beak style is a modification of the curvilinear style illustrated in a mask (Fig. 279) and two gable ornaments (Fig. 280) from the Sepik River. We note the same emphasis on curves and the same stressing of the long ridge of the nose. In place of the slanting eyes of the beak style, the curved style favors circular eyes or eyes set horizontally as in Papua Gulf examples (Fig. 281). Though the style in each is followed through consistently, there is variation from one example to another. There is also a variation in effectiveness; a design may be a masterpiece of concentration, bringing out a grotesqueness of conception with extraordinary power, or the design may be more loosely spotted.

The variety of mask designs of the Sepik River tribes is greater than in any other region of New Guinea. Four different types of Sepik River masks have been described: (1) house masks attached to the gable ends of houses, wood-carved or made of palm leaves or of areca palm blossoms; (2) wood-carved face masks; (3) wood-carved masks attached to canoes; and (4) masks made for attachment to dance costumes or to large hoods covering the head or the upper part of the figure. There is such a variety of styles that the beak and curve style division hardly covers all types. Many sources contributed to produce such multiplicity. Noses may be reasonably normal, or they may be broad like tubers or long like trunks (Fig. 282); eyes may be round, disc-shaped or tube-like; mouths may be large or small, straight or crescent-shaped; and cheeks and foreheads may recede or project (Wirz).

In a Sepik River carving of a human figure surmounted by a frigate bird (Fig. 283), the painted decorations of the head and the carved scrolls on the torso recall the curvilinear style. A pointed chin, a high ridge nose, round eyes, are curvilinear style elements; the squatting posture is more like that of the *korovar* style. Essentially, these characteristics in a less extravagant form may be seen on a head carved in the round (Fig. 284), with a high ridge nose, a projecting mouth, and a pointed end used to stick the head in the earth.

The use of color in the Sepik River region is strikingly represented on a large female figure of the Abelam tribe (Color Plate 30). Bright reds and oranges against clear blues give a fresh, scintillating effect. The design is dazzling, a mosaic of small color areas, each contributing its sparkle to the total impression. Color is supported by a pattern of curves, zigzags and dentated lines enclosing larger and smaller shapes. These are ingeniously graduated in scale, the larger areas being in the head. In that way the head attracts attention first, and we examine it before we turn to the other, more involved, shapes. Carving defines the major sub-divisions; color enlivens the surface and adds to the effect.

Dance masks of bent sticks covered with bark cloth of the Baining tribe from the Gazelle Peninsula of New Britain are among the startling creations of Oceania (Fig. 285). Curved shapes grow directly out of structure and materials. Being light, the masks could be large; some are over three feet high, not counting those with fitted bamboo poles. The masks suggest insects as much as the crocodiles the heads may have been intended to represent. Painted designs, red and black on white, conforming to the curves of the framework are used sparingly in lines and borders; the large eyes are accented by the decorative treatment of adjacent areas. The lightness of construction is paralleled by the style of the decoration, which is also light and spacious.

An entirely different type of Melanesian mask was used on the islands of the Torres Straits, between New Guinea and Australia. These islanders depended on the sea for their livelihood, and used plates of tortoise shell for masks. This unwieldy material was bent into shape, perhaps under the application of heat. Noses, tops and perforated side pieces were laced on. The hair is human; the eyes are of pearl shell and black paste; and teeth were set into the open mouth. In the example in Fig. 286, the effect is obtained with the least modification of the raw material. Its colorful, mottled surface is the most striking part of the mask. The technique of cutting out shapes is suitable to the material, and highly effective.

The curved noses and broadly based heads are still in evidence in New Caledonia door jambs (Fig. 287), representing ancestral spirits. In breadth and vigor these jambs are comparable to Northwest

Pacific Coast carving, but they have a style of their own. A mighty head, carved in deeply grooved horizontals, puts a determined stop to the equally emphatic chevrons below. Fine examples are in the British Museum and in the Denver Museum.

Pottery plays a comparatively minor part in Oceanic art. A fine example, however, a water jar from the Sepik River region, shows the characteristic curvilinear style in modeled and painted decorations (Fig. 288). Compared to the wealth of forms in Melanesia, the remaining regions are almost homogeneous in their art styles. This is particularly true of Micronesia.

MICRONESIA

These islands include chiefly the Mariana, Marshall, Caroline and Gilbert Islands. Due to their small size and more limited resources, Micronesian art does not compare in complexity and richness with the arts of Melanesia. Sculpture was developed only to a limited extent, partly due to the scarcity of wood. The available supply was used for canoes, drums, bowls and other utensils, leaving no surplus for sculpture. Even where wood was available, sculpture remained largely undeveloped. Where wood was used for carving, as in statues and masks, the figure was highly stylized. A statue of a deity, about five and a half feet high, from Nukuoro Island (of the central Caroline Islands) was carved by Polynesians who came from the east (Fig. 289). The head lacks features; there are no hands or feet; the torso is reduced to minimum essentials. This extreme severity happens to coincide with our own contemporary taste.

The same is true of a mask under four feet high from Satoan Island, of the Mortlock group of the central Caroline Islands. The surface is covered with white chalk and the features are emphasized in black. A black zigzag border surrounds the shield-shaped head. The mask is said to represent a good spirit; it was used in dances to ward off the danger of typhoons and probably for promotion of the breadfruit harvest (Tischner). If this mask had been made to our own order, to a generation acquainted with Modigliani, it could not have been more convincing. To that extent we have absorbed the functional point of view, which Micronesian art represents so well. A simpler version of this type, three feet high, shown in Fig. 290, was used as a gable ornament on a house.

A wooden dish, about a foot and a half long, from Wuvulu (also known as Matty) Island, is distinguished for its simple form, which is left unpainted and uncarved. In excellence of construction these wooden utensils could hardly be improved upon. A coconut grater, two feet long, is made in the form of a stool (Fig. 291). A piece of rough coral or a shell was fastened to the end against which the person seated on the stool could grate the coconut.

Lack of raw materials in Micronesia imposed handicaps on the arts. Even canoes had to be built up of small pieces fitted together to produce virtually watertight joints. As canoe builders and as navigators the Micronesians were famous. They undertook long sea voyages, and the Marshall Islands pilots constructed maps made of thin strips of wood and shells to indicate ocean currents. House building was also highly developed and the largest of the ceremonial houses would seat several hundred people.

To sum up, it can be said that the art of the Micronesians remained undecorated and depended for its appeal on a forthright expression of function and good craftsmanship. Their artistic sense is reflected in utensils, tools and weapons.

THE HAWAIIAN ISLANDS

Monumental free-standing wood sculpture is rare in the South Seas. Although such a style once was common in the Hawaiian Islands, only three large examples of war gods are known to exist today. One in the Peabody Museum of Salem (Fig. 292) is about seven feet high. A huge head shows a figure-eight mouth, eyes pinched out of sight, and a flowing mane down the back. The body is vigorous in carving and stands out in surprising contrast to the stylized head. The style is different from other known Hawaiian carving, as an "aristocratic style that served the restricted portion of the old Hawaiian Temple." The head suggests a certain resemblance to a Japanese Kamakura period mask or a lantern-bearing goblin. Fenollosa points out that the slanting and staring eyes are of the "Pacific" school of art. Whatever its origin, there is here a naturalistic intent, however stylized. Making faces at an enemy was a Polynesian way of winning battles. Snarling faces of warrior ancestors, however monstrous, were meant to seem alive; ferocity as an expression in art was cultivated.

Wood carving in Hawaii is also believed to have been linked to an earlier Micronesian and a later Central Polynesian settlement (Linton-Wingert). The ornamental-stylized elements, especially the large heads, with figure-eight mouths, recall the Marquesan and Maori style. The treatment of the figure may relate to the Micronesian inheritance. Thus, Hawaiian wood carving combined these two contributions. The large temple figures with their stylized heads reflect the aristocratic culture of the ruling caste. A more naturalistic head and the treatment of the figure, based on the Micronesian contribution, prevailed in the household gods of the common people. These two styles of figure carvings, the ornamental temple figure, and naturalistic popular house gods, existed side by side. The war god, Kukailimoku, was represented in the carved wood stationary temple figures, which were kept in one place, primarily for the chiefs and priests. The common people were admitted only to the public section of the temple enclosure.

Figures of the aristocratic war gods were also constructed of wicker work covered with red feathers (Fig. 293). Some of these figures, which were portable, were from six to eight feet high. They were covered with red feathers, and the large heads, with piercing eyes and large mouths, were set with sharks' teeth to make them as awe-inspiring as possible. Few examples of temple figures of either type exist today. They were destroyed in the native uprising of 1819. On that occasion, the suppressed populace rose in arms against the chiefs and priests, defeated their army and destroyed temples and statues. The many taboos which had become irksome were abolished as a result of the uprising, but the folk beliefs continued even after the introduction of Christianity.

The carved wood figures with the more nearly realistic heads represent the popular deities presiding over families and occupations. Hawaiian wood carving is sculpturesque, even a small piece looks larger than it really is. A game board (konane) on a massive central pedestal connected to figure-carved legs, and ending in stubby feet, is only eight inches high with a top slightly over a foot long and less than a foot wide (Fig. 294). The compact, bulky support contrasts with the slender top. Beside the well-rounded heads with wide-open mouths, these shapes still suggest tree trunks and roots only slightly modified by man.

A female figure, twenty-seven inches high (Fig. 295), emphasizes the figure rather than the head.

The form, narrow at the waist, expands across the shoulders and below the knees. The same proportions prevail in a smaller figure of the same type in the Oldman Collection.

Hawaii produced the best-made bark cloth in the South Seas. It was decorated in many colors by means of small bamboo stamps in angular geometric designs. These were combined by making large motifs out of the small stamp which by itself covered about one square inch. Stripes and large designs were painted. A number of early pieces of Hawaiian bark cloth, or tapa (Fig. 296), reveal excellent taste. Bark cloth was used for robes and blankets.

The finest kind of cloaks and capes used by chiefs on special occasions were made of feathers fastened to overlap on a net. Yellow, red and some black were the characteristic colors. Fans and wicker constructed helmets were also covered with feathers. The attraction is in the color and the beauty of the surface, design being subordinated to simple geometric shapes, like borders, diamonds and crescents.

The Central Polynesian islands, with the Samoa and Tonga groups in the west and the Cook, Harvey, Society, Rarotonga, Tahiti and Austral Islands in the east, should be mentioned. The Cook Islands produced an abstract style of wood carving represented by carved staffs showing conventionalized human heads of clan and national deities. A fine example from the Cook Islands is a ceremonial adze, 34 inches long, in the Smithsonian Institution. Finely proportioned neck-rests were carved in the Samoan Islands and carved fly whisk handles on Tahiti.

EASTER ISLAND AND THE MARQUESAS

Perhaps the best known of all South Seas art objects are the large stone images of Easter Island (Fig. 297) cut with stone tools from soft tufa, which material came from the crater of the extinct volcano Ranoraraku. The largest figure, weighing many tons, stands nearest the crater; others in groups of six to a dozen stand on stone platforms, most of them facing the sea.

Easter Island was visited in the late eighties of the last century by W. J. Thompson, paymaster in the U. S. Navy, who has given a detailed account of what he saw at that time. Within the crater Thompson found stone images in all stages of completion. Carving was done in the native rock; the statues were then cut loose from the bed. Workshops were both inside and outside the crater. Inside the crater he counted 93 statues, 40 of which were standing up ready for transport to the platform. On the slope of the crater 155 images stood, ready for removal. One unfinished image measured 70 feet. They were memorials to distinguished persons; each one had a name. Arms were carved in low relief, and crowns of red tufa were placed originally on top of each head. The largest crown measured twelve and one-half feet; to put it in place an inclined roadway had to be built. Rectangular projections on the side of the head represented ears, which were longer on the older images.

As wood was scarce, carved wooden figures are small in size. Some seem to be based on mummies (Fig. 298), and the carving is artistically impeccable. An example of a bird god found on Easter Island probably owes its form to a piece of wood that was shaped like the finished product before the carving began. The carver's problem here was to adapt a figure of his imagination to the available shape. A crooked stick of driftwood became a man-like bird.

The Easter Islanders are Polynesians and seem to be related to the Marquesans. The early explorers, Cook (1774) and Marchand (1791) found in the Marquesas a Neolithic culture, which continued to the nineteenth century. Stone in large blocks weighing many tons was also used in the Marquesas for house platforms and retaining walls. Carved stone images vary from a few inches to ten feet in height. Thus stone carvings became a combination of a rudimentary shaping of the figure on which details were superimposed by shallow surface carving. The head of the figure is invariably large; the smaller the figure, the larger in proportion is the head (Fig. 299). Eyes are large circles, representing, perhaps, mother-of-pearl discs placed in skulls over the eyes. The wide mouth may also have a skull origin. Whether the stylization is based on some relation to appearance as suggested by the skull resemblance, or a result of gradual simplification, is not definitely known. Resemblances to comparable stylizations elsewhere, as in the Huon Gulf *tami* style mask (shown in Color Plate 27), suggest that these stylizations may not be local developments. In the modern version of the style the details are standardized and repeat within a narrow range in about the same way.

Carved and drawn figures in the Marquesas are called *tikis*. They represent ancestors, chiefs or priests. An ancestor veneration with human sacrifice may at some unknown date have replaced the ancient gods of nature. If we glance back at the Indonesian ancestor figure from Nias (Fig. 255), we note that the posture is about the same, and details like fingers are in the same pattern. Tikis often have feet, or they may be anything between a bust and a full length figure.

Marquesan war clubs conform to a type. Carved of ironwood, they are about five feet long and end in a head above a shelf-like projection (Fig. 300). Within the limits of this general pattern there are variations in details. Each club has the same three small heads, two within the "eyes" and one placed where the tip of the nose would be if the head should be meant to have features. Over eighty different designs have been published and yet there seems to be no duplication, though perhaps some slight variation in craftsmanship.

THE MAORI OF NEW ZEALAND

The Maori, who inhabited New Zealand before the coming of the white man, hold high rank among the great wood carvers of the world. Each of the major styles, on the continents here discussed, had its own specialty in which it had no equal. Negro African masks and figures, and Pacific Northwest Coast totem poles are paralleled by Maori canoe prows and ancestor figures. Maori carvings are particularly successful in the elaboration of intricate details; in design and craftsmanship they are among man's most ambitious achievements.

New Zealand, consisting of North Island and South Island, is a mountainous and rugged country about 1200 miles southeast of Australia. The mountains of South Island form a snow-capped range with peaks more than 12,000 feet high. North Island reaches into the subtropics in its northern tip, and the rest of New Zealand has a healthy temperature and cool climate. Originally, New Zealand had no land mammals except bats, and no snakes, but lizards, two primitive species of frogs and many birds. Hardwood forests furnished excellent wood for house and canoe building.

Maori is the collective name for Polynesian tribes, probably from the Cook Islands or the Marquesas, who settled the islands. By the fourteenth century the Polynesians had reached the northern shores in successive voyages. White settlement began after Cook's explorations (1779), and after 1839 the influence of Christianity began to make itself felt. In 1840 the islands were peacefully attached to Great Britain, and in 1852 were granted self-government, but final peace between the British and the Maori did not come until 1871. The Maori have since become an integral part of the population, and New Zealanders look upon Maori art as a part of their national heritage.

Even though the tribes had no writing, their history and legends were handed down by word of mouth from generation to generation. The names of the large outrigger canoes in which early crews arrived were remembered, the "Arawa" being well known. The original plank canoes were replaced in New Zealand by dugout canoes up to eighty feet long.

Maori wood carving was attached chiefly to canoes, to the exteriors and interiors of houses, to staffs, feather boxes, and burial chests, shaped in outline like human figures. War clubs were carved of whale bone and wood, and ornaments called *hei-tiki* were carved of green jade. Tattooing for men, on face (Fig. 301) and thighs, was highly developed as an art. New Zealand had featherwork and flax coats, made by twined weaving; loom weaving was unknown. A hard New Zealand jade, greenstone, that takes a fine edge, was used for carving and cutting tools. Much of the work still in existence was carved with iron tools, as wood carving did not cease with the occupation of the country by the white man.

For the Maori, carving was so important that the art was attributed to Rauru, a deity comparable to a patron saint of mediaeval Europe. House posts represented revered ancestors, and every stage of the construction of a house was accompanied by a religious ceremony. When the logs were cut, Tame, the god of the forests, had to be propitiated, and when the house was finished there were special incantations to make it warm. For an important house human sacrifices were made, a slave or even a favorite child. Art was achieved literally at the cost of human anguish and suffering, in addition to the labor that went into its creation. It is not surprising, therefore, that carvings were treasured and in times of danger moved to safe places.

Each village had its council house, rectangular in plan, and with an open porch at one of the gable ends. The barge boards along the slanting eaves, as well as interior posts, ridge poles and wooden slabs set between the reed panels to form the walls, were carved. The rafters in the interior were painted with scroll designs.

The perishable nature of wood has put us in touch only with a fairly recent phase of this art. These carvings were produced, bought or traded in modern times; even the early ones are hardly before the beginning of the nineteenth century.

Some houses carved during the nineteenth century have been preserved. The Turanga house, completed in 1843, was acquired by the government in 1867 as a house of exceptional merit, and is now part of the Colonial Museum at Wellington. Another historic example is the Te Kuiti house, which was dismantled four times, removed twice and recarved by native craftsmen. As late as 1939 thirteen houses were still standing in one section of the North Island. Of these the Te Ore Ore house, built in 1878, near Masterton, is outstanding. Food stores received special attention as late as 1856, when natives built such a store for Witako, which was later taken to London.

Skilled carvers were held in high regard, and even chiefs engaged in carving. To complete a fine canoe or an important house is believed to have taken years. The Turanga house took eighteen carvers (using steel tools) six months to complete. This house is about forty-four by eighteen feet in the interior and has thirty-two carved figures on the side walls in addition to other carvings for the end walls.

The most characteristic aspect of Maori carving is its use of curves, though straight lines also occur. Angular designs were used on baskets, textiles and feather robes. A linear character is emphasized in a mingling of grotesque human and animal motifs. Where the human figure is used, it appears in frontal position (Fig. 302). Slanting eyes, figure-eight mouths with protruding tongues, three fingers on hands or bird-like claws and three- or four-toed feet, suggest a creature as much animal as human (Fig. 303). Spirals and other curves, in places where shoulders and knees would normally be, overwhelm and almost obscure the figure. Maori wood carving has these characteristics: (1) it tends to reliefs; low and high relief (Fig. 304), and high relief combined with sculpture in the round; (2) it favors perforations, so that open spaces also take on well-defined shapes. Where this is carried furthest, as in canoe prows and canoe sterns, the voids contribute to the effect by emphasizing the pattern; (3) it uses the motif of the protruding tongue in figures, fitting this motif into the pattern; (4) it is essentially curvilinear and given to scrolls and spirals (Fig. 305).

Polychrome painting had no place in such a style; the surface is usually covered with a red ocher, and the eyes of figures are inlaid with paua shells, which closely resemble abalone shells.

The spiral motif is so developed that simple and compound spirals can be differentiated. In some spirals, the curves come close together in the center; they are only partially closed in old carvings, but an S-curve can be made out. The spiral motif was probably developed and perfected in New Zealand, and owes little to outside influences. It has also been suggested that the spiral motif was inspired by coiled rope, as has been claimed for the Ionic volute of Greek architecture.

In carvings of ancestors a human aspect is apparent. In canoe design a purely linear, ornamental character predominates, and in some lintels placed over doors or windows figure and ornament are of about equal importance. Minor variations in style were developed locally. In some carvings heads are pointed and bodies ridged horizontally, in others heads are flat or concave on top. Different tribes or different periods may account for such variations. Where several figures are represented in a row, as in the case of five figures on a lintel, the central figure would be the ancestor, the figures on either side his two ghosts, and the end figures mythical beings called *manaias*. They are recognized by a single dot, the eye, placed within the top scroll.

Canoe prows were carved out of single blocks that were lashed to the canoe. In a type represented in the University Museum, Philadelphia (Fig. 306) and also in the Musée de l'Homme, Paris, the central panel contains two large perforated spirals. The carving is carried through on several planes, from the full width of the original block to the inner filling below the level of the large spirals. The design seems calculated and precise, but alive at the same time with no suggestion of mechanical monotony. Such carvings were carried through without drawings on paper; the carver depended on his ability to visualize the design. This was not an uncommon practice wherever fine wood carving was produced in any style; full-size blueprints are a modern invention. The stern rose vertically, constructed like a bird's feather with a strong central rib around which delicate spirals fill in the width of the plank from which the stern was carved.

In house carving the progenitor of the tribe was represented in the central post (Fig. 307). Facial tattoo marks were the only details that referred in any realistic way to the person who was honored by the carving. The carved house post, about four feet high, shown in Fig. 303, is extraordinarily vigorous. Deep cuttings set off divisions within the head against flat, low relief for the larger areas. Precision, elegance, richness of textures and a strong, rhythmical flow of line are the qualities that make a direct appeal to the eye.

A work of major importance is a carved lintel, three feet wide, in the Peabody Museum of Salem (Mass.). All characteristics of Maori art are fully developed in this lintel. An ancestral figure in the center is flanked by highly conventionalized *manaias*. The motif of the main figure of three-fingered hands resting on the abdomen is traditional to the Marquesas, the original home of the Maori. That there is probably a meaningful relation between central and side figures is suggested by the connecting links that touch head and shoulders of the ancestor. The carving is exuberantly vigorous. It is also extravagantly rich in the lace-like surface enrichment of the figures; at the same time the character is stern and determined, rather than soft and languid. A controlled and disciplined imagination, skill and a determination to carry through so complicated a work are reflected here.

The character of the Maori people is virile and aggressive; they were warlike, and the South Seas' best fighters. As we see them through their art, they appear intellectual and energetic, given to carrying out projects that required much planning and great sustaining power to realize. How different is the impression made by this well-thought-out, highly symmetrical design from that of the freer, more spontaneous, wood carvings of New Ireland or the Sepik River.

The same general style, but less florid, is represented in the lintel shown in Fig. 304. The spirals have come to rest, each in its own place, without carrying the eye to other parts; the figure too assumes a static posture. Its sturdy monumentality suggests that it belongs to a different region or is perhaps from an earlier period.

A New Zealand whalebone club was conceived as a weapon, but impresses us also as a work of art. Design and craftsmanship vie with each other for attention in the example shown before in Fig. 263. The perfection of the cutting in smooth curves, enclosing rows of evenly placed notches, is as admirable as the disposition of the spirals, the treatment of the handle and the profile of the club—a ceremonial object of luxury and distinction.

A wood-carved dressing box, from the Smithsonian Institution, reveals the full richness of Maori scroll carving. Though the general effect is one of flatness, the carving varies in depth. Grooved scrolls in triple bands are filled in by notched center ribs, each like a flexible chain of vertebrae. At either end a mask-like face may be detected, though so well integrated into the pattern that one cannot be certain of any specific meaning.

Small ornaments, around six inches long, carved out of nephrite, the greenstones used for tools, were worn around the neck as highly prized amulets (Fig. 308). These *hei-tiki*, or neck tikis, take on a variety of shapes suggestive of an embryo. Heads are large; limbs and torso are more or less fused into a single perforated shape. The three-fingered hand indicates a supernatural being. The heads may be twisted out of line with the body, and the eyes are inlaid with shell; the spaces left between limbs and body are usually no more than narrow slits.

South Seas art emphasized decoration in simple as well as in extravagantly grotesque shapes. The natural environment made its influence felt more in the choice of materials and less in the selection of motifs. Craftsmanship maintained a high quality. Styles varied from a less mature level to distinguished art forms, comparable to outstanding achievements elsewhere. Basic motifs seem to have been distributed from west to east; some of them possibly going back to the Asian mainland, but, essentially, styles were elaborated locally, even when motifs have been imported. The over-all impression of Oceanic art is one of fantastic variations, even though raw materials and techniques were limited.

AUSTRALIA

Australia, some 7,000 miles southwestward from San Francisco, is about as large as the United States without Alaska. It was connected with New Guinea and smaller islands to the north and with Tasmania to the south as recently as 30,000 to 40,000 years ago. The northern portion of Australia is within the tropical, the rest in the south temperate zone. All central Australia is a great desert due to insufficient rainfall. Among the many strange animals, the kangaroo is the best known. There are many varieties of kangaroos; in addition to the long-legged, man-sized red and gray kangaroos, there are smaller varieties, the wallabies. Most of the Australian aborigines, or "Black-fellows," are hunters or fishermen, without permanent settlements or domestic animals except the dog. The first white settlers from England arrived in 1788; in 1901 Australia became a self-governing dominion of the British Empire.

Rock painting on vertical walls under overhanging ledges was still being done in Australia, in regions untouched by the white man, as late as 1936; even in New South Wales rock paintings were created up to 1845. There are few instances where white men have witnessed rock painting being executed. It was confined to a few sites in any region, and the religious significance of the art did not encourage the presence of strangers. Where the art still flourishes, old paintings are kept fresh as part of a ritual, but freshness and preservation cannot be taken as a proof of antiquity. So far, no method has been found to determine age. Whether centuries or millennia are involved is unknown. The dry and warm climate of Australia may have preserved paintings, even in open rock shelters.

Generally speaking, engravings were not painted; each art, engraving and painting, was separate from the other, but the two techniques follow the same styles. There is no evidence to indicate which technique is older. Both are found in each of the mainland states of the commonwealth, except Victoria, from which no carvings have been reported.

Australian rock paintings are naturalistic in spirit, but they appear stylized to us. Compared to European paleolithic paintings, as well as to Bushman painting, Australian rock paintings are static; they attempt no movement and show no details. Human and anthropomorphic figures are in front view, animals in side view, or as if seen from below. There is a basic similarity of style throughout the continent; even when representations of the figures are separated by 1500 miles, as are those of New South Wales and north Australia, the style is broadly the same. The most elaborate paintings are from north Australia, of which Delamere is one of the two known sites. Though the basic style is widely distributed, individual designs are limited in use. In one instance a key-pattern was used by the members of the Karad-jeri tribes (La Grange, northwestern Australia) because they alone knew the chant which gave the design meaning, and which imbued with magical power the object on which it was engraved. As so often in primitive cultures, art and magic are closely related.

The techniques include three types: (1) outline drawings; (2) silhouettes, with or without borders; and (3) polychrome painting, using four colors. Painted hand stencils are also common, particularly in New South Wales.

One of the largest and most imaginative rock paintings represents "The Lightning Brothers"

(continued on page 311)

(Fig. 309). The larger of the two is the younger brother, Yagtchadbulla, who is about twelve feet high, including his headdress. The red and yellow stripes on the body and arms represent body painting. Hands are missing and toes are indicated by lines. Even though the human character is recognizable, the paintings are still symbolic. This symbolic abstract style of painting does not apply to animals which are not sacred totems; they are painted more realistically. According to the natives the figures were painted by the mythical persons represented who still exist and return to the paintings at the totemic center during the rainy season.

Painting for the Australian is either religious and magical or secular and informational. If magical, it is held sacred and valued for the power it invokes in connection with a ritual, but after the ceremony is over, the painting is neglected. Secular painting is informational and includes bark paintings, though some bark paintings are also sacred. The painter often includes what is not visible but known to be present, like the interior organs of an animal, the spinal column and the alimentary canal. Associations with objects may also be included in the paintings, like footprints with animals.

The meaning of a sacred drawing was explained to two investigators, Frank M. Setzler and F. D. McCarthy, by a native, Wondjuk, of Yirrkale, who stated, in effect: An apparently abstract design was in reality a series of symbols. The branches and roots of the tree were the black and cross-hatched horizontal bands. White dots above stood for bees, white and yellow dots below for their droppings. The horizontal string of white and yellow dots was the hard wax. The vertical cross-hatched panels across the middle were the "sugar bags" (of which the left and center ones happen to be women's, the rest are men's). The first discovery a boy makes of wild honey has great magical significance for his future.

Another bark painting (Fig. 310) is by Banjo, of Umba Kumba, and shows two crocodiles and one wallaby in red, white, and yellow on black.

A plain red kangaroo, called "Koopoo, the old man kangaroo" by the natives, is represented in a bark painting, in a heavy-handed, broadly painted style. This particular "Koopoo" plays a part in a legend according to which "Koopoo led a tribe of Kangaroo-black-fellows from the Timor Sea along a river to the Eastern Sea." The persistence of this legend is believed to be a trace of some ancient tribal movement.

In a bark painting of a turtle hunt from Groote Eylandt (Fig. 311), the fishermen in a boat have speared a seagoing turtle. One man at the bow is holding the rope to which the spear is attached. In its primitive force—the huge boat and large turtle against the diminutive men—the artist may have unconsciously projected his own respect for the magnitude of the expedition onto the turtle and the boat.

From the point of view of design and technique, a recent bark painting of a hunting scene has considerable charm (Fig. 312). It was collected in 1946-47 in N. E. Arnhem Land, by R. and C. Berndt of the Department of Anthropology of the University of Sydney. These explorers give the following interpretation: In the center a male kangaroo sleeps under the shade of a palm; about him, female kangaroos keep watch until it is their turn to sleep and be guarded by the male. Kangaroo tracks along the lower edge of the bark balance those of emus at the upper left and right. Emus to the left are feeding on the nuts of the dalpi palm. Between the tree where the kangaroo sleeps and the right edge of the painting a spider has slung its web, and dispersed throughout the design are short-tailed goannas, wagtails, pigeons and yams.

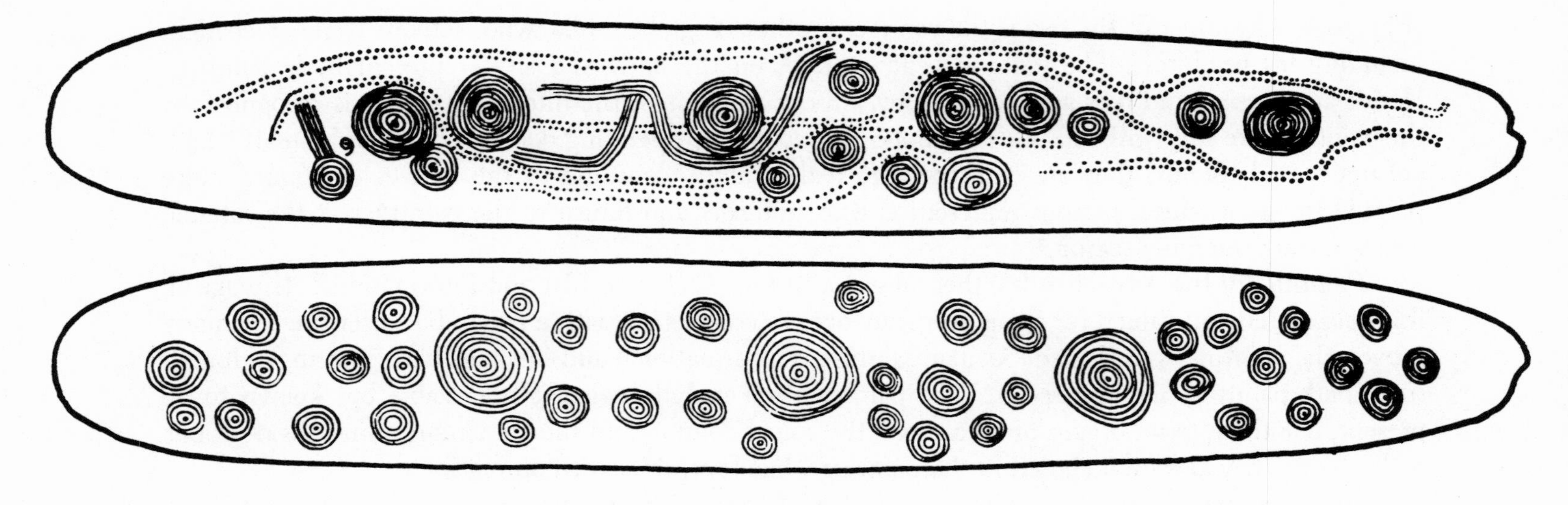

Ill. 35. Cricket Churinga of Ungwamina, Western Aranda, Australia. *After Geza Róheim. Hungarian Ethnographical Museum. Courtesy, International Universities Press, New York.*

In addition to rock and bark painting, Australian primitive art has engraved shells and pendants, oval plaques of wood or stone, called *churingas,* as well as ground paintings done with charcoal and red and yellow ocher, and eagle down glued on with human blood.

Churingas (Tjurungas) represent mystical bonds between a man and his totem ancestor. They must be kept safe and not shown to women, lest men become ill or die. Every person, it is believed, has two bodies—a body of flesh and one of wood or stone (Strehlow); the *churinga,* which also symbolizes the mother (Fry), is regarded as part of her supernatural deathless body (Strehlow). *Churingas,* are virtually notations in regard to a person's totemic ancestor, though they may look like mere decorations to the uninformed. Roheim gives these explanations on a cricket *churinga* of Ungwamina, Western Aranda (Ill. 35), in the Hungarian Ethnographical Museum. The four separate parts of the drawings have these meanings: the large concentric circles may be the tree on which the crickets sat; the small concentric circles may be the chrysalis stage from which they flew up to the trees; the wavy lines may be the footprints in the sand; the dots may be the body decoration on the grub ancestors.

It appears from this that the attached meanings are more important than the thing itself. We get the impression that unless a stone has been dedicated, set aside and treated with respect and secrecy, it is probably not a *churinga.*

In the case of the Australian aborigines, we have a people who wear no clothes, but paint their bodies; who build no houses but paint on rock walls, slabs of stone, bark and the ground itself. Primitive art in Australia hardly attains the high level that prevails in other regions. However, it has a religious character and is attractive, in spite of its limitations. In contemporary aboriginal Australia we arrive at the same conclusions as in Africa and the Americas: Art is deeply imbedded in the human spirit, it reflects man's beliefs, and is closely related to other cultural achievements.

VI

EUROPE AND AFRICA: CAVE PAINTINGS, CARVINGS AND ROCK ENGRAVINGS

EARLY MAN'S MOST SIGNIFICANT ACCOMPLISHMENTS ARE PAINTING AND SCULPTURE. FROM WHAT WE know of the prehistoric period in Europe, a sense of form is present even in his unpolished stone tools and bone implements. We have only the vestiges of whatever rude dwellings he may have had, and not even pottery can be traced back that far. It may be that song and dance antedate art, but art alone has survived. Prehistoric man's most spectacular accomplishments, the Ice Age pictures of large animals of the hunt, drawn or painted on the bare rock surfaces of caves, have been preserved, in some cases remarkably well. These paintings of the so-called Franco-Cantabrian style, in the caves of southwestern France and the Cantabrian mountains of northern Spain, are masterpieces of prehistoric art.

PREHISTORY

Prehistory is the period before the development of the art of writing. This means roughly about 3000 B.C. for Egypt and Sumer, somewhat later in China, and only a few centuries before the Christian era for most of the European continent.

The historic period of some five millennia is very short compared to the much longer Old Stone Age, or Paleolithic period. During the greater part of the Old Stone Age, Europe is believed to have been inhabited by a primitive type called Neanderthal man. He disappeared during the later period and the modern type of man, "Homo sapiens," arrived at the very end of the Old Stone Age. In appearance he is believed not to have been too different from man today. The late Old Stone Age, also known as the late or upper Paleolithic or Ice Age, is divided into the Aurignacian, Solutrean, and Magdalenian periods. Two of these periods are important for art, the Aurignacian and the Magdalenian.

The Ice Age we are here concerned with was the last of four glaciations of which the first has been dated back to 600,000 B.C. to 1,000,000 B.C., long before the appearance of man or art. According to some estimates the Aurignacian period has been placed around 60,000 B.C. to 40,000 B.C.; the following Solutrean period at about 40,000 B.C. to 30,000 B.C.; and the Magdalenian period at 30,000 B.C. to 10,000 B.C. Until the last glaciers melted down to their present location, around 10,000 B.C., northern Europe, including the British Isles, Scandinavia, and all mountainous regions from Spain across Europe and parts of Asia and North America were covered with ice.

During the prehistoric period, progress was slow. Man aimed to make himself safe against starvation, and achieve some measure of security. In his struggle for survival he invented tools and weapons, but long before prehistory had come to a close he had established himself as an artist. It may seem strange that primitive man painted and carved before he had permanent houses to live in. Whatever his shelters, tents or wattle huts may have been like, certainly less effort was expended on them than on painting. It is a fact that prehistoric man had artists before he had masons, for the use of stone for architecture does not appear until the Neolithic period.

During the first part of the late Old Stone Age the climate was intensely cold. Animals of cold climates like mammoth, cave bear, woolly rhinoceros and reindeer lived in temperate parts of Europe. As the climate warmed up toward the end of the Aurignacian period wild horses, oxen, bison and a few deer tended to replace the other animals. When the second cold era returned in the Solutrean period, the reindeer, musk ox, lemming and, to a lesser extent, the mammoth were among the dominating species. This last cold period gave way to the warm climate of the Magdalenian period, which continued through some ten thousand years into our own historic era. Throughout these periods of changing climates southern Europe was less affected and remained more temperate, and cave paintings are concentrated in the southwestern regions.

Though certain species of animals are typical of certain climates and are most numerous under their preferred climatic conditions, they also occur in other periods. The presence of certain animals in paintings does not by itself indicate the period.

CAVES AND ROCK SHELTERS

The limestone caves and open rock shelters in southwestern France, the center of prehistoric engravings and paintings, are in two regions comprising some seventy sites. One region is that of the river Dordogne and its tributary the Vezère; the other, to the south, is in the French Pyrenees. The Dordogne region includes, among others, the sites of Pair-non-Pair, Limeuil and Les Eyzies. Nearby are many well-known rock shelters like La Madelaine, Le Moustier, Laussel, Laugerie-Basse, the site of Cro-Magnon, and the caves of Les Combarelles and Font-de-Gaume. The region of the French Pyrenees

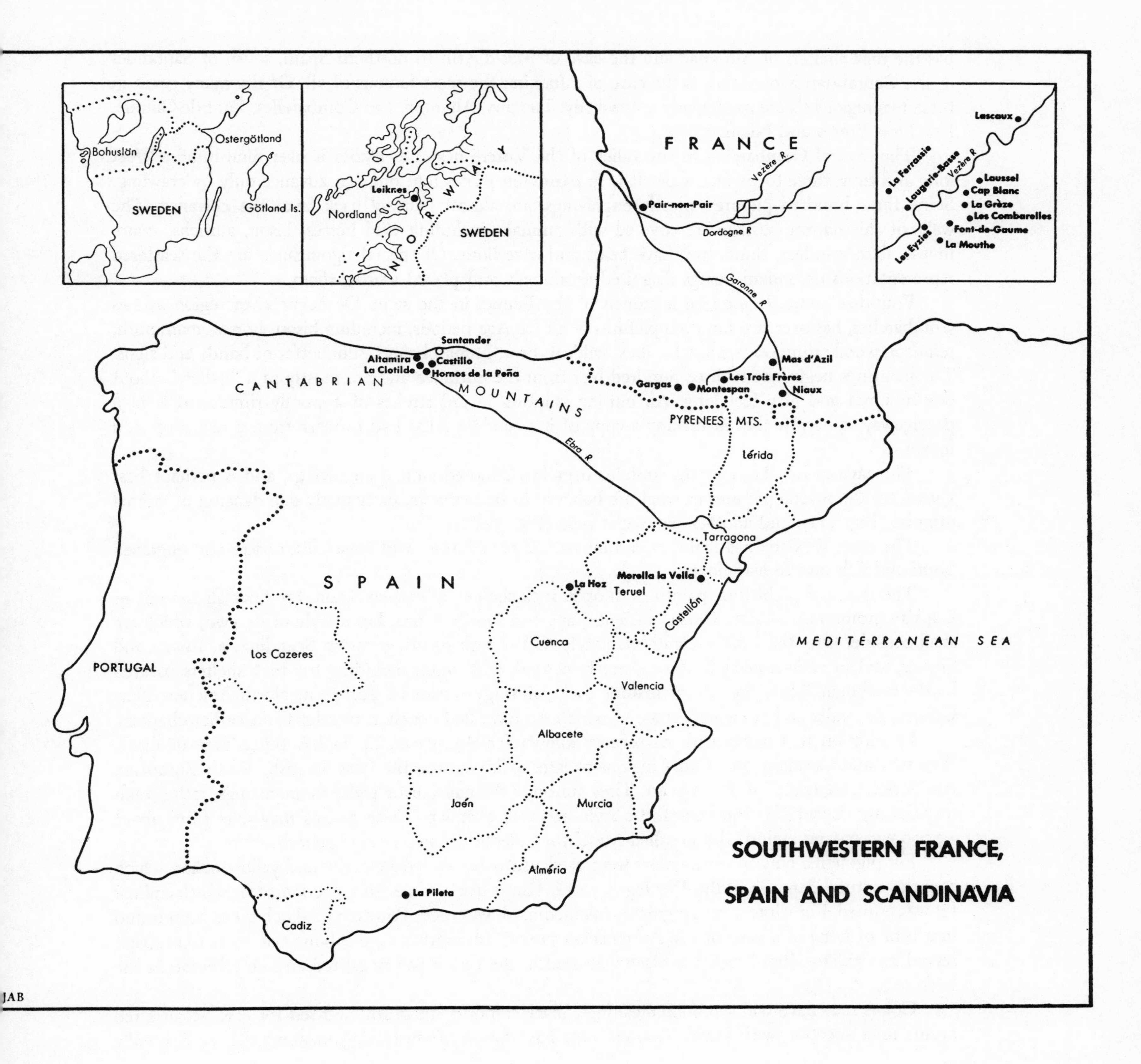
Bohuslän
Ostergötland
SWEDEN
Götland Is.
Leiknes
Nordland
NORWAY
SWEDEN
FRANCE
Vezère R.
Pair-non-Pair
Dordogne R
Garonne R
Lascaux
La Ferrassie
Laugerie-Basse
Vezère R
Laussel
Cap Blanc
La Grèze
Les Combarelles
Font-de-Gaume
Les Eyzies
La Mouthe
Santander
Altamira
Castillo
La Clotilde
Hornos de la Peña
CANTABRIAN MOUNTAINS
Gargas
Montespan
Les Trois Frères
Mas d'Azil
Niaux
PYRENEES MTS.
Ebro R.
Lérida
Tarragona
SPAIN
La Hoz
Morella la Vella
Teruel
Castellón
MEDITERRANEAN SEA
PORTUGAL
Los Cazeres
Cuenca
Valencia
Albacete
Jaén
Murcia
Almería
La Pileta
Cadiz
SOUTHWESTERN FRANCE, SPAIN AND SCANDINAVIA
JAB

has the rock shelters of Aurignac and the cave of Mas-d'Azil. In northern Spain, south of Santander in the Cantabrian Mountains, is the cave of Altamira, the most famous of all. Of the many caves in these two regions six are particularly noteworthy: Lascaux, Altamira, Les Combarelles, Font-de-Gaume, Les Trois Frères and Niaux.

The cave of Combarelles in the valley of the Vezère near Les Eyzies is over nine hundred feet long and from three to six feet wide. It is so narrow in places that one can advance only by crawling. Some three hundred pictures, mostly engravings, are almost halfway back from the entrance. The walls of this narrow passage are covered with animals, including wild horses, bison, aurochs, mammoths, ibex, reindeer, rhinoceros, cave bears and cave lions. Of special significance are the scattered representations of human beings disguised as animals and placed among them.

Font-de-Gaume, located on a branch of the Beune, in the same Dordogne river region as Les Combarelles, has over two hundred pictures of all Ice Age periods, including bison, horses, mammoth, reindeer, woolly rhinoceros, aurochs, ibex, wildcat, bear, human beings, silhouettes of hands and signs. The paintings begin about three hundred feet from the entrance and are mostly in a "gallery" about one hundred and fifty feet long. An outline painting in red strokes of a woolly rhinoceros is in a passageway so narrow that in making a copy of it a modern artist had to work from a reflection in a mirror.

The cave of Les Trois Frères contains over five hundred animal engravings, and is perhaps best known for the several pictures of what are believed to be sorcerers, particularly one dancing in animal disguise (Fig. 321), and another blowing a pipe (Fig. 322).

The cave of Niaux has many important paintings of bison, wild horses, ibex, deer and engraved bison and fish on the clay floor.

The group of prehistoric paintings in open rock shelters in eastern Spain, the Spanish Levant, or Capsian group, named after Gafsa (ancient Capsa) in North Africa, has a style of its own, which we shall consider after the Franco-Cantabrian style. Other rock paintings are in Scandinavia, Russia and Siberia, and in various areas in Africa, north, central, and south, including the rock shelters painted by the Bushmen. There are also prehistoric rock paintings outside of Europe in North America, New Guinea, Australia and elsewhere, some of which we have had occasion to refer to in earlier chapters.

In addition to France, with its seventy known Ice Age caves, Spain has thirty-three or more, Italy two, and Germany one. Other regions of later rock pictures, the East Spanish, North European, and African, are related to Ice Age art. They continue the naturalistic styles in engravings, rather than in paintings. Eventually the naturalistic style becomes abstract. These groups may date from about 10,000 B.C. on and include the so-called Mesolithic, Neolithic, and Bronze periods.

For pigments, natural earth colors were used; red ocher or red hematite and yellow ocher, which occur as natural deposits in the Dordogne caves. Lamp black came from the lamps in which animal fat was burned. For white, a rare pigment, calcined marl, was used. Powdered red ocher has been found in a tube of bone in a cave of the Aurignacian period. In another cave a bone has been found that served as a palette. Breuil believes black was used in the earlier paintings, red and polychrome in the later ones.

Colors may have had symbolic meanings, black standing for death, and red for life. Because red occurs in connection with burial sites, red may have had a life-sustaining meaning. There is usually

Ill. 36 (right). Lines drawn in clay with a toothed implement. Length of panel, ca 18 in. Altamira cave, Spain. *"Four Hundred Centuries of Cave Art," Breuil-Boyle-Windels,* (1952).

Ill. 37 (center). Herd of reindeer, engravings on bow, ca 4 in. long, from Teyjat, south France, late Magdalenian period. *Courtesy, American Magazine of Art. University of Minnesota.*

Ill. 38 (below). Painted ceiling at Altamira, Spain. *After Breuil. "Prehistoric Cave Paintings," by Max Raphael, Pantheon Books* (1945).

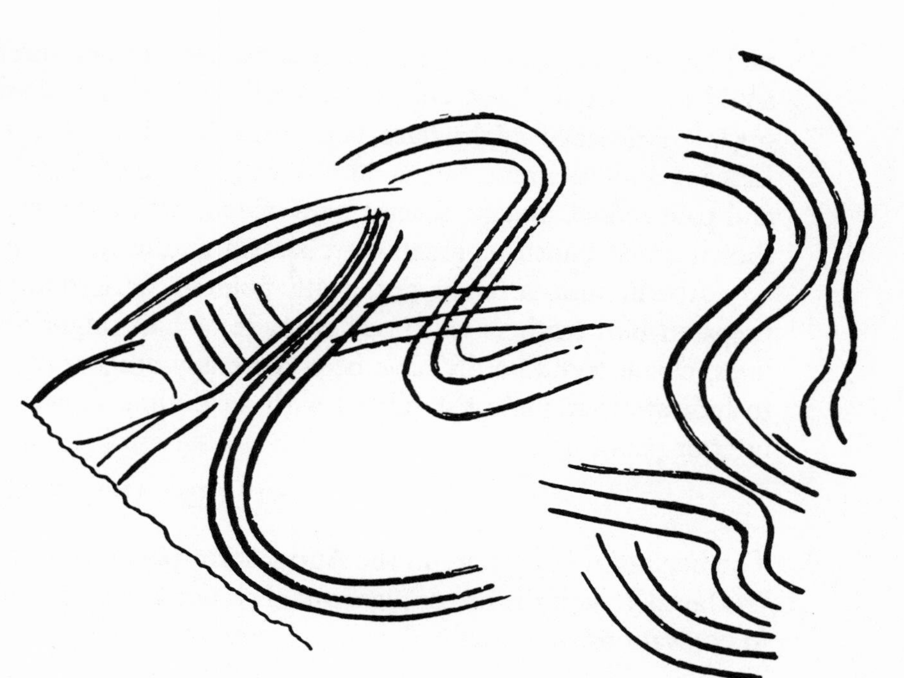

no blue or green, but as the prehistoric painter seemed interested in animals and not in landscapes, he could do without these colors. However, it is also possible that green and blue pigments made of organic substance might have been used in other cases and faded out with time. Purple occurs at Lascaux and Altamira, but is rare. A wide range of colors is seen in the Noilles cave, where brilliant and pale yellow, orange, several hues of red, dark and purple browns, blue and greenish blacks occur, showing that bluish pigments were known and in this case have survived.

At Altamira earth crayons, neatly pointed, were found lying on a stone bench. For actual painting prepared bird feathers and brushes made of hair might also have been used, especially for very thin lines, which could hardly have been done any other way. Some unfinished paintings at Lascaux seem to indicate that the artist started with an outline drawing, which disappeared during the process of interior painting.

STYLES AND PERIODS

The beginnings of art are in the Aurignacian period, but during the preceding Mousterian period man was familiar with the use of pigments. It is not known for what purpose pieces of coloring matter found in excavations were used, whether for cosmetics, body painting, or for use on walls or on implements. Though isolated examples of bones and stone slabs showing traces of pattern and paintings have been found in France, Germany and Czechoslovakia, on sites earlier than the late Paleolithic period, Breuil and Obermaier place the earliest art in the middle Aurignacian period.

The evolution of engraving and painting can be demonstrated accurately and objectively by comparing pictures known to be early from the positions in which they occur in the various layers on the walls. As the same rock surfaces were painted over and over again, one painting superimposed on top of the other, the lowest painted layer must be the earliest. On such a basis hand silhouettes (Fig. 313) and finger-drawn or painted lines (Ill. 36) stand at the beginning before any pictures of animals. They were followed by simple engraved or painted contours of animals, showing only the legs on the near side (Fig. 314). As the development progressed lines tended to become less rigid and strokes began to vary between thick and thin. On some examples contours broadened to cover parts of the animal and in others the whole animal was painted over.

Gradually the style changed from a hard, continuous profile with two front legs only, to a free posture, showing legs and horns virtually correct. The silhouette lost its sharp contour and merged with interior modeling. The animals adhere to side views; there are no front, rear, or three-quarter views in the European Paleolithic period.

Engravings and paintings were found side by side, but engraving is the preferred technique, producing superior examples into the late Magdalenian period, as in the mammoth at Font-de-Gaume (Fig. 315), and the reindeer at Teyjat (Ill. 37). Painting reached its fullest development in the middle Magdalenian at Altamira (Ill. 38). After this climax of a realistic style, simplification set in; it progressed to more stylized forms and finally ended in an ornamental pattern-like style in the Neolithic and Bronze periods. In prehistoric painting we cannot ascribe a particular painting to a specific date. We can distinguish which is earlier and which is later, but we cannot say how much earlier or how much later.

The relative chronology of periods and styles within the whole late Paleolithic period is fairly

Fig. 268. Melanesian painting with bird motifs, in black, red and white; Middle Sepik River *für Völkerkunde, Basel, Switzer-* region, New Guinea. *Museum land.*

Fig. 269. Melanesian float in shape of a frigate bird, inlaid with mother-of-pearl, Solomon Islands. L. 21¼ in. *Collection, Lt. John Burke, U.S.N.R. Photo: Museum of Modern Art.*

Fig. 270. Melanesian mortuary figure, Dutch New Guinea. H. 12 in. *University Museum, Philadelphia.*

Fig. 271. Melanesian wooden mask (*korovar* style), central New Britain. *Chicago Natural History Museum.*

Fig. 272. Melanesian female figure (*korovar* style), Trobriand Islands, Massim area, New Guinea. H. 16 in. *Peabody Museum of Salem, Massachusetts.*

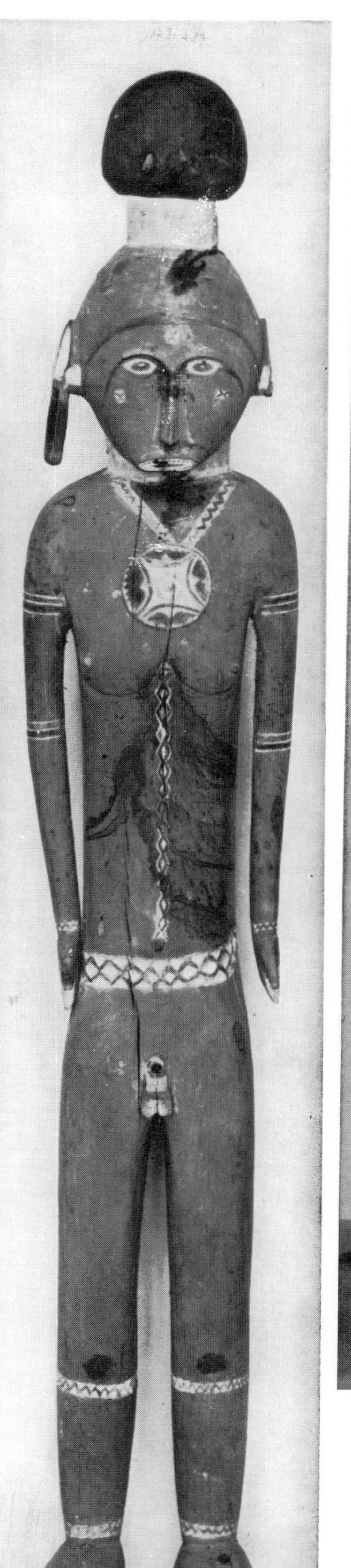

Fig. 273. Melanesian canoe prow ornaments, seated human figures (*korovar* style), Solomon Islands. H. 13½ in. *Chicago Natural History Museum*. Fig. 274 (right). Melanesian male figure (*tami* style), Admiralty Islands. H. 60 in. *Chicago Natural History Museum*. Fig. 275 (extreme right). Melanesian female figure (*korovar* style), Solomon Islands. H. 24 in. *University Museum, Philadelphia*.

Fig. 276 (top left). Melanesian *uli* figure (*uli* style), central New Ireland. *Brooklyn Museum*. Fig. 277 (lower left). Melanesian mask, wood with fiber top, New Ireland. H. 18 in. *Denver Art Museum*. Fig. 278 (middle). Melanesian ceremonial stool, Sepik River region, New Guinea. H. 6½ ft. *University Museum, Philadelphia*. Fig. 279 (right). Melanesian mask, Sepik River region, New Guinea. *University Museum, Philadelphia*.

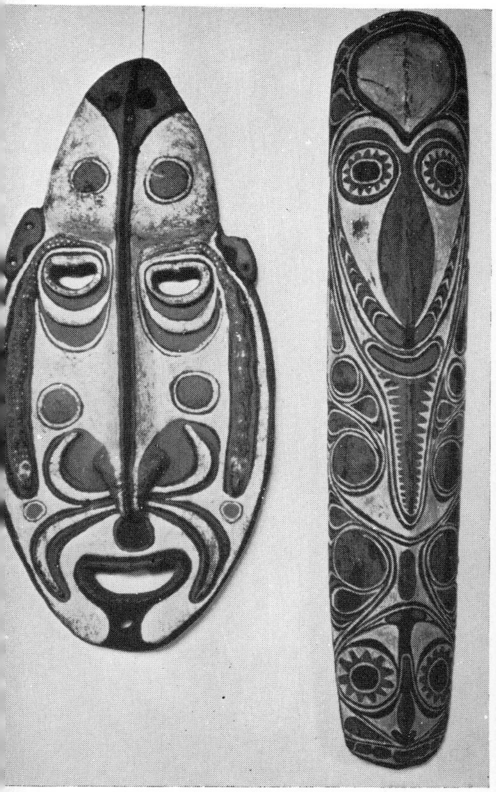

Fig. 280. Melanesian gable ornaments, Sepik River region, New Guinea. *University Museum, Philadelphia.*

Fig. 281. Melanesian dance mask covered with bark cloth, Gulf of Papua, New Guinea. *Collection, Mr. and Mrs. Ralph Altman, Los Angeles.*

Fig. 282. Melanesian figure, Sepik River region, New Guinea. H. 18½ in. *University Museum, Philadelphia.*

Fig. 283 (right). Melanesian figure surmounted by a frigate bird, Sepik River region, New Guinea. *Washington University, St. Louis, Missouri.*

Fig. 284. Melanesian wood-carved head, Sepik River region, New Guinea. *University Museum, Philadelphia.* Fig. 285 (above, right). Bark cloth mask, Baining tribe, Gazelle Peninsula, New Britain. H. 18 in. *Chicago Natural History Museum.* Fig. 286 (right). Melanesian design, tortoise-shell mask, Torres Straits. H. 14 in. *Philadelphia Commercial Museum.*

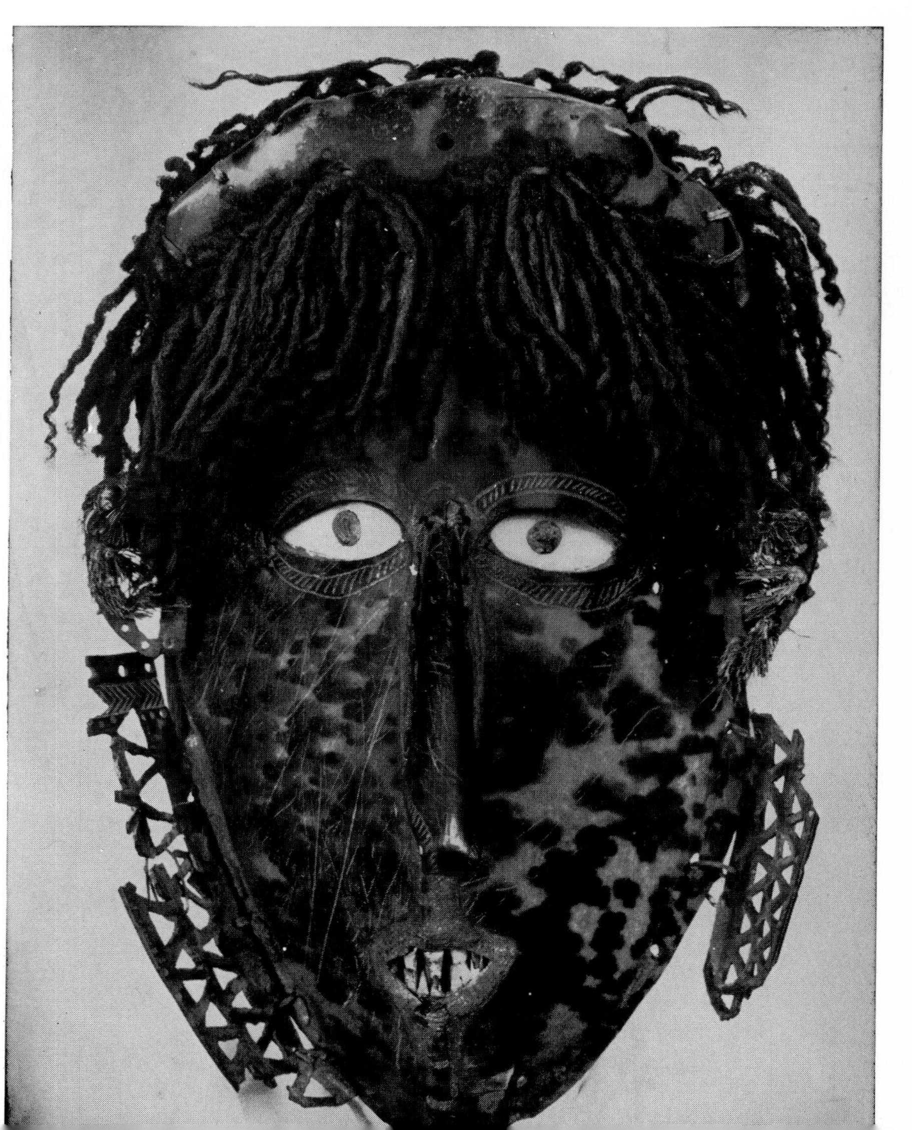

Fig. 287. Melanesian doorpost, New Caledonia. *British Museum.*

Fig. 288 (right). Melanesian pottery water jar, painted red, yellow ocher, black and white, middle Sepik River region, New Guinea. H. 27½ in. *Museum für Völkerkunde, Basel, Switzerland.*

Fig. 289 (extreme right). Micronesian female figure, Nukuoro. *Honolulu Academy of Arts, Hawaii.*

Fig. 292 (left). Polynesian sculpture, figure of a war god. H. ca 6½ ft. *Peabody Museum of Salem, Massachusetts.*

Fig. 293 (below). Polynesian featherwork on wicker, with dogs' teeth and composite eyes of shell and wood, representing the war god Kukailimoku, Hawaiian Islands. *British Museum.*

Fig. 290 (top left). Micronesian house mask, Mortlock Island. *University Museum, Philadelphia.*

Fig. 291 (left). Micronesian coconut grater, Mariana Islands. H. 24½ in. *American Museum of Natural History.*

Fig. 294 (above). Polynesian game board (konane), Hawaiian Islands. *Collection, Mrs. Vaid McHattie Forbes, Honolulu. Photo: Honolulu Academy of Arts.*

Fig. 295 (extreme right). Polynesian design, female figure from Hawaii. H. 27 in. *Collection, Mrs. Vaid McHattie Forbes, Honolulu. Photo: Honolulu Academy of Arts.*

Fig. 296 (right). Polynesian tapa from Hawaiian Islands. *Peabody Museum of Salem, Massachusetts.*

Fig. 297 (top). Polynesian stone images on outer slope of Ranoraraku, Easter Island. *Photo: American Museum of Natural History.* Fig. 298 (extreme left). Polynesian ancestral figure, Easter Island. H. 17 in. Fig. 299 (center). Polynesian stone sculpture, tiki, Marquesas Islands. H. 8 in. Fig. 300 (right). Polynesian sculpture, head of a war club, ironwood, Marquesas Islands. Total with handle, ca 5 ft. long. *University Museum, Philadelphia.*

Fig. 301 (above). Polynesian sculpture, carved head showing tattooing, Maori, New Zealand. H. 9 in. *Chicago Natural History Museum.* Fig. 302 (extreme right). Polynesian wood-carved figure, from a Maori chief's home, New Zealand. *British Museum.* Fig. 303 (right). Polynesian sculpture, carved house post, Maori, New Zealand. H. 47 in. *Royal Ontario Museum of Archaeology, Toronto.*

Fig. 304 (left). Polynesian sculpture, lintel fragment, Maori, New Zealand. *University Museum, Philadelphia.*

Fig. 305 (above). Polynesian sculpture, Maori carving, New Zealand. *New Zealand Embassy, Washington, D. C.*

Fig. 306 (below). Polynesian sculpture, canoe prow, Maori, New Zealand. *University Museum, Philadelphia.*

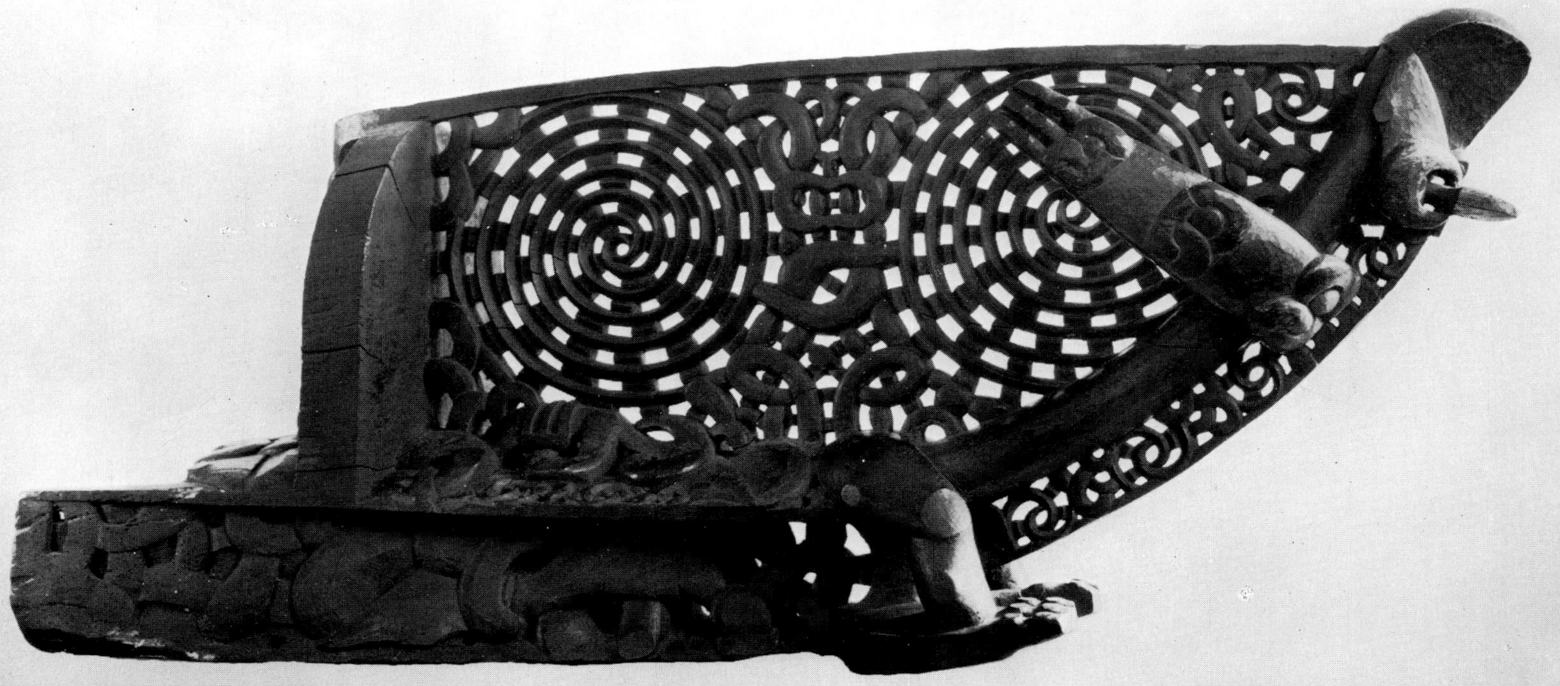

Fig. 307 (right). Polynesian sculpture, carved section of a house post, Maori, New Zealand. *Smithsonian Institution.*

Fig. 309 (below). Australian rock painting, representing the Lightning Brothers, Yagtchadbulla, Teabuinji and the latter's wife, Karnanda (under his arm), after the original at the Lightning Totem Center near Delamere, North Australia, after Davidson (1936). *American Philosophical Society, Philadelphia.*

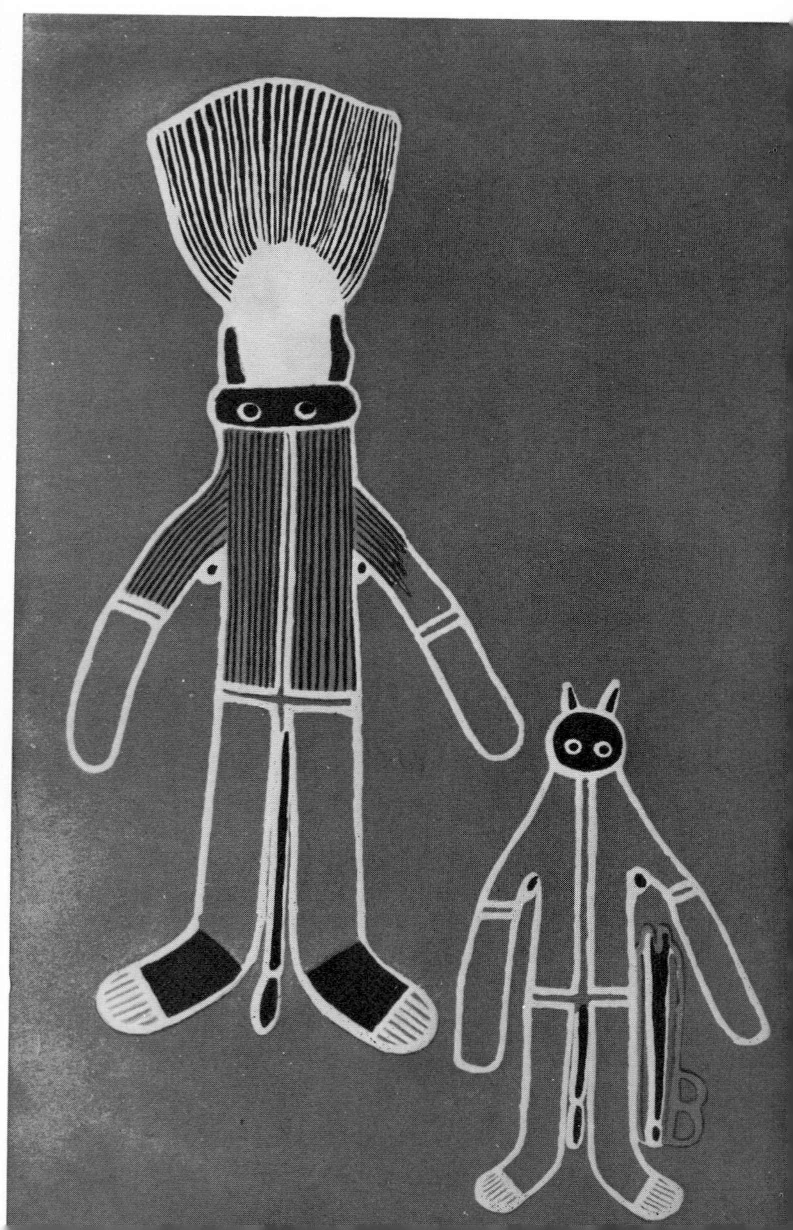

Fig. 308 (below). Polynesian sculpture, greenstone (nephrite) neck ornament (hei-tiki), Maori, New Zealand. *Peabody Museum of Salem, Massachusetts.*

Fig. 310. Australian bark painting of two crocodiles and one wallaby, in red, white and yellow on black, painted by Banjo of Umba Kumba, Groote Eylandt, Northern Territory. Collected by Frank M. Setzler. *Smithsonian Institution.*

Fig. 311 (left). Australian bark painting, "The Turtle Hunt." Collected by Charles P. Mountford, Arnhem Land Expedition.

Fig. 312 (below). Australian bark painting, hunting scene by Mauwunboi. Collected by R. and C. Berndt in N. E. Arnhem Land, 1946-1947. Department of Anthropology, University of Sydney. *Photo: Australian News and Information Bureau, New York.*

Fig. 313. Hands stenciled in red; superimposed bison in yellow are of a later Aurignacian period, cave at Castillo, Spain. *"Four Hundred Centuries of Cave Art," Breuil-Boyle-Windels (1952).*

Fig. 314. Rock engraving, bison in profile, at La Grèze (Dordogne), France. *Photo: Caisse Nationale des Monuments Historiques, Archives Photographiques, Paris.*

Fig. 315 (below). Rock paintings of mammoth and bison from the cave of Font-de-Gaume, Dordogne, France. *From a pastel by H. Breuil. Photo: Institute de Paléontologie Humaine, Paris.*

Fig. 316. Horse with flying arrows, Lascaux cave, France. L. ca 4½ ft. *Photo: Caisse Nationale des Monuments Historiques, Archives Photographiques, Paris.*

Opposite: Fig. 317. Head of the large bull at Lascaux cave, France. *"Four Hundred Centuries of Cave Art," Breuil-Boyle-Windels (1952).*

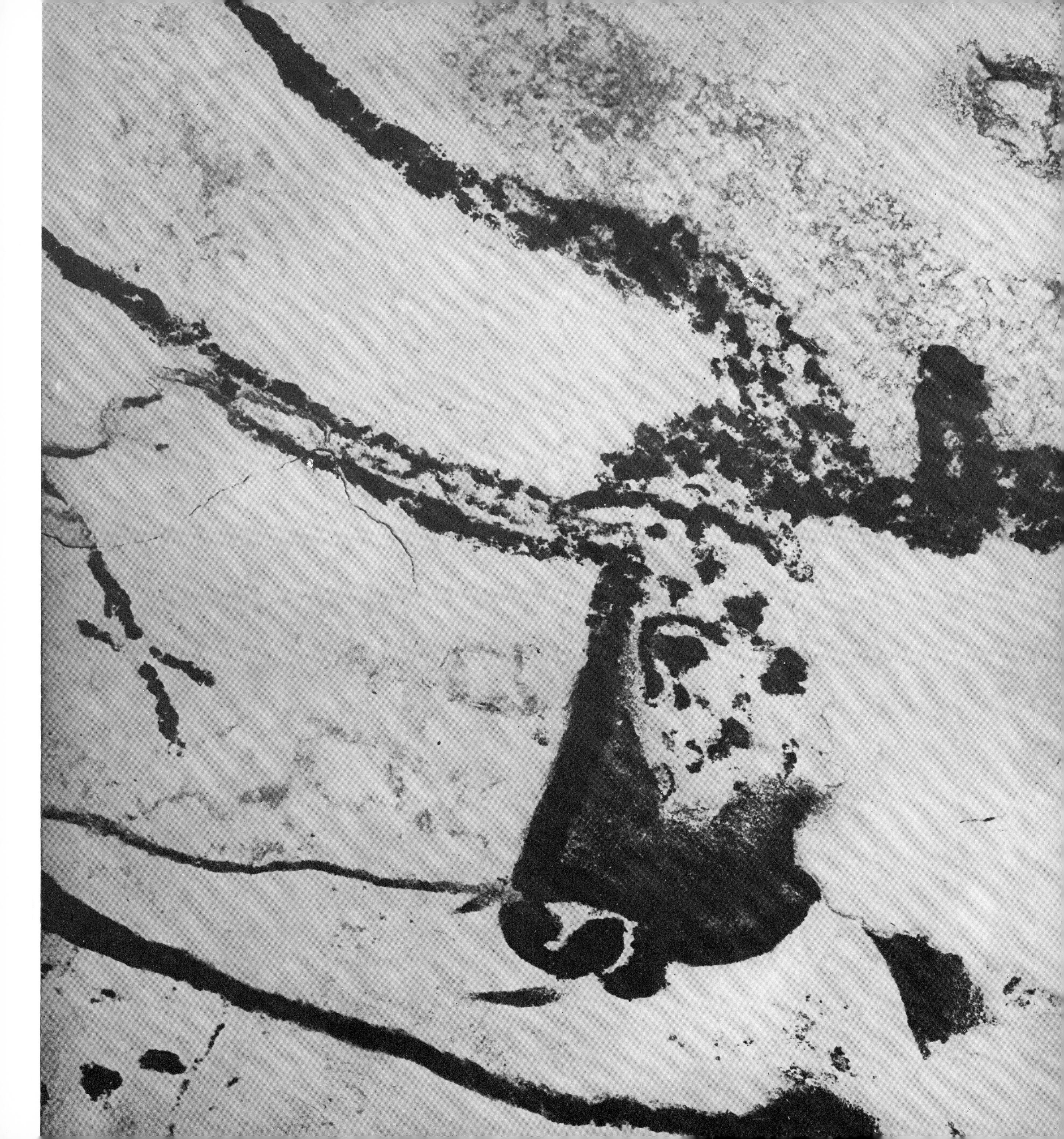

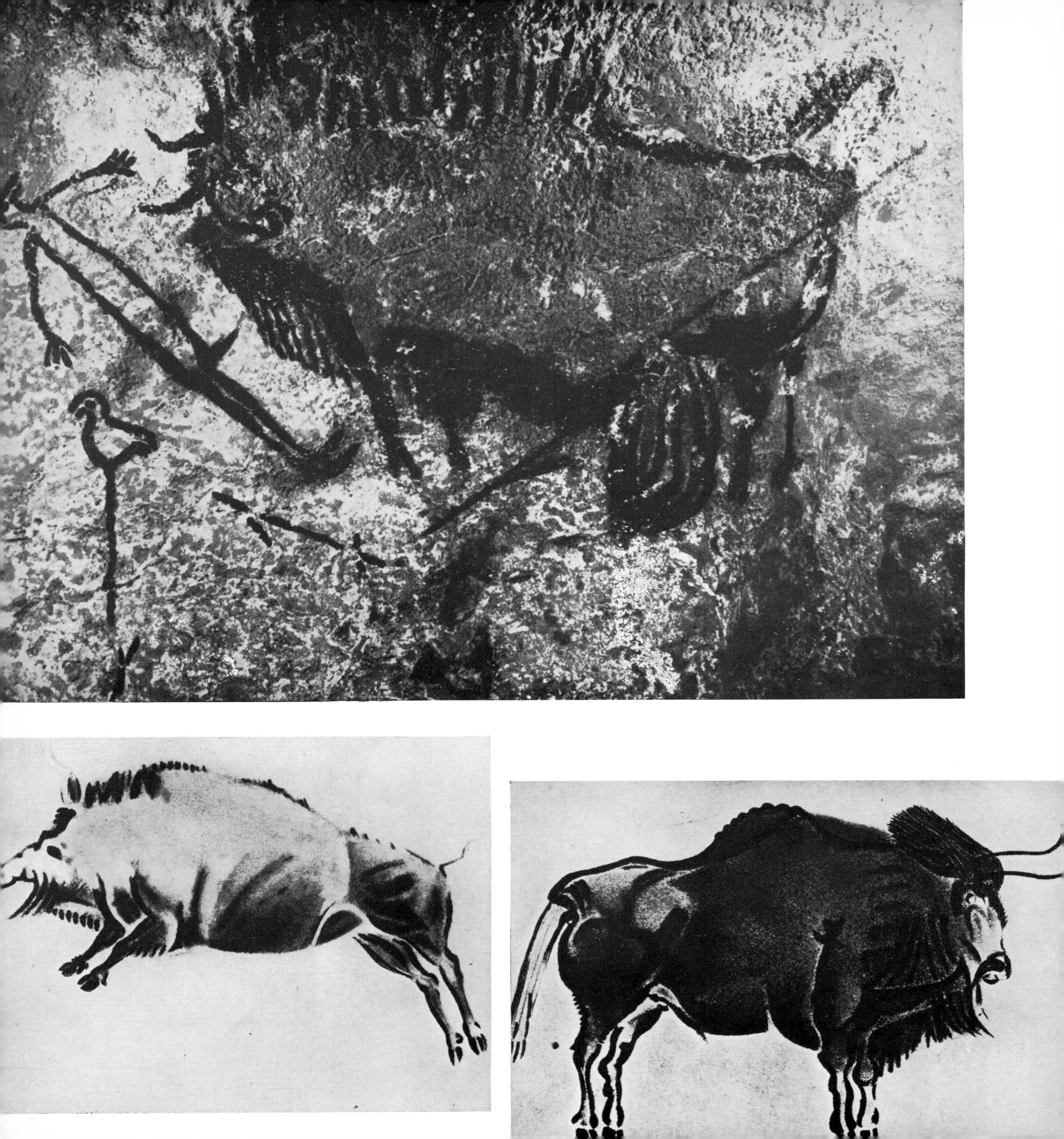

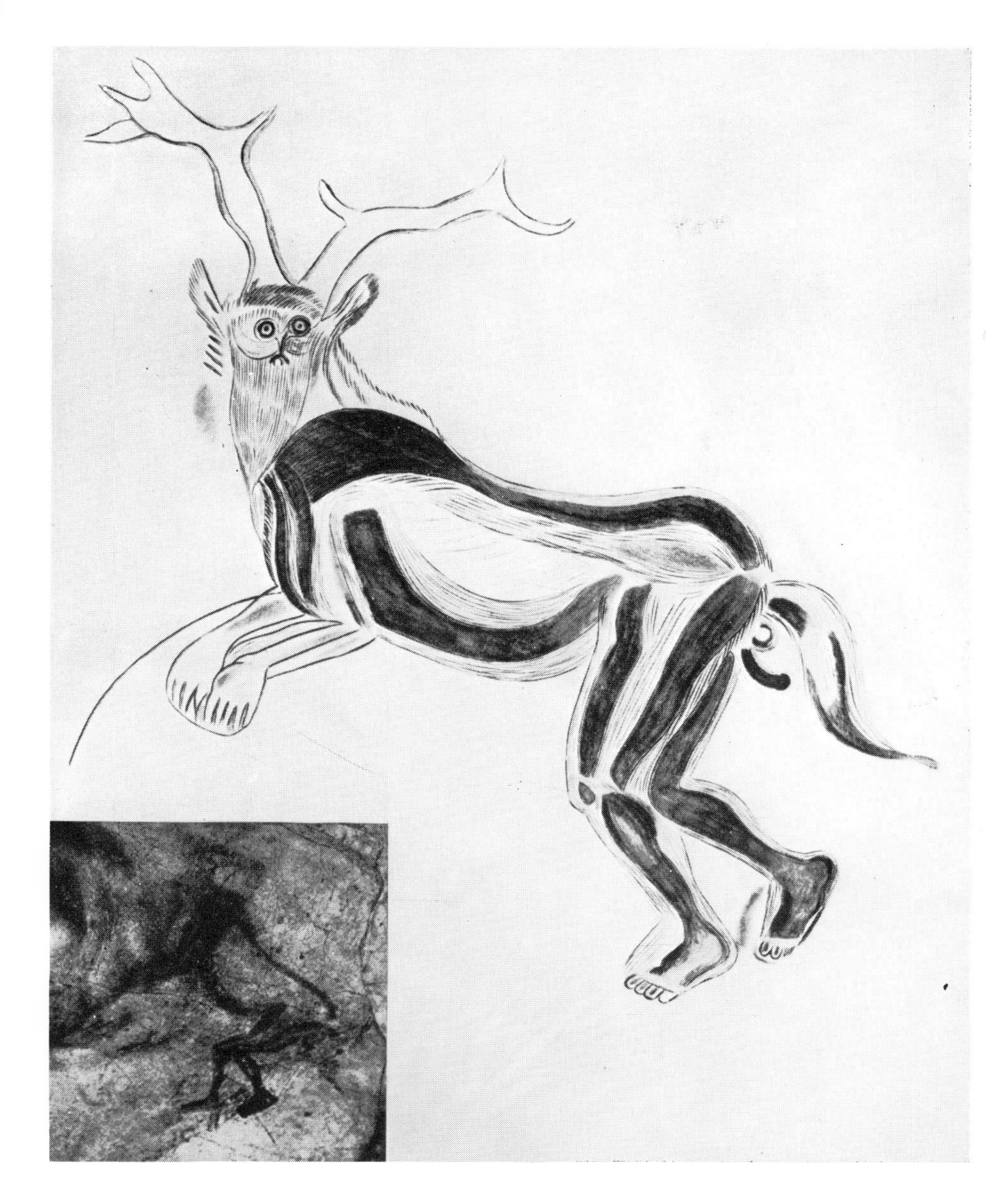

Fig. 321. Painting of a "sorcerer," a figure in a stag's pelt and with a horse's tail, at the cave of Les Trois Frères, France. *"Four Hundred Centuries of Cave Art," Breuil-Boyle-Windels (1952).*

Fig. 322 (below). Rock painting, or "sorcerer," from the cave of Les Trois Frères, France. *"Four Hundred Centuries of Cave Art," Breuil-Boyle-Windels (1952).*

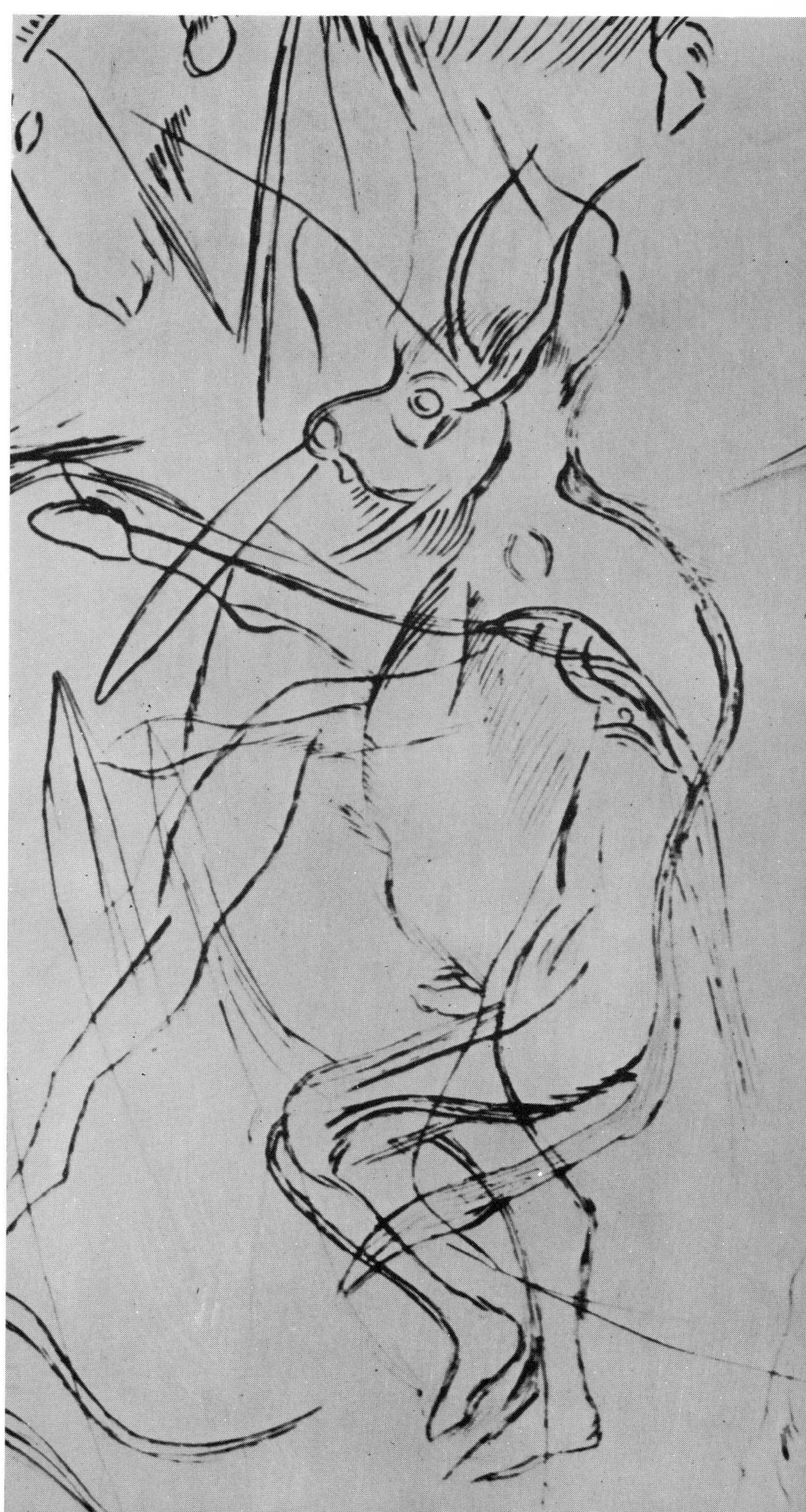

Opposite page:

Fig. 318 (top). Gorged bison, man and bird on post, Lascaux cave, France. *Photo: Caisse Nationale des Monuments Historiques, Archives Photographiques, Paris.*

Fig. 319 (lower left). Galloping wild boar, Altamira cave, Spain. L. ca 5 ft. *Photo: Caisse Nationale des Monuments Historiques, Archives Photographiques, Paris.*

Fig. 320 (lower right). Bison standing, Altamira cave, Spain. L. ca 5 ft. *Photo: Caisse Nationale des Monuments Historiques, Archives Photographiques, Paris.*

Fig. 323 (above). Two elks, rock engravings, at Jämtland, Sweden. *Frobenius Collection, Frankfurt am Main, Germany.*

Fig. 324. Brown bear, polished rock engraving, after a facsimile reproduction, from Valle near Lödingen, Nordland, Norway. *Museum of Modern Art.* L. 7½ ft.

Fig. 326 (right). Rock painting of running bowmen, from Cueva Saltadora, Valtorta Gorge, East Spanish style. Upper right figure, H. 4¼ in., W. ca 5½ in. *Photo: Frobenius Institute, Frankfurt am Main, Germany.*

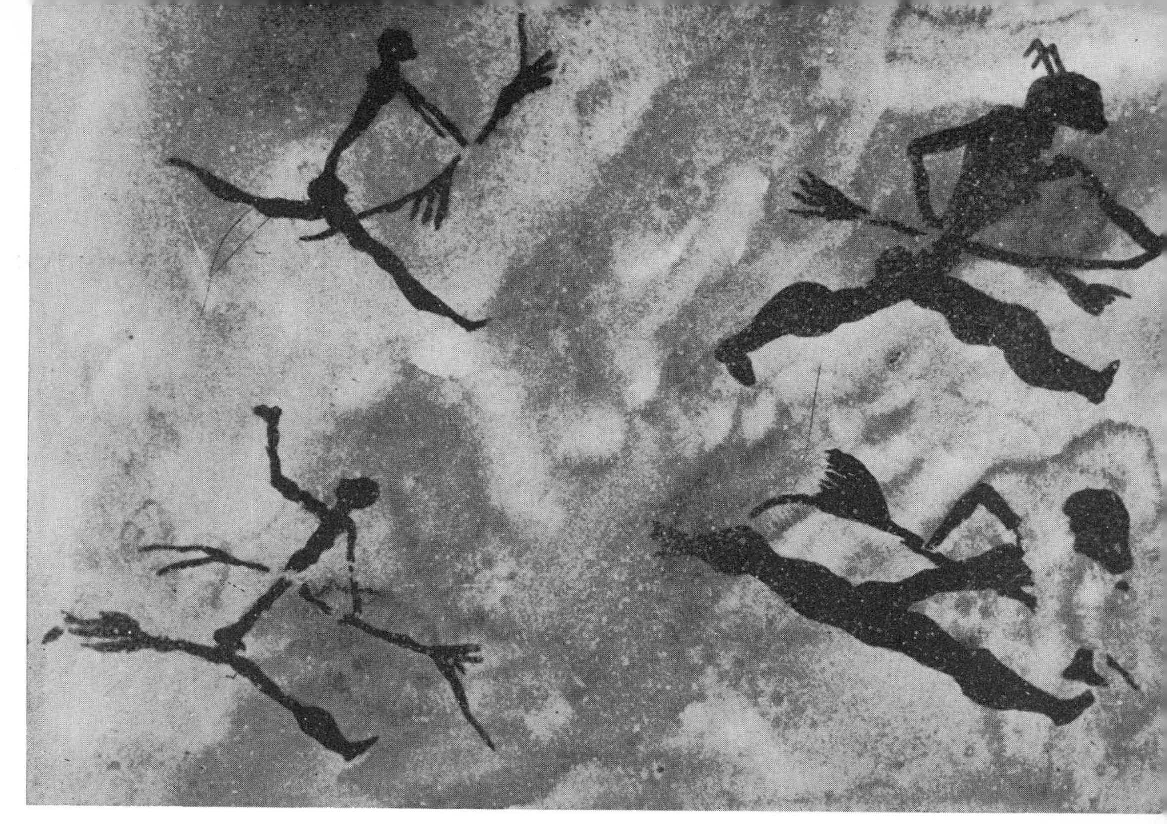

Fig. 325 (above). Aurignacian sculpture, "Venus of Willendorf." H. 4½ in. *Photo: Naturhistorisches Museum, Vienna.*

Fig. 327. Rock painting of a bowman, from Cueva Saltadora, Valtorta Gorge, East Spanish style. *Photo: Frobenius Institute, Frankfurt am Main, Germany.*

Fig. 328 (above). Rock painting of masked warriors, La Mola Remigia shelter, Gasulla Gorge (Castellón), East Spanish style. *Transatlantic Arts, Inc., New York.*

Fig. 329 (left). Rock painting, Cueva Más del Joseph, Valtorta Gorge (Castellón), East Spanish style. *Photo: Frobenius Collection, Frankfurt am Main, Germany.*

Opposite: Fig. 330. Rock engravings, naturalistic style, North Africa, in Habeter, Fezzan. *Photo: Frobenius Institute, Frankfurt am Main, Germany.*

Fig. 331 (right). Rock painting, representing a fight for a bull, from Khargur Tahl, Uwenat Hills, Libyan Desert, North Africa, after Frobenius Collection facsimile. *Photo: Museum of Modern Art.*

Fig. 332 (below). Rock painting, adoration scene, Wadi Sora, Libyan Desert, North Africa. H. 6 in., W. 12½ in. *Frobenius Collection, Frankfurt am Main, Germany.*

Fig. 334 (above). Rock painting, Kafirs running, Stormberg, South Africa. *After Stow and Bleek (1930).*

Fig. 333 (left). Rock painting, battle between animal-headed bowmen, from Ain Dua, Libyan Desert, North Africa. *Frobenius Institute, Frankfurt am Main, Germany.*

Fig. 335 (left). Rock painting, Bushmen driving off cattle pursued by Kafirs. *After Stow and Bleek (1930).*

Fig. 336 (below). Rock painting, Kafirs pursuing Bushmen driving off cattle. *After Stow and Bleek (1930).*

Fig. 337 (left). Rock painting from a slate grotto, Salt River Valley, Southern Kaoko Veldt, southwest Africa. *After Obermaier and Kühn. Photo: Humphrey Milford, Oxford University Press, London and New York.*

Fig. 338. Rock painting, hunting scene disturbed by a rhinoceros, at Naukluft, southwest Africa. *Museum of Modern Art.*

Fig. 339 (below). Rock painting, hunting scene from Marandellas, Southern Rhodesia, South Africa. *Frobenius Institute, Frankfurt am Main, Germany.*

Fig. 340 (below). Rock painting, hunting scene, Rhodesia, South Africa. *Denver Art Museum.*

Figs. 341 and 342. Rock paintings, animals, formlings and figures, Mtoko Cave, Southern Rhodesia, South Africa. *Frobenius Institute, Frankfurt am Main, Germany.*

Fig. 343 (below). Rock painting of a procession of men, from Sassa (Makaha Road), Southern Rhodesia. *Frobenius Institute, Frankfurt am Main, Germany.*

Opposite page:

Fig. 344 (top left). Rock painting, hunting scene from Mrewa, Southern Rhodesia, South Africa. *Frobenius Institute, Frankfurt am Main, Germany.*

Fig. 345 (top right). Neolithic pottery bowl, Lower Austria, ca 2500 B.C. *Photo: Naturhistorisches Museum, Vienna.*

Fig. 346 (bottom). Bronze Age rock engraving (1000 B.C.–500 B.C.) from *Bohuslän*, Island of Götland, Sweden. *Photo: Lars Jevbratt, Göteborg Art Museum, Göteborg, Sweden.*

Fig. 347. Bronze Age rock engraving (1000 B.C.–500 B.C.) from Bohuslän, Island of Götland, Sweden. *Photo: Lars Jevbratt, Göteborg Art Museum, Göteborg, Sweden.*

Fig. 348. Bronze Age rock engraving (1000 B.C.–500 B.C.) from Bohuslän, Island of Götland, Sweden. *Photo: Lars Jevbratt, Göteborg Art Museum, Göteborg, Sweden.*

definite. We have an example of rock pictures at La Grèze (Fig. 314), definitely known to be early, or of the Aurignacian period. When the cave was first discovered these pictures were still buried beneath Ice Age layers of the later Magdalenian and Solutrean periods. Ampoulange, the archaeologist, at work in the cave, had been searching for tools and utensils, and in the course of his excavations uncovered the hidden wall pictures. They could have been executed only at a time before the Solutrean and Magdalenian layers had accumulated, or, in other words, in the Aurignacian period. Excavations made in other caves, at Pair-non-Pair and at Gargas, also reveal clearly the character of the Aurignacian style. Incised drawings on reindeer horn show animals, ornaments and sex symbols; and drawings on other implements, like spear throwers, have been dated from the layers in which they were found. In turn, these styles have served to confirm the dates of other rock engravings where the dates of the layers were not assured by the place they occupied in the various superimpositions.

AURIGNACIAN ART

At La Grèze the animals are engraved in outline on the surface of the rock in a flat silhouette manner showing one front and one hind leg only. But along with contour engravings there are also polychrome paintings. Some animals are engraved, others painted, the two styles existing side by side. At this early stage there is no action, foreshortening or feeling for volume in either engravings or paintings.

What has proved to be the most important cave of Aurignacian paintings is the one found at Lascaux near Montignac, France, as recently as 1940. Four boys were looking for a lost dog. They dug innocently into a hole, and suddenly fell into this fantastic Paleolithic world. To their amazement they found rock-walled caverns covered with painted animals in huge friezes of bulls and horses, all of them colorful and lifelike. Other paintings attributed to the Aurignacian period have been found elsewhere in France and Spain, but these are quite often covered with the work of later artists of the Magdalenian period. The Lascaux paintings, however, on a pure white rock surface, are free from superimpositions and are in excellent condition. The good state of preservation is in part due, according to Breuil, to the fact that the warm air, condensing dew, does not penetrate the cave to the depth at which the paintings are located.

The paintings at Lascaux are more advanced than those at La Grèze, they have also more action and greater monumentality than the otherwise equally fine Magdalenian paintings of Altamira. The largest Lascaux paintings measure up to eighteen feet in length. Here bulls and galloping wild horses (Fig. 316) are drawn in broad outline but with little interior modeling. Fluent contours and broadly painted surfaces in flat tints establish for Lascaux a style different from the compact masses of the later Altamira paintings. The horses have small heads, short legs and heavy-set bodies. The indication of the horns is usually sensitive, and the structure of the joints of the animals' legs is well understood.

In some paintings there is a blurring of detail, as in animals' hoofs. This is part of a general softness of technique, due possibly to the use of dry powder applied with a blowgun (perhaps in the form of a hollow bone) rather than with a brush and liquid pigment. The combination of brush and blowgun technique is well illustrated in the painting of a pregnant wild horse. Contours and arrows are brush-drawn; head, mane and the broad surface across the body itself are rendered in soft tone apparently achieved by spraying on powdered pigment so that the dust settled on the damp surface.

Horses of two kinds, a short Shetland pony type and a larger type, are the most frequently painted animals at Lascaux. There are about sixty of them. In addition, Lascaux has about twenty paintings of oxen, several bison, a few deer and ibex, and one each of rhinoceros, wolf, bear, unicorn and bird. These animals of a temperate climate would fit either into the Aurignacian or the end of the Magdalenian period.

In this later Aurignacian period (also named by Breuil, the Perigordian period), represented by Lascaux, contours rather than interior modeling determine the effect. There is movement; all four legs of animals are represented, and the horns are more nearly in perspective. The drawing of the horns in what Breuil calls "twisted perspective," front rather than side view, was the criterion that led to the attribution of Lascaux as Aurignacian. The fact that this particular detail varies considerably at Lascaux has made the dating of Lascaux less certain, Windels admitting that the "Lascaux sequence will fit into the Magdalenian cycles as easily as into the Aurignacian."

The head of a large black bull (Fig. 317), in the great hall at Lascaux shows technique and drawing in a close-up view. An arrow has struck the muzzle, a throwing-stick is to the left of the horns. A broad, heavy contour describes the shape which is filled in with color. What control the painter had of his brush is seen in the way he indicated the horns, each with a curvature of its own, to differentiate between the foreshortened near horn and the horn on the far side of the head. The ragged edge is perhaps due to the uneven surface, the eye is in front view, as one would expect. Though styles differ from one cave to another, stylistic differences in the same cave are also discernible. The loose, fluffy lines of a running horse, for instance, are stylistically different from the strokes used in a "gorged bison" (Fig. 318), with its lowered head and backward-slanting legs. From the underside of the bison, entrails flow out in a huge, balloon-shaped mass. A lance is drawn across the hindquarters, a rhinoceros walks off to the left and a human figure, presumably the hunter, leans back with arms outspread. We could conclude that the lance or the rhinoceros nearby had dealt a fatal thrust to the bison and that the man had been killed. His head has been replaced by a mask or a bird, and a bird surmounts a vertical line, a stick or post close by.

The most recent and plausible explanation as to the meaning of this, offered by Horst Kirchner and quoted by Herbert Kühn, suggests a kind of shamanic incantation in which the shaman falls into a trance and in this condition experiences the killing of the animal. The bird on the post would be the embodiment of the spirit migration of the shaman in his trance. Kirchner points out that this shamanic act is still customary with Siberian tribes before the beginning of a hunt and that a bird is a symbol of the shamanic trance.

As this painting involves a group and represents a hunting incident, it could be another link to the second style of prehistoric painting, the East Spanish style, which represents groups of men with animals. Such incidental resemblances between Lascaux and the East Spanish style are well known. The figure in this painting (Fig. 318) is close to the East Spanish (Alpera) style, and the group of bison, man and bird is more definitely a composition, one of the few examples in the Franco-Cantabrian style, which departs from the practice of painting rows or friezes of animals.

Such friezes exist at Lascaux, Font-de-Gaume and elsewhere. At Font-de-Gaume, in the main gallery, is a polychrome frieze of bison over which later and smaller mammoth are engraved, as shown in Fig. 315. As the animals are superimposed, one over the other, it is difficult to see any single animal, and yet the group stands out in bold contours. Large masses and delicate outlines are effectively combined, and tusks, horns, hoofs and eyes are clearly visible. There is some deterioration which accounts for a lack of precision, as in places where the legs fade out. What is particularly impressive is the sense of confidence and mastery of the mighty sweeps in the lines of the backs drawn without hesitation. Of the six most important caves, three, Font-de-Gaume, Les Trois Frères and Altamira, have paintings and engravings of all periods.

MAGDALENIAN ART

Of the many thousands of engravings and paintings only a limited number have been studied. For every fine example there are many that are inferior or difficult to decipher. Individual animals are represented almost exclusively (Figs. 319 and 320) in the Franco-Cantabrian region. The human figure appears rarely, and then masked and in animal disguise. According to an inventory published by Herbert Kühn on the total number of representations of human beings in Paleolithic art, including engravings on bone and ivory, only some ninety-nine were listed. Considering the many engravings and paintings, this is a small percentage. Paleolithic painting began with the animal as the chief topic; man was incidental.

The same spaces, presumably sacred, were used over again by succeeding artists; hence, superimpositions are frequent. It may have taken thousands of years for painting to develop the skill and elaboration of the Magdalenian period. This style is best represented in the cave of Altamira. The paintings of Altamira were discovered in 1879, and as in the case of Lascaux, by chance.

When the Spanish archaeologist and landowner Don Marcelino S. de Santuola first entered this limestone cave, he completely overlooked some black pigment marks on the wall. The cave entrance had been discovered by a hunter in 1868; then, too, these marks had been disregarded. It was Don Marcelino's young daughter who, eleven years later, first noticed that the rough ceiling and walls were covered with paintings of animals. In prehistoric times, a landslide had evidently sealed the opening to the cave, with the result that the Altamira paintings are as fresh as if they had been painted yesterday.

At first people could not believe that the bison and wild boars at Altamira belonged to a period that ended ten thousand years ago. The painted animals seemed to be represented with so much action, details were so precise and the postures so lively that it seemed impossible the murals could be so old. Sceptics declared shepherds must have painted them in the more recent past. But it was not long before similar paintings were discovered in France, particularly in caverns at Font-de-Gaume and Les Combarelles. It then became clear that these paintings could not be recent, because frequently they were covered with incrustations that formed transparent layers over the pigment.

The Magdalenian style of Altamira is based on the effect of mass and depth entirely replacing sharp contours; line is no longer a factor. Rigidly enclosed shapes give way to a style of rendering that uses spots and disconnected strokes to suggest changes in surface modeling; a sense of form replaces mere outlines that cling to profiles. The La Grèze bison of the Aurignacian style encourages the eye to follow the outline which is the only element that describes the animal; at Lascaux we have an impression of the whole animal, contour and interior surface, and at Altamira the paintings show still more gradations of modeling and color.

The principal paintings at Altamira are on the ceiling of the entrance vestibule, in what might be called the "Picture Gallery." Here the uneven rock surface is covered closely with animals, chiefly bison, close to life-size. These paintings extend over a length of more than forty feet.

The colors are remarkably fresh; whatever soot from torches, lamps or hearths that might have settled on the paintings has disappeared in the course of time through oxidation. In the moist atmosphere of the cave the pigments seem to have been applied thickly and are damp to the touch. They were painted on a damp wall, and this resulted in their preservation. The original paintings are, if anything, more brilliant than any reproductions that have yet been made.

The suggestion of spontaneity which the cave paintings have is in part due to the method employed. Modeling for form and painting for color were two operations, done more or less at the same time. Two techniques, direct and indirect, have been used throughout the course of history. In the indirect technique, modeling and color were applied in separate layers, probably the effect was attained directly by applying liquid pigment and dry pastels in the form of natural earths.

In a side view of the cave ceiling, when illuminated by a single electric light, shadows are cast by the boulder-like projections on which the animals are painted. Reproductions usually fail to bring out the relief effect and make the animals appear to be painted on a flat surface. The artist took advantage of this bumpy ceiling and painted an animal on each hummock, adapting the outlines of the animal as well as he could. The combination of painting and natural relief was certainly deliberate, presumably to produce a more lifelike effect. What strikes our eye, in a photograph or color reproduction, is the bulk of each animal, but we may not realize that each painted animal corresponds to a bulge of rock projecting from the ceiling.

In the paintings, heads all but disappear under the weight of flesh and fat. Most of the animals are standing, but they are not rigid or inert. Heads are lowered, more in some cases than in others; tails are either up or down, and in contours and proportions there is considerable variation. If we accept the traditional interpretation, four bison are painted as if lying down; one boar is running, but otherwise there is perhaps less suggestion of motion than was thought to be the case when the paintings were first seen by modern man. The legs of the standing animals, though well drawn, seem suspended from the body; partly because the hoofs have no ground to stand on. Curved horns, manes and tufts of hair, the formation of mouth, nostrils and the joints of hind legs—all such details are sensitively painted. There is some interior drawing in which black is used for outlines, a simplified means of suggesting modeling and roundness of form. There is extraordinary realism, considering the primitive tools used on a rough surface.

The raised head, the uplifted tail, the undulating line of the back and especially the suggestion of action in the farther front leg of the young bellowing bison (Color Plate 31) all suggest life. Contours are hard and reinforced by black where the bony structure comes to the surface. Elsewhere, the profile is kept soft to suggest fur and flesh. Flat and modeled portions are differentiated; there is a sense of volume and a feeling for anatomical structure. To our eyes this suggests stylization, combined with realism.

How the available space cramped the drawing is indicated by the unnatural forward placement of the hind legs of the bellowing bison. In the allover sketch of the ceiling (Ill. 38) it will be seen that the bison to the right takes up the available space. In the painting the bison turns his head back because there was not enough space left on the boulder for any other view. A desire to fit each animal as fully as possible to a boulder may explain, without prejudice to other explanations, the postures of four bison with legs drawn up to the body.

This searching of the surface for possibilities of relief effects may find its explanation in magic, which called for realistically rendered animals to make magic more potent. The basic idea of magic is the natural sympathy throughout the world between things that resemble each other. Like attracts like; what is done to one object will affect another distant object if the two resemble each other. Applying this notion to the animals the hunter wished to attract, he painted a near-life-sized bison on the cave ceiling on top of a projecting boulder so that this replica would have not only the visual appearance but also something of the bulk of a real bison. The artist was eager to give magic every chance to operate, and he made the resemblances between paintings and live animals as convincing as possible.

Since prehistoric man utilized natural reliefs where he found them, one would expect him also to have carved reliefs out of the rock. There are indeed a number of such reliefs of animals, and a few of human beings. There are genuine rock-carved reliefs on the walls of open rock shelters or half-caves and on large blocks of stone. They vary in size from about a foot and a half high, as in an Aurignacian female figure from Laussel, to horses seven feet long in the rock shelter of Cap Blanc, where four horses form a frieze about forty feet long. They belong to a small group of well-known Magdalenian reliefs of excellent quality. When first discovered, they still showed traces of red paint. Though engravings and paintings out-number reliefs, both natural and man-made, the fact that the Magdalenian painter at Altamira still took advantage of natural reliefs is an argument for magic. Artistically, the paintings would have been sufficient in themselves; the natural relief did not improve the art but contributed to the magic. Smooth surfaces do not seem to have been sought out by the artists; often projections in the rock were drawn into the picture, not only at Altamira, but in other caves as well. Such a projection is used for the back of a primitive ox in the cave of Covalanas, in the province Santander in Spain. Other examples have been reported from the caves at Nancy, Niaux, Mas d'Azil, Le Portel, Tuc d'Audoubert, Pinal, Hornos de la Peña and La Pasiega.

On the Altamira ceiling (Ill. 38), we note some twenty-five animals. In Altamira, as in other caves, the animals are unrelated to each other, with a few exceptions. There is no composition of any apparent artistic significance, and neither ground nor space is suggested. The animals are turned this way and that, so that some animals are difficult to relate to any imaginary observer or to each other. The placing of an animal may have depended on the position taken by the artist while drawing. As we shall see, this traditional point of view has been questioned more recently by Max Raphael, who has attempted to demonstrate for the Altamira ceiling not only a definite composition, but also a specific content. Even so, these paintings were probably not meant for spectators, though Altamira, like other caves, could have accommodated small gatherings for rituals. In a sense this places painting outside the realm of representative art in our sense of the word. Painting, as we know it, directs itself broadly to other human beings, and includes representation of space or is decorative. In the Ice Age caves, there was no room for any large audience, and a setting in space, and a decorative effect are also generally lacking.

Instead of this we have realistic relief-images affixed to the earth and intended presumably for the magic multiplication of the animals. Some deeply engraved strange beings, probably sorcerers, are no longer easily visible at Altamira. We get a clearer impression of this man-beast, sorcerer, in the cave of Les Trois Frères (Fig. 321) where a human figure, disguised as an animal, apparently participates in rituals connected with the abundance of the animals.

Supporting evidence for ritual dances was found in the cave of Tuc d'Audoubert by Herbert Kühn, who explored this cave accompanied by Count Begouen, the original discoverer. Penetrating cautiously into the unknown depths, sometimes by crawling, then again walking erect, they came upon the skeleton of a cave bear, stepped upon the skeleton of a snake, and, finally, noted footprints of human heels. The heel prints had been left there by men who lived thousands of years ago. These early discoverers may well have felt some of the awe and mystery that the Ice Age men experienced.

According to the evidence of the rock pictures, primitive religion in the form of magic began with sanctuaries in the form of caves and rock shelters set aside as holy places. Of the many caves, shelters and rock surfaces of France, Spain and Scandinavia, only certain ones were painted, most of them were not. Invariably, succeeding generations painted the same rocks in the same locations, presumably because the sites themselves were sacred. The caves are not only dark and gloomy, but there is about them something eerie and fear-inspiring. Shut off and separated from the outside world, the caves suggest secrecy and may have been open only to the few. Breuil and Kühn agree in stressing this religious aspect of the caves. The fact that the entrance was often narrow and difficult of access emphasizes that concealment was sought deliberately, even though the main "galleries" are more spacious. Today, the cave of Altamira has been provided with a new entrance and something of the original effect has been lost. The modern electric light installations necessarily reduce the uncanny effect the cave previously possessed.

That a religious atmosphere pervaded particular caves in various regions—France, Spain and Africa—may be indicated by the fact that natives today have at times refused to go near the caves for fear of the demonic power of the paintings. In the case of rock pictures at Lake Onega, between the Baltic and the White Sea, Christian monks, at some early date, painted crosses over the paintings to rob them of their power. Other caves, once heathen sanctuaries, were turned into Christian places of worship; Lourdes, in France, is perhaps the best known example. We should not assume that rock paintings were unknown until stumbled upon in our own period. Some rock paintings were known before our day and a tradition of their sacred character lingered on to more recent times. Thus, a religious intent can be demonstrated for rock paintings in Europe, Africa and no doubt elsewhere.

Some caves may even have served as art studios. At Limeuil a quantity of slabs, incised with animals, have been found, many small and some medium-sized. Various degrees of skill are shown; some have contours that appear to be corrections; others have the same head repeated, as if done by master and pupil. A three-inch slab of limestone with what looks like a sketch for a large bison three and one-half feet long, in the cave of Font-de-Gaume, was found two hundred miles away at Genière. The head of a hind engraved on a bone appeared as part of a finished painting on the cave wall at Altamira. The fact that the same types reappear on the paintings seems to indicate that the engraved bones served as sketches for paintings. It has been suggested that painting may have served as teaching material for magic in which the spoken word, music, dance and masks were involved (Fig. 322).

We may presume that the painters were aided by memory images. The artists, who were also hunters, probably had a capacity for eidetic, virtually identical, imagery. It is known that some hunters can recall with photographic clarity retinal images of animals seen during a hunt. Eidetic persons have been able to reactivate images after a week's lapse. This may help to explain how the prehistoric artist could paint in dark caves, only dimly lighted by primitive fat lamps. Boudon, who worked on prehistoric lamps, mentions more than ten lamps found in caves.

On the other hand, eidetic imagery does not explain prehistoric rock paintings. It could not have functioned as a mechanical device enabling the painting to come into existence like a transfer from retinal impression to cave wall. At best, we may assume that eidetic imagery was of some assistance to the painters.

MAGIC

We have indicated that painting served the purposes of religion, but other reasons have also been advanced as to why prehistoric man created these animal paintings and put them in such inaccessible places. It has been suggested that man painted to amuse himself, or possibly he wished to decorate his caves as we paper our walls. That this type of primitive art is primarily "art for art's sake" is the explanation offered by Hoernes and Boule, who believed that whatever magical beliefs existed became attached to paintings that were already in existence. That art may have been a leisure time activity is a theory that should not be discarded too hastily, even if it may not explain Altamira. But the fact that animal paintings were placed deep down in caves and crevices of the earth is difficult to understand. Perhaps this was done after more accessible wall spaces in caves and shelters had been used and any paintings placed near the cave entrances had long since disappeared. Against this stands the fact that many paintings are in such inaccessible places that lack of space is not convincing.

The most reasonable and most widely held theories so far advanced are that the paintings themselves, and the process of painting them, had a magical significance involving the animals which were hunted for food. Magic is here used in the sense of primitive religion. A magical explanation was first stated by S. Reinach and has been accepted with reservations by other scholars. Reinach contends that "the impulse behind art was bound to the development of magic."

A number of cave paintings show figures that have been thought to be "sorcerers," or medicine men. Such a figure, in the cave of Les Trois Frères, wears a stag's pelt and horse's tail, and is surrounded by animals. Posture and action suggest that he is participating in a ritual, or perhaps casting a spell over the animals rather than trying to ambush them. Luquet calls this sorcerer the chief piece of evidence in support of magical dances during the Magdalenian epoch. As recently as 1930 Obermaier and Kühn had reported thirty-four rock pictures of masked dancers.

It may be argued that the prehistoric hunter employed magical principles in his art in three ways: (a) to create new animals, or fertility magic; (b) to assist the hunter's aim, or death magic; (c) to appease dead animals, or propitiation magic.

The very fact that the painted animals were concealed in the depths of caves suggests that they were placed there for a purpose. Perhaps caves were considered as convenient points of access to the earth, the seat of fertility? To man the world over, the earth has been the source of life. The cave may have taken on a magical significance as a symbol of the womb, associated with fertility and the origin of life. Caves may have been sanctuaries in which primitive man painted in order to furthe· the creation of new animals for his food supply. The closer the contact between painting and cave, the more certain the magic. In support of the idea that caves had a fertility significance, it has been pointed out that engraved blocks of triangular female fertility symbols, of an early date, have been found in a cave, in a position facing downward (Levy).

As fertility magic was directed to the multiplication of the animals, so death magic was intended to assist the hunter in trapping and killing his prey. We find that in various caves javelins, spearheads and boomerangs were painted on animals, while lines standing for blood are shown coming from mouth and nostrils of a bear in the cave of Les Trois Frères. In the cave at Montespan a sculptured figure of a bear shows a number of holes, apparently representing wounds. An engraving of a horse in the same cave shows twenty-two arrow marks. These painted weapons and actual holes in the painted and carved animals suggest shooting at the paintings as a ceremonial exercise before the hunt. Moreover, the animals painted are mainly those that were hunted for food; cave lions and bears occur more rarely. Paintings may have existed before belief in magic caused the spears to be added, according to Hoernes.

Luquet argues that a magical intent can be assumed for only two specific groups; for those animals which show the painted weapons and for those which have intentional damages to the surface, which are believed to show that the animal was wounded. All others may well have been meant as artistic expressions and no more; there is nothing to prove a magical purpose. If prehistoric artists used animal drawings so that magic might bring them to life, they must have first had the idea of representation. Artists must therefore have existed before their pictures could be used for the purpose of magic.

We must now take another look at the composition of the Altamira ceiling (Ill. 38), which is generally accepted to be accidental. Raphael's interpretation of four bison at Altamira as part of a propitiation ceremony does not seem entirely plausible simply because the bison look more like lying down than being propped up. Their legs are drawn up close to the body; they are not used to support the body. The emphasis was perhaps not on resting but on the desirability of getting the whole bison onto the boulder. On the other hand, as Raphael has pointed out, an upright bison with what has been termed "votive offerings" is represented at Niaux. Here the hind legs are used to sit upon, they are not drawn up under the body as at Altamira (Ill. 39).

Perhaps for want of a better explanation the idea of resting bison (Ill. 38) has been followed, since it was first proposed. Though resting animals might be easier to kill, death magic is not represented as there are no painted weapons or actual holes on the Altamira animals.

The problem is made more difficult by the fact that Breuil's sketch leaves out the sorcerers or "anthropoids" who conceivably might be assigned the task of doing the actual propitiating. Without propitiators, the "propitiation" theory lacks the visual evidence. Another difficulty is the fact that Raphael's demonstration of a composition is based on drawings and ignores the actual relief of the ceilings. As we have pointed out, these boulders may have been significant. At best, one can only suggest plausible explanations, one cannot be too positive about any one theory; perhaps the truth lies between several of these interpretations.

Ill. 39. Rock painting of upright bison with votive offerings, Niaux Cave, France.
"Prehistoric Cave Paintings," by Max Raphael, Pantheon Books (1945).

To bring this discussion up to date, José Camón Aznar (1954) also points out that the bison turning his head is an attempt on the part of the artist to get the animal completely onto the boulder. Bison heretofore described as "resting" are explained as animals fleeing in fear. Whether the postures are interpreted as resting or leaping may be less important than the fact that they are closely identified with the boulder. For reasons of magic we believe this endeavor to suggest bulk may have been of basic significance.

ORIGINS OF ART

Even though painting and magic may have been closely connected, magic does not explain how drawing and painting originated. Art appears to be linked to man's need for religion; therefore, we have focused attention on the religious significance of the cave paintings and the secrecy which surrounded them. Other ideas as to the origins of art—as a desire for ornamentation, as a drive to imitate, as a play instinct—formerly projected on a theoretical basis, now have to be squared with the evidence of archaeology, in order to retain validity. What we know of prehistory as to the uses if not the origins of art favors religion as a strong motivation, without necessarily eliminating other causes.

Drawing may have originated accidentally by lines made by man playfully, comparable to the scribble stage of children's drawings. The recognition of accidental resemblances may have led to conscious efforts to produce resemblances to animals. Such man-made markings on cave walls have been found, and have been interpreted by Luquet as coming close to man's first attempts at drawing. Lines left by nature on rock surfaces at times suggest the shapes of animals. By adding a touch here and there, the hand of man could have completed the likeness. On the other hand, such additions could have been made at various times and may not relate to the origin of drawing.

The oldest interlaced lines at Hornos de la Peña, finger-drawn or drawn with a many-pronged tool, as at Altamira (Ill. 36), appear to be meaningless, but contours of oxen drawn with the finger on the clay surface in the caves of La Clotilde and at Hornos are purposeful attempts to create a resemblance to the animals. Stenciled hand silhouettes (as was shown in Fig. 313) in red and black, interlaced lines and primitive outlines of animals occur on clay-covered walls in numerous caves of Aurignacian dates, at Gargas, Castillo, Altamira (Ill. 40) and others. The hand silhouettes (Fig. 313) are mostly left hands; the right hand presumably was used to blow or spatter on the liquid coloring matter. The hands occur as groups or in rows; at Gargas 150 well-preserved hand silhouettes have been counted.

One view links hands to the magic significance of the hand which began in prehistory. Through his hand man dominated the animals. According to another view, the hand means "contact or prerogative" and not a dedication of the hand, as the means by which hunter or artist achieves his success, nor private ownership or achievement. Hand signs as indicating private ownership are ruled out only by an assumption that private ownership was "hardly understood at this stage of social development" (Levy). Various signs, though of no artistic interest, are significant as a kind of sign language that must have had a definite meaning. They appear on cave walls often in connection with painting. The stenciled hands belong to this group of signs; others are signs that may be conventionalized hands (pectiforms); weapons of various types (claviforms); and traps or huts or tribal emblems (tectiforms).

Hand silhouettes, the earliest cave paintings, if they can be called paintings, gradually disappeared and were replaced by line drawings. Even though hand silhouettes are early they may represent one form of magic without necessarily having played a part in the development of drawing.

According to another theory as to the origin of drawing, the first and oldest "picture layers" are said to be imitations of the claw marks made by the cave bear. This is said to represent more than mere play and simple external impulses, because man was already endowed with talent to react artistically to cave bears' claw marks, which gave him the idea of drawing with his fingers (Maringer-Bandi). But it is hardly plausible that man's superior endowment should have needed claw marks to inspire him to create with his own fingers. The lines might possibly have been drawn deliberately in imitation of claw marks in order to bring sympathetic magic into play, man thereby aiming at some benefit for himself.

Ill. 40. Drawings done by finger tracings on the clay of the ceiling of the gallery, L. ca 15 ft., Altamira cave, Spain. *"Four Hundred Centuries of Cave Art," Breuil-Boyle-Windels (1952).*

The Franco-Cantabrian style of the Ice Age did not disappear as suddenly as was believed even a generation ago. The Scandinavian rock pictures are later examples of the same hunting culture art that flourished in France and Spain (Fig. 323). For that reason they may be discussed here, before we turn to figure sculpture and the minor arts. It must have taken thousands of years to develop Aurignacian profile engravings into fully rounded middle Magdalenian paintings. The late Magdalenian style again took on a linear character. Realism still lingered (Fig. 324), but gradually contours became firm where they had been rounded, and developed into a simplified geometric style, finally ending in the Bronze Age in a stylized abstraction. We have seen this development in its beginning and in its maturity, and we now turn to a late stage of this still basically realistic style.

Hunting art moved north into Scandinavia, but no remains have been found between the Franco-Cantabrian area and northern Europe. The interlying countries, northern France and Germany, have been settled so long that any rock paintings which may once have existed there have largely disappeared, except in secluded places or isolated regions. The Scandinavian sites must be later than the Franco-Cantabrian style, as during this period a large part of Northern Europe was still covered with glaciers. Hence the earliest realistic engravings must date from a period after the melting of the ice, or from between 8000 B.C. and 6000 B.C., to the beginnings of the Bronze Age of about 1600 B.C., or even 1000 B.C. They are not to be confused with the Bronze Age rock engravings in both south and north Scandinavia. The Ice Age engravings still belong to a hunting culture; the later Bronze Age pictures represent the period of an agricultural life.

For the first glacial period in Scandinavia Kühn distinguishes three periods; a period of realistically rendered animals of the hunt, a second transitional period of strongly conventionalized animal renderings, and a third period of entirely schematic drawings of animals and stylized human figures. This sequence is clearly indicated by superimpositions. A good example is a particular rock at Bardal on which Bronze Age engravings of ships are on top of two earlier layers of engravings of animals (Ill. 41). In the earlier pictures the lines are ground in and made smooth for pigment to adhere to. Traces of red color have been found on one engraving at Leiknes in Nordland (Norway). Later engravings are composed of dots hammered in with stone implements. The grinding technique of contours suggests the Neolithic period, for an age that could grind contours of engravings to a smooth surface was probably familiar with the grinding of stone tools.

The subjects include reindeer, fish, signs and human beings carved on hard, glacier-worn horizontal surfaces of rock, pecked out with stone chisels.

The Norwegian engravings have some characteristics not found in the Franco-Cantabrian groups like a shorthand device of adding a second and different head to the rear end of one animal, thereby letting one body represent two different kinds of animals. In one style, the animals show only two legs in profile, as in the brown bear from Valle (Fig. 324), somewhat like the Aurignacian style in the bison of La Grèze, shown in Fig. 314. In spite of this simplified technique, the contour retains the character and action of a bear. The Norwegian rock paintings are often found near water. It has been suggested that the hunted animals were driven over a cliff into the water, to become the easy prey of men operating from boats.

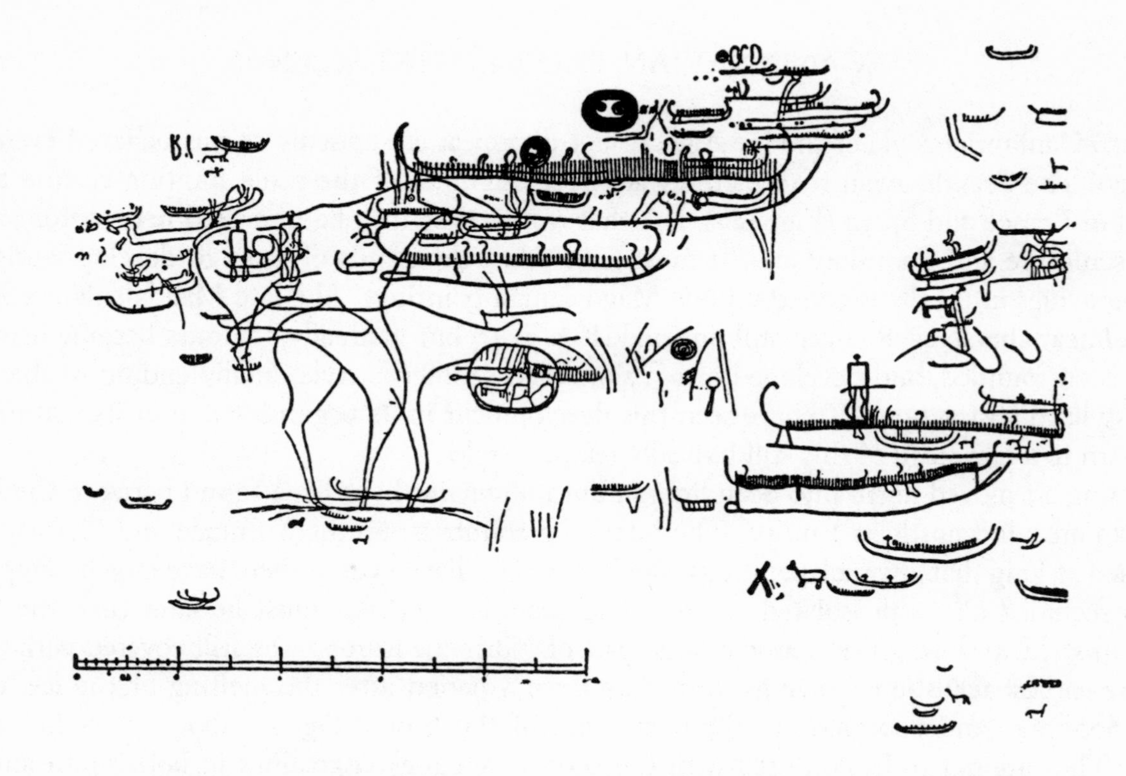

Ill. 41. Rock engravings near Bardal, in northern Norway. *After Hoernes. "Urgeschichte der Bildenden Kunst in Europa," Anton Schroll, Vienna* (1925).

FIGURE SCULPTURE AND MINOR ARTS

Works of sculpture of the Aurignacian period are found in various places across Europe. They consist of stone or ivory statuettes of nude women. Among them is a limestone statuette, four and one-half inches high, the so-called "Venus of Willendorf" (Fig. 325) found in lower Austria. It is an extraordinarily fleshy figure with large hips, loins and breasts. Face and limbs are neglected, the breasts are almost as large as the head, and the hair is arranged in schematic fashion in parallel rows of small tufts. Such statuettes are believed to have been used in connection with a cult of human fertility. Assuming that the figure never had a face, as is commonly taken for granted, such neglect points to a lack of interest in what is individual in human beings. On the other hand, the emphasis is particularly one of obesity. Sex, fertility and obesity are underscored in what might be called an ascending scale. Sex, in the way we use the term, is perhaps least important. Fertility, in the sense of pregnancy, may be related to the pregnant animals in the cave paintings, expressing race preservation as a desirable objective. Obesity finds its counterpart in the massive animals of the cave paintings with their extra supply of fat. Obesity may demonstrate security against starvation, a triumph for self-preservation.

We may look upon the "Venus of Willendorf" in two ways, as a scientific specimen and as a work of art. As a specimen, this statuette may throw some light on the state of mind of our early ancestors. Virtually, life itself, and its preservation, were raised to a level above the ordinary. Man had the capacity for creation; unlike his nearest relatives among the primates he could externalize his emotions, his fears and hopes, creatively, and engage in art. From a larger point of view the "Venus of Willendorf" is art as well as scientific specimen, as any work of art may become the object of scientific inquiry. Though this statuette does not conform to our ideal of beauty, it does not lack artistry. This naturalistic type, short and rotund, differs from a more abstract elongated type, best represented in one from Lespugue, now at the Musée de l'Homme, Paris.

We thus find that naturalism as well as abstraction occurs in prehistoric art. Though statuettes like the "Venus of Willendorf" are early, they are neither the first nor the only examples of prehistoric sculpture. To the reliefs in stone, previously discussed, may be added high reliefs of two bison carved in a clay bank in the cave of Tuc d'Audoubert, represented by casts in leading museums of Natural History.

Though we are here concerned primarily with painting and sculpture, the minor arts represented by engraved slabs of stone, bone and ivory should be mentioned. Bodily ornamentation involving beads, pierced animal teeth and the like also belongs to the subject. Some caves like Laugerie-Basse have yielded a considerable number of engravings on reindeer antlers. Small engravings found in the cave of Les Eyzies were largely on stone. This kind of "mobilary art" probably served different purposes such as hunting charms, sketches for the use of artists, personal ornamentations and other uses. The fact that these arts were practiced shows that painting did not stand alone, but received support from an activity in art that was probably broad and widely diffused.

Objects of art were valued by prehistoric man intrinsically and not solely for reasons of magic. That he preferred order in his ornaments and was sensitive to aesthetic principles like sequence and balance is proved by the jewelry he wore. Aurignacian graves of Mentone (Italy), Cromagnon (France) and Brünn (Moravia) have yielded many necklaces, bracelets, head and kneebands, hairnets, aprons of shells, animal teeth and fish vertebrae. An important necklace was discovered in the Grimaldi (Italy) cave of Barma Grande in connection with one of three skeletons of late Paleolithic date. When found, it was preserved in its original position in a clay deposit. It consisted of fish vertebrae, nassa shells and perforated deer teeth. Though the materials themselves seem neither rare nor conspicuous, they were arranged in orderly fashion according to size and shape to form an attractive design which demonstrates the above-mentioned principles of art. An artistic effect was produced which is as satisfying as it is unusual. Many simpler necklaces, in which the elements were strung together haphazardly, must have preceded this one, that had been developed into a pattern. Thus, on the evidence of archaeology, it appears that Paleolithic man was impelled by aesthetic as well as religious motivations.

Through painting, the artist of the Ice Age has bridged the intervening millennia and put himself in touch with his fellow artist almost of our own day. Considering conditions and materials the prehistoric painter had to work with, it is difficult to see how any painter of whatever period could have solved his problems better. Lascaux and Altamira stand as the first among the great schools of painting the world has seen, they belong clearly to the Paleolithic period. Of the styles to follow there is less certainty on the periods each style may be assigned to. Some regions in Africa may relate to the Paleolithic period according to some opinions; on the other hand later periods are also indicated in other instances. Certain Swedish rock engravings are definitely of the Bronze Age, and for the East Spanish style the most recent trend of opinion favors a Neolithic date.

During the prehistoric period in Europe, painting developed another and different style in eastern Spain in the mountainous heights back of the Mediterranean coast from Lérida in the north to Cadiz in the south. This Spanish Levant or Capsian style of painting was first heard of in our own day, in 1903, when J. Cabre Aguila first saw a painting of a deer at Calapata in the province of Teruel. Since then new discoveries have increased the number of sites; about forty are known to date with close to seventy rock shelters, mostly in the provinces of Lérida, Tarragona, Teruel, Castellón, Cuenca, Valencia, Albacete, Murcia, Jaén and Almería.

These paintings are in open rock shelters rather than in caves. Groups of men and animals, each one only two and one-half to six or more inches high, appear as silhouettes, showing no interior details. In contrast to the Franco-Cantabrian style, they are executed in flat tones within an outline drawing. The small miniature-like paintings are usually monochromatic, in reddish browns, black and occasionally in white, and are well preserved.

The East Spanish style represents figures and animals mostly in action, usually loosely scattered on the rock surface, but there are paintings in which the figures are related in groups and some groups are well composed.

It is possible to differentiate several figure types, depending on the shapes of the bodies. There is a thin-line type, a more nearly straight-line type which seems to relate to Lascaux, and a type with a wedge-shaped torso and thick legs (Fig. 326), as in the Valtorta Gorge.

No specific dates or periods can be assigned to any of these styles. The difficulty in dating is due to the fact that this region lacks caves with the floors covered with superimposed datable layers of debris, as found in France. The small engravings on stone that could be dated by the layers they were found in and compared with larger wall pictures are less plentiful. But excavations in the Parpallo cave in Valencia (1929-31) yielded small objects painted in the Franco-Cantabrian animal style. On the basis of the archaeological evidence, Obermaier (1937) was led to believe that the East Spanish and Franco-Cantabrian styles had been contemporary. According to his view, the two races lived in the same region of the Iberian peninsula during the same Ice Age, each race developing its own style independently with no influence of one upon the other.

Kühn, on the other hand, has recently (1952) called attention to additional Franco-Cantabrian excavations (1934) in two caves at Los Cazeres and La Hoz, in the vicinity of Madrid which, like Parpallo, are located within the East Spanish area. The question is: Was this occupation contemporary, or did one follow the other? The evidence of these additional Paleolithic finds seems to indicate that the two races occupied the same region. The reason for this is that the more Paleolithic caves are found within the East Spanish region, the less likely it would seem that the two styles could have existed at the same time and still retained their identity over thousands of years. Kühn and Maringer and Bandi now hold that one race must have followed the other, and that the East Spanish must be later, as the Franco-Cantabrian is known to be of the Ice Age.

Julio Martinez Santa-Olalla (1941) is also of the same opinion that the East Spanish followed the Franco-Cantabrian style. On a painting in Villar del Humo (Cuenca), a man is represented leading a horse by a halter, and a man on horseback occurs among the paintings of Gasulla Gorge at Ares del

Maestre. The presence of domesticated animals would point to a period that was transitional to a mode of life based partly on pasture and agriculture.

Further evidence in support of a later date for the East Spanish style comes from North Africa where, more recently, clay vessels in the East Spanish style were found, indicating a Neolithic date. Excavations in the Valtorta Gorge and beneath rock pictures on two other East Spanish sites, Albarracin and Bicorp, yielded post-glacial tools and a Neolithic ax, indicating a post-glacial period for the East Spanish style.

We are still not clear in regard to the origin of the East Spanish style. Maringer and Bandi (1952), among others, have suggested that the East Spanish style may represent a fusion of the late Paleolithic Perigordian style of France with another style that entered Spain from North Africa. The appearance of wild bulls in both the Perigordian (Lascaux) and the East Spanish styles is pointed out as indication of a relation between France and eastern Spain. For the figures of the East Spanish style there are parallels in Africa. There is no certainty as yet as to how to account for the variations of style within the East Spanish style, whether they are regional or racial. The principal phases of the East Spanish style can be traced in the Minateda shelter, in the province of Albacete. Here the paintings appear in thirteen superimposed layers. They include animals in both the Franco-Cantabrian and the East Spanish styles. Eventually the East Spanish style developed into a schematic manner and became abstract during the Bronze period. This Bronze Age style is found particularly in northwest Spain (Galicia). Obermaier, and Breuil and Burkitt have published studies in that field, but the most comprehensive survey is by Breuil (1933-35).

Comparatively few of the East Spanish rock paintings have been reproduced, as many cannot be photographed easily. One of the finest examples of the East Spanish style is a painting of three walking figures (Ill. 42). This is in the Cueva Saltadora in the Valtorta Gorge, an important site, which may be said to be for the East Spanish what Altamira is for the Franco-Cantabrian style. It is located in the mountains of Castellón, beginning several miles north of the village Albocacer, and ends in the valley of San Mateo. In this painting, published by Herbert Kühn, the figures are about nine inches high. The composition is so excellent that it could hardly be the result of an accident. There is here a feeling for rhythm in the way the figures are related to one another. They advance in a lively manner that seems fresh and spontaneous. All incline forward, but the one on the right seems to hesitate as if to restrain the figure in the center. In this middle figure the head is tilted back, which gives the whole group a sense of easy freedom. Unless the artist who painted these figures was aware of what he was doing, he could hardly have achieved such a positive artistic effect. His success could not have been due to chance, because these wedge-shaped torsos, massive hips and curved thighs constitute a mature style. A good artist, working within a definite pattern, aimed for a rhythmic expression much in the manner of artists everywhere.

A remarkable representation of action is shown in a running bowman (Fig. 327) from the Valtorta Gorge, Cueva Saltadora. Posture and details of anatomy are not visually correct. In place of realistic proportions the artist has substituted a series of strokes that suggest vividly the man running. Refinements, as in the thighs, exist side by side with clumsy details, as in the lower legs and feet. But the strokes are so sure, the sense of movement so compelling, we are hardly aware of any inaccuracies. This is the same cave as that shown in Fig. 326 where thin- and thick-legged figures appear side by

Ill. 42. Rock painting of three women walking, from Cueva Saltadora, Valtorta Gorge, East Spanish style. *"Die Felsbilder Europas," Herbert Kühn* (1952).

Opposite page: Ill. 43. Rock painting of a deer hunt, from Los Caballos shelter, Valtorta Gorge (Castellón), East Spanish style. *After Mellado.*

side. All show the figure running, carrying what might be intended as bows. The upper right-hand figure is four and a half inches high and five and a half inches wide.

Equally accomplished is another group of five figures in motion at the shelter of La Mola Remigia in the Gasulla Gorge, province Castellón (Fig. 328). Five figures are combined into a closely knit, well-integrated combination of shapes, lines, solid masses and open spaces. The rhythm of the dance may have helped the artist to create a composition in space. More attention than usual is here paid to the heads, which bring out different profiles, perhaps through the use of masks. In the proportion of the figures and in the technique used, the style differs from the preceding group of three women.

A magnificent deer hunt (Ill. 43) with eight full-grown animals and two fawns is also represented in the Valtorta Gorge. Here is a convincing representation of movement in both hunters and animals. The character of the animals is indicated with a good deal of variety in posture; the hunters have a light, almost fluid sketchiness, typical of the style.

Another deer hunt (Fig. 329) from the Cueva Más del Joseph, in Valtorta Gorge, shows a slightly different style. The drawing brings out the anatomy of the animals; hoofs, joints and heads are rendered with a delicate precision. In addition, the lines are flowing and the hunter is drawn with an amazing dash and swing.

An important early discovery (1908), a painting, two yards long, on the wall of a rock shelter close to the village of Cogul (Lérida), shows bulls, stags and nine women in skirts surrounding a small naked man. Perhaps a ritual is represented, or a dance, or this may be merely a group of women watching animals. It may even be doubtful that the animals were intended to form part of the group. If we accept this as a group, it lacks the convincing effectiveness of the battle and hunting scenes, where the group effect is unmistakable.

In a battle between bowmen at Morella la Vella (Castellón), men are represented in forward-plunging postures with bent knees. Bows are extended, and arrows placed for shooting are like action lines. The string-like bodies are weightless; there is an all-over attention given to arms, bows, legs, torsos and head, with no particular stress on any one. This represents one of the variations of the East Spanish style, in which the emphasis is not so much on distortion in proportions of the figure, but rather on exaggerated action. But there are also paintings in which the variations from the normal proportions of the figure are pronounced.

In the Cueva del Civil in the Valtorta Gorge (Ill. 44), men armed with bows and arrows represent a figure style in which wedge and string-like torsos, wide hips, thick thighs and pin heads are used. Movement is either constrained or extravagant. Several postures suggest that the artist had reached a stage where a few formulae had been mastered. This applies especially to the type in which the widely separated legs form a V-shape. Other postures show enough differences to make it appear that the artist was also striving for variety of movement. A few figures are incomplete, as if the artists had been practicing. Of the others, about half are studies in action, in which the thin, spider-like arms suggest postures that occur when men hunt with bows and arrows. In addition to action, the thinness of bows and arrows and the calves of the legs are indicated correctly and realistically. It is significant that realism appears in the bows and arrows and in legs, because all three were particularly needed for survival. It is not surprising that the artists excelled in what was of greatest interest to them. In comparison, the other parts of the figure were perhaps incidental; dots, wedges and thin and thick strokes were used to com-

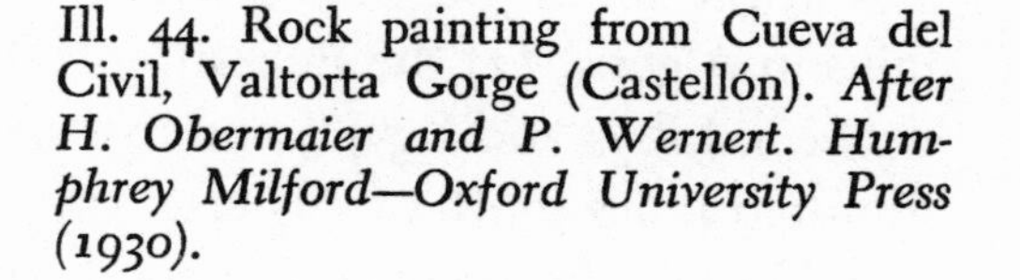

Ill. 44. Rock painting from Cueva del Civil, Valtorta Gorge (Castellón). *After H. Obermaier and P. Wernert. Humphrey Milford—Oxford University Press* (1930).

plete the figure according to a formula. A selective realism was combined with an emphasis on movement in the drawing of the human figure. This is true more or less for all styles of figure representation. Animals were drawn more consistently in their correct proportions, as they appeared to the hunters. The variations of styles are pronounced in the figures, and less so in animals.

The East Spanish style includes not only scenes of hunting and warfare, but also incidental scenes of ritual and genre, and figures that may have had a religious connotation. There is a well-known painting of two men climbing a rope to remove wild honey from a hole in a wall, with bees swarming about (Cueva de la Arana, province Valencia). In another, a woman, wearing a dress and holding a smaller figure by the hand, looks like a scene of mother and child (Minateda, province Albacete). A man wearing an animal mask could be a sorcerer (Raco, Gasulla Gorge, province Castellón), and a man lying prostrate on the ground transfixed with arrows, while a group of men nearby hold up their bows as if in triumph, has been interpreted as part of a scene of execution.

The men are represented as nude, but they wear different kinds of headdresses, shoulder capes, loin covers, belts, kneebands, made probably of furs or plant fibers. We can only conjecture as to the purpose of the paintings. They may have served as death magic, as offerings, as records of events, or they could have been done as an expression of some need for communication.

However we may interpret the archaeological evidence, the East Spanish paintings seem to reflect a worldly spirit less exclusively devoted to magic, though magic probably continued to function. The use of weapons, in this case bows and arrows, is more apparent than in the Franco-Cantabrian style.

A spirit of aggression, not felt in the Franco-Cantabrian style, stands out in the way man fights man. Though the hunter's attention is still focused on the animals, he also appears in his own right. In the paintings he is neither disguised as a sorcerer nor is he given a careful objective study. This is still reserved for the animals. The East Spanish style reflects an expanding culture, but through a new style without the power and monumentality of the old. Polychrome fresco painting and near-miniature outline drawings are hardly comparable. Each style should be judged by its own best standards.

NORTH AFRICAN ROCK PICTURES

Africa, like Europe, has its prehistoric rock pictures. They are located in the north, in the central part, and in the south. Beginning with north and central Africa, the main regions are (1) the Atlas Mountains in Algeria, (2) the Fezzan, in Libya, south of the province of Tripolitania, (3) the Libyan desert between Libya and Egypt, and (4) the Ahaggar (Hoggar) Mountains in the central Sahara, about nine hundred miles south of Algiers.

During the prehistoric period, the Spanish peninsula, Morocco, Algeria and Tunisia appear to have formed a unit. The tops of the Atlas Mountains were then covered with glaciers, volcanoes were still active in central Morocco and the lower altitudes were subject to rain periods. What is desert today was bush and grassland then. Among the extinct animals that appear in the rock pictures are the ancient buffalo, two species of elephant and a species of lion.

Many of the rock pictures of the Atlas Mountains are in the Susfana Valley. Certain sites represent the last remaining vestiges of cultures that flourished before a change of climate dried up the rivers and lakes. Remains of ancient graves, old wells and ruined oases existed up to the recent past in Tarhit in the southwest and in the Susfana Valley. The sand dunes progressing from east to west have destroyed the fertile soil. The prehistoric art centers are on the slopes of the valleys, which resisted the general desiccation. The engravings are on boulders and rock walls which have slid down into the ravines wherever the foundations disintegrated.

There are two major styles represented in the Atlas Mountains region, a naturalistic style of large engravings of animals, at times in groups and without human beings (Fig. 330), and a later geometric style of the so-called Libyan-Berber group. The earlier naturalistic style is believed to be Paleolithic. It combines the monumental character of the Franco-Cantabrian style with the movement of the East Spanish style. One of the best of the early period is the elephant mother defending her young against a leopard (Ill. 45) at Ain Safsad (eastern Algeria). Another elephant, not included here, stands behind the leopard. A realistic intent is clearly indicated by the suggestion of markings on the leopard. The way the elephant mother gathers in her offspring under her trunk is entirely natural. It is so realistic that we are surprised to note that each animal has only two legs. One is inclined to assume a conscious simplification by the artist, perhaps in part an economy measure in view of the large size of the drawing. The whole group, including three elephants, is twenty-five feet wide.

Essentially the same naturalism appears in an engraving of two buffalo fighting (Ill. 46), located at Enfous at the eastern end of Susfana valley. Behind the larger animal is a small figure executed in a sketchy manner and wearing a mask. As in the Franco-Cantabrian style, the human element is slighted, suggesting a parallel to the figures of sorcerers in French caves. In an engraving of a lion at Djattou over

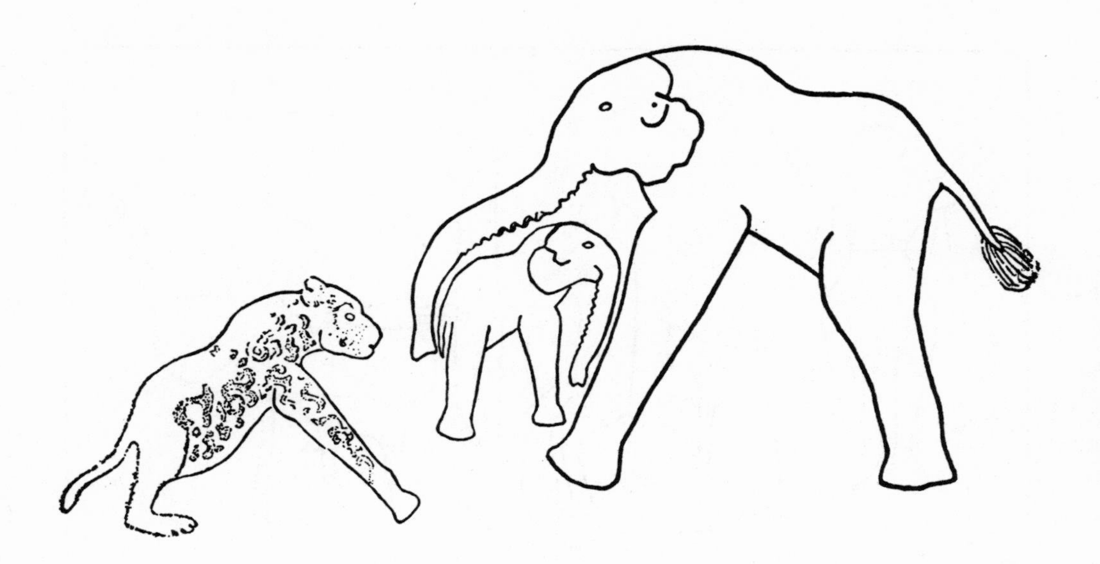

Ill. 45. Rock engraving, elephant mother defending her young, at Ain Safsad, eastern Algeria, North Africa. *After Frobenius — Obermaier (1925). Drawn by Carl Arriens.*

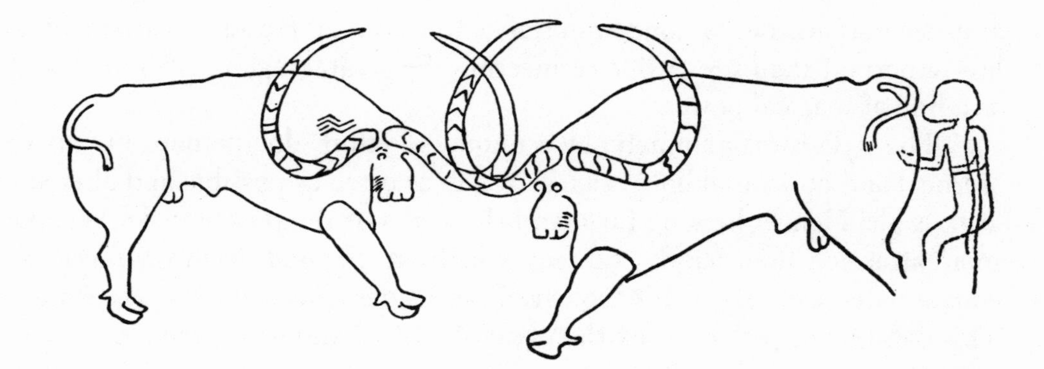

Ill. 46. Rock engraving, two buffaloes fighting, at Enfous, eastern Algeria, North Africa. *After Frobenius — Obermaier (1925).*

six feet long and more than four feet high, the body is in profile, the head is turned toward the spectator. Though a degree of naturalism is still retained in a suggestion of movement, stylization is also present, without as yet having reached the schematic stage. Between the naturalistic and the schematic stage is another group of half-naturalistic animals. In this style the lines are simplified but still suggest the natural appearance of the animals.

Some engravings show human figures in pairs, with raised arms, and a line connecting the genital regions. In a stylized engraving (Ill. 47), we see a man on an ostrich hunt, accompanied by his dog. The presence of a cow suggests the domestication of animals. The wife stays home and performs a ritual to insure the hunt's success. The engraving tells a story and indicates that the woman wears

Ill. 47. Rock engraving of a man on an ostrich hunt, accompanied by his dog. At Tiout, Sahara Atlas, North Africa. *After Frobenius—Obermaier (1925). Drawn after W. Fisher by Jean Brown.*

arm decorations, but is noncommittal as to costume. Heads are a part of the body silhouette and are less important than sex. A line connecting the genital regions of hunter and wife has been interpreted as a line of magical power.

The style is diagrammatic by economy of effort, due perhaps in part to the hardness of the rock. Vertical and horizontal lines are resorted to as often as possible and altered in direction as infrequently as possible. Hence the long torso and short legs of the profile male. Weapons, like the arrowhead, get more attention than hands and feet, which are slighted. Man's survival, through hunting, is given a concentrated expression; his biological necessities, food and sex, are stated with unmistakable clarity. This monument perhaps took the place of a ritual and was given a permanent form to serve as a magical preparation for good hunting.

On the basis of the patination of North African rock engravings and the representation of horses and camels, some dating has been attempted. The darker coloration, according to one theory, indicates earlier, the lighter color later, periods. In one instance a camel shows a light patination. As there were no camels (dromedaries) in Africa before 500 A.D., some of these rock engravings link up with a comparatively late historical period. The development in North Africa appears to have been from naturalism to schematic drawing. An engraving might be an early work, or a later work by a less competent artist. Kühn places greater emphasis on style as an indication of period.

Adjoining Algeria to the east is Libya. Here a highly schematic linear Libyan-Berber manner is believed to be comparatively late; it is represented by rock engravings of animals and animals with riders. They are static, almost geometric, though the intent of the primitive artist may have been realistic. Rock paintings discovered in the Libyan desert in the rock shelters of the Khargur Valley, in the Uwenat Hills, represent a fight for a bull (Fig. 331). They show a general resemblance to the East Spanish style and to the paintings of South Africa largely in the fact that the figures are silhouette drawings of bowmen in action. There are as many differences as there are resemblances. Comparing the bowmen of the East Spanish Cueva del Civil (Ill. 44) with the African bowmen of Uwenat Hills (Fig. 331), we note that heads, arms, torsos, thighs, lower legs and feet are by no means the same. The use of thin and thick lines is different, each site has its own style. Even within the basic simplicity of these styles, which limits the range of expression, variations are possible. It also happens that widely separated regions have produced individual drawings that are stylistically indistinguishable.

These rock paintings of Khargur Valley, as well as others in the Libyan desert, were discovered or further explored on two expeditions (1933-35) of the Forschungs Institut für Kulturmorphologie, DIAFE XI and XII. Important sites are Ain Dua and Wadi Sora, both within the Uwenat Hills. At Ain Dua pictures with cows with exaggerated udders seem to point to livestock and dairy industries. At Wadi Sora the paintings are under overhangs, rather than in caves. The subjects include acrobats, dancers, swimmers and hand prints. Obermaier attributed these paintings to the late Paleolithic period and pointed out that the styles of Ain Dua and Wadi Sora are practically identical with the East Spanish style.

At Wadi Sora agitated bowmen engaged in battle seem to constitute a variation of the East Spanish style. The bowmen wear animal masks, have wedge-shaped torsos and feet, where shown, and have prominent heels. Another painting of the same site, only about six inches high (Fig. 332) and a foot long, shows a group of figures with backs bent and arms raised behind a horned animal. It has been entitled "Adoration Scene" as if the men were humbling themselves behind the huge beast; there are no weapons. This touching scene may indeed have a religious significance. At Ain Dua (Fig. 333) massive animals are placed beside wiry figures. The figures are defined as to style, but the scene lacks the vigor and convincing drive which is present in the best.

Some of the most attractive African rock paintings were found in the central Sahara in the Ahaggar Mountains, at Oued Mertoutek. These show groups of speckled cattle and of graceful, slender human figures holding bows, or with raised arms and bent knees as if performing a dance. The variety and the ease of the postures painted in silhouette make these figure paintings outstanding in prehistoric African art.

In addition, there are sites with Bushman-like rock paintings on Lake Tanganyika, in the eastern part of the Iramba plateau, and in the Lake Chad region in the valley of Telizzharen (Telis'share).

SOUTH AFRICAN BUSHMAN PAINTINGS

Of short pygmy-like stature, Bushmen have remained unchanged in their physical development for thousands of years. It is generally believed that some of the rock paintings in South Africa were painted by the Bushmen, the last ones at a comparatively recent date. Rock paintings and engravings in South Africa occur on the rock walls of the hills and mountains of Southern Rhodesia, the states of the Union of South Africa and Southwest Africa.

This larger area of the whole of South Africa falls into four separate style regions; central, south (Fig. 334), southwest (Fig. 338), and east (Rhodesia) (Fig. 343), together forming the Union of South

Africa. An eastern region of Southern Rhodesia shows rock paintings in three or four layers, one over the other. The oldest ones are monochromatic red or yellow. Polychromy appears in the third layer, meaning at some later period, as yet not determined.

Of the remaining Bushman cultures, a central style group is artistically the most developed. At various times copies have been made of rock pictures by individuals and in connection with expeditions. These illustrations of Bushman paintings of the central group (reproduced in Figs. 334, 335, and 336) are after copies made by G. W. Stow, between 1867 and 1882, in the Eastern Freestate, and in the southeastern part of the Orange Free State in the Union of South Africa.

A southern group is characterized by pictures in monochromatic red and by paintings of the human hand. The fourth or western group of the former German colony of Southwest Africa is related to the Southern Rhodesian group. The rock paintings in this group are characterized by the use of color, representations of groups and the painted white beads worn by individual figures.

Bushman paintings, like other rock paintings, are found in layers one over another, but the older ones are not necessarily better than those of more recent date. Stow reports that "old Bushmen assert that the productions of an artist were always respected as long as any recollection of him was preserved in his tribe." Calculating that the memory of an artist would be preserved for at least three generations, the oldest paintings in the Imvani rock-shelter might be about 500 years old; many may be much older. Sir John Barrow, while traveling in the Cape Colony in 1797, definitely related the rock paintings to the Bushmen. Stow had no doubt that these paintings were by the Bushmen, even though their descendants had often lost all knowledge of the paintings. A painting of a group of men on horseback, from a Boer community, is as recent as 1869. It is known to have been by a painter who is remembered as having "carried two or three of his horn paint-pots on his belt." Hugo Obermaier (1930) concluded that at least a very important share of South African rock pictures may be assigned to the Bushmen.

The usual earth pigments were used everywhere, pulverized in mortar and mixed with animal fat to form oil colors. Hollow cylindrical bones, split from larger bones to form spatula-like ends, took the place of brushes. This is an important detail reported by Obermaier and Kühn, and is said to be based on eye-witness account. It goes far to explain the Bushman painting technique, which does not look brush drawn, as it lacks the soft, pliable touch that comes from a brush. Instead, the lines and shapes have a slightly edgy and rigid character typical of a spatula-drawn stroke.

Stow reports that a Bushman who had discovered a painting of an ostrich hunt called it "very good." Here is a documented instance where our own and native appreciation agree. There is no separate logic and no special aesthetics that apply only to primitive man.

Bushman paintings are closer to the East Spanish style than to the Franco-Cantabrian. They represent various animals, hunting scenes, dances, battles and other activities of the people. There is little indication of the environment; plant life and utensils appear only incidentally as part of human activity. Here, too, men are in action, in long streaky proportions with tiny heads, feet and hands, or without hands and feet, which are not essential to illustrate group action. Hunters fling themselves forward with legs extended (Fig. 334). They are silhouettes in a variety of postures, well observed though exaggerated. The emphasis is on action; animals and figures are elongated, almost as if drawn over actual shadows, as has been suggested, though this was probably not the case. In the painting of Kafirs running (Fig. 334), showing broad-toed feet, Stow sees a caricature.

In one of the paintings some Bushmen are driving off a herd (Fig. 335), while others act as a rear guard to hold back the advancing Kafirs. The attacking Kafirs are huge in relation to the Bushmen.

The pleasure experienced by the artist in making the most of his tool may have encouraged elongated proportions, hence these long, spindly figures. If his bone implement was like a spatula, one readily appreciates this preference for long straight lines and curves that come together in a point where thigh meets calf behind the knee.

Weapons, like bows, javelins and shields, and the necklace that marks the enemy chieftain, are emphasized. The reserve supply of javelins fastened to the chieftain's shield and the prominent markings of the cattle are visually of equal prominence. Bushman painting has a tendency to seize upon some details for special emphasis to the total exclusion of others.

Bushman-painted animals are quite unlike the large Altamira bison, weighed down by surplus fat. Bushman painting recorded hunting expeditions in a small scale, adapted to the capacity of a single artist. Paintings could have been made in order to communicate experiences, without excluding painting for the sake of magic. Three figures painted in red (Fig. 337), about twenty inches high in the original, are composed in a pleasing manner. The repetition of elongated torsos, and thin, spider-like arms is so attractive as to point to a definite aesthetic intent on the part of the artist. Smaller figures in between the larger figures could be accidental remains from earlier paintings, as in this particular grotto paintings occur in three super-imposed layers.

ROCK PAINTINGS OF SOUTHERN RHODESIA

The rock pictures of Southern Rhodesia differ from those of the Bushmen. They belong to a high state of culture which included stone buildings like the largest one, the "Great Zimbabwe" near Fort Victoria, and stone houses, underground tin and copper mines, and stone terraces. They represent not only hunting scenes (Fig. 339), but also religious and mythological themes, as well as trees, plants and landscapes.

A burial (?) scene from Rhodesia (Ill. 48) shows a large recumbent figure surrounded by smaller standing figures. A bird mask or bird head, and a bird perched on one knee, recall the bird on a stick symbol at Lascaux. The difference in scale between large and small figures may indicate rank, and the careful rendering of the torso contrasts with the curved lines used for the arms. It has been suggested that the custom of ritual regicide is here represented (Douglas C. Fox). According to this concept the ruler's function is not to rule on earth, but to prepare himself for his divinity, so that he may provide for his people's welfare from the hereafter.

A facsimile of a rock painting from Mtoko Cave in Southern Rhodesia (Figs. 340 and 341) represents an assemblage of animals and figures in action, one about as important as the other. They are too scattered for a hunting scene; though some figures carry bows there is little actual shooting. The figures suggest the Egyptian type in their wedge-shaped torsos, but the rendering is less systematized; some bodies are mere strokes, others are rounded off, bag-like. A few are running or dancing or about to turn a cart-wheel like acrobats, but the most typical posture suggests a slightly stiff, constrained walk. They are more like animated symbols than studies based on observation. Heads are like points on a pin; some suggest animal masks (Fig. 340). In contrast to the schematic figures, the animals are realistic

Ill. 48. Rock painting, burial scene of a king (?), W. ca 10 in., at Rusape, Southern Rhodesia, South Africa. *Frobenius Institute, Frankfurt am Main, Germany.*

and based on close observation. Some are very beautiful, like the zebras expressed in a sophisticated technique in which the stripes combine to build up into animal shapes (Fig. 341). The great variety of poses shows how closely animal life was studied and how vividly it was reproduced in silhouette fashion by means of a flat tone. The long oval-shaped objects have been called "formlings" and are assumed to have had a ritual significance (Fig. 342).

Essentially, this is the same style as in the "burial of a king" and is related to, but not identical with, Bushman painting and the East Spanish style.

An effective rock painting from Sassa (Makaha Road) Southern Rhodesia, represents a procession of ten men (Fig. 343). Five in one group carry bows and arrows, the others raise their arms and seem to be swaying as if in a dance. This may be accidental and within the range of variations, which are also found in the shapes of the torso and legs. The major proportions are repeated as in the long, wedge-shaped torsos and the short legs, plump in the hip and tiny in the feet. The composition in a row points to a ritual and suggests an interest beyond an exclusive concern with hunting. But where hunting scenes alone are represented, they are often of considerable interest. They may be in a freely disposed, naturalistic vein, in which the animals are shown as silhouettes, vividly and convincingly (Fig. 344). Some reflect a life-like quality seemingly based on close observation of the animals, whereas others are stylized without loss of a suggestion of movement.

SCANDINAVIAN BRONZE AGE ROCK ENGRAVINGS

The European Old Stone Age hunting culture developed into the New Stone Age, the Neolithic period, with the change of climate following the Ice Age. Flora and fauna became approximately what they are today.

The same races did not necessarily remain in the same regions throughout these many millennia. The Magdalenian people probably followed the cold-loving animals northward as the ice retreated. Other races like the less well-known Azilians took their place in southern Europe. Caves continued to be used, even while agricultural life began with the domestication of animals and with the cultivation of cereals. With the increase in population, specialization began. Man started to develop special skills, with the result that society divided itself into occupational groups: warriors, hunters, agriculturalists and artisans. Stone implements were polished, built-up pottery was produced and cloth was woven.

The change from a hunting culture to agriculture is reflected in the rock paintings. In Swedish and Italian examples, pictures of cows and ploughs become plentiful. The Paleolithic period had chiefly lance and bow and arrow; the Neolithic period the polished stone ax; the Bronze period, bronze weapons. Each of these periods has left an art style of its own, at times fine in design and superior in craftsmanship and technique, though Neolithic art has no parallels to the life and color of the paintings of Altamira and Lascaux.

Neolithic art differs from Paleolithic in its geometric character. In spite of the length of these periods, the many regions, the differences of use and technique and material, the style everywhere remained geometric for several thousands of years, during the European Neolithic, Bronze and Iron periods. Motives of a naturalistic or pictorial origin became conventionalized, or abstract.

As man invented the crafts that now became necessary for survival, invention put a premium on ideas. Ideas could be suggested by abbreviated pictures, out of which writing developed. Basket-making and loom-weaving introduced repeating strands. These designs were transferred to pottery and in time produced early ceramic decoration (Fig. 345). The regularity of the seasons became significant because they determined the time for sowing and harvesting. The course of the sun across the sky and the changing phases of the moon left their mark in symbols which were incorporated in the arts and acquired a religious significance.

In the Middle Stone Age (Mesolithic), the New Stone Age (Neolithic) and the Bronze Age, figures increase. Sacred symbols, ceremonials, and, finally, gods in human form with spears or hammers occur in the rock engravings of Scandinavia.

We meet a different kind of stylized figure drawing in rock engravings of the Scandinavian Bronze Period, found along the shoreline of south Sweden between Bohuslän and Ostergötland and the island of Götland (Ill. 49, and Figs. 346, 347 and 348). They also occur elsewhere in north Europe from England to the Alps. In the above-mentioned Swedish region there are well over two hundred groups of such engraved pictures. Vestiges of reality are fused with simplifying short-cuts; drawing is here on the road to a pictographic sign language. Ships, sleds, wagons can be recognized; men with spears. axes or hammers are probably varied manifestations of the sun god. Interpretations of meaning are hazardous and there is probably no strict separation of secular and religious representation. Perhaps pictures were votive offerings to gain favor with the gods.

The places where these rock engravings are found are still called "dance or sun hills." There was no more intent to decorate the rocks than is the case with votive offerings in Christian chapels. Such engravings may have served as communications, expressive of beliefs or supplications, but not of art in our sense. They served as a pictorial language, expressing what is known, not what is experienced emotionally in the way of mature art.

Some Swedish scholars believe these engravings may have started out as having a death cult significance, followed by a fertility cult, and that they finally came to have a purely secular meaning as memorials. Throughout these changes in meaning, the style itself did not change.

We have traced the beginnings of rock painting and engraving from the naturalistic style of the

Ill. 49. Bronze Age rock engravings, from the region between Bohuslän and Oster-Götland, Island of Götland, Sweden. *After Hoernes. "Urgeshichte der Bildenden Kunst in Europa," Anton Schroll, Vienna, (1925).*

Ice Age through the conventionalized and more abstract manners of the Neolithic period of southwestern Europe, the Scandinavian countries and various sections of Africa. We have seen that during these periods art not only helped man to sustain life but also helped him to adjust himself to the animal world wherever hunting magic cultures were dominant.

With the appearance of animistic beliefs during Neolithic periods, naturalism receded in favor of more nearly geometric styles, encouraged through a changing economy. What we look upon as masterpieces of painting were perhaps the by-products of a search for magic; nevertheless a measure of aesthetic appreciation must also have been present. Altamira and Lascaux appear as the first of the great schools of painting that the world has produced.

ACKNOWLEDGMENTS

IN THE PREPARATION OF THE MANUSCRIPT FOR THIS BOOK THE AUTHOR HAS BENEFITED FROM THE RESEARCH OF MANY specialists. To arrive at a reasonably accurate summary of what modern research has contributed as a foundation proved to be a task of considerable magnitude. In his effort to avoid the many opportunities for error the author has availed himself of the constructive criticisms of a number of colleagues in art and anthropology. The books that contributed directly to the work are listed in the selected bibliography.

Professor Paul S. Wingert of Columbia University has read the manuscript, and I am indebted to him for many comments and criticisms in connection with the text. Dr. Perry B. Cott, of the National Gallery of Art, has also read the manuscript and been helpful with suggestions. Mr. J. B. Eggen, of Hurlock, Maryland, read parts of the manuscript and has contributed data on the anthropological side and advised in regard to the text itself. I am indebted to Dr. Ben Karpman, Chief Psychotherapist of St. Elizabeth's Hospital, Washington, D. C., and to Dr. A. L. Kroeber, Professor Emeritus of the Department of Anthropology, University of California, for their kindness in reading portions of the second chapter dealing with the psychological approach in its bearing on totemism. I have benefited from this assistance and herewith extend my thanks. Any errors or omissions are due entirely to the author and are not the responsibility of the several persons here mentioned.

For assisting me with special information, I am grateful to the following persons: Dr. Matthew W. Stirling, Chief of the Bureau of American Ethnology (the Olmec section); Mr. René Batigne, Director, and Miss Louisa Bellinger, Curator, of the Textile Museum of the District of Columbia (Peruvian textiles), Mr. Batigne (for an advance proof of the manuscript of Dr. Junius Bird's Catalogue Raisonné of *Paracas and Nazca Needlework, 3rd Century, B. C.–3rd Century A. D.*, of the Textile Museum of the District of Columbia 1955); Dr. Stirling (for an early copy of "Stone Monuments of the Rio Chiquito, Veracruz, Mexico" [1955]); Mrs. G. Philip Bauer (for an advance copy of the Carnegie Institution of Washington publications on *Ancient Maya Paintings of Bonampak, Mexico* [1955]); Mr. William Fagg, of the British Museum (Yoruba sculpture); Dr. Melville J. Herskovits, of Northwestern University (Dahomey art); Dr. Stanley Stubbs, of the Laboratory of Anthropology, of Santa Fe, New Mexico (Navaho rugs and Navaho and Zuñi silver); Dr. J. Eric S. Thompson, Carnegie Institution of Washington (Maya sculpture); Dr. Terah L. Smiley, Geochronologist, Laboratory of Tree-Ring Research, University of Arizona, Tucson, Arizona (for information in regard to the Douglass tree-ring calendar).

In connection with study in museums and collections, I am indebted to the following directors and curators for having given me of their time: Mrs. Willena D. Cartwright, Denver Art Museum; Mr. J. Ed. Davis, Indian Arts and Crafts Board, United States Department of Interior, Washington, D. C.; Mr. Richard S. Finley, Santa Barbara Museum of Natural History, Santa Barbara, California; Mr. F. F. Latta, Kern County Museum, Bakersfield, California; Miss Dorothy C. Miller, Museum of Modern Art; Mr. George Mills, The Taylor Museum, Colorado Springs, Colorado; Dr. Frederick R. Pleasants, Brooklyn Museum; Mrs. Ruth De Ette Simpson, Southwest Museum, Los Angeles, California.

The Smithsonian Institution, Department of Ethnology, has kindly made available to me for study objects kept in storage, for which I express thanks. I am grateful to the Belgian Embassy and the Embassy of New Zealand for printed information and for photographs, and to Mr. Reginald Barrett, Liaison Officer of Nigeria, and to Mr. W. A. R. Walker, Liaison Officer of the Gold Coast. Mr. James V. Herring, Professor Emeritus of Art of Howard University, has kindly oriented me in regard to contemporary African wood carvers.

Many museums, private collectors, and dealers have kindly furnished me with black-and-white photographs of works in their collections. Likewise, I have been furnished with color plates by various sources. I am grateful for permission to reproduce all of these and have given credit with the photographs. Mention should be made of the Hon. Robert Woods Bliss Collection of Mexican and Peruvian works on Loan to the National Gallery of Art, Washington, and the Edward Gaffron Collection of Peruvian works on loan to the Art Institute of Chicago.

In my search for photographs, I have received the assistance of the following persons, to whom I wish to express thanks: Mr. Marius Barbeau of the Ministere des Mines et des Ressources (Canada); Dr. John O. Brew, Director, Peabody Museum, Harvard University; Mr. E. K. Burnett, Museum of the American Indian, Heye Foundation, New York; Miss Willena D. Cartwright, Denver Art Museum; Mr. Carlos Chapoy-Vidaurri, Secretary, Mexican Embassy, Washington, D. C.; Mrs. Katherine B. Edsall, Peabody Museum, Harvard University; Dr. William N. Fenton, Director, New York State Museum, Albany, New York; Mr. Robert P. Griffing, Jr., Director, Honolulu Academy of Arts; Dr. Melville J. Herskovits, Northwestern University, Evanston, Illinois; Mr. Robert Bruce Inverarity; Mr. Pal Kelemen, New York; Dr. Clarence Kennedy, Smith College; Dr. G. Montell, Statens Etnografiskia Museum, Stockholm, Sweden; Dr. Hermann Niggemeyer, Frobenius Institute, Germany; Prof. Dr. Frans M. Olbrechts, Director, Musée Royal du Congo Belge; Dr. Cornelius Osgood, Department of Anthropology, Yale University and Peabody Museum of Natural History; Mr. Eugene B. Power, Eskimo Art Inc., Ann Arbor, Michigan; Mr. Ladislas Segy of New York; Professor Julian H. Steward, Department of Anthropology, University of Illinois; Dr. Robert Wauchope, Director, Middle American Research Institute, Tulane University of Louisiana; Mr. E. S. Whitman, United Fruit Company, New York; Mr. F. Windels, Montignac, France; Mr. R. M. Younger, Director, Australian News and Information Bureau, New York; Dr. Eduardo Noguera, Director de Monumentos Prehispánicos of the Instituto Nacional de Antropologia e Historia, Mexico, D. F.; Dr. Alfred Westholm, Director, Göteborg Art Museum, Göteborg, Sweden.

Special thanks are due the photographers who have furnished me with the photographs of superior quality. They are: Mr. Henry B. Beville (National Gallery of Art), Mr. Richard Brittain (The Art Institute of Chicago), Mrs. Justine M. Cordwell (Chicago), Mr. Wyatt Davis (Santa Fe), Mr. Eliot Elisofon (New York), Mr. Floyd W. Faxon (Los Angeles), Mr. Reuben Goldberg (University Museum, Philadelphia), Mr. Vagn Guldbrandsen (Copenhagen), Mr. Robert Bruce Inverarity; Mr. Ernest Johansen (Museum of International Folk Art, Santa Fe, New Mexico), Dr. Clarence Kennedy (Smith College), Mr. Floyd R. Kestner (Smithsonian Institution), Mr. Clarence John Laughlin (New Orleans), Mr. Peter Moeschlin (Basel), Mr. Frederick P. Orchard (Peabody Museum, Harvard University), Mr. Mickey Pallas (Chicago), Mr. Myron Wood (Colorado Springs).

The maps have been drawn by Mr. Jean A. Brown of Washington, D. C. I am indebted to Mr. Brown for his careful work in recording the place names mentioned in the text.

Several publishers have kindly allowed me to quote from their works or make reproductions from plates. I wish to thank the following for permission to use these sources: The American Museum of Natural History, New York (for illustrations from *Bulletin*, Vol. 9, article 10 [1907]); Columbia University Press (for drawings of Melanesian Kapkaps); Denver Art Museum (for drawings from leaflets, Department of Indian Art), Fisk University Press, Nashville, Tennessee (for quotations from Sahagun); International Universities Press, New York (for illustrations from *The Eternal Ones of the Dream*, by Géza Roheim [1945]); Dr. Herbert Kühn of The University of Mainz, Germany, and the W. Kohlhammer Publishing Company, Stuttgart, Germany (for the frontispiece illustration); Anton Schroll & Co., Vienna (for illustrations of cave paintings); Mrs. K. M. F. Scott of Marshfield, Rondeborch, Cape, South Africa (for reproductions of Bushmen paintings); Smithsonian Institution, Washington, D. C. (for drawings from *Annual Reports* in Eskimo and Middle American art); Stanford University Press, Stanford, California (for Maya art); Mrs. Helen M. Whiting, Peabody Museum of Archaeology and Ethnology, Harvard University (for drawings on Mimbres pottery); Dr. Kurt Wolff, Pantheon Books, Inc. (for Altamira ceiling drawing and other drawings); Dr. Heinrich Ubbelohde-Doering, Munich, and Frederick A. Praeger, Inc., New York (for a drawing of Raimondi monolith); University of Minnesota and American Magazine of Art (for drawings of Maya murals at Chichén Itzá).

For translations from foreign languages, I am grateful to Mr. Ernest R. Fiedler, Administrator of the National Gallery of Art, and to Mrs. Britta (Linder) Bornbaum of Stockholm (Swedish); to Dr. Katherine Shepard, National Gallery of Art (Spanish); and to Miss Johanna van Nierop, of Washington, D. C., and Mr. Ralph C. Altman of Los Angeles (Flemish).

I owe thanks also to Mr. Raymond MacNamarra and Edna Florance Christensen for their general assistance and to H. Felix Kraus for the layout of the book.

A large number of footnotes for each chapter, containing page reference to the selected bibliography, were deleted from the final manuscript. Specialists will recognize the sources and the general reader would probably have no occasion to use them.

SELECTED BIBLIOGRAPHY

Only those references are listed which have contributed to this book. Comprehensive bibliographies will be found in those books where noted.

GENERAL

Adam, Leonhard; *Primitive Art.* Harmondsworth, Middlesex, England (Penguin), 1949. (Bibliography)

Bidney, David; *Theoretical Anthropology.* New York (Columbia University Press), 1953.

Benedict, Ruth; *Patterns of Culture.* Mentor Books, New York (The New American Library), 1934.

——; "Animism." *Encyclopaedia of the Social Sciences,* New York (Macmillan), Vol. 13, 1930-44, pp. 65-67.

——; "Magic." *Encyclopaedia of the Social Sciences,* New York (Macmillan), Vol. 10, 1930-44, pp. 39-44.

Boas, Franz; *Primitive Art.* Oslo, 1927. Also new ed. Irvington-on-Hudson, New York (Capitol), 1951.

——; "Anthropology." *Encyclopaedia of the Social Sciences,* New York (Macmillan), Vol. 13, 1930-44, Art: pp. 89-93.

Burland, C. A. and Hooper, J. T.; *The Art of Primitive Peoples,* London (The Fountain Press), 1953.

Cairns, Huntington; *Law and the Social Sciences.* New York (Harcourt, Brace), 1935.

Collier, John; *Indians of the Americas.* Chicago (W. W. Norton and Co.), 1947.

——; also, same title (slightly abridged); Mentor Books. The New American Library, 1953.

Frazer, Sir J. G.; *The Golden Bough* (Vols. 1 and 2), *The Magic Art and the Evolution of Kings.* 3rd. ed., New York (Macmillan), 1935.

Freud, Sigmund; *Totem and Taboo.* The Basic Writings of Sigmund Freud. Tr. and ed. with an introduction by Dr. A. A. Brill, New York (Random House Modern Library), 1938.

Goldenweiser, Alexander; "Form and Content in Totemism." *American Anthropologist,* 1918, pp. 280-295.

——; "Totemism." *Encyclopaedia of the Social Sciences,* New York (Macmillan) Vol. 13, 1930-44, pp. 657-660.

Herskovits, Melville J.; *Man and His Works; the Science of Cultural Anthropology.* New York (Knopf), 1948.

Heydrich, M. and Fröhlich, W.; *Plastik der Primitiven,* Stuttgart (Wolf Strache), 1954.

Jaensch, E. R.; *Eidetic Imagery and Typological Methods of Investigation.* Tr. by Oscar Oeser, London (Routledge), 1930.

Jung, C. G.; *Two Essays on an Analytical Psychology.* New York (Pantheon), 1953.

Kempf, E. J.; "The Probable Origin of Man's Belief in Sympathetic Magic and Taboo." *Medical Journal and Record,* Vol. CXXXIII, No. 1, New York, Jan. 7, 1931.

Kris, Ernst; *Psychoanalytic Explorations in Art.* New York (International Universities Press Inc.), 1952.

Kroeber, A. L.; *Anthropology.* New York (Harcourt, Brace), 1948.

——; "Primitive Art." *Encyclopaedia of Social Sciences,* New York (Macmillan) Vol. 1, 1930-44, pp. 226-229.

Lesley, Parker; "Primitive Art and the Contemporary Point of View." *University of Minnesota Gallery Exhibition Catalogue,* 1940, pp. 7-12.

Lévy-Bruhl, Lucien; *The "Soul" of the Primitive.* Tr. by Lillian A. Clare. New York (Macmillan), 1928.

Linné, Sigvald, Ed.; *Primitiv Konst.* Konst och Konsthantverk hos Primitiva Folk. Stockholm (Aktiebolaget Bokverk), 1947.

Linton, Ralph; " 'Primitive' Art." *The American Magazine of Art,* Jan. 1933, pp. 17-24.

Lowie, Robert H.; *The History of Ethnological Theory.* New York (Farrar and Reinhardt), 1937.

Lublinski, Ida; "Der Mythos von der Geburt." *Zeitschrift für Ethnologie,* Berlin, 1932, pp. 112-125.

Luquet, G. H.; "Le Réalisme Intellectuel dans l'Art Primitif." *Journal de Psychologie,* Tome 34, Paris, 1927.

Malinowski, Bronislaw; *Magic, Science and Religion.* Garden City, New York (Doubleday), 1954.

Mandelbaum, David G.; "The Art of Primitive Peoples." *University of Minnesota Gallery Exhibition Catalogue,* 1940, pp. 3-6; 16-35.

Marett, R. R.; *Faith, Hope and Charity in Primitive Religion.* New York (Macmillan), 1932, p. 204.

Moloney, James Clark; *The Magic Cloak.* A Contribution to the Psychology of Authoritarianism. Wakefield, Mass. (Montrose), 1949.

Montague, Ashley; "Some Anthropological Terms. A Study in the Systematics of Confusion." *American Anthropologist,* Jan.-Mar., 1945.

Osborn, Fairfield; *The Pacific World.* New York (W. W. Norton & Co.), 1944.

Pijoán, José (Cossió-Pijoán); *Summa Artis; Historia General del Arte,* Vol. I. *Arte de los Pueblos Aborígenes.* Madrid (Espasa-Calpe, S. A.), 1944.

——; Vol. X. *Arte Precolombiano, Mexicano y Maya.* 1946.

Primitive Art; A Guide Leaflet to Collections in the American Museum of Natural History, No. 15, New York, supplement to American Museum Journal, Vol. IV, No. 3, July, 1904.

Róheim, Géza; *The Eternal Ones of the Dream; A Psychoanalytical Interpretation of the Australian Myth and Ritual.* New York (International Universities Press), 1945.

Spinden, Herbert J.; "Power Animals in American Indian Art." *Selected Papers of the XXIX International Congress of Americanists,* Chicago, 1952, pp. 195-199.

———; "Sun Worship." *The Smithsonian Report for 1939,* Washington, D. C., pp. 447-469.

Stagner, Ross and Karwoski, T. F.; *Psychology.* New York (McGraw-Hill), 1952.

Storch, Alfred; *The Primitive Archaic Form of Inner Experiences and Thought in Schizophrenia.* New York and Washington, 1924.

Sydow, Eckart von; *Die Kunst der Naturvölker und der Vorzeit.* Berlin (Propylaen), 1923.

———; *Kunst und Religion der Naturvölker.* Oldenburg, I. O. (Gerhard Stalling), 1926.

———; *Primitive Kunst und Psychoanalyse.* Leipzig-Vienna-Zürich (Internationaler Psychoanalytischer Verlag), 1927.

Taylor, Edward B.; *Primitive Culture.* Vol. I, London (John Murray), 1871.

Thompson, Edward Herbert; *People of the Serpent.* Boston, 1932.

Thurnwald, Richard; *Des Menschengeistes Erwachen, Wachsen und Irren. Berlin* (Duncker & Humblot), 1951.

Vatter, Ernst; *Religiöse Plastik der Naturvölker.* Frankfurt, 1926.

White, Leslie A.; *The Science of Culture; A Study of Man and Civilization.* New York (Farrar, Straus), 1949.

CHAPTER ONE

Andersson, Efraim; *Contribution à l'Éthnographie des Kuta.* Studia Ethnographica Upsaliensia VI, Uppsala, 1953.

Clarke, J. D.; "The Stone Figures of Esie." *Nigeria* (Lagos), No. 14, 1938.

Cordwell, Justine M.; "Some Aesthetic Aspects of Yoruba and Benin Cultures." Doctoral Dissertation, Northwestern University, 1952, Evanston, Illinois.

———; "Naturalism and Stylization in Yoruba Art." *Magazine of Art,* May 1953, pp. 220-225.

Duckworth, E. H.; "Recent Archaeological Discoveries in the Ancient City of Ife." *Nigeria* (Lagos), No. 14, 1938.

Fagg, William; *The Webster Plass Collection of African Art.* British Museum, London, 1953.

———; "Observations on Nigerian Art History. Masterpieces of African Art." *Exhibition Catalog,* Brooklyn Museum, 1954-1955, pp. 11-16.

———; "The Antiquities of Ife." *Magazine of Art.* April 1950, pp. 129-133.

Farrow, Stephan S.; *Faith, Fancies and Fetich.* London, 1926.

Frobenius, Leo; *Die Masken und Geheimbünde Afrikas.* Halle, 1898.

———; *The Voice of Africa.* 2 Vols., London (Hutchinson & Co.), 1913.

———; *Das Unbekannte Afrika.* Munich, 1923.

Gaffé, René; *La Sculpture du Congo Belge.* Paris-Brussels (Éditions du cercle d'art), 1945.

Gaskell, W.; "The Influence of Europe on Early Benin Art." *The Connoisseur,* London, June, 1902.

Germann, Paul; "Die Afrikanische Kunst." Anton Springer, *Handbuch der Kunstgeschichte,* Vol. VI, *Die Aussereuropäische Kunst,* Leipzig (Alfred Kröner), 1929, pp. 551-591.

Griaule, Marcel; *Folk Art in Black Africa.* Paris and New York (Les Éditions du Chêne and Tudor), 1950.

Guillaume, Paul and Munro, Thomas; *Primitive Negro Sculpture.* New York (Harcourt, Brace), 1926.

Hall, H. V.; "Great Benin Altar." *University of Pennsylvania Museum Journal,* Vol. XIII, June, 1922, pp. 105 ff.

Herskovits, Melville J. and Frances S.; "The Art of Dahomey. I. Brass Casting and Appliqué Clothes." *The Magazine of Art,* Feb. 1934, pp. 67-76.

Heydrich, Martin; "Afrikanische Ornamentik." *Internationales Archiv für Ethnographie,* 1914. Supplement to Vol. XXII, pp. 1-84.

Himmelheber, Hans; *Negerkünstler.* Ethnographische Studien über die Schnitzkünstler bei den Stämmen der Atutu und Guro im Innern der Elfenbeinküste. Stuttgart (Strecker and Schröder), 1935.

Karutz, R.; "Vom Wesentlichen in der Afrikanischen Kunst." *IPEK,* Leipzig, 1927.

———; "Weitere Afrikanische Hörnermasken." *Internationales Archiv für Ethnographie,* Vol. XVI, 1903, pp. 121-127.

Kjersmeier, Carl; *Centres de Styles de la Sculpture Nègre Africaine.* 4 Vols. Paris (A. Morancé), 1935-38.

———; *African Negro Sculpture.* New York (Frederick Praeger), 1948.

———; "Bambara Sculptures." *Man,* London, 1934.

Kochnitzky, Leon; *Negro Art in Belgian Congo.* Belgian Government Information Center, New York, 1952.

———; *Shrines of Wonders; a Survey of Ethnological and Folk Art Museums in Central Africa.* New York (Clark and Fritts), 1952.

Lange, Julius; *Darstellung des Menschen in der Alteren Griechischen Kunst.* Tr. by Mathilde Mann, Strassburg (C. T. H. Ed. Heitz), 1899. (French excerpt from 1892 Ed.) pp. X-XXXI.

L'Art nègre du Congo Belge; various authors. Published by the Belgian Government under the auspices of a commission for the protection of the native arts and crafts. 1950 (in French).

Lavachery, Henry; "Essays on the Style in Statuary of the Belgian Congo." *Negro,* London, 1934.

Lem, F. H.; *Sudanese Sculpture.* Paris (Arts et Metiers Graphiques), 1949.

———; The Art of the Sudan Masterpieces of African Art. *Exhibition Catalog,* Brooklyn Museum, 1954-1955, pp. 17-21.

Ling-Roth, H.; *Great Benin: Its Customs and Horrors.* Halifax, England, 1903.

Lips, J. E.; *Die Plastik der Naturvölker,* Cologne, 1930.

———; *The Savage Hits Back.* New Haven (Yale University Press), 1937.

Lommel, Andreas; "Afrikanische Kunst." *Introduction, Exhibition Catalog,* Munich (Völkerkunde Museum and America House), 1953.

Luschan, Felix von; *Die Altertümer von Benin.* 3 Vols. Berlin, 1919.

Maes, J.; "La Psychologie de l'Art Nègre." *IPEK,* Leipzig, 1928.

Maesen, A.; "Traditional Sculpture in Belgian Congo." *Vatican Exhibition, The Arts in Belgian Congo,* Brussels (CID), 1950, pp. 9-33.

Marquart, Jos.; *Die Benin-Sammlung des Reichsmuseums für Völkerkunde in Leiden.* Leiden, 1913.

Murray, K. C.; "The Stone Images of Esie." *Nigeria* (Lagos), 1951, No. 37, p. 45.

———; *Our Art Treasures.* Public Relations Department, Lagos (Nigeria), Crownbird Series No. 28, (n.d. but after 1951).

Olbrechts, Frans M.; "Contributions to the Study of the Chronology of African Plastic Art." *Africa,* London, Oct. 1945.

———; *Westersche Invloed op de Inheemsche Kunst in Afrika?* Brussels, 1942.

———; *Plastiek van Kongo.* Antwerp (Standaard-Boekhandel), 1946.

Perier, G. C.; *Les Arts Populaires du Congo Belge,* Brussels, (Office de Publicité), 1948.

Pleasants, F. R.; "African Sculpture in the Peabody Museum of Cambridge, Mass." *IPEK,* 1936-37, pp. 117-124.

Rattray, R. S.; *Religion and Art in Ashanti.* Oxford (Clarendon Press), 1927.

Read, C. H. and Dalton, O. M.; *Antiquities from the City of Benin and from other parts of West Africa, in the British Museum.* London, 1899.

Schmalenbach, Werner; *Die Kunst Afrikas.* Basel, Switzerland (Holbein), 1953. (Bibliography).

Schweeger-Hefel, Annemarie; *Afrikanische Bronzen.* Vienna (Wolfrum), 1948.

Segy, Ladislaw; *African Sculpture Speaks.* New York (A. A. Wyn) 1952. (Bibliography)

———; "Circle—Dot Symbolic Sign on African Ivory Carvings." *Zaire.* Vol. VII, No. 1, 1953.

———; "Primitive Negro Art." *Art and Archaeology,* XXXIV, May-June, 1933, pp. 130-136.

Siroto, Leon; "Baulé and Guro Sculpture of the Ivory Coast." Masterpieces of African Art, *Exhibition Catalog,* Brooklyn Museum, 1954-1955, pp. 26-30.

Stillman, E. Clark; "The Traditional Art of the Belgian Congo." *Exhibition Catalog,* Brooklyn Museum, 1954-1955, pp. 31-36.

Storms, D. Arnold; "Contemporary Christian Art in Belgian Congo." *Vatican Exhibition, The Arts in Belgian Congo.* Brussels (CID), 1950, pp. 64-73. (Bibliography)

Sweeney, James Johnson; *African Negro Art.* New York (Museum of Modern Art), 1935.

———; (and Radin) *African Folk Tales and Sculpture.* New York, (Pantheon), 1952. Bollingen Series XXXII.

Sydow, Eckart von; *Handbuch der Westafrikanischen Plastik.* Vol. I, Berlin (Dietrich Reimer; Ernst Vohsen), 1930. (Bibliography)

———; *Afrikanische Plastik.* New York (George Wittenborn, Inc.) 1954.

Thomas, T.; "Variation on a Theme. Analysis of Small Carved Figures from Bali, Cameroons, Africa." *Man,* XXXVIII, 1938, pp. 33-37.

Trowell, Margaret; *Classical African Sculpture.* New York. (Frederick A. Praeger), 1954.

Underwood, Leon; *Masks of West Africa.* London (Alec Tiranti), 1948.

———; *Bronzes of West Africa.* London (Alec Tiranti), 1948.

———; *Figures in Wood of West Africa.* London (John Tiranti), 1949.

Wannijn, Rob. L.; "Ancient Religious Insigniae in Bas-Congo." *Vatican Exhibition, The Arts in Belgian Congo,* Brussels, (CID), 1950, pp. 41-53. (Bibliography)

Werth, E.; "Die Afrikanischen Schafrassen und die Herkunft des Ammon Kult." *Zeitschrift für Ethnologie,* 1944, No. 6, p. 317, Fig. 14.

Wingert, Paul S.; "African Negro Sculpture." *Catalog,* M. H. De Young Memorial Museum, San Francisco, 1948. (Bibliography)

———; *The Sculpture of Negro Africa.* New York (Columbia University Press), 1950. (Bibliography)

———; "The Wurtzburger Collection of African Sculpture." *Catalog,* The Baltimore Museum of Art, 1954.

CHAPTER TWO

Adam, Leonhard; "Nordwest Amerikanische Indianer Kunst." *Orbis Pictus,* Vol. 17, Berlin (n.d.).

———; "Parallèle Entre les Masques du Nord-Ouest de l'Amérique et les Masques Japonais. *Cahiers d'Art,* 1928, No. 9, pp. 376-379.

———; "Northwest American Indian Art and Its Early Chinese Parallels." *Man,* London, Jan. 1936, No. 3.

Barbeau, Marius; "The Modern Growth of the Totem Pole on the Northwest Coast." *International Congress of Americanists Proceedings,* 23rd Session, 1928, pp. 505-511; also from *The Smithsonian Report for 1939,* pp. 491-498 (with 5 plates), Washington, D. C., 1940.

———; "Totem Poles." A Recent Native Art of the Northwest Coast of America. *Smithsonian Institution Report,* Washington, D. C., 1931, pp. 559-570.

———; "Totem Poles." *Bulletin No. 119,* Vol. 1, Totem Poles According to Events and Topics, Vol. II, Totem Poles According to Location, National Museum of Canada, Anthropological Series No. 30, Ottawa, 1950.

Boas, Franz; "The Use of Masks and Head-ornaments of the Northwest Coast of America." *Internationales Archiv für Ethnographie,* Vol. III, 1890, pp. 7-15.

———; "The Social Organization and the Secret Societies of the Kwakiutl Indians." *U. S. National Smithsonian Report for 1895,* Washington, D. C., 1897.

———; "The Decorative Art of the Indians of the North Pacific Coast." *Bulletin of the American Museum of Natural History,* Vol. IX, pp. 123-176, New York, 1897.

———; "Methods in Woodwork." *The Red Man,* Vol. 2, No. 8, pp. 3-10.

———; "Tsimshian Mythology." Based on texts recorded by Henry W. Tate. *Thirty-first Annual Report of the Bureau of American Ethnology,* 1909-1910. Smithsonian Institution, Washington, D. C., 1916.

British Museum; *Handbook to the Ethnographical Collections.* London, 1925.

Davis, Robert Tyler; *Native Arts of the Pacific Northwest.* From the Rasmussen Collection of the Portland Art Museum, Stanford, California (Stanford University Press), 1949.

Douglas, Frederic H.; "Totem Poles." Leaflets 79, 80, Denver Art Museum, Denver, Colo., 1936.

Drucker, Philip; "The Antiquity of the Northwest Coast Totem Pole." *Journal of the Washington Academy of Science,* Dec. 15, 1948, Vol. 38, pp. 389 ff.

Emmons, George T.; "The Kitikshan and their Totem Poles." *American Museum of Natural History,* Vol. 25, No. 1, pp. 33-48, New York, 1925.

———; "The Art of the Northwest Coast Indians." *Natural History,* May-June, 1930, pp. 282-292.

Emmons, George T. and Boas, Franz; "The Chilkat Blanket with Notes on Blanket Design." *American Museum of Natural History, Memoirs,* Vol. 3, Pt. 4, New York, 1907, pp. 329-400.

Garfield, Viola E. and Forrest, Linn A.; *The Wolf and the Raven.* Seattle (University of Washington Press), 1948.

Goddard, Pliny Earle; "Indians of the Northwest Coast." *American Museum of Natural History, Handbook 10,* New York, 1934.

Himmelheber, Hans; *Eskimokünstler.* Eisenach, Germany (Erich Roth), 1953.

Hoffman, W. J.; "The Graphic Art of the Eskimo." *Smithsonian Report for 1895,* Washington, D. C., 1897.

Houston, James A.; "Eskimo Sculptors." *The Beaver,* Winnipeg, Canada, June 1951, pp. 34-39.

Inverarity, Robert Bruce; *Art of the Northwest Coast Indians.* Berkeley and Los Angeles (University of California Press), 1950. (Bibliography)

———; *Movable Masks and Figures of the North Pacific Coast Indians.* Cranbrook Institute of Science, 1941.

Keithahn, Edward L.; *Monuments in Cedar.* Ketchikan, Alaska (Roy Anderson), 1945.

Krickeberg, Walter; "Malereien auf Ledernen Zeremonial Kleidern der Nordwest Amerikaner." Jahrbuch für Prähistorische und Ethnographische Kunst, *IPEK,* Leipzig, 1925, pp. 140-150.

———; "Das Kunstgewerbe der Eskimo und der Nord-Amerikanischen Indianer." H. Th. Bossert, *Geschichte des Kunstgewerbes aller Zeiten und aller Völker,* Vol. II, 1929, pp. 155 ff.

Krieger, H. W.; "Some Aspects of the Northwest Coast Indians' Art." *Scientific Monthly,* Vol. 23, 1926, pp. 210-219.

———; *Archaeological and Ethnological Studies in Southwest Alaska.* Smithsonian Miscellaneous Collection, Vol. 78, No. 7, Explorations and Fieldwork of the Smithsonian Institution, Washington, D. C., 1926, publ. 1927.

———; "Indian Villages of Southeastern Alaska." *Smithsonian Report,* Washington, D. C., 1927, publ. 1928, pp. 467-494.

Kroeber, A. L.: "American Culture of the Northwest Coast." *American Anthropologist,* Vol. 25, pp. 1-28.

Levi-Strauss, Claude; "The Art of the Northwest Coast Indians." *Gazette des Beaux Arts,* Vol. 24, 1943, pp. 175 ff.

Mason, J. Alden; "Eskimo Pictorial Art." *The Museum Journal,* Philadelphia, Sept. 1927, pp. 248-283.

Murdoch, John; *Ethnological Results from the Point Barrow Expedition.* Alaska 1881-1883. Smithsonian Institution. Washington, D. C., 1892.

Nelson, Edward William; "The Eskimo about Bering Strait." *Eighteenth Annual Report of the Bureau of American Ethnology*, Smithsonian Institution, Washington, D. C., 1900.

Niblack, Albert D.; "The Coast Indians of Southern Alaska and Northern British Columbia." *U. S. National Museum Report*, Washington, D. C., 1888.

Smith, Harlan L.; "Totem Poles of the North Pacific Coast." *Journal*, American Museum of Natural History, Vol. II, No. 3, 1911, pp. 76-82.

Waterman, T. T.; "Observations among the Ancient Indian Monuments of Southeastern Alaska." *Exploration and Field Work of the Smithsonian Institution in 1922*, Vol. 74, No. 5, publ. 1923, pp. 115-133.

——; "Some Conundrums in Northwest Coast Art." *American Anthropologist*, Vol. 25, pp. 435 ff.

Woodcock, George; "Masks of the Pacific Northwest Indians." *The Burlington Magazine*, April 1954, pp. 109-113.

CHAPTER THREE

Alexander, Hartley Burr; *L'art et la Philosophie des Indiens de l'Amérique du Nord*. Paris (Ernest Leroux), 1926.

Amsden, Charles Avery; *Navaho Weaving*. Albuquerque (University of New Mexico Press), 1949.

Archer, W. G.; *The Vertical Man; a Study in Primitive Indian Sculpture*. New York (Macmillan), 1947.

Bunzel, Ruth L.; *The Pueblo Potter, A Study in Creative Imagination In Primitive Art*. New York (Columbia University Press), 1929.

——; "Zuñi Katcinas." *Forty-seventh Annual Report of the Bureau of American Ethnology*, Washington, D.C., 1932.

——; "Introduction to Zuñi Ceremonialism." *Forty-seventh Annual Report of the Bureau of American Ethnology*, Washington, D. C., 1932.

Chapman, Kenneth Milton; *Pueblo Indian Pottery of the Post-Spanish Period*. Bulletin No. 4, Laboratory of Anthropology, Santa Fe, New Mexico, 1950.

Colton, Harold S.; *Hopi Katchina Dolls; with a Key to Their Identification*. Albuquerque (University of New Mexico Press), 1949.

Cosgrove, H. S. and C. B.; "The Swarts Ruins." *Papers*, Peabody Museum of American Archaeology and Ethnology, Vol. XV, No. 1, 1932, *Report on Seasons* 1924-1927.

Covarrubias, Miguel; *Mexico South*. New York (Knopf), 1946.

——; *The Eagle, the Jaguar, and the Serpent*. New York (Knopf), 1954.

Douglas, E. A.; "Tree Rings and their Relation to Solar Variations and Chronology." *Annual Report*. The Smithsonian Institution for 1931, published Washington, 1932, pp. 304-313.

Douglas, Frederic H.; *Hopi Pottery*. Enjoy Your Museum Pamphlet III-A. Pasadena (Esto), 1933.

——; Denver Art Museum, Department of Indian Art, Leaflets: *Northwest Coast Indians*, No. 1, 1930; *North American Plain Indians, Hide, Dressing and Bead Sewing Technique*, No. 2, 1930; *Navaho Spinning, Dyeing, and Weaving*, No. 3, 1930; *Pima Indian Close Coiled Basketry*, No. 5, 1930; *Navaho Silversmithing*, No. 15, 1930; *Hopi Indian Basketry*, No. 17, 1931; *Santa Clara and San Juan Pottery*, No. 35, 1931.

Douglas, Frederic H. and d'Harnoncourt, René; *Indian Art of the United States*. New York (Museum of Modern Art), 1942.

Dunn, Dorothy; "The Development of Modern American Indian Painting, Southwest and Plains Area." *El Palacio*, November 1951, pp. 331-353.

Ewers, John Canfield; *Plains Indian Painting*. A Description of an Aboriginal American Art. Stanford University, California (Stanford University Press), 1939.

——; "Blackfeet Crafts." *Indian Handcrafts* 9. United States Indian Service, Department of the Interior, 1945.

Fenton, William N.; "Masked Medicine Societies of the Iroquois." *Smithsonian Report for 1940*, pp. 397-430. Smithsonian Institution, Washington, D. C.

Fewkes, Jesse Walter; "Prehistoric Pottery Designs from the Mimbres Valley, New Mexico, U.S.A." *IPEK*, Leipzig, 1925, pp. 136-139.

——; "Archaeological Expedition to Arizona in 1895." *Seventeenth Annual Report of the Bureau of American Ethnology*, Washington, D. C., 1898, pp. 519-752.

——; *Mimbres Pottery, Design on Prehistoric Pottery from the Mimbres Valley, New Mexico*. Smithsonian Miscellaneous Collection, Vol. 74, No. 6, Washington, D. C., 1923.

——; "Hopi Catchinas." *Report of Bureau of American Ethnology*, 1899-1900, publ. 1903, pp. 3-126.

Holmes, William H.; "Ancient Art of the Province of Chiriqui." *Sixth Annual Report of the Bureau of Ethnology*, 1884-85. Smithsonian Institution, Washington, 1888, pp. 13-187.

——; "Aboriginal Pottery of the Eastern United States." *Twentieth Annual Report of the Bureau of American Ethnology*, 1898-1899. Smithsonian Institution, Washington, 1903.

Kelemen, Pal; *Medieval American Art*, a Survey in Two Volumes. New York (Macmillan), 1943. (Bibliography)

King, Jeff; *Where the Two Came to Their Fathers.* A Navaho war ceremonial, given by Jeff King, New York. Text and paintings recorded by Maud Oakes, Commentary by Joseph Campbell, New York (Pantheon), 1943.

Kirkland, Forrest and Marriott, Alice L.; "Indian Pictographs in Texas." *Catalog,* Dallas Museum of Fine Arts, 1943.

Klah, Hasteen; *Navajo Creation Myth,* the Story of the Emergence. Recorded by Mary C. Wheelwright. Santa Fe, New Mexico (Museum of Navajo Ceremonial Art), 1942.

Latta, F. F.; *Handbook of the Yokuts Indians,* Kern County Museum, Bakersfield, California, 1949.

Lublinski, Ida; "Der Mythos von der Geburt." *Zeitschrift für Ethnologie,* Berlin, 1932, pp. 112-125.

Lyford, Carrie A.; *Quill and Beadwork of the Western Sioux.* Indian Handcrafts 1. U. S. Office of Indian Affairs. Department of the Interior, 1940.

Mallery, Garrick; "Pictographs of the North American Indians"; a Preliminary Paper. *Fourth Annual Report, Bureau of American Ethnology,* Washington, D. C., 1886.

——; "Picture-Writing of the American Indian." *Annual Report of the Bureau of American Ethnology,* Vol. X, Washington, D. C., 1893.

Mills, George; *Kachinas and Saints.* Taylor Museum of the Colorado Springs Fine Arts Center (n.d.).

Mills, William C.; *Certain Mounds and Village Sites in Ohio.* Vol. 2, Part 3, Exploration of the Tremper Mound, Columbus, Ohio, 1916.

——; *Exploration of the Tremper Mound in Scioto County, Ohio.* Holmes Anniversary Volume, Washington, D. C., 1916, pp. 334-358.

Reichard, Gladys A.; *Navajo Medicine Man; Sandpaintings and Legends of Miguelito.* New York (J. J. Augustin), 1939.

——; *Navaho Religion, a Study of Symbolism.* 2 Vols. New York (Pantheon), 1950.

Setzler, Frank M.; *Archaeological Perspectives in the Northern Mississippi Valley.* Reprinted from Smithsonian Miscellaneous Collections. Vol. 100 (whole volume). Smithsonian Institution, Washington, 1940.

Shead, Ralph B.; *Engraved Shells of the Spiro Mound.* Reprint from the Seventh Annual Report of The Museum of the University of Oklahoma, Norman, Oklahoma, 1950-1951.

Spinden, Herbert J.; "The Making of Pottery at San Ildefonso." *The American Museum Journal,* April 1911, pp. 192-196.

Steward, Julian H.; "Petroglyphs of the United States." *Smithsonian Report for 1936,* pp. 405-425, Smithsonian Institution, Washington, D. C.

Tschopik, Harry, Jr.; *Indians of North America.* Science Guide No. 136. Man and Nature Publications. The American Museum of Natural History, New York, 1952.

Underhill, Ruth; *Pueblo Crafts.* Indian Handicrafts 7, Bureau of Indian Affairs, Department of the Interior, 1953.

Vaillant, George C.; *Indian Arts in North America,* New York (Harpers), 1939.

Willoughby, Charles C.; *The Art of the Great Earthwork Builders of Ohio.* Holmes Anniversary Volume, Anthropological Essays, Washington, D. C., 1916, pp. 469-480.

——; *Indian Masks.* The Exposition of Indian Tribal Arts, Inc., New York, 1931.

Wingert, Paul S.; *American Indian Sculpture,* a Study of the Northwest Coast. New York (J. J. Augustin), 1949. (Bibliography)

Wissler, Clark; *The American Indian.* An Introduction to the Anthropology of the New World, New York (Oxford), 1922.

Wyman, Anne; *Cornhusk Bags of the Nez Percé Indians.* Southwest Museum Leaflets, No. 1, 1935, Los Angeles, California.

CHAPTER FOUR

Adam, Leonhard; "Le Portrait dans l'Art de l'Ancienne Amérique." *Cahiers d'Art,* 1930, No. 10, pp. 519-521.

Ancient Maya Paintings of Bonampak, Mexico. Supplementary Publication 46. Carnegie Institution of Washington, Washington, D. C., 1955.

Basler, Adolphe; and Brummer, Ernest; *L'art précolombien,* Paris, 1947 (Librairie Gründ).

Bennett, Wendell C.; "The Archaeology of Colombia, Handbook of South American Indians." Vol. 2, *The Andean Civilization,* Bulletin 143, Bureau of American Ethnology, Washington, D. C., 1946, pp. 823-850.

——; *Ancient Arts of the Andes.* New York (Museum of Modern Art), 1954.

Bennett, Wendell C.; and Bird, Junius B.; *Andean Culture History.* American Museum of Natural History, Handbook Series No. 15, New York, 1949.

Bird, Junius; and Bellinger, Louisa; *Paracas Fabrics and Nazca Needlework,* 3rd Century, B.C.—3rd Century A.D. Catalogue Raisonné. Washington, D. C. (The Textile Museum), 1954.

British Museum Guide to the Maudslay Collection of Maya Sculptures, Casts and Originals from Central America. London, 1938.

Burland, C. A.; "Civilization of Pre-Columbian Mexico." *History Today,* London (Studio), Sept. 1952, pp. 589-597.

Cahill, Holger; *American Sources of Modern Art.* New York (Museum of Modern Art), 1933.

Caleti, Augustin Villagra; *Bonampak, Mexico* (Instituto Nacional de Anthropologia e Historia), 1949.

Caso, Alfonso; *Thirteen Masterpieces of Mexican Archaeology.* Tr. by Edith Mackie and Jorge R. Acosta, Mexico, 1938.

Charlot, Jean; "A XII Century Mural." *Magazine of Art,* November 1938, pp. 624-629, 670.

Compton, Carl Benton; "The Cult of the Female Among the Tarascans." *Magazine of Art,* Feb. 1953, pp. 75-79.

Covarrubias, Miguel; *Mexico South.* New York (Knopf), 1946.

Danzel, Theo. W.; "Psychologie Altmexikanischer Kunst." *IPEK,* Leipzig, 1925, pp. 124-135.

Dieseldorff, E. P.; "A Pottery Vase with Figure Painting from a Grave in Chama." *Bulletin 28, Bureau of American Ethnology,* pp. 635-644, Washington, D. C., 1904.

Disselhoff, H. D.; *Frühe Kunst Amerika's.* Catalog edited by Stefan P. Munsing, Munich, 1952.

Doering, Heinrich, Ubbelohde; *The Art of Ancient Peru,* New York (Frederick A. Praeger), 1952.

Ekholm, Gordon F.; "The Probable Use of Mexican Stone Yokes." *American Anthropologist,* New Series, Oct.-Dec. 1946, pp. 593-606.

Feuchtwanger, Franz; *The Art of Ancient Mexico.* London and New York (Thames and Hudson), 1954.

Fogg Museum of Art Catalogue; *An Exhibition of Pre-Columbian Art.* Cambridge, Mass., 1940. (Bibliography).

Gold Museum; *80 Masterpieces from the Gold Museum.* Banco de la Republica. Bogotá, Colombia, 1954.

d'Harcourt, Raoul; *Primitive Art of the Americas.* Paris, and New York. (Les Editions du Chêne and Tudor), 1950.

Holmes, W. H.; "Masterpieces of Aboriginal American Art." V. The Great Dragon of Quiriguá. Part I, *Art and Archaeology,* Washington, D. C., July, 1916.

Joyce, Thomas Athol; *Maya and Mexican Art.* London, (The Studio) 1927.

Kidder, A. V.; "The Pottery of the Casas Grandes District, Chihuahua." *Holmes Anniversary Volume,* Washington, D. C. 1916, pp. 253-268.

Kroeber, A. L.; "Great Art Styles of Ancient South America." *Selected Papers of the XXIXth International Congress of Americanists,* pp. 207 ff. Edited by Sol Tax, Chicago, 1951.

Kubler, George; *The Louise and Walter Arensberg Collection. Pre-Columbian Sculpture.* (Philadelphia Museum of Art), 1954.

Leal, Castro; *Twenty Centuries of Mexican Art.* Mexico and New York (The Museum of Modern Art in Collaboration with the Mexican Government), 1949.

Lehmann, Walter; "Ein Goldener Adlerschmuck aus Costa Rica." *IPEK,* 1945, pp. 165-197.

Lothrop, Samuel Kirkland; *An Archaeological Study of Central Panama.* Pt. I, Historical Background, Excavations at the Sitio Conte, Artifacts and Ornaments. Memoirs, Peabody Museum, Harvard University, Volume VII, Cambridge, 1937.

———; *Ancient America, Gold and Jade Cultures.* The Taft Museum, Cincinnati (Ohio), 1950. Exhibition Catalog.

Maudslay, A. P.; *Archaeology. Biologia Centrali-Americana.* 4 Vols., 1889-1902, and Appendix by J. T. Goodman, 1897, London (Porter and Dulan).

Mason, J. Alden; The Ancient Civilization of Middle America." *University Museum Bulletin,* June, 1943, University of Pennsylvania, Philadelphia.

Means, Philip Ainsworth; *A Study of Peruvian Textiles in the Museum of Fine Arts,* Boston, 1932.

Médioni, Gilbert and Pinto, Marie-Therese; *Art in Ancient Mexico.* Diego Rivera Collection. New York (Oxford), 1941.

Morley, Sylvanus Griswold; *Guide Book to the Ruins of Quiriguá.* Washington, D. C., 1935.

———; *The Ancient Maya.* Stanford University, California and London (Stanford University Press–Oxford University Press), 1946. (Bibliography)

Morris, E. H., Jean Charlot, and A. A. Morris; *The Temple of the Warriors at Chichen Itza, Yucatan.* Carnegie Institution of Washington, Publication No. 406, Washington, D. C., 1931.

National Gallery of Art Catalogue; *Indigenous Art of the Americas.* Collection of Robert Woods Bliss, 1947.

Plesants, Frederick R.; "Pre-Columbian Art at the Fogg." *Magazine of Art,* 1940.

Prehispanic Art of Mexico; Mexico DF. Instituto Nacional de antropologia e historia, 1946.

Proskouriakoff, Tatiana; *A Study of Classic Maya Sculpture.* Publication No. 593, Carnegie Institution of Washington, Washington, D. C. 1950.

Rivet, Paul; *Cités Maya,* Paris (Albert Guillot), 1954.

Rowe, John Howland; "Inca Culture at the Time of the Spanish Conquest. Handbook of South American Indians." Volume 2, *The Andean Civilizations,* Bureau of American Ethnology, Bulletin 143, Washington, D. C., 1946, pp. 183-330.

Ruppert, Karl; Thompson, J. Eric S.; Proskouriakoff, Tatiana; *Bonampak, Chiapas, Mexico.* Publication No. 602. Carnegie Institution of Washington, Washington, D. C., 1955.

Sahagun, Fray Bernardino de; *A History of Ancient Mexico.* Tr. by Fanny R. Bandelier, Vol. 1, Nashville (Fiske University Press), 1932.

Satterthwaite, Linton; "The Piedras Negras Expedition." *University Museum Bulletin,* Vol. 4, No. 5, October, 1933, University of Pennsylvania, 1933, pp. 121-126.

Saville, Marshal H.; *The Goldsmith's Art in Ancient Mexico*, New York (Museum of the American Indian), 1920.
——; *Turquoise Mosaic Art in Ancient Mexico.* Contributions, Heye Foundation, Vol. 6, New York (Museum of the American Indian), 1922.
Sawyer, Alan R.; *Handbook. The Nathan Cummings Collection of Ancient Peruvian Art*, Chicago, 1954.
Schmidt, Max; *Kunst und Kultur von Peru.* Berlin (Propylaen), 1929.
Seler-Sachs, Coecilie; "L'architecture et la Sculpture Chez les Aztèques." *Cahiers d'Art*, 4th year, 1929, No. 10, pp. 457-464.
Spinden, Herbert J.; "A Study in Maya Art, Its Subject Matter and Historical Development." *Memoirs of the Peabody Museum of American Archaeology and Ethnology*, Harvard University, Vol. VI, Cambridge (Peabody Museum), 1913.
——; "Portraiture in Central American Art." *Holmes Anniversary Volume*, Washington, D. C., 1916, pp. 434-450.
Stephens, John L.; *Incidents of Travel in Central America, Chiapas and Yucatan.* New York (Harper), 1841.
——; *Incidents of Travel in Yucatan.* New York (Harper), 1843.
Steward, Julian H.; Editor, *Handbook of South American Indians*, Vol. 2. *The Andean Civilizations*, Smithsonian Institution, Bureau of American Ethnology, Bulletin 143. Washington, 1946.
Stirling, Matthew W.; "Great Stone Faces in the Mexican Jungle." *The National Geographic Magazine*, Sept. 1940, pp. 309-334; Sept. 1943, pp. 321-332.
——; "Stone Monuments of the Rio Chiquito, Veracruz, Mexico." *Anthropological Papers*, No. 43. Smithsonian Institution, Bureau of American Ethnology, Bulletin 157. Washington, D. C., 1955.
Thompson, J. Eric S.; *The Civilization of the Mayas.* Chicago Natural History Museum, Popular Series, Anthropology, Number 25, Chicago, 1953.
——; *The Rise and Fall of the Maya Civilization.* Norman (University of Oklahoma Press), 1954.
Strong, William Duncan; "Finding the Tomb of a Warrior-God." *The National Geographic Magazine*, Apr. 1947, pp. 453-482.
Toscano, Salvador; *Arte Precolombiano de Mexico de la America Central.* Mexico (Instituto de investigaciones esteticas), 1944. (Bibliography)
——; *El Arte y la Historia del Occidente en Mexico.* Mexico (Secretaria de Educacion publica), 1946.
Trimborn, Herman; *Indianische Welt in geschichtlicher Schau.* Iserlohn (Silva), 1943.
Vaillant, George C.; *Artists and Craftsmen, in Ancient Central America.* Guide Leaflet Series, No. 88, The American Museum of Natural History, New York, 1935.
——; *The Aztecs of Mexico, Origin, Rise and Fall of the Aztec Nation.* Harmondsworth-Middlesex (Penguin), 1950. (Bibliography)
Weiant, C. W.; *An Introduction to the Ceramics of Tres Zapotes, Veracruz, Mexico.* Smithsonian Institution, Bureau of American Ethnology, Bulletin 139, 1943.
Wilson, Lucy L. W.; "Hand Sign or Aranyu." *American Anthropologist*, Vol. 20, 1918, pp. 310-317.
Wray, Donald E.; "The Historical Significance of the Murals in the Temple of the Warriors, Chichen Itza." *American Antiquity*, July 1945, pp. 25-27.

CHAPTER FIVE

Apollinaire, Guillaume and Tzara, Tristan; *L'Art Oceanien*, Paris (Apam), 1951.
Archey, Gilbert; "Maori Carving Patterns." *Journal of the Polynesian Society*, June 1936, New Plymouth, New Zealand, pp. 49-62.
Balfour, Henry; *The Evolution of Decorative Art.* London (Percival and Co.), 1893.
Barrett, Charles and Croll, Robert Henderson; *Art of the Australian Aborigines.* Melbourne (The Bread and Cheese Club), 1943.
Chauvet, Stephen; *Les Arts Indigenes en Nouvelle-Guinée.* Paris, 1930.
Clauzot, Henri; "Sur l'Art Maori." *Cahiers d'Art*, 1929, p. 99.
Davidson, Daniel Sutherland; *Aboriginal Australian and Tasmanian Rock Carvings and Paintings.* Philadelphia (American Philosophy Society), 1936.
——; *Oceania.* University Museum Bulletin, June 1947, University of Pennsylvania, Philadelphia.
Duff, R. S.; "Moas and Man." *Antiquity*, Vol. 22-23; 1948-49, pp. 172-179.
Emory, Kenneth P.; *Hawaii: Notes on Wooden Images.* Ethnologia Cranmorensis, Cranmore Ethnological Museum, Chislehurst, England, 1938.
Firth, Raymond; *Art and Life on New Guinea.* London, New York (Studio), 1936.
Frobenius, Leo; "Ozeanische Masken." *Internationales Archiv für Ethnographie*, Vol. 10, 1897.
Haddon, A. C.; *The Decorative Art of British New Guinea.* Dublin, 1894.
Hambly, Wilfrid D.; *Primitive Hunters of Australia.* Leaflet 32. Field Museum of Natural History, Chicago, 1936.

Hamilton, Augustus; *The Art Workmanship of the Maori Race in New Zealand*. Dunedin, N. Z. (University of Otago), 1896 and 1900.

Hamsbruch, Paul; "Das Kunstgewerbe in Australien, in der Südsee und Indonisien." T. H. Bossert, *Geschichte des Kunstgewerbes*, Vol. 1, Berlin, 1928, pp. 290-366.

Handy, E. S. Craighill; *L'art des Iles Marquises*. Paris (Les éditions d'art et d'histoire), 1938.

Helbig, Karl; " 'Sichtbare' Religion in Bataklande auf Sumatra." *Zeitschrift für Ethnologie*, Berlin, 1934, No. 4-6, pp. 231-241.

Hough, Walter; "The Buffalo Motive in Middle Celebes Decorative Design." *Proceedings of the U. S. National Museum*, Vol. 79. Washington, D. C., 1932, pp. 1-8.

Kraemer, Augustin; *Die Málanggane von Tombára*. Munich (G. Müller), 1925.

Krieger, H. W.; "Design Areas in Oceania Based on Specimens in the U. S. National Museum." *Proceedings of the U. S. National Museum*. Vol. 79, Washington, D. C., 1932, pp. 1-47.

Kühn, Herbert; *Die Kunst der Primitiven*. Munich (Delphin), 1923. (Bibliography)

Level, André; "Isles Marquises." *Cahiers d'Art*, 1929, pp. 105-108.

Lewis, Albert B.; *New Guinea Masks*. Leaflet No. 4, Field Museum of Natural History, Chicago, 1922.

———; *The Melanesians, People of the South Pacific*. Chicago Natural History Museum, 1951.

Linton, Ralph; "Ethnology of Polynesia and Micronesia." *Guide*, Part 6, Field Museum of Natural History, Chicago, 1926.

———; and Wingert, Paul S.; *Arts of the South Seas*, in Collaboration with René d'Harnoncourt. New York (The Museum of Modern Art), 1946.

Luquiens, H. M.; *Hawaiian Art*. Bernice P. Bishop Museum. Special Publication 18, Honolulu, Hawaii, 1931.

McCarthy, F. D.; *Australian Aboriginal Decorative Art*. Sydney (Australian Museum), 1938.

Metraux, Alfred; "Easter Island." *Smithsonian Report for 1944*, Washington, 1945, pp. 435-452.

Meyer, A. B.; *Masken von Neu Guinea und dem Bismarck Archipel*. Dresden (Stengel and Markert), 1889.

Nevermann, Hans; *Südseekunst*. Staatliche Museen zu Berlin (Guide), Berlin, 1933.

Peabody Museum of Salem Catalogue; *Polynesian Collection, The Hawaiian Portion*. Salem, Mass., 1920.

Phillipps, W. J.; *Maori Art*. Wellington, New Zealand (Harry H. Tombs Limited), 1946.

Reichard, Gladys A.; *Melanesian Design*. 2 Vols., New York (Columbia University Press), 1933.

Rhead, Sir Herbert; *Australia; Aboriginal Paintings, Arnhem Land*. New York (N.Y. Graphic Society and UNESCO), 1954.

Röder, J. "Felsmalereien aus dem Mac Cluer Golf." *IPEK*, 1941-1942, Vol. 15-16, pp. 198-219.

Schnitger, F. M.; "Megalithen vom Batakland und Nias." *IPEK*, 1941-42, Vol. 15-16, pp. 220-252.

Skinner, H. D.; "Evolution in Maori Art." *Journal of the Royal Anthropological Institute of Great Britain and Ireland*, London, Jan.-June, 1916, pp. 184-196. July-Dec. pp. 309-321.

———; "A Ngaitahu Carved Skull Box." *The Journal of the Polynesian Society*, New Plymouth, N. Z., June 1936, pp. 63-66.

Söderström, Jan; *Die Figurstühle vom Sepik-Fluss auf Neu-Guinea*. Stockholm (Statens Etnografiska Museum), 1944.

Speiser, Felix; "Über Kunststile in Melanesien." *Zeitschrift für Ethnologie*, Berlin, 1937, pp. 304-369.

———; "Versuch einer Kultur-Analyse von Neukaledonien." *Zeitschrift für Ethnologie*, Berlin, 1933, Vol. 65, pp. 173-192.

———; "L'Art Plastique des nouvelles Hebrides." *Cahiers d'Art*, 1929, pp. 91-94.

Steinen, K. v. d.; *Die Marquesaner und ihre Kunst*. 3 Vols., Berlin (D. Reimer), 1925-1928.

Stephan, E.; *Südseekunst*. Berlin (D. Reimer), 1907.

Thompson, W. J.; "The Pito Te Henna or Easter Island." *Report of the United States National Museum, Smithsonian Institution for 1889*, Washington, D. C., 1891, pp. 447-552.

Tischner, Herbert; *Oceanic Art*. New York (Pantheon), 1954.

Walden, E.; and Nevermann, Hans; "Totenfeiern und Malagane von Nord-Neu Mecklenburg." *Zeitschrift für Ethnologie*, Berlin, 1940, Publ. 1941, pp. 11-38.

Wingert, Paul S.; *Art of the South Pacific Islands*. A Loan Exhibition. M. H. De Young Memorial Museum, 1953, San Francisco, California.

———; *An Outline Guide to the Art of the South Pacific*, New York (Columbia University Press), 1946. (Bibliography)

———; See Linton (1946).

Wirz, Paul; *Kunstwerke vom Sepik*. Guide to an exhibition, 1954. Museum für Völkerkunde, Basel, Switzerland.

Wölfel, Dominique Joseph; "Le style de l'art, Néo-Calédonien." *Cahiers d'Art*, 1929, pp. 95-97.

CHAPTER SIX

Aznar, José Camón; *Las Artes y los Pueblos de la España Primitiva.* Madrid (Espasa-Calpe, S.A.), 1954.

Braidwood, Robert J.; *Prehistoric Men.* Popular Series, Anthropology Series, Number 37, Chicago (Chicago Natural History Museum), 1950.

Breuil, Abbé H.; *Four Hundred Centuries of Cave Art.* Tr. by Miss Mary E. Boyle, Realized by Fernand Windels, Montignac, Dordogne, 1952.

——— and Daniel, Glyn; *Cave Drawings.* An Exhibition of drawings by the Abbé Breuil of paleolithic paintings and engravings. The Arts Council, 1954. (Paleolithic Cave Art)

Brodrick, Alan, Houghton; *Prehistoric Painting.* New York (Transatlantic Arts), 1948.

Cartailhac, Emile and Breuil, Henri; *La Caverne d'Altamira à Sentillane près Santander, Espagne,* Monaco, 1906.

Frobenius, Leo; *Erythräa, Länder und Zeiten des Heiligen Königsmordes.* Berlin-Zurich (Atlantis), 1931.

Frobenius, Leo and Fox, Douglas C.; *Prehistoric Rock Pictures in Europe and Africa.* New York (Museum of Modern Art), 1937.

Frobenius, Leo and Obermaier, H.; *Hádschra Máktuba.* Munich (K. Wolff), 1925.

Herberts, Kurt; *Anfänge der Malerei.* Wuppertal-Barmen (Bädecker), 1941.

———; *Wände und Wandbild.* Stuttgart (Stahle and Friedel), 1953.

Hoernes, M. and Menghin, O.; *Urgeschichte der Bildenden Kunst in Europa.* Vienna (Schroll), 1925.

Karutz, Richard; *Die Ursprache der Kunst.* Stuttgart (Strecker-Schröder), 1934.

Kirchner, Horst; "Ein Archäologischer Beitrag zur Urgeschichte des Schamanismus." *Anthropos,* Vol. 47, 1952.

Klaatsch, Hermann; *Die Anfänge von Kunst und Religion in der Urmenscheit.* Leipzig (Unesma), 1913.

Kühn, Herbert; "Die Bedeutung der Prähistorischen und Ethnographishen Kunst für die Kunstgeschichte." *IPEK* (Jahrbuch für die Prähistorische und Ethnographische Kunst), Leipzig, 1925, p. 3.

———; "Alter und Bedeutung der Nordafrikanischen Felszeichnungen." *IPEK,* 1927, pp. 13-30.

———; Kunst und Kultur der Vorzeit Europa's. Vol. I, *Das Paleolithikum,* Berlin, 1929.

———; *Die Felsbilder Europas.* Zürich-Vienna, 1952.

———; See Obermaier (1930).

Laubat, F. de Chasseloup; *Art Rupestre au Hoggar.* Paris (Librairie Plon), 1938.

Levy, Gertrude Rachel; *The Gate of Horn.* London (Faber and Faber), 1948.

Luquet, G. H.; "Le Réalisme Intellectuel dans l'Art Primitif." *Journal de Psychologie,* Vol. 24, Paris, 1927.

Maringer, Johannes and Bandi, Hans-Georg; *Art in the Ice Age.* New York (Frederick A. Praeger), 1953.

Nelson, N. C.; *South African Rock Pictures.* Guide Leaflet Series of the American Museum of Natural History, No. 93, New York, 1937.

Obermaier, Hugo; "Altamira. The Caverns of the Stone Age Artists." *Natural History,* Vol. XXX, 1930, New York, pp. 426-434.

———; and Kühn, Herbert; *Bushman Art, Rock Paintings of Southwest Africa.* London (Oxford), 1930.

Parkyn, Ernest; *An Introduction to the Study of Prehistoric Art.* London and New York (Longmans, Green and Co.), 1915.

Passemard, Luce; *Les Statuettes Féminines Paléoliques Dites Venus Steatopyges.* Nîmes. (Imprimerie cooperative), 1938.

Raphael, Max; *Prehistoric Cave Paintings.* New York (Pantheon), 1945.

Rhotert, Hans; *Libysche Felsbilder.* Darmstadt (L. C. Wittich), 1952.

Rosenthal, Eric; and Goodwin A. J. H.; *Cave Artists of South Africa.* Cape Town, South Africa (A. A. Balkema), 1953.

Santa-Olalla, Julio Martinez; "Neues über Prähistorische Felsmalereien in Frankreich, Spanien und Marokko." *IPEK.* 1941-42, pp. 1-24.

Scheltema, Frederik, Adama, van; *Die Kunst Unserer Vorzeit.* Leipzig (Bibliographisches Institut), 1936.

———; *Die Kunst der Vorzeit.* Stuttgart (Kohlhammer), 1950.

Spearing, H. G.; *The Childhood of Art.* New York (Putnam), 1913. Also two vol. edition, London (Ernest Benn), 1930.

Stow, George Wm. and Bleek, Dorothea F.; *Rock Paintings in South Africa from Parts of the Eastern Province and Orange Free State.* London (Methuen), 1930.

Windels, Fernand and Laming, Annette; *The Lascaux Cave Paintings,* London (Faber and Faber), 1949.

INDEX

Abelam, 288
Abomey, 25
Accra, 55
Acoma, 129, 133
Adam, Leonhard, 70, 75
Adena, 116, 117
Admiralty Islands, 280-284
Afotobo, 16
Africa, 10 (map), 11-55, 321-326, 356-362
aggression, 356
Aguila, J. Cabre, 350
Ai-Apec, 232, 263 (*237*)
Ain Dua, 359
Ain Safsad, 356
Alaska, 56-64; 61 (ill. 2)
Albarracin, 351
Altamira (*see also* painting, rock), 302, 304, 337, 339-346, 346 (ill. 40), 349, 361, 363
American Museum of Natural History, (*190, 216-217, 228, 237*)
Ammon, 51
Anasazi, 115
ancestors, veneration of (*see also* figures, ancestral), 13, 14, 19, 275
Andersson, Efraim, 31
animism, 53, 59, 162, 169
Antubam, Kofi, 55
Apache, 57 (map), 124, 127, 136, 139, 142
aprons, leather, 75, 77
Arawa, 293
architecture, 12, 17, 116, 171-172, 223-224, 228, 279, 293, 300
Arnhem Land, 297
Art Institute of Chicago, 232
art, origins of, 345-346
artists (*see also* potters), 18, 54, 55, 62, 77, 79-80, 142-143, 185, 278, 351, 361
Ashanti, 10 (map), 12, 24, 25
Atutu, 15, 16
Aurignac, 302
Aurignacian period (*see also* engraving, rock; painting, rock), 300, 304, 337, 338, 339, 347, 349
Austral Islands, 275, 291
Australia, 296-298
Awatovi, 125, 143
awe, feeling of, 19
"ax gods," 210, 218
axes, 201 (*166*), 204 (*178*)
Azilians, 362
Aznar, Jose Camón, 345
Aztecs, 162, 163 (map), 164, 214-218

Badjokwe, 10 (map), 33, 52-53
Bafum, 31
Baga, 10 (map), 21-22, 35 (*7*)
Baining, 288
Bakota, 10 (map), 18, 19, 31
Bakuba, 10 (map), 12, 18, 49, 50-51
Bali, 15, 31
ball-court marker, 195 (*154*)
Baluba, 10 (map), 16, 49, 51-52, 83 (plate 6)
Bambara, 10 (map), 20-22, 31, 33 (*3*)
Bamum, 10 (map), 31
Bandi, Hans-Georg (*see also* Maringer, Johannes), 350, 351
Bangwa, 10 (map), 31
Banjo, 297
banner stones, 119
Bapende, 10 (map), 49-50
Barbeau, C. Marius, 65
Bardal, 347
bark cloth, *see tapa*
Barma Grande, 349
Barnes Collection, 20
Barotse, 10 (map), 53
Barradas, José Perez de, 221
Barrier Canyon, 125
Barrow, Sir John, 360
Bascom, William R., 29
"Basket Makers," 115
basketry, 135, 136
baskets:
  Apache, 155 (*132*)
  California, 155 (*131*)
  Pima, 137 (ill. 20)
Basonge, 10 (map), 15
Bateke, 10 (map), 32, 49-50
Batshioko, see Badjokwe
Baulé, 10 (map), 21, 23, 24, 31
Bayaka, 10 (map), 32, 49-50
beadwork, 122-124
beak style, 284, 287
"Bear Mother," 79, 108 (*92*)
Begouen, Count, 342
Bekom, 10 (map)

Note: Italic numbers in parentheses indicate photograph figure numbers.

Belgian Government Information Center, 55
beliefs:
Africa, 13-14
(animalistic) animistic, 346
Eskimo, 59-60, 166-169
Iroquois, 119
Middle and South America, 165-169
Navaho, 125
Northwest Pacific Coast, 66-68
Oceania, 275-279
Bella Colla, 57 (map), 65
Bena biombo, 52
Bena Lulua, 10 (map), 49, 51
Beni, 10 (map), 16, 26-28
Benin, 12, 15, 23, 24, 25-30, 29 (ill. 1), 44 (27), 54-55
Benin City, 54
Bennett, Wendell C., 225
Berlin Museum, 121
Berndt, R. and C., 297
Bicorp, 351
Bird, Junius, 235-236
Blackfeet, 123, 127
"bladder festival," 59
blankets:
Chilkat, 75, 76-77, 80, 101 (79), 137
Navaho, 137-139, 150 (133, 134)
Bliss, Hon. Robert Woods, Collection of, 174, 209-210, 216, 221, 223-224, 234, 237
blowgun, 337
Boas, Franz, 65, 66, 68-70, 74
Bobo, 10 (map), 20
Bohuslän, 363
Bonampak (*see also* painting, mural), 165, 184-186
Bope Pelenge, 50
Boston Museum of Fine Arts, 238-239
Boudon, 343
Boule, 343
bowls:
Admiralty Islands, 271 (261), 280
Baluba, 52, 81 (50)
Central America, 219 (ill. 27)
Northwest Pacific Coast, 78, 104 (83), 105 (85)
United States (Alabama), 111 (98), 118
bows, fire-drill, 60
box, Northwest Pacific Coast, 78, 106 (87)
brasses, Dahomey, 25, 40 (20)
Breuil, Abbé H., 302, 304, 337, 338, 342, 344, 351
British Museum, 26, 27, 29, 52, 180, 181, 217, 289
Bronze Period, 302, 304, 347, 349, 362-363
bronzes:
Benin, 26-28, 43 (plate 4), 44 (24-26), 45 (28)
Ife, 29-30, 45 (30)
Brooklyn Museum, 239
Brünn (Moravia), 349
Buffalo Museum of Science, 23, 282
Buli, 52
Bundu Society, 14, 22
Bunzel, Ruth L., 129, 133
Burkitt, Miles, 351
Bushman (*see also* painting, rock), 10 (map), 321-336, 359-360, 361
Bushongo, *see* Bakuba

Cairns, Huntington, 167
Calapata, 350
calendars, Aztec and Maya, 165-166
Caleti, Augustin Villagra, 185
Calima Style, 223
Calusa Indians, 120
Cameroons, 13, 15, 19, 23, 30-31, 46 (35)
canoes, 289, 293
paddles, 283
prows, 272 (266), 283, 285, 294, 307 (273), 317 (306)
Cap Blanc, 341
Capsian, 302, 350
carbon 14 method, 166
Carnegie Institute of Washington, 183-184
Caroline Islands, 289
Carriso Rock, 125
carving, see sculpture; wood carving
carving, architectural, 18, 46 (35), 88 (63), 160 (146), 195 (152), 198 (161), 283, 288, 293, 294, 309 (280), 312 (287), 313 (290), 318 (207)
Casas Grandes, 127
Caso, Alfonso, 209, 211
Castillo, 346
Catherwood, Frederick, 165
Celebes, 275, 280
Central and East Africa, 13
ceramics (*see also* pottery), 218, 226-227
ceremonies, initiation, 125, 283
champlevé, 180
Chancay, 22
Chavín de Húantar, 166, 221, 224
Cherokee, 142
Cheyenne, 122, 124
Chibcha, 117, 163 (map), 223, 229-230
Chicago Natural History Museum, 119, 285, 287
Chichén Itzá, 165-166, 183, 185-186
Chichimec, 213
Chihuahua, 65
Chimakuan, 65
Chimu style, 163 (map), 164, 171, 223, 229-230
Chinookan, 65
Chiricahua, 125
Cholula, 213
Chorotega Indians, 218-219
churingas, 298, 298 (ill. 35)
cire perdue process, 24, 209, 221
Cleveland Museum of Art, 190, 238
clubs:
war, 78, 106 (86A), 156 (130), 315 (300)
whalebone, 271 (263), 295
Coatlicue, 168, 172, 208 (192, 193), 214
coats, flax, 293
Cochiti, 129, 134
coconut grater, Micronesia, 313 (291)
Colonial Museum, Wellington, 293
color, use of, 17, 19, 121, 123, 126, 142, 178, 184, 220, 233, 237, 288, 302, 340
Columbus, voyage of, 221
Comanche, 121, 142
conchas, 141, 158 (138)
Congo, 12, 13, 16, 18, 23, 31-55
contemporary art:
in Africa, 54-55
on Northwest Pacific Coast, 79-80
in United States, 142-143
Cook, Captain, 70, 292
Cook Islands, 275, 291
Copán, 165, 175-176, 178, 180-182, 183
copper, Ife, 29-30, 45 (31)
Cordwell, Justine M., 16, 17, 30, 55
Cortez, 165, 215
Cosgrove, H. S. and C. B., 128
Covalanas, 341

Covarrubias, Miguel, 189
Cree, 122
Creek, 142
Cromagnon (France), 349
Cueva de la Arana, 355
Cueva del Civil, 354, 359
Cueva Más del Joseph, 354
Cueva Saltadora, 351
cults (*see also* beliefs), 363
cultures, prehistoric, 56, 115, 118, 127, 233, 234-235, 268
Cupisnique, 230-231
curvilinear style, 284, 287, 288

Dahomey, 12, 13, 18, 25-26; 40 (20)
Dan, 10 (map), 23
Dapper, Olfert, 27-28
Darmstadt Museum, 52
Delamere, 296
Denver (Colo.) Museum, 289
designs, *see* motifs
distortions, 17, 127, 227
Djattou, 356
Doering, Heinrich U., 165
Dogon, 10 (map), 13, 20
dolls, *see* Kachinas
Douglas, Fredric H., 123
drawing (*see also* painting):
  cave, 303 (ill. 36)
  Northwest Pacific Coast, 75-76
  Peru, 232
Drucker, Phillip, 171
drums, 62, 269 (256), 272 (265), 282

East Spanish style, 338, 343, 344, 349, 350-356, 359, 360
Easter Island, 274, 275, 291
effigy jars, 84 (54), 112 (*100, 102*), 118, 150 (116)
Egypt, 11, 31-32, 50, 53, 165
Ekholm, Gordon F., 211
Ekoi, 10 (map), 15, 18, 19, 30-31
Enfous, 356
engraving, bone, 342
engraving, rock, 302, 304, 337
  Font-de-Gaume, 321 (315)
  North Africa, 328 (330), 356-359; 357-358 (ills. 45-47)
  Scandinavia, 326 (323, 324), 335-336 (346-348), 348 (ill. 41),
    362-364, 364 (ill. 49)
engraving, shell, 110 (94, 95), 117
engraving, walrus ivory, 60-61, 61 (ill. 2)
Enwonwu, Ben, 53
Esie, 26
Eskimo, 56-64, 68, 80
Eweke II, 54
Ewers, John C., 121, 122, 123

Fagg, Bernard, 29
Fagg, William, 16, 28
Fang, 10 (map), 31
fear, 13, 68, 279
featherwork, 239, 243 (plate 24), 268 (253), 291, 293
Fenollosa, 290
Fenton, William N., 119-120
Fewkes, Jesse Walter, 134, 142
figure carving, *see* figures; sculpture; wood carving
figure styles, Melanesia, 284-286, 285 (ill. 34)
figures, 18-19, 175-177, 271
  Ashante, 39 (17)
  Badjokwe, 84 (53)
  Bakuba, 46 (42)
  Baluba, 81 (49)
  Bena Lulua, 84 (51)
  Cameroon, 45 (36)
  Haida, 98 (74)
  Inca, 256 (219)
  Melanesian, 307 (275)
  Mochica, 242 (plate 21)
  New Guinea, 254 (plate 30), 310 (283)
  New Hebrides, 251 (plate 29)
  Quinault, 100 (77)
  Yoruba, 40 (22, 23)
  Zapotec, 202 (170)
figures, ancestral, 14, 20, 22-24, 27, 30-31, 51, 278, 285-286, 287,
    294
  Baluba, 46 (45-46)
  Baulé, 38 (12, 13)
  Congo, 46 (41)
  Dogon, 33 (2)
  Indonesia, 269 (255)
  New Ireland, 308 (276)
figures, fetish, 14, 24, 49
figures, funerary, 30, 32, 46 (40)
figures, mortuary, 20, 306 (270)
figurines:
  Maya, 182, 198 (159)
  Olmec, 201 (167)
  Tarascan, 173-174, 159 (140)
Fiji Islands, 275, 281
Firth, Raymond, 278
float, Solomon Islands, 305 (269)
flutes, 280
Font-de-Gaume, 300, 302, 304, 338, 339, 342
Forschungs Institut für Kulturmorphologie, DIAFE XI and XII,
    359
Fox, Douglas C., 361
Franco-Cantabrian, 302, 338, 339, 347, 350-351, 355, 356, 360
Frazer, Sir James George, 68
frescoes:
  Maya, 183, 184-186, 213
  Toltec, 212
Frobenius, Leo, 29

Gabun, 31
Gaffron Collection, 234-235, 237
Gafsa, 302
Gallinazo, 230-231
game board, Hawaii, 290, 314 (294)
Gargas, 337, 346
Gasulla Gorge, 328 (328), 350, 354, 355
"Gate of the Sun," 226, 238-239
Gauguin, 275
Gazelle Peninsula, New Britain, 288
Geh, 22
Genière, 342
Ghana Empire, 12
Gilbert Islands, 289
Gio, 22
gods:
  Africa, 26
  Aztec, 166-167, 214-217
  Hawaii, 313 (292, 293)
  Inca, 168
  Maya, 186-187
  Scandinavia, 363
  Toltec, 212
Gold Coast, 14, 24, 54-55
Gold Museum, Bogota, 220
gold weights, bronze, 24-25, 39 (18)

Goldenweiser, Alexander, 120
gold work:
Africa, 25, 40 (19)
Central and South America, 203 (174), 209, 220-223, 249-253 (210-217)
gorgets, shell, 117, 110 (94)
"Great Zimbabwe," 361
Grimaldi (Italy), 349
grinding stones (metates), 219, 248 (206)
Groote Eylandt, 297
Guetar Indians, 218-219
guilt, sense of, 67
Guro, 10 (map), 24

Haddon, Alfred C., 282
Haida, 57 (map), 65, 66, 70, 74, 77, 79
Hall, H. U., 121
Harvey Islands, 291
Hausa merchants, 54-55
Hawaiian Islands, 274, 275, 290
headdress, Yoruba, 82 (plate 3)
headpiece, Bambara, 33 (3)
headrest, Baluba, 83 (plate 6)
heads:
"baby face," 172, 190-191
Colima, 159 (143)
New Guinea, 311 (284)
"smiling," 205 (180-181), 210-211
Tarascan, 159 (143)
head-styles, Oceania, 285 (ill. 34)
Healey, Giles G., 185
Hereros, 10 (map)
Herskovits, Melville J., 18, 25, 29
Himmelheber, Hans, 14, 16, 59, 79
Hoernes, M., 343, 344
Hoffman, Walter James, 60, 79
Hohokam, 115
Holmes, William H., 65, 218
Hopewell, 115, 116, 118, 119
Hopi, 57 (map), 115, 124, 125, 127, 129, 136, 139, 142, 143
Hornes de la Peña, 341, 345, 346
Hottentots, 10 (map)
house posts (*see also* carving, architectural), 70, 71-72, 88 (62, 63)
Houston, James A., 80
Howe, 143
Hoyle, Rafael Larco, 230
Huasteca, 162, 163 (map), 211-212
Hungarian Ethnographical Museum, 298

Ibibio, 10 (map), 30
Ibo, 10 (map), 19, 30
Ibudor, Felix, 54
Ica, 22
Ife, 15, 18, 30
Ikerre, 26
imagery, eidetic, 343
Inca, 163 (map), 164, 166, 223-224, 234-235
incense burner, Andean, 226, 256 (220)
Indian Arts and Crafts Board, 134
Indians, North America, 65-80, 116-144
Ingalik, 58
insecurity, 13
Iroquois, 57 (map), 119-120, 126
Isla de Sacrificios, 217
ivory:
Benin, 27, 28 (ill. 1), 28-29, 42
Eskimo (walrus), 60
Mangbetu, 53
Warega, 53
Ivory Coast, 13, 16, 23

Jacobson, O. B., 142
jades, 188, 218, 293
pre-Columbian, 199 (162)
jars:
Aztec, 245 (200)
Inca, 265 (245)
Maya, 91 (plate 13)
jars, effigy, *see* effigy jars
Jemez, 125
jewelry:
Central and South America, 203 (174), 221, 222, 223, 253 (212, 213, 216, 217)
European prehistoric, 349
Navaho and Zuni, 140-141

Kabah, 181
Kabotie, Fred, 142, 143
Kachina dolls, 114, 140, 157 (135)
Kachinas, 90 (plates 10, 11, 12), 139, 140, 143
kapkaps, *see* ornaments, breast
Karad-jeri, 296
Karutz, R., 51
Kata Mbula, 50
Kawaika, 125
Key Marco, 120
Khargur Valley, 158-159
Kiowa, 142
Kirchner, Horst, 338
Kjersmeier, Carl, Collection, 31
korovar style, 284, 288
Kraemer, Augustin, 287
Kuaua, New Mexico, 125
Kubler, George, 166, 174, 211
Kühn, Herbert, 338, 339, 342, 343, 347, 350, 351, 358, 360
Kukailimoku, 290
Kukulcán, 166
Kwakiutl, 57 (map), 65, 73, 74, 75, 98 (75)

La Clotilde, 346
La Grèze, 337, 339, 347
La Hoz, 351
La Madelaine, 300
La Mola Remigia, 354
La Pasiega, 341
La Venta, 162, 189-191
Lacondon Indian, 185
Lagos, 27, 55
Lambayeque, 230
language, pictorial, 363
Lascaux, 302, 304, 322-324 (316-318), 337, 338, 339, 340, 363
Latta, F. F., 124-125
Laugerie-basse, 300, 349
Laughton, Charles, Collection, 174
Laussel, 300, 341
Le Moustier, 300
Le Portel, 341
Lehmann, Walter, 165
Leiknes (Norway), 347
Les Combarelles, 300, 302
Les Eyzies, 300, 302, 349
Les Trois Frères, 302, 339, 342, 343, 344, 365 (321, 322)
Lespugue, 349
Lewis, Albert B., 278
Levy, Gertrude R., 344, 346
Leyden (Netherlands) Museum, 177

Liberia, 13, 22, 38 (11)
lime tube stopper, New Guinea, 270 (260), 280
Limeuil, 300, 342
lintels, 160 (146), 195 (152), 198 (161)
Linton, Ralph, 290
Lorogho, 21
Los Cazeres, 350
Lothrop, Samuel K., 211, 219-221
Lunda Empire, 53
Luquet, G. H., 343, 344, 345
Luschan, Felix von, 24, 27
Lyford, Carrie A., 124

Ma-Pe-Wi (Velino Shije), 142, 143
Machu Picchu, 224
Magdalenian Period, (*see also* engraving, rock; painting, rock), 300, 304, 337, 338, 339-343, 347, 362
magic, 59, 118, 119, 124, 167, 169-170, 275, 280, 296, 297, 341, 342, 343-345, 355, 358, 364
Makonde, 10 (map), 53
malagan, 273, 286
Malekula, New Hebrides, 285
mana, 275
manaias, 294-295
Mandan, 121, 122
Mangbetu, 10 (map), 15, 33, 53
Mano, 22
mantles, 246 (plate 25), 266 (246, 248)
manuscripts, Maya, 94 (plate 15), 186-187, 187 (ill. 26)
Maori, 292-296
maps:
- Africa, 10
- Australia, 276-277
- France (southwestern) and Spain, 301
- Middle America and the Andean Regions of South America, 163
- North America, 57
- Scandinavia, 301
- South Seas and Australia, 276-277

Marajão, 235
Marchand, 292
Mariana Islands, 289
Maringer, Johannes, 346, 350, 351
Marquesas, 274, 275, 291-292
Marshall Islands, 289
Martinez, Crescencio, 142
Martinez, Julian and Maria, 135
Mas-d'azil, 302, 341
masks:
- Africa, 18, 19, 21, 22, 23, 24, 25, 26, 28, 30, 31, 32, 34 (5), 36-38 (10, 11, 14), 39 (15, 16), 41 (21), 43 (29), 44 (32-34), 45 (38, 39), 46 (40, 43), 47 (44), 48 (47), 49-50, 51, 52, 53, 82-83 (plates 1, 5, 7), 84 (52)
- Aztec, 244 (201), 245 (203)
- Eskimo, 58, 59-60, 62-64, 64-65 (ills. 5, 6), 81 (57-59)
- Melanesia, 250 (plates 27, 28), 269 (257), 270 (259-260), 278, 279, 283, 286, 288, 306 (271), 307 (277, 279), 309 (281), 310 (282), 311 (285, 286), 312 (287)
- Micronesia, 289, 313 (290)
- Middle America, 95 (plate 17), 204 (177), 210, 213, 217, 218, 244 (198), 245 (202, 204)
- Northwest Pacific Coast, 69, 73-74, 77, 79, 86 (plate 8), 89 (64), 92 (65, 66), 93 (67-70), 96 (71), 99 (76), 105 (84)
- Peru, 223, 239, 268 (254)
- Southwest United States, 139-140, 157 (136, 137)

Masterton, New Zealand, 293
Maudslay, Alfred P., 165, 180
Mauny, 30
Maya, 162, 163 (map), 164, 166, 168, 175-188, 175 (ill. 21), 177 (ill. 22), 179 (ills. 23, 24), 187 (ill. 26)
Mayne and Duncan, 68
McCarthy, F. D., 297
Melanesia, 273, 274, 280-289
Melle Empire, 12
Melville, Herman, 275
memorial boards, Melanesia, 269 (257), 287
Menché, see Yaxchilán
Mendi, 10 (map), 14, 22
Menomini, 136
Mentone (Italy), 349
Mesolithic Period, 312, 363
Metraux, Alfred, 117
Mexico, 117, 118, 159, 200
mica, 119, 145 (103)
Micronesia, 273, 274, 289
Mimbres, 128, 129-131 (ills. 15-17)
Minateda, 351, 355
Minneapolis Institute of Arts, 232
Mixtec, 162, 163 (map), 164, 209, 217
Mochica, 163 (map), 166, 227-228, 230-232
Mogollon-Mimbres, 115
Mohammedans, see Moslems
Mohave, 128
Monomotapa Empire, 12
Monte Alban, 162, 166, 191-192
Montespan, 344
Montezuma, 216, 220
Montignac, 337
Morella la Vella, 354
Morley, Sylvanus Griswold, 168
mortars, 78, 107 (89, 90), 242 (plate 20)
mosaic work, 217, 245 (204)
Moslems, 12, 20
Mossi, 20
motifs:
- Andean, 226
- animal, 31, 61, 67, 69, 70, 238, 287
- bird, 133 (ill. 19), 222, 282
- blankets, Navaho, 138
- cat demon, 237
- cat head, 234
- centipede, 237
- crocodile, 222, 280
- Eastern woodlands, 116, 117
- god, multiple-headed, 237
- goldwork, Quimbaya, 226
- Maori, 294
- Maya, 176
- Oceania, 281, 282 (ills. 30, 31), 295
- pottery, 127, 129, 133, 227, 231, 233
- quillwork, 123
- sandpainting, 126
- serpent, 178, 224
- textiles, Peru, 237-238
- Toltec, 212
- Totonac, 210-211

Mound Builders, 117-119
Mousterian, 304
Mtoko Cave, 361
Murdoch, John, 80
Muschenge, 55
Musée de l'Homme, Paris, 249, 294
Museo de America, Madrid, 181
Museum of Navaho Ceremonial Art, Santa Fe, New Mexico, 126
Museum of New Mexico, 142
Museum of the American Indian, New York, 117, 125

Museum of the University of Oklahoma, 117

Nampeyo, 134-135
Nancy, 341
Nash, Wesley, 143
National Gallery of Art, Washington, D. C., 174, 190
National Museum of Guatemala City, 182
National Museum of Mexico, 168, 174, 181, 212, 215, 217
Navaho (*see also* blankets; painting, contemporary; silver), 57 (map), 115, 125, 126-127, 136, 144
Nazca, 166, 227, 233-234
Neanderthal, 300
neck-rest, Melanesia, 272 (*267*)
Nelson, Edward W., 59, 60, 62, 79
Neolithic Period, 302, 304, 349, 351, 362, 363, 364
New Britain, 282, 284, 285
New Caledonia, 283, 288
New Guinea, 275, 276 (map)
  Geelvink Bay, 274, 280
  Huon Gulf, 276 (map), 281, 292
  Massion area, 276 (map), 282
  Papua Gulf, 276 (map), 287
  Sepik River, 276 (map), 280, 282, 288, 289
  Torres Straits, 276 (map), 288
New Ireland, 282, 286, 287
New Zealand, 275, 281, 292-296
Newark (N. J.) Museum, 26
Nez Perce, 136
Nias, 275, 292
Niaux, 302, 341, 344
Nigeria, 13, 15, 16, 18, 19, 26, 30, 54, 55
Noilles, 304
Nok culture, 15, 18, 33 (*1*)
Nootka, 57 (map), 65, 68, 70, 74
Nukuoro Island, 289
Nunivak, 59

Oaxaca Museum, 192
Obalufon II, 29, 43 (*31*)
Obermaier, Hugo, 304, 343, 350, 351, 359, 360
Ogowe River tribes, 10 (map), 31
Ohio State Museum, Columbus, 119
Olbrechts, Frans, 33, 56
Oldman Collection, 291
Olmec, 94, 162 (plate 16), 163 (map), 189-191
Olokun, 29, 45 (*30*)
Onondaga, 142
ornaments:
  breast, 282, 283 (ills. 32, 33)
  gable, 309 (*280*)
  headdress, 97 (*72*)
Osiris, 31
Ostergötland, 363
Oued Mertoutek, 359
oval style, 284

Pacheco, 230
Pahouin, see Fang
painting:
  bark, 297, 319 (*310-312*)
  contemporary Indian, 142-143
  Eskimo, 62, 65 (ills. 3, 4)
  hide, 146 (*107*), 147 (*108*)
  Maya, 183
  mural, 91 (plate 14), 125, 150 (*112*), 186 (ill. 25)
  negative, 227
  Northwest Pacific Coast, 75-76, 101 (*78*)
  Oceania, 280, 282, 305 (*268*)
  Plains Indian, 120-122
  prehistoric, 302, 304, 342
painting, rock, 350-356, 358-359
  Altamira, 255 (plate 31), 303 (ill. 38), 325 (*319, 320*), 345 (ill. 39)
  Australia, 250, 251, 254, 269-272, 296, 305-318, 318 (*309*), 319 (*310*)
  Bushman, 330-332 (*334-338*)
  East Spanish, 327-328 (*326-329*), 352, 353, 355 (ills. 42-44)
  La Greze, 361 (*314*)
  Lascaux, 362 (*316, 317*), 364 (*318*)
  Les Trois Frères, 325 (*321*), 343
  North Africa, 329 (*331, 332*), 330 (*333*), 356-359
  Southern Rhodesia, 332 (*339, 340*), 333 (*341-343*), 334 (*344*), 361-362, 362 (ill. 48)
  Southwest United States, 148 (*110-111*)
painting, sand, 126-127, 149 (*113*)
Pair-non-pair, 300, 337
Palenque, 175, 177-178, 181
Paleolithic Period, 299, 304, 349, 350, 356, 359
palmas, 205 (*179*), 210
Pangwe, see Fang
Papago, 57 (map), 124, 136
Papantla, 210
Paracas Cavernas, 228, 235, 236
Paracas Necropolis, 166, 235-237
Paracas style, 246 (plate 25)
Parpallo, 350
Peabody Museum, Harvard University, 125, 181, 221
Peabody Museum, Salem (Mass.), 280, 295
pendants, 243 (*172*), 245 (*199*), 248 (*205*)
Perigordian, 338, 351
petroglyphs, 70, 148 (*110, 111*), 224-225
Philadelphia Museum of Art, 219
Picuris, 234
Piedras Negras, 175-177, 179, 182
pigments, 15, 74, 178, 321, 324, 337, 340, 344, 360
Pima, 57 (map), 61 (map), 124, 129 (ill. 20), 136, 137 (ill. 20)
Pinal, 341
pipes, 60, 78, 85 (*55, 56*), 108 (*91*), 111 (99), 118, 145 (93)
Pizarro, 165
Polelonema, Otis, 142
poles, mortuary, 69, 72
poles, totem, *see* totem poles
Polynesia, 273, 274, 290-296, 316 (*300*), 318 (*307*)
Pomo, 57 (map), 136
Poro, 22
Portland (Oregon) Art Museum, 74, 76, 174
Portrero Nuevo, 189
potlatch, 66, 70, 77
potters, Pueblo, 129-135
pottery:
  California, 150 (*117*)
  contemporary, 129-135
  Europe, prehistoric, 334 (*345*)
  Middle America, 95 (plate 18), 160 (*144*), 187-188, 198 (*160*), 214, 248 (*208*)
  Mimbres, 128, 129-131 (ills. 15-18), 151 (*118, 119*)
  Oceania, 279, 289, 312 (*288*)
  Pueblo, 57 (map), 129-135, 133 (ill. 19), 151 (*120-122*), 153 (*123-128*)
  South America, 226-235, 242, 243, 247 (plates 19, 22, 26), 256-259 (*224-230*), 260 (*231, 232*), 261-265 (*234-244*)
  United States, prehistoric, 112 (*101*), 118-119, 127-128, 149 (*114*), 150 (*115*)
Prehistoric Museum, Rome, 209-217
prehistory, 299-300
Proskouriakoff, Tatiana, 176, 181

Pueblo Bonito, 115

Quetzalcoatl, 166, 212-213, 216
Quiché, 118
quillwork, 122-123; 148 (109)
Quimbaya, 162, 163 (map), 231-232
Quinault, 75
Quiriguá, 175, 178-179, 188, 191

Raimondi, Stela, 224, 225 (ill. 28)
Ranoraraku, 291
Raphael, Max, 341, 344
Rarotonga, 291
rattles, Northwest Pacific Coast, 77, 102-103 (80-81)
Rauru, 283
regicide, ritual, 361
Reinach, S., 343
religion, see beliefs; gods; magic
Rhodesia, Southern, 361-362
rock shelters, 300, 350
Rockefeller, Nelson A., Collection, 237
Róheim, Géza, 298
Romain-Desfosses, Pierre, 55
Roth, H. Ling, 26

sacrifices, human, 165, 167-169, 214, 217
Sahagun, Fray Bernardino de, 167-168, 191, 217
Saiyatasha, 140, 157 (137)
Salinar, 230-231
Salish, 57 (map), 65, 75, 137
Samoa, 275, 281, 291
San Idlefonso, 125, 129, 142, 224
San Juan, 224
San Lorenzo, 189-190
sand painting, see painting, sand
Santa Ana, 129, 134
Santa Clara, 129, 134
Santa-Olalla, Julio Martinez, 350
Santarem, 235
Santo Domingo, 129, 134
Santuola, Don Marcelino S. de, 339
Sassa (Makaha Road), 362
Satoan Island, 289
Scandinavia, 326 (323, 324), 335 (345, 346, 347), 336 (348), 347, 348 (ill. 41), 362-364, 364 (ill. 49)
schools:
  Africa, Muschenge, 55
  United States, Mt. Edgecombe, 79
sculpture (see *also* figures; sculpture, stone; stelae; wood carving), 18, 135
sculpture, stone, Africa, 11, 36 (9)
sculpture, stone, European prehistoric, 348-349, 327 (325)
sculpture, stone, Middle America:
  Aztec, 208 (*190, 191*), 214-216, 241 (*194-197*), 244 (*201*), 245 (*203*)
  Costa Rica, 248 (207)
  Huasteca, 206 (*186*)
  Maya, 160 (*145*), 175-181, 175, 177, 179 (ills. 21, 22, 24), 195 (*153*), 196 (*155, 156*), 197 (*158*)
  Olmec, 94 (plate 16), 189-191, 200 (*163-165*)
  Toltec, 207 (*187, 188, 189*), 212, 213
  Totonac, 172, 203 (*175*), 204 (*176*), 205 (*180-181*), 206 (*183, 184, 185*), 210
  Zapotec, 191, 192, 202 (*171*), 203 (*173*)
sculpture, stone, Northwest Pacific Coast, 98 (*75*), 102 (*81*), 108 (92)
sculpture, stone, Oceania:
  Easter Island, 291, 315 (297)
  Marquesas, 292, 315 (299)
  New Hebrides, 251 (plate 29)
  New Zealand, 318 (308)
sculpture, stone, South America:
  Andean, 224-226, 256 (*221, 222*)
  Mochica, 243 (plate 23), 261 (*233*), 262 (*234*)
sculpture, stone, United States, 109 (93), 110 (96), 111 (97), 116-118, 135, 155 (129)
security:
  feeling of, 13
  need for, 67
Seibal, 180
Seneca, 120
Senufo, 10 (map), 20-21, 25
Senungetuk, Ronald, 79-80
Setzler, Frank M., 297
Shamba, Bolongongo, 50
Shango, 26
Sherbro Island, 13, 22
Shije, Velino, see Ma-Pe-Wi
shirt, ceremonial, 76, 77, 87 (plate 9)
Sierra Leone, 13, 22
Sikyatki, 115, 125, 134, 135, 143
silhouettes, hand, 337 (*313*), 346, 346 (ill. 40)
silver:
  Inca, 223, 253 (*218*), 256 (*219*)
  Navaho, 140-142, 158 (138, 139)
  Zuñi, 142-143
Sioux, 57 (map), 121, 122, 135
Skaows-Ke'ay, 79
skull derivation, preservation of, 19, 30-32
"smiling heads," see heads, "smiling"
Smithsonian Institution, Washington, D. C., 291, 295
Society Islands, 275, 291
Solomon Islands, 275, 282, 284, 285
Solutrean Period, 300, 337
"sorcerers," 342, 343
Spanish Levant, 302, 350
spatulas, Melanesian, 270 (295), 279, 280
Speiser, Felix, 284
Spinden, Herbert J., 177-178
spindle whorl, 78, 107 (88)
Spiro Mound, 117
spoon, horn, 78, 106 (86)
Stela Bennett, 225
Stela Raimondi, 225 (ill. 28)
stelae, Maya, 179 (ill. 23), 193 (*147, 149*), 194 (*150, 151*)
stencils, 296, 346
Stephens, John Lloyd, 165
Stirling, Matthew W., 189-190
Stockholm Museum, 192
stools, ceremonial, 48 (48), 287, 308 (278)
Stow, G. W., 360
Strehlow, T. G. H., 298
Struck, B., 28
stucco, Maya, 182
styles, Central America, 218
Sudan, 12, 13, 15, 18, 20, 21
Sumatra, 275, 280
sun worship, 280
Susfana Valley, 356
Sydow, Eckart von, 61
symbolism, 136, 234, 278, 280, 302, 338
symbolism, animal, 69, 72, 119, 168, 217, 238
symbols, sacred, 363

Tahiti, 275, 291
Tajin, 166

talents, 15-17
tamborines, 62
Tame, 293
Tami Island, 281
tami style, 281, 281 (ill. 30), 284, 285, 292
Taos, 134
tapa, 270 (258), 271 (262), 274, 279, 314 (296)
tapestries, 236
Tarascan, 118, 159 (*141*, *142*), 162, 163 (map), 164, 172-174
tattooing, 293, 294, 316 (301)
Te Kuiti house, 293
Te Ore Ore house, 293
Técali, 217
techniques, 14-15, 19, 180, 183, 211, 214-215, 227-228, 236
Tello, Julio C., 235
Temple of the Jaguars, 185, 186 (ill. 25)
Temple of the Warriors, 186
Temples, Father, 16
Tenochtitlan, 214
Teothuacán, 162, 166, 188, 212-213
Tervuren Museum, 52
Tesuque, 129, 134
Textile Museum of the District of Columbia, 236-237
textiles, Peru, 235-239, 246 (plate 25), 266-267 (246-252)
Teyjat, 303 (ill. 37), 304
Thompson, W. J., 291
Tiahuanaco, 166, 224-225, 227-228
tikis, 292, 295, 318 (308)
Tilden, Bennie, 143
Tischner, Herbert, 289
Tlaloc, 167, 172, 212
Tlingit, 57 (map), 64, 65, 66, 72, 74
Togo, 13
Toltec, 162, 163 (map), 166, 212-214
Tonga Islands, 275, 281, 291
totem animals, 67, 71 (ills. 7-14)
totem poles, 70-72, 80, 88 (60-62)
totemism, 67-68, 275
Totonac, 162, 163 (map), 164, 166, 205 (176), 209-211
tree trunk theory, 17, 31-32
Tremper Mound, 118
Tres Zapotes, 162, 189-190
triangular style, 284
Trobriand Islands, 282, 284
Trujillo, 224
Tsimshian, 57 (map), 65, 66, 70, 73, 74
Tsireh, Awa, 142
Tuc d'Audoubert, 141, 142, 149
Tula, 166, 213
Tulane University, 181, 182, 188
tumbaga, 221-222
Turanga house, 293
Twoitsie, 143

Uaxactun, 183
uli style, 273, 284, 286
United Fruit Company, 185
University Museum, Philadelphia, 120, 221-222, 226, 228, 294
University of Sydney, 297
urns, funerary, 201 (168), 202 (169)
Uxmal, 183

Valle, 347
Valtorta, George, 81 (326, 327), 328 (329), 350-355, 352, 353, 355 (ills. 42, 43, 44)
vases, 91 (plate 13), 196 (157), 219 (ill. 27), 229 (ill. 29), 249 (209), 257 (223)
"Venus of Willendorf," 327 (325), 348-349
Verité Collection, 21
Villar del Humo (Cuenca), 350
Viracocha, 168, 172, 229, 238-239, 257 (226)

Wadi Sora, 359
Wakashan, 65
Warega, 10 (map), 33, 52
Warua, 10 (map), 33
weaving, 136-139, 279
Weiant, Clarence W., 190
West Africa, 13
Wheelwright, Mary C., 126
Wied, Maximilian von, 121
Windels, Fernand, 338
Wingert, Paul S., 22, 51, 65, 279-280
Wirz, Paul, 280, 282
Witako, 293
wood carving (see *also* canoes; carving, architectural; clubs; figures; figures, ancestral; masks; totem poles):
  Africa, 33 (4), 34-36 (6-8), 47 (37)
  Northwest Pacific Coast, 68-75, 97 (73), 105 (84)
  Oceania, 271 (264), 284-290, 293-295, 306 (272), 307 (274), 312 (289), 314 (295), 315 (298), 316-317 (302-305)
  Peru, 231-232, 239-240
  technique, 17, 18, 23, 30-31, 188
Wukchumme, 124
Wuvulu (Matty Island), 289

Xipe, 167
Xochicalco, 213

Yassi Society, 14, 22
Yaxchilán, 175, 180-182
yokes, stone, 205 (182), 210
Yokuts, 124
Yoruba, 10 (map), 13, 16, 17-18, 25-26, 42 (plate 2), 55

Zapotec, 162, 163 (map), 164, 166, 191-192
Zeltner, D. F., Collection, 219
Zia (Sia, Tsia), 129, 134
zoomorph P, Quiriguá, 160 (148)
Zuñi, 57 (map), 124, 127, 129, 133, 133 (ill. 19), 135, 139-140, 143